Abnormal Psychology Casebook

A New Perspective

Andrew R. Getzfeld, Ph.D.
New Jersey City University

PEARSON
Prentice
Hall

Upper Saddle River, New Jersey 07458

Library of Congress Cataloging-in-Publication Data

Getzfeld, Andrew R.

   Abnormal psychology casebook: a new perspective/Andrew R. Getzfeld.

     p. cm.

   Includes bibliographical references (p.).

   ISBN 0-13-093787-8

     1. Psychology, Pathological—Case studies. 2. Mental illness—

   Case studies. 3. Psychiatry.

   I. Title.

RC454.G45 2004

616.89′09—dc22   2003061625

Senior Acquisitions Editor: Jeff Marshall
Editor-in-Chief: Leah Jewell
Editorial Assistant: Jill Liebowitz
Marketing Manager: Sheryl Adams
Marketing Assistant: Jeanette Laforet
Assistant Managing Editor: Maureen Richardson
Production Liaison: Fran Russello
Manufacturing Buyer: Tricia Kenny
Cover Design: Bruce Kenselaar
Cover Illustration/Photo: David Muir/Masterfile
Composition/Full-Service Project Management: Lithokraft/Marty Sopher
Printer/Binder: RR Donnelley & Sons Company
Cover Printer: Phoenix Color Corp

Credits and acknowledgments borrowed from other sources and reproduced, with permission, in this textbook appear on page 295.

Pearson Education LTD., London
Pearson Education Singapore, Pte. Ltd
Pearson Education, Canada, Ltd
Pearson Education–Japan
Pearson Education Australia PTY, Limited

Pearson Education North Asia Ltd
Pearson Educación de Mexico, S.A. de C.V.
Pearson Education Malaysia, Pte. Ltd
Pearson Education, Upper Saddle River, New Jersey

10 9 8 7 6 5 4 3 2 1
ISBN 0-13-093787-8

Dedication

*I dedicate this book to the memory of my father,
Robert B. Getzfeld, whose endless love, compassion,
and support always pushed me to surpass my potential.*

A. R. G.

Contents

Preface

There exist many casebooks of abnormal psychology. Some of these casebooks have been around for many years and have gone through many revisions. Some do not include patients who did not succeed in treatment (some psychologists use the term "client;" the terms, for me, are interchangeable). Some of the casebooks use famous people for their cases, such as Charles Manson, Jack the Ripper, Jeffrey Dahmer, Theodore Bundy, and "Sybil." These are all fascinating people, but I asked myself, "What would the purpose be if I decided to rehash famous serial killers and such?" After all, there are only so many ways one can assess Charles Manson, although Jack the Ripper is still a very popular subject today. (Ask Patricia Cornwell how much of her own money she spent trying to deduce his true identity.) I decided that the field needed a book that included real-life individuals from a wide variety of racial, ethnic, and geographical backgrounds with whom you might easily identify.

As a practicing psychologist and a practicing social worker for over 15 years, I have been fortunate to have encountered a wide variety of patients. Students often ask me how many patients I have had, and to this date I have counted over 400 different cases! Compared with other psychologists who have been practicing this is not a large number. But when I was first approached to write this book, I realized that I had a great sample size from which to draw the cases you are about to read.

The format of this book is also rather unique. Each case is related with as much of the original narrative as is possible (all cases were interpreted using <u>DSM-IV-TR</u> diagnostic criteria). This will allow you to get a more complete and accurate picture of the client "in his/her own words." Verbatim is a key word for school psychologists, and I am putting this concept to use in this book. Thought questions appear midway through each case, and review questions at the end of each chapter. I suggest you use these questions to think further about the disorders being discussed. These questions in general do not have right or wrong answers. You will also be briefly exposed to the field of psychopharmacology, a crucial treatment modality in today's world of managed care and "quick fixes" for mental health problems and concerns. This section, which occurs with each case, will be as current as possible.

This book presents two cases per chapter. This will allow instructors to pick between two cases in each chapter if one case is not to their liking. Additionally, should an instructor decide to emphasize a particular disorder, s/he can use both cases to ensure comprehension and retention. Chapter 11 allows the student to apply what s/he has learned in class by providing two cases without the solutions (<u>DSM-IV-TR</u> diagnoses). The solutions, which should be discussed and debated in class, can be found on the book's web site (**www.prenhall.com/getzfeld**).

Writing a book such as this made me realize that it is impossible to satisfy all needs. Thus it is impossible, short of writing a virtual encyclopedia, to include every <u>DSM-IV-TR</u> diagnostic category. My editor and I have decided that, should you desire future disorders in the next revision, please email me (**del238de@verizon.net**) or my editor (**Jeff_Marshall@prenhall.com**). We will collect this data and use it to determine the cases and/or changes to be made in the second edition. If there is enough demand for a particular disorder, Prentice-Hall will consider posting an additional case to the book's web site.

Finally, a word about the treatment modalities you will encounter. The modalities selected only represent some of the many possible ways to treat the mental disorders discussed here. In some instances the modalities selected worked well, in others, not well at all. As you will see, perfect success is not guaranteed in the fields of psychology and psychotherapy. By the time you have completed your studies, the success percentage will have hopefully increased.

This book has been a long endeavor and I am proud and pleased with the results. I would like to hear your impressions. Tell me what you liked and disliked about the book. What changes should be made in the second edition? What should be kept? All emails will be read; you will receive a reply (although not instantaneous).

My goal was to make this learning experience as enjoyable as possible while presenting you with real-life examples of a variety of mental illnesses. Some of these people may be close to you in age; some may sound like you, your family, or friends. All of them are real people with real concerns, and in most cases their strongest motivation is a desire to get better. The patients wanted their stories to be told so that other could learn from them, and devise even more effective treatment modalities, or perhaps conduct research to discover cures for their disorders. Before we meet our first patient, some thanks are due.

Acknowledgments

Many individuals have both helped and encouraged me as this project took shape. This book would not be possible without the patients described within, and their generosity in allowing me to use their situations so that others can learn from them is boundless.

I wish to also thank the following reviewers, whose trenchant comments helped me to shape the book you now hold in your hands:

Joseph A. Davis, San Diego State University
Sara DeHart-Young, Mississippi State University
Elizabeth McPhaul-Moore, Piedmont Community College
Christiane Turnheim, Massachusetts Bay Community College

I wish to express special thanks to the wonderful people at Prentice-Hall who took a chance on an unknown author and helped him gingerly along the path to completion. Thanks to Jayme Heffler, who took a chance and signed me to my first contract. I extend my special appreciation to Stephanie Johnson, who provided guidance and kind words during difficult times and the initial roadblocks. I extend special thanks and appreciation to Jeff Marshall, my editor, and to Jill Liebowitz, his editorial assistant, for their ability to put up with email bombardments and endless questions, and for pushing me to meet the deadlines. Finally, thanks to the other hard working people at Prentice-Hall who worked on this book: Sheryl Adams and Ronald Fox. A word of thanks to Marty Sopher at Lithokraft: You always kept me abreast as to the book's status.

Of course this book would have been impossible without the continued and invaluable support of my family. I am indebted to my lovely wife Gabriella, to our new daughter Anya Rose Getzfeld, and to my mother Paula Getzfeld. Thanks for having the patience to put up with my writer's block and grumpiness, my endless late hours seeing the sun rise, and for putting up with me trying to split my duties among being an author, university professor, husband, new father, and a son. I realize that I have not been a barrel of laughs at times, but I think it was worth it! I will be forever indebted to my late father Robert B. Getzfeld, who always encouraged me to challenge myself and taught me to persevere no matter how overwhelming the odds might be. This book is for you, guys!

Andrew R. Getzfeld, Ph.D.
April 2003

About the Author

Andrew R. Getzfeld received his B.A. in Psychology from Vassar College, his M.S.S.W. from the University of Wisconsin-Madison, and his Ph.D. in School Psychology from the University of Tennessee-Knoxville. He is a frequent presenter at APA and NASP, and has chaired poster sessions for Psi Chi at EPA. Andrew holds licenses in both New York and New Jersey, as a Certified Social Worker in New York, and as a Certified School Psychologist, Certified School Social Worker and a Certified Alcohol Counselor in New Jersey. Presently teaching in the Psychology Department at New Jersey City University, Andrew's areas of interest include eating disorders and addictions, abnormal psychology, child development, and psychopharmacology. Andrew also serves as a Psi Chi Faculty Consultant and is the Psi Chi Faculty Advisor at New Jersey City University. In his limited leisure time he enjoys travel, swimming, reading voraciously, writing books, and spending as much time as possible with his family, especially his daughter Anya Rose.

Chapter 1

Anxiety Disorders I

Anxiety disorders are so pervasive, and also eminently treatable in certain instances, that we will discuss four cases across the next two chapters. According to a recent report from the *National Institute of Mental Health (NIMH)*, anxiety disorders affect about 14% of the United States population (National Institute of Mental Health, 1999). Fortunately, the first disorder we will discuss, *Panic Disorder With Agoraphobia*, "only" affects about 2% of the United States population. However, *Phobic Disorders* affect about 8% of the United States population. One could possibly say that we are a phobic population. In light of the terrorist attacks on September 11, 2001, and because of fear of retaliation over the war in Iraq, one suspects that these numbers will increase.

The positive side of many phobic disorders is that they often respond well to treatment and can be extinguished. Panic disorder with agoraphobia, on the other hand, is more difficult to treat and may require medications. We will first examine Paula*, who first developed panic disorder and then subsequently developed *agoraphobia* (fear of open places). We will conclude with Robert, who demonstrates a very common phobia, one from which many people suffer!

---

*In order to protect their privacy, all first and/or last names of all individuals discussed and/or described within this book, have been changed.

Panic Disorder With Agoraphobia

The Case of Paula:
One Woman in Search of an Exit

Presenting Problem

Paula is a 27-year-old white female who lives in a large city. Paula is single and has never been married. She works as a securities and bond trader for a major financial institution and has done so since she graduated from college. "I got my BA in Economics, and the economy was doing really well. This company sent recruiters to campus, we had a good match, and so here I am." Paula has "shown loyalty to this firm; I've worked for them since I graduated. The hours can be nuts at times but look at what I have to show for it! They're great in that they're going to pay for me to get my MBA. I was all set to go for it when the problems started getting worse."

Paula was 5'6" tall, wore glasses, and was somewhat thin. She made good eye contact and had a *blunted affect* but often appeared tense in the sessions. For example, she would have a frightened look in her eyes at the start of each session, similar to the "look a deer has when it's caught in the headlights. I know how I look when I'm scared." She did not smile much and always seemed on edge. We noticed that her hand would often go to her neck to check her pulse, or over her heart. She would perform these behaviors about four times each session. Paula wore no jewelry except for a Phi Beta Kappa Key attached to a small wrist chain.

We asked Paula for some clarification, and for the reason(s) she came in. "Well, if you thought you were having constant heart attacks and dizzy spells, you'd look for help also. Lately my heart beats so fast, I get dizzy, have chest pains, and I'm short of breath. I feel like I'm dying and the world is ending. I've gone to the emergency room a number of times and each time they tell me it's in my head and nothing is wrong. I went to a *cardiologist* for a sonogram and *echocardiogram* and he found nothing wrong at all with my heart. He also told me that the problem was psychological. He told me to get some hypnosis and relaxation training, cut out caffeine, and maybe exercise and do yoga or Tai Chi. He also suggested that I try and not spend as much time at home with mom."

"I got a bit worried and of course I went to another doctor when I got the next attack. He told me the same thing and told me to relax more. He also gave me some *Xanax (alprazolam*)* to help me relax. I used it a lot and it really zonked me out. I was like the walking dead. It helped, but once I stopped taking Xanax because I couldn't work while on it, the attacks came back. My mom and my best friend at work got worried and told me to see someone. My general practitioner recommended you, so that's why I came in. I need to get this thing under control and over, and I'm afraid to not use Xanax, since it worked before. I can't drive while taking it, so hopefully there are some logical answers to this."

Background Information

Paula's mother is a homemaker, and her father owned a car dealership. He died "shortly after I graduated. He knew I had a job so at least he lived to see that. He died from *congestive heart failure*; I hope that doesn't run in the family. My dad had a huge insurance policy, and when we sold the business, my mom was set for life. She does painting as a hobby and sells it to a store in the neighborhood. She's really good at it." Paula is an only child, but there is a story behind that.

"I had a younger brother who was very sick when he was born. He had a heart defect and other birth defects that I really don't wish to discuss. He died when he was three. The doctors tried everything but it was basically hopeless. The defects were not picked up while he was in the womb, so we were upset and thought about suing the doctors. My dad, who was too soft, said to forget it and move on. They tried to get pregnant again but it didn't happen. They were still too devastated by his death to consider adoption, and they didn't want to wait at least five years. My mom is still affected by this."

Paula reached all of her developmental milestones at the age-appropriate levels with one exception. "I was reading when I was four; they considered this early. They put me in a special program at school and I was always the best reader. I still love to read. I guess that's why my eyes are so bad. My dad was a math whiz and my mom, well, she's the intuitive one in the family." Paula lives at home with her mother "to take care of her and watch out for her."

Paula was unattached at the start of the sessions and said "it's probably because of three things: I work too hard and too many hours, I live at home, and my problems prevent me from going out a lot. They come and go, but they've really gotten bad lately. I'm not sure what's happening. I stopped using caffeine, but that gave me the shakes and it made me tired

---

*All medications are listed first with their trade name (the first letter is capitalized), and with their generic name in lowercase and in parentheses.

all the time. It's hard to give that up. I also stopped smoking, figuring that might help. It did, a bit." At this point Paula appeared on the verge of tears but none were noticed.

We then asked Paula for some more family background. "My mom has had health problems, but nothing psychological that I know of. Her father's father, who was from Poland, had a bad drinking problem. Other than that, nothing. My dad was the same way, no psychological stuff. His health was quite bad. Here was a man who was never sick when I was young. He hits 50 and bang! All of a sudden everything breaks down. He got cancer, then emphysema, and then the heart failure. He always said that the cigarettes caused his troubles, but cancer also ran in his family. His mother died from breast cancer, and his father from colon cancer. I have a lot to look forward to. That's one reason I stopped smoking, and I don't drink. I have enough bad seeds in me." Paula was reluctant to continue at this point and said she needed "some air. I'll come back next week if that's okay." We were about to answer when she flew out of the office. She called later that day to confirm her appointment for the following week.

So far it seems like Paula's concerns are straightforward. She feels like she's having heart attacks, yet all of her medical doctors tell her it's psychological. They have found nothing physiologically wrong with her heart. If we were to stop here, we could make a fairly confident diagnosis of *Panic Disorder*. However, as you will see throughout this book, rarely is all as it seems at the beginning of a case. Psychologists and other helping professionals make sure to gather as much information as they can before making a diagnosis, and they are not afraid to change diagnoses later on during an active case. Let us take our first break as we ponder some questions.

Thought Questions

1. What is going on with Paula?
2. What other physiological possibilities might explain Paula's behavior?
3. Paula seems like a very bright woman. How could someone so bright possibly have a mental illness?
4. How important is Paula's family history?
5. Paula works in a high-pressure job. How might that be related to her symptoms?

Assessment and Evaluation

Paula was assessed through an *unstructured diagnostic interview* and a *psychiatric evaluation*. The advantage of using an unstructured interview is that the clinician is not restricted to follow an ordered set of questions. This format allows for a lot of variance and is preferred by many. New therapists or interns often prefer a *structured diagnostic interview,* since it puts less pressure on them.

Paula returned the following week and told us "I am sorry about what happened. You were going into some sensitive areas and I felt like the walls were closing in on me. I felt like I was being choked, so I had to book. I can handle things now, so fire away." We asked Paula more questions to get some clarification on certain issues. See if her replies clear up her situation for you.

We first asked her to tell us when her *panic attacks* began. "Well, if that's what you call them, they began shortly after I entered college. The work, the pressure of guys, all of these things caused me to get really stressed. I had no good outlets, no good support systems. I was always babied at home, and I went home often. School was only 90 miles away from home, and the train was reliable. I also went to a very small college, so everyone knew everyone else. I graduated from a large high school where I could stay hidden if I wanted."

"Things got worse when my dad got sick. I was always worried about him and was afraid he was going to die early, which he did of course. He didn't live long enough to see me become a success (she begins to cry here). He had a rough life, getting so sick so suddenly, losing his only son. Life is not fair." We gave Paula some time to compose herself. If someone cries in your office, you should let them cry; don't try and stop them prematurely. The patient will usually feel better afterwards. Generally speaking new or novice therapists get scared when a patient cries. The natural tendency is to make them feel better and to stop the tears quickly. Paula took about three minutes and while sniffling and still teary-eyed, she continued.

"I felt my brother's death as well. I really withdrew from people for a long time. We didn't believe in therapy, so we all helped each other. Business was bad for my dad as well, and then this . . . no wonder he got sick. The attacks really started after John's death (her brother), but they were not as bad as they are now. Of course since my dad died from a heart condition, it makes sense that I have one as well."

"I would flip out in school. I would get dizzy before a presentation or before going out with a new guy and I'd get all dizzy and sweaty. Just before I lost my virginity it happened also. If nothing else it's a great way to get out of tough things (laughs). But I still believe that this is a heart thing with me. Things did get a lot worse once I got my job." We asked Paula to clarify this.

"Well, my job is high pressure, so I'd get the dizzy spells, faints, and attacks more often at work, and sometimes at home. The real problem began one day last year. I had an attack at work. A co-worker asked me out, and soon after a major client fell through. I got the blame but it had to do with the client. My boss was livid, a guy was interested in me, I freaked, so I had an attack. I got dizzy and felt faint and ran to the bathroom. Co-workers saw me, and my secretary saw me and followed me in. She put cold compresses on my head and took me to the company doctor. He sent me to the emergency room since he wanted to be sure I was okay. Of course they did the usual 'Nothing's wrong with you, Ms. X, go home and see a shrink.' I went home then and took the next two days off. I was horrified, since no one had ever seen me get an attack before."

"It got to the point where my mom would walk me to the car, ride with me to work sometimes, and pick me up at night. I started to stay away from crowded spots, movie theaters, and social gatherings. I always know how to quickly get out of a place if I need to. I checked out all of the exits here. My mom is in the waiting room in case I freak again. I had to take medical leave from work because things got so bad that I couldn't get myself in to work. It's real hard to leave the house now. You have no idea what it took to come here by car. My mom drives now, since I can't do it. If I had an attack while driving I'd kill both of us."

"I've come really far at work and I'm petrified they'll can my rear if I stay on extended medical leave. But I can't go in there. My attacks were the worst at work, as much as I love it. I can't have an attack there again. Everyone will laugh, 'Look at retard Paula, at it again. This is a trader? Better move her to the mail room.' You have no idea how this is. No matter what I do it gets harder and harder to leave home. And the attacks haven't stopped." (She begins to cry again.)

We asked her how she manages to cope. "I've lost some weight because of the attacks, even though my mom's a fab cook. Since I was 'discovered' at work, and since I've rarely left the house, I've lost twenty pounds. I could use it, but I'm not eating. My mom is my life. No guy will come near me. I can't be alone. And I watch my mom on top of it all. I have thought of other ways to cope." Can you guess what those might be?

"Well, I've tried alcohol. Getting drunk helped a bit, but how the hell can I go to work that way? I feel like crap the next day, and the attacks come back again if I'm sober. I tried taking *Contac* (an over-the-counter *allergy pill/antihistamine;* these type of pills will normally make you drowsy), but that zonks me beyond reason. I can't do anything with those, and they constipate me as well. Plus I have difficulty peeing. So I thought of a solution. I thought I'd finally do it and kill myself." She looked directly at us, her eyes intent and narrowly focused. She did not appear to be looking for a reaction from us at this point.

We need to stop here for a moment. Some patients will have *suicidal thoughts and tendencies,* but fewer will have actual *suicidal behaviors.* Regardless, any time you hear a patient mention suicide, it needs to be immediately checked out and determined whether this is a viable threat or not. Suicidal thoughts are not unusual for patients whose conditions do not get better, or whose conditions cause chronic physical or psychological pain. At times these individuals may try anything to shut off the pain, and suicide at times seems like the only option. We asked Paula to clarify.

"I decided, once it was impossible for me to work, date, or get in a car, to off myself. I couldn't take the pain anymore, and I was hurting my mom. Life made no sense, living made no sense and was too much of an effort. I hated my life and myself. I was a weak woman who was giving in to a stupid problem. How awful is that? My dad would've killed me if he were alive. So I decided to do it." We then asked Paula when this was and if she had a plan, important questions.

"This was about four months ago. I was going to swallow a bottle of aspirin. I read somewhere that it's easy to O.D. (overdose) on aspirin and it's painless, so that made sense. Just lie down in my room, put on some sad tunes like The Doors, and take them all and sleep forever. I decided to do it while my mom was out shopping, so it would be complete when she got home. I was all set to do it and had everything ready. I wrote a long love letter to my mom, telling her how sorry I was and how disappointed she must be in me."

Obviously, Paula changed her mind. We needed to discover the reasons for this. "The reasons? My mom and dad. My dad didn't sacrifice everything . . . his life . . . to raise me and then see me off myself because of a stupid problem that no one can figure out. I know I'd go to Hell if I killed myself. When I do die I want to be in Heaven with my mom and dad and brother, not down there. I'd look like a coward, unable to face my weaknesses. My folks did not raise me like that. The real reason I didn't do anything, and why I'm here now, is because of my mom." She began to cry again and she paused for a moment before continuing.

"I thought about how she might benefit not having to deal with my crap anymore. How is it that I can't even go out because I'm petrified of having an attack, and how easy it would be if I were dead? Well, I thought about it and saw that by doing it I'd hurt her so much she might kill herself. To lose one child early, a husband, and then your last child . . . no one could deal with that, no one. I'll never leave my mom by choice. You know, for once in my life I was not selfish. I love my family but I really haven't been as good to them as I could have been."

"I told my mom about all of this and she was concerned but not alarmed. She said, 'Paula, now we must see someone. Tell them at work, but I've stayed out of your life long enough. It's time to get some help before this gets completely out of hand. I'll take you. I'll even help to pay if you need it.' That's my mom. Did I tell you she's here with me in the waiting room?"

We then asked Paula if she had any suicidal thoughts or, of greater concern, a set plan since then. "I've had some thoughts but no way will I do anything; I've got no plans at all. I will not be damned to Hell, and I will not hurt my mom. I will suffer through anything in order not to hurt my family. So no, nothing really since then. I hate feeling like a failure and having no control over my body, so I do need help. I just don't know what to do. Suicide is not the answer." We told Paula that if she ever has these thoughts while in treatment to call the police or the clinic immediately. This particular clinic always has a therapist on call 24 hours a day, 7 days a week. We believe that it is more sensible to err on the side of caution than not when it comes to suicidal thoughts and behaviors.

Paula also met with the psychiatrist after we completed our *initial intake assessment*. We expected the psychiatrist to agree with our preliminary impressions, which she did. In sum, "Paula is seen as having Panic Disorder With Agoraphobia. She has a long history of panic attacks that have led to crippling avoidance behaviors, such as avoiding dating and social situations, and now being unable to go to work. Paula is still somewhat convinced that these issues are cardiac related, so I recommend contacting her primary care physician and cardiologist, as well as the private hospital she visited for their input and records. Paula is not actively suicidal now and is not seen as a viable threat at the present time. She should engage in weekly sessions and see us for a follow-up in two weeks, sooner if need be." The psychiatrist followed up with her diagnosis, which matched ours. See if you agree:

Panic Disorder With Agoraphobia   300.21

Theoretical Etiologies

There are many *theoretical etiologies* (hypothesized causes and/or origins) for the anxiety disorders, and many of these etiologies have been subjected to extensive research. Freud made his name by treating anxiety disorders, and the psychodynamic perspective is still embraced today by some therapists. In deference to Freud, we will begin with his viewpoint.

Freud and his followers view anxiety as a warning signal that dangerous or threatening *id* impulses (either sexual or aggressive) are about to enter consciousness. In order to prevent this from occurring, the *ego* will activate its *defense mechanisms* and the person will do his/her best to avoid the feared object or situation. Focusing specifically on panic disorder, Freud would probably say that because the aggressive and sexual id impulses are so close to the conscious portion of the mind, the *psyche* becomes so stressed that a panic attack occurs. When repression occurs, the panic subsides. As we will note throughout this book, the psychodynamic perspective is difficult to research accurately and is given little credence today.

Learning (or behavioral) etiologies have a simpler explanation for the anxiety disorders: The fears and anxieties are learned behaviors, either acquired through *classical conditioning* or *operant (instrumental) conditioning.* In classical conditioning, a previously neutral stimulus such as a spider or a cockroach acquires a negative value when it is paired with a noxious event. If the spider bites a little boy and spins a web on him (unlikely except in the movies), this model states that the boy will likely acquire a phobia for spiders (*arachnophobia;* see the movie). If an adult breaks a tooth while biting an apple, apples may become an acquired phobia.

Operant conditioning can also be involved with acquiring phobias. Anxiety relief negatively reinforces the avoidance behavior (*negative reinforcement* occurs when a behavior is strengthened due to the removal of a reinforcer). If the person is petrified of the dentist (and justifiably so), avoiding him/her will alleviate the anxiety and thus the avoidance behavior will become negatively reinforced. A Darwinist would point out that humans are predisposed to fear certain species that can harm us, such as spiders and snakes. This is called *prepared conditioning.* Finally, panic attacks are seen as occurring due to subtle environmental cues. Learning theories cannot and do not explain all anxiety disorders and their etiologies.

The last two perspectives include a lot of concepts. In the interest of space, we will briefly examine each of them. Cognitive psychologists theorize that dysfunctional patterns of **thinking** may lead to anxiety disorders. Albert Ellis is a proponent of this concept. Ellis' *Rational Emotive Therapy (RET)* states that humans get into trouble because of their irrational beliefs and thoughts. For example, they may have a commitment phobia because they believe that to be in a marriage they (and the marriage) must be perfect. Anything less is considered a failure. Of course this individual is doomed to fail, since nothing is ever one hundred percent in life! Ellis would focus on these irrational beliefs and work with the patient to correct the beliefs, and thus the behavior would change. Paula has already demonstrated this concept, since she cannot go back to work because her co-workers saw her having a panic attack and thus they think she is crazy.

People who have anxiety disorders may also misread the amount of fear they will bring to a situation. Women may fear childbirth or an *amniocentesis (amnio)* because of the perceived excruciating pain associated with both. In fact, myths abound about the length of the needle used during an amnio, and many women do not consider it to be that painful. However, this increased expectation of fear leads to avoidance and does not teach the individual how to cope with these situations.

Oversensitivity to threat is a key symptom of anxiety disorders. Phobic individuals see threats and/or danger in everyday, generally safe situations (e.g., bridges, tunnels, crossing the street). We have an inherent tendency to be wary of certain situations, which Darwin might say has allowed the species to survive. For example, we have a tendency to avoid dark places because danger may lurk (Bouton, Mineka, & Barlow, 2001). Clark (1996) hypothesized that these individuals may be overly sensitive to dangerous situations and thus may overreact and see danger where none exists. That is, these individuals may interpret these normal physiological reactions in an alarmist way, presuming they are signaling an impending catastrophe. Thus, they will experience a panic attack and this will recur once the "feared" situation is re-experienced.

Research has also begun to confirm the hypothesis that biology plays an important role in anxiety disorders, especially in panic disorder. Some of these theories can be quite complex, so we will continue with a brief summation. Genetics seems to play a role in anxiety disorders, specifically in agoraphobia and in panic disorder (Barlow, 2002). We seem to inherit a tendency to be tense, and we also seem to inherit the tendency to panic. The genetic predisposition may not cause the panic attack but it might leave the individual more vulnerable to such attacks.

The *GABA system* also seems to be involved. GABA is a neurotransmitter that reduces anxiety specifically by inhibiting neurons from exciting neighboring neurons. The hypothesis here is that depleted GABA levels lead to increased anxiety caused by neurons firing too often. A class of medications used to treat anxiety disorders (*benzodiazepines*; e.g., *Valium*, generically called *diazepam*) works to excite the GABA system, thus making decreased anxiety levels more likely. However, the GABA system and its dysfunction are not directly related to anxiety disorders, but it certainly appears to contribute to them. Panic disorder specifically seems to be linked to depleted serotonin levels; this hypothesis is supported by the fact that some *antidepressant medications* (such as *Paxil (paroxetine)* and *Zoloft (sertraline)*) seem to be beneficial in treating panic disorder. Indeed, Paxil and Zoloft are approved for the treatment of Panic Disorder With or Without Agoraphobia (Bezchlibnyk-Butler & Jeffries, 2002).

Finally, some fascinating recent research points to a biological implication for panic disorder. People who have panic disorder appear to suffer increased anxiety when faced with biologically dangerous situations, such as increased carbon dioxide levels in the blood or hyperventilation. Klein (1994) believes that a brain defect leads individuals who are more likely to panic to misinterpret cues related to suffocation, such as increased carbon dioxide levels. This will lead to what Klein calls respiratory alarm, which leads to the symptoms of a panic attack: Hyperventilation, rapid heartbeat, nausea, and hot or cold flashes. This perspective has gathered support both for and against its views.

In sum, the best way to view the etiology of anxiety disorders is from a combination of biological and psychological perspectives. Cognitive and learning theories have support, as do biological perspectives. This integrated approach will serve practitioners well, and researchers even better. Further research is presently being conducted and it will be exciting to see the results.

Treatment Plan

We decided to use *individual therapy* with Paula, with the option of *family therapy* a bit later. *Group therapy* for someone with Panic Disorder With Agoraphobia is not a wise idea. It is difficult enough to get someone like Paula to leave the house. The clinic staff believed that putting her in a group situation would be destructive. We also monitored Paula's suicidal thoughts and behaviors by checking with her each session to see if they were recurring. Early on in treatment we discovered some key information about Paula's background. Paula told us "My mom, who is fully supportive of treatment, wants to speak with you to give you some additional background information. I told her anything to help me, so can she come in for this one time?" We stopped the session at this point and checked with the clinic supervisor, since this could pose a potential conflict of interests. Ed told us it was okay with him, and clinic policy did not forbid this situation, so we invited her mother in to the session. What did her mother tell us?

"Well, I think I had panic attacks when I was younger. (Paula responds with a shocked look and is about to say something.) Paula, let Mom speak to the doctor. I did some reading and it seems like that is what happened. They began when I was a teenager. I had heart palpitations and I would get dizzy, cold sweats, and I would sometimes faint. Of course back then I was told I had a heart condition and diagnosed with an *arrhythmia*. I was also told that since I was a woman I tended to be overly sensitive to certain situations. I lived a normal life and they went away when I met my late husband. He took care of me and made me feel so secure, so confident, the attacks stopped. I know they were in my head because the doctors lately have found nothing wrong with my heart. It couldn't be stronger, and no arrhythmias are there either. Back then if a lady got an attack, she would be 'swooning, have the vapors', stuff like that. No one made anything of it. I only know they stopped once I met Jack. It's odd, but when he passed they didn't come back. I had to watch Paula and myself. I'm really lucky I guess." *Spontaneous remission,* as seen with her mother, is not unheard of. Of course we had no way to verify any of this, so we needed to be cautious in accepting this information. At the very least, it makes Paula's situation a bit clearer.

Paula then spoke. "I am really upset that you never told me this, Mom. Do you know how much trouble you could have saved me from? There's no reason for this at all. (She is screaming at this point and pointing her finger at her mother). If I didn't need you to get me home I would throw you out and have you walk home." Her mother then left the session and waited for Paula outside of the building.

Paula continued, "I don't know what to say. This blew me away. I guess it makes sense, since these have to come from somewhere." We told Paula that anxiety disorders, especially panic disorder, may have a genetic predisposition and are more common among women (APA, 2000). "That really doesn't help. We have some major issues along with my crap to deal with here." At that point the session ended and Paula walked angrily out of the office. We could hear the yelling between them as they waited for the elevator. This was the last time Paula invited her mother into a session; her mother subsequently never returned to the sessions.

Over the next few individual sessions we monitored Paula's suicidal thoughts and her panic attacks. Paula told us that she no longer had suicidal thoughts, especially since she began treatment and realized "how foolish committing suicide might be." Her panic attacks had subsided a bit, and at this time she returned to the psychiatrist for her second follow-up visit. This time she decided to prescribe Zoloft (sertraline), one of the antidepressants we previously mentioned. Zoloft is used to treat depressive disorders (a class of *Mood Disorders*) and is indicated for the treatment of panic disorder. Zoloft has a faster onset than *Tofranil (imipramine),* produces fewer side effects, but causes sexual dysfunction in about 75% of those who use it (decreased libido, anorgasmia, *clitoral priaprism* (constant erection)). "I'm really resistant to taking any kind of meds, but I'll try this stuff. You have to understand I'm not depressed, so I doubt this will work. But I need to get this thing fixed once and for all, so let's go for it."

For some of the disorders we will discuss, the most effective treatment methodology is a combination of psychological and biological, i.e., medications along with psychotherapy. This approach also sees the etiologies of most (if not all) disorders as having biological **and** psychological/ environmental origins. This is known as the *interactionist or integrated* *approach,* and works well with treating panic disorder. We worked with Paula to help her understand the origins of these attacks as well as to help her realize what they really mean and do. We also worked with Paula on helping her deal with stress in her life. We used *hypnotherapy* and *progressive muscle relaxation techniques,* and *cognitive restructuring* to help Paula. These can be classified as cognitive behavioral techniques and have been proven to be quite effective when used properly and for a length of time (Barlow, Gorman, Shear, & Woods, 2000). Paula made some nice progress as the sessions progressed.

"The hypnosis and relaxation really helped, but the best help was learning that these attacks are not, finally, heart attacks, and that I'm not going crazy or freaking out. I can control them and not have them control me. Stress was killing my life: job stresses, meeting a good guy, my mom, bills, my dad's death . . . all of these things were wearing me out. I spent the weekends at home either catching up or hanging with my mom. That's no life!" Paula started to become more at ease when the attacks did occur, which were much less often. The "Zoloft helped significantly. The attacks rarely happen, so I may go off of it soon, since the therapy helps a lot too."

"I know now what an attack means, what it resembles, and how to handle it. I'm also able to go out now, but that was the hard part. The meds and the therapy really helped there. I saw that since I wasn't getting as many attacks I could chance going out alone and it worked! The first time made it a lot easier. It's like riding a horse. Once you've done it once it gets a lot easier. I then got a lot less stressed, and then I finally graduated to going to the supermarket alone in my car. That was tough! But I didn't have an attack, so I decided to call my boss at work and tell him I'll be back in one week. I've been working at home but they need me back at work. That's the real test."

Paula passed that test as well. She learned how to control her stress and how to react once an attack occurred. "I know I'm not going crazy and that I don't have to be perfect anymore. It's okay if I say 'No' to my mom or to my job . . . or to anyone! I know what to say to myself when I feel an attack coming on." At the clinic's request she remained on Zoloft until she was discharged, but at discharge Paula told us "I don't need it anymore, but I know where to go if I do need it again. The hypnosis and relaxation techniques are just as good and less harmful to my health!"

Paula remained in treatment for 7 months. Her mother never returned to engage in family therapy, but Paula told us "not to worry about that. We still love each other very much, but I need to handle this myself, not with her help. I need to grow up, and so does Mom. I intend to move out and buy an apartment when I have enough bucks, which my mom likes. I'll live close to her, but we need some separation. That's probably a partial cause of the attacks, that we've lived together for 27 years." She laughs at this point.

"I'm also going out with friends more often on the weekend and trying to meet a decent guy, but that's another problem. I thought my panic attacks were rough! And my agoraphobia is also under control. It still happens but like the panic attacks it is not as severe anymore. I can deal with it and the fear and nausea. I thank the clinic and me for that. I just need a cure now." We used the *gradual exposure technique* to treat Paula's agoraphobia. She gradually exposed herself, in a stepwise fashion, to the real-life situations that caused her agoraphobia and panic attacks, and when she discovered that the attacks were not occurring, she was able to enter these places (like her car, work, and so on.). She used her best friend Gil to help her. Eventually Gil left Paula to do these exercises on her own.

Paula was discharged from us after seven months and had made very nice progress with a lot of hard work on her part. "It took many years, but I now know that I've got a mental illness that can come back, not a physical problem. You know, perhaps I'm lucky. I bet heart problems are harder, and more dangerous, to treat."

We previously discussed antidepressants, and how effective Zoloft and Paxil are in treating Panic Disorder. *Tofranil (Imipramine)* is a *tricyclic antidepressant* that is also effective in treating panic disorder. The major concern with Tofranil is twofold: The length of time before clinical efficacy is attained, and the potential side effects. Paula's psychiatrist did not wish to prescribe Tofranil for these reasons. Additionally, while waiting for the therapeutic onset, the side effects can lead the patient to cease taking the medications. Some of the side effects of Tofranil and some other tricyclic antidepressants include sedation and drowsiness, decreased *libido* (sexual desire), and *anticholinergic side effects.* This last group includes side effects such as constipation, blurred vision, confusion, poor memory, and hypotension (Maxmen & Ward, 1995). Most of these side effects drop out after one to two weeks. Many of these effects are also called *antihistamine effects,* since they are similar to those produced by over-the-counter allergy pills such as Contac. It is highly unlikely for one to become dependent on antidepressants.

As mentioned, a more effective class of antidepressant to use includes Zoloft and Paxil. These are the *Selective Serotonin Reuptake Inhibitors (SSRIs).* They produce fewer side effects than Tofranil, have a faster period of onset, and are likely to be used for a longer period of time. Zoloft appeared to work well for Paula.

One other possible type of medication to use would be *anxiolytics (anti-anxiety medications).* Medications in this category include Xanax (alprazolam) and Valium (diazepam). The Food and Drug Administration (FDA) recently approved Xanax for the treatment of panic disorder with or without agoraphobia (Bezchlibnyk-Butler & Jeffies, 2002). Xanax acts faster than Tofranil and also has fewer side effects. However, Xanax poses its own set of problems.

First, Xanax is highly addictive, unlike antidepressants. Second, anxiolytics such as Xanax can cause drowsiness and withdrawal symptoms if stopped abruptly or after using long-term. Finally, drinking grapefruit juice (or using other foods) while taking Xanax can elevate Xanax's blood levels. This means that your body will feel like more of the Xanax is in it than is actually the case (Bezchlibnyk-Butler & Jeffies, 2002).

In sum, the medications discussed are effective, but each type has its own set of cautions and side effects. The psychiatrist needs to decide which is most appropriate for the patient.

Prognosis

Paula's prognosis is listed as "good." She was able to return to work and reduce her panic attacks to a "manageable number. I can handle them now and I'm not housebound, not an emotional and mental cripple." Paula, after many years, gained insight into what was causing her panic attacks and came to terms with her father and brother's deaths. She realized how important her mother was, but not to the extent of limiting her own life. She also worked hard at getting better and at gaining insight "because I had to get better. I have my whole life ahead of me."

We told Paula that by going off of Zoloft so soon, her chance at relapse was much higher than if she stayed on it for a longer period of time (Bezchlibnyk-Butler & Jeffries, 2002). Paula took this under consideration and shortly returned to the clinic to see the psychiatrist. She stopped in to see us and told us "I decided that I can't take chances, so I'll go back on the Zoloft. I hate the stuff and I hate meds, but I can't go back to where I was, not at all."

At last report Paula had switched psychiatrists and was still taking her Zoloft "with no real problems." She told us that the ultimate test of her mental health occurred on September 11, 2001 and "I got very weak and almost came back in to see you. But I knew I had to be strong for me and for my mom. I'm hanging in there, but it's been rough. I've come too far to let some primitive maniacs spoil my progress." Paula was still "searching for a decent guy, but I'm young and have lots of time. I still live at home, but there's time for these things. And my mom? She's doing great! She's got more energy than I have!" It sounds like Paula's recovery is continuing very well.

Specific Phobia, Situational Type
The Case of Robert:
A Traveling Salesman with a Concern

Presenting Problem

Robert is a 33-year-old white male who has been married for 5 years. He received his bachelor's degree in chemistry from a well-known university and has a law degree. "I had some trouble passing the bar. I tried twice but the third time was the proverbial charm. That was big for me. I don't like failing at anything more than once." Robert works for a major pharmaceutical firm and "enjoys the work. I am a *detail rep*, a glorified drug pusher, if you will (laughs). I travel around the United States in my focus area, visiting with doctors, hospitals, and clinics. I provide literature and lots of free samples to all of my clients, usually doctors. Of course I give them the freebies as well: The pens, pads, cool stuff. The goal, of course, is to get them to use our products. I've been quite successful at that. I guess it's my legal skills at persuading them to use our products, but of course our products are good."

Robert is 5'11" tall and has curly hair that is going gray. He wears glasses and has a friendly demeanor with a wry sense of humor. Robert is thin but has a bit of a belly "from too much chocolate! I love my sweets and cakes. I can tell you where the best bakeries are; I know them all!" Robert made excellent eye contact and displayed appropriate affect. He was verbally open and easily answered all of our questions. Robert would come in to the sessions wearing his company identification.

We asked Robert to tell us what brought him in to see us. "Well, there are two reasons, basically. First, it's been more and more difficult for me to get into airplanes. First it was boats, and then it was planes. I can do cars because I have to but I get a choking feeling when I'm in a plane. Because it gets so bad I've been confined to a smaller section of the country for my work. I can use trains but not planes. Lately I've had some problems with elevators, so I almost always use the stairs. Thank goodness we're only on the fourth floor! I don't know what I would do otherwise."

"The other issue is my stage fright. It's getting worse and worse. I never had a serious problem with this before, but lately I'm forgetting key details about our products when I present. That's NOT good. I suspect it's common, especially since Fran, my wife, has been on my back about cutting back on the travel. But if I keep on doing this, professionals will laugh at me, and the company will not be able to turn away. I feel like when I'm pitching a product, I get that choking feeling again and I need to get out of the situation. I've told them I'm afraid to fly because of the recent plane crash." (At Robert's request, the date of that crash cannot be divulged for confidentiality purposes). "They accept that. It's true anyway. I get so closed in when I fly, and then that happens. They don't know what caused it. The more often you fly, the greater the chances you'll go down. But the real problem is the stage fright. I don't think this is normal."

Background Information

Robert and Fran have a 2-year-old son Hank. "It's been amazing. I still can't believe that I'm a father. We didn't try very long and look what happened. He's certainly a handful. I hate being on the road and not seeing him a lot, but I need to work to support the family. Fran works at a non-profit agency in a large metropolitan area, and she works part-time because of Hank. She didn't want to stop working, and we needed the extra money to pay for childcare." Robert reports that he and Fran are "happily married, but we have our problems, like anyone does."

Robert's development history is unremarkable; he reached all of his developmental milestones at age-appropriate levels. Robert received excellent grades in college. He graduated with a 3.6 average (out of a possible 4.0), and he graduated with honors. "I worked hard in school, since I was the first in my family to attend college. That's one reason why I went on to law school, to make my family proud and do my name justice. I was also interested in law of course. The money also seemed good, and besides, how many chem majors enter law school? I wanted to do law for pharmaceutical companies, since they paid well and it fit with my school background."

"Well, once I got into that, I soon realized that law was not for me. I started to get some problems, so I thought it had to do with the job. My problems got worse, so I decided to change careers and become a detail rep. I guess it's like seeing someone who is an English major go on to get a masters in Psych. The company had no problems with this change. I guess they realized how good I was (laughs), but they do that for a lot of good employees. You just had to promise you'd stay with them, which I did. The job was interesting, it provided security, and it paid well. I still can give them legal advice if they wish. I'm usually on the road a lot which is one of the reasons I'm here. Fran is not happy that I'm on the road so much. She IS happy about the six figures I bring in."

Robert's parents emigrated from Moscow, Russia. "My dad is still alive, but my mom passed away three years ago. She had a bad case of angina and died from heart failure. She lived in pain the last few years of her life. My dad's been on his own for three years, and he's doing okay. He's a tough SOB. Being a vet helps. He was in the army and saw action. What a nightmare. He talks about it sparingly. My son loves him. I only wish that my mom were alive to see my son."

Robert reports no known history of mental illness in his family "but then you never know. My dad either won't talk about his family a lot, or he doesn't remember. The Russians didn't keep good records back then, and my dad said he'd never return to Moscow. We have no idea what happened to his father. My dad came over with his mother, sister, and brother. My mom took a lot of her information to the grave. She also didn't want to talk about it. I guess it's part of the culture."

Robert has an older sister Molly. "Molly never went to college. She went to high school and got married shortly afterwards to Arthur. He was an entrepreneur. They lived quite well, so there was no need for further schooling on her part. Molly lives pretty close to us. She has two girls. One lives here and the other recently moved to Florida. Molly never seemed to have any mental or extreme physical problems. I guess I'm the first in my family in a lot of things (laughs)."

Thought Questions

1. What is going on with Robert?
2. Discuss the possible relation between Robert's concerns and his failing the bar exam.
3. What might the relationship be between the birth of Robert's son and his concerns?
4. Might there be a relationship between Fran's "pressuring" Robert to cut back on his travel and his fear of airplanes?
5. How might the airplane crash be related to Robert's concerns?

Assessment and Evaluation

Robert was assessed with an unstructured diagnostic interview and a *psychiatric evaluation*. Additionally, we asked Robert to get a complete physical for two reasons. First, he had not seen a doctor for a checkup for six years, which for a male is not that unusual. Second, we wanted to be certain that physically, everything was okay with him. It is possible that the "choking" that he described may be a physiological problem. Regardless, we wanted to be certain.

We questioned Robert further to get a clearer picture of his *phobias*. We asked Robert to clarify Fran's pressures on him regarding work. "Well, this has been occurring lately, especially since our son was born. The problem? Fran wants me home all of the time and does not want me to travel. That's not possible with my job. I might as well quit, or take a desk job and be miserable, or go back to law. I can't do the latter since I hate practicing law. So that's what's happening. We get into a lot of fights over this. We fight on the phone, and then we fight a lot during the weekend when we both need to rest. Like most fights, it revolves around time and money. I'm doing this job for our son's future. Fran needs to get that."

We then asked Robert if his problems worsened after his mother's death. "Well, that was a hard time for everyone. I was very close to her, and what made it worse is that she never saw our son. That made me more anxious and depressed of course. I still managed to go to work and get things done, and presenting was actually easier. It took my mind off of my sorrow. But we still had these arguments, I can tell you that much." We asked Robert how his sex life was with everything occurring.

"Well, it ain't the best, that's for sure. We still make love, but it seems . . . forced, like we need to do it to tell us that everything's okay. Like it's our responsibility as married people. But it's not that frequent. I'm very tired at the end of a long week, and Fran's lost a lot of her spontaneity. We're not burning down the house, if you know what I mean. But we do make love about once a month or so." Does any of this new information give you any clues as to what might be occurring with Robert?

We then focused on Robert's apparent *claustrophobia*. Be aware that sometimes a fear of flying might in fact be claustrophobia. Robert seems to have this since not only is he afraid of flying, but also of boats and closed-in spaces in general. "Well, as I said, I've always been a bit wary of flying. The more you fly the more likely you'll go down in a crash. But it's gotten a lot worse lately, especially after the plane crash. I still get nauseous when I think I have to fly. My boss understands this, but he told me last week that I better get some help and fly or else I'll get demoted and/or fired. At least since I'm seeking help they can't touch me." (Legally, they cannot.)

"Once the crash occurred Fran was all over me about not flying again. You know the drill, 'you're a father now, and I can't raise this child alone,' and on and on. Honestly, I've never had airplane fears like I've got now. The elevator fears seemed to come after the airplane fears. It makes life a lot easier for me if I'm not cramped. I need a lot of space to feel comfortable. It's also gotten more difficult for me to cross bridges which is a major issue living where we do."

So far it seems that Robert suffers from a *specific phobia, situational type*. Robert demonstrates insight that his fears are unreasonable and that they interfere with his life, specifically his marriage and career. The specific phobia as we saw it is claustrophobia (fear of closed in places). Before our next session, Robert went for his physical and, as we suspected would occur, his doctor found nothing wrong with him that might be causing these concerns. "He told me the usual stuff, to lose a bit of weight and exercise, but all was fine otherwise. A waste of time and money (smiles)."

We turned our attention to Robert's stage fright, which may be another type of phobia. "The stage fright was always there. Once I began to present in law school and later, I managed to control it. I'm a naturally shy person. I know, I know . . . so why do I sell for a living? I enjoy it, and I enjoy people. I just hate screwing up in public. My dad is a perfectionist and he expects us to be like that too. I'll blame him for this. But this is a real problem." We asked him when it came back and got worse. "Well, since my mom died, and since our son was born. Fran's bugging me made it worse. I saw that connection. It's like she wants me to foul up, and I'm doing so. We'll lose the house if I get fired because of this, but I'll be home!" He laughed sarcastically here.

We asked Robert to tell us if there was a specific situation that may have worsened this condition. It may seem like we are "badgering" Robert, but it is crucial to try and discover, if possible, when a patient began to manifest symptoms and why. "As I told you I never liked to present, which is one reason I did not pursue law after passing the bar. I just get all uptight when I present. Things got better once I passed the bar and I was working only as a consultant, but I realized that law wouldn't do it for me. My stage fright had decreased, so being a detail rep would be possible. There was one episode that may have worsened things."

"I had been doing sales for about 7 months and at this promotion I was selling a new product. This was a 'miracle drug' for treating weight problems, and I was asked to pitch it to a weight loss clinic in a hospital. I was excited and of course I knew the material. I did a great job at first but there was a medical resident who was a total ass. He kept asking impossible questions, and of course I'm not a doctor. Finally, I just froze and blanked on the material. He started to yell at me, called me unprofessional, and stormed out. The chief of staff apologized for his behavior and promised that he would be severely punished. That didn't matter. After that incident I began to doubt my skills and myself. I never liked being criticized, especially in public. In this case it was unwarranted, since I always know my material before presenting. It never seemed to get really better after this. So I guess it began there."

"I really know I'm acting crazy, and I need help for my job, marriage and most importantly for my son's sake. I'll do whatever it takes; just tell me what I need to do. I can't take this anymore. Life has ceased being fun, and it should be a blast as a new father."

We felt like we had a grasp on Robert's situation, but he still had his psychiatric evaluation ahead, and a *case conference* where all of the helping professionals in the clinic would discuss his case. The psychiatrist ". . . enjoyed speaking with Robert. He is a man who has good insight into his problems and suspects he knows their origins. He realizes that his behaviors are irrational, and he honestly seems to want help. No medication is warranted at this time. He will set up an appointment if he wishes to discuss *anxiolytics* (antianxiety medications)." The diagnoses then followed. The psychiatrist's report was presented at the case conference, and the other clinicians agreed with our impressions and with the psychiatrist's diagnoses:

Specific Phobia, Situational Type	300.29
Rule Out (R/O) Social Phobia	300.23

Theoretical Etiologies

We had an extensive discussion of the possible etiologies of anxiety disorders when we examined Paula. There appear to be some additional etiological hypotheses when discussing specific and social phobias, and we will focus on those. Claustrophobia, which Robert seems to have, tends to develop later than the other phobias, most of which develop in childhood. The development of a phobia is easy to understand. The individual, when they first encounter the object, experiences extreme fear and arousal, almost similar to (but not) a panic attack. The next step is the strong desire and attempt to escape the situation and avoid it in the future. In Robert's case, his fears significantly impact his life, so much so that he made lifestyle changes and risked his job because of this phobia. Situational phobias such as claustrophobia tend to have a familial component, but whether the disorder itself is inherited, or a predisposition (called the *diathesis*) is inherited is unclear.

How can we tell that Robert does not have panic disorder? Let us presume that his panic attacks were related to his presentations or having to fly, and were related to nothing else (calling his reactions panic attacks might be a bit of a reach). We can then safely say that he does **not** have panic disorder. However, if he were having panic attacks outside of the specific phobic situations (in an open place, with Hank in the park, etc.), then he would be diagnosed with panic disorder.

Some research, as we have noted, states that specific phobias develop because of direct experience. Robert's choking could have been real initially, and it might have occurred on a plane or during a speaking engagement. Specific phobias can also develop by watching someone else experience extreme fear (a concept on "Fear Factor"), experiencing a panic attack or a false alarm about a situation, and perhaps being told about a specific danger (don't go to Afghanistan or Iraq for a few years). If an unexpected panic attack occurs in a certain situation, that situation may be linked in the future with panic attacks and thus become phobic.

Humans also seem to be predisposed to developing phobias (or at the least fears or cautions) involving certain situations. Research has shown that fears of snakes, heights, and flying are the most common fears, and can thus become the most common phobias. *Darwinists* might state that these fears are related to survival and adaptation. It makes sense for all humans to fear snakes since they can poison us; we should be wary of heights since we can fall and die or injure ourselves.

The individual also needs to develop anxiety about the possibility that the event will recur. There remains much anxiety as to when the next terrorist attack will occur in the United States. People who completely alter their lives based on this anxiety would be considered phobic.

We also need to consider social and cultural factors. Culturally men are not "supposed" to report phobic behavior. Men are supposed to be strong and display "machismo"; expressing a fear or a phobia would make the man look weak. Fears of magic, spirits or other apparitions are considered normal in some cultures and should not be taken out of context when diagnosing a phobia.

Treatment Plan

One of the nicer features of working with Specific and Social Phobias is that they are easier to treat than other types of mental disorders. A helpful aspect when treating any phobic disorder is to try and discern when the phobia began to surface. Usually there is a precipitating event(s). Knowing it/them will not ensure a successful treatment, but it gives clinicians more useful information to apply.

The clinic decided to engage Robert in individual therapy. Robert was, as you have seen, very willing to participate in therapy so he could "get cured, or get control or something like that. I'll try anything, even medications if I need to. I could probably get the appropriate ones myself (laughs)!" One of the best ways to treat specific phobias is by using *systematic desensitization techniques,* in this instance structured and supervised exposure exercises. If this occurred unsupervised, Robert might try to do too much too soon (we figured he would do this because he is so motivated to get better quickly) and thus would end up avoiding the phobic situation, reinforcing the avoidance behavior.

The concept behind this method is to gradually expose the patient to the phobia-producing stimuli; in Robert's case, closed-in spaces. We discussed Robert's fears and began by showing him photographs of elevators, cramped offices, and airplanes, asking him to tell us what was occurring with him. "Well, the photos made me nervous. I imagined being in them and I got all sweaty, like I was going to have a panic attack. I got very squirmy and squeamish." We showed the photos to him at the next session and "I feel a bit better, because I told myself between sessions that my reactions to photos—photos!—were foolish. I can handle this now."

We next asked Robert to imagine himself in a claustrophobic setting, although not the worst one he could possibly imagine. We again were looking for feedback. "Well, again I'm getting nauseous and sick here. I don't like this feeling. I have a vivid imagination, and it seems real to me. I'm trying to block the reactions." We took a break and began to teach Robert *progressive muscle relaxation techniques.* These are relaxation techniques that, with practice, can be readily learned. Our goal was to tell Robert to use these techniques whenever he felt claustrophobic. We did them for a few sessions with him while asking him to imagine, first, stressful situations.

"The techniques are working, but not as fast as I would like. I can now, after six sessions, imagine some easy situations and stay relaxed, but the tough ones like planes are still hard. I do like the feelings when I'm using the relaxation techniques." We continued on this path with Robert. Eventually, we exposed him to a very claustrophobic situation, the elevator in our clinic. We stopped it and had the doors stay closed. Robert told us "I felt panicky, but I didn't pass out. I used the relaxation and deep breathing techniques and they kind of worked. I'm amazed, to be honest." Robert was assisted in many of these exercises outside of the clinic by his lifelong friend Dick, "as good a guy as you could possibly meet. I don't want Fran to help because she would rush me and be critical if I failed." Once he conquered the elevator, Robert exposed himself to more and more threatening situations with Dick's help until he felt comfortable at work, and eventually in an airplane. "I'll never be totally at ease in a plane, but people say if flying was totally safe, we would have no fear of flying. So I'm justified I think."

Robert also learned through the exposure exercises that elevators rarely pose a threat, just like boats and airplanes. Albert Ellis would call Robert's past beliefs *irrational,* since they really do not make much sense. In other words, Robert, like others with phobias, exaggerates his anxieties and fears. One of the goals for Robert was to get him to face his fears and the feared situations directly. Avoidance only makes things worse.

What about Robert's social phobia? This got better as we taught him the relaxation techniques and his claustrophobia got better. Robert also used a key treatment suggestion as you will see. Robert was asked to use exposure exercises and rehearsals to combat his social phobia. He first had to present in front of an imaginary person, then a small group, and finally an imaginary large audience. He was videotaped (with his permission of course) so he could get feedback on his *nonverbal behavior.* The tapes showed that Robert was very nervous, sweating, and making poor eye contact during the rehearsals. Once Robert learned to use the relaxation and rehearsal techniques, he graduated to rehearsing for real people, in this instance the clinic staff.

We followed the same pattern. Robert first rehearsed and presented in front of us, then in front of all of the psychologists, then in front of all of the clinicians, and finally in front of all of the clinic staff. The presentations were brief and Robert again was videotaped. "I noticed that I was sweating a lot initially but as the number of people increased my tension eased somewhat. The deep breathing is so helpful. Being able to practice is also very helpful."

"I think my social fears are tied to my claustrophobia, and to Fran's bugging me about traveling too much. It's like I'm being self-destructive, but Fran would be happy to see me home. I used what I've learned and I rehearsed my next presentation before colleagues and co-workers. This helped a lot because they pointed out flaws in my delivery and in my style. I'm a better presenter, but the proof comes next week, when I go out on the road again by car. I'm not totally there yet." What do you suspect happened?

Ideally, Robert would have been placed in a *cognitive-behavioral* group setting to treat his social phobia. He would be with other socially phobic individuals; a key goal of such a group is to rehearse the situations in front of each other. At the same time, the therapist(s) focus on *cognitive* restructuring, changing the underlying misperceptions and fears that accompany these phobic-producing social situations. These misperceptions are presumed to be automatic and/or unconscious. The clinic did not have such a group but if we did, Robert would have been an excellent addition. Perhaps such a group would **not** have made a significant difference. Hoffman and Barlow (2002) recently discovered that the exposure-based rehearsal, which occurred with Robert, is more effective and thus more important than the cognitive therapy.

The next week Robert filled us in about his presentation. "Well, it went okay. I got nervous and was afraid I would forget things and get yelled at, so I paused, took some water, did a short relaxation technique for 10 seconds, and went on. It made it easier. I still got criticized, but I realized after they were criticizing the **product,** not me! That really helped. Like you guys said, I was misinterpreting a lot of things. I expect the next one to go much better."

We were not surprised at Robert's progress. When a patient is as motivated and as insightful as Robert, treatment, if effective, should work rather quickly. Since we were also using cognitive, *behavioral,* and cognitive-behavioral techniques, we expected to see results quickly. If no positive changes occurred, then the therapist(s) need to change the intervention(s). The final issue that we wanted to discuss was Robert's concerns with Fran.

"Well, yes, Fran is still pressuring me, but at least I'm on the road to recovery. Fran does not want to come in and see you guys. She hates therapists and thinks you're all very very weird. She told me this is my problem and that any problems we have at home stay there, for us to work out alone. I can see her point, but she's being silly. I know where to go if we need to come in. Fran is still immature in many ways. Being a mother hasn't changed that aspect of her."

Robert continued in therapy for four months. "I realized where my silly fears came from, especially my social fears. The claustrophobia took a bit longer to handle. I also wanted to make sure I was basically better before I quit here. Coming back a month later saying 'Oops, I left too early' would really be embarrassing. As for Fran, little has changed. She's still at me, and I really think we need marital therapy. I've told her that if she doesn't let up she will damage the marriage and our son. Our sex life is still not great either. I've decided to hire someone to watch our son one weekend a month so we can go away and be alone. I hope that helps. She's just not willing to compromise."

At the end of four months, we felt comfortable in discharging Robert. The psychiatrist felt no need to see him after his initial visit. "I'm about to take my first plane trip in a long time. I'm scared, but I'm excited. It's a trip to San Francisco and, get this. Fran and our boy are coming along. We're spending the money and making this a working vacation. We'll let you know what happens."

We previously examined anxiolytics and a subclassification of these medications, the benzodiazepines (specifically Xanax). Other drugs that fall into this classification are Valium (diazepam) and *Ativan (lorazepam)*. These drugs are effective in alleviating anxiety, and may have helped Robert. They act quickly; however, they have some significant problems.

First, these medications are highly addictive and therefore can cause *withdrawal symptoms*. Second, anxiolytics are really designed for short-term and infrequent use. In other words, because they are highly addictive, one can easily become physiologically and psychologically dependent on them. One problem would be treated, but another one might arise. These drugs cause the patient to sometimes become drowsy, unable to concentrate (which is interesting, since those who have excessive anxiety or phobias usually have problems concentrating), and cause *central nervous system impairment*. In other words, do not use these drugs and operate a motor vehicle. We could have prescribed Valium to Robert, but since he was confined to his car in order to not get fired, we would have a problem.

Psychiatrists are usually reluctant to prescribe anxiolytics to patients with phobic disorders, and with good reason. These drugs are effective, but their addictive potential and side effects are cause for concern. In addition, Robert had no desire to take these medications, and since he was a detail rep, he knew better than most people.

Beta Blockers (drugs that lower blood pressure and heart rate) such as *Inderal (propranolol)* seem to be effective in treating anxiety disorders and are seen by some as successfully treating social phobia (Bezchlibnyk-Butler & Jeffries, 2002), but the field is undecided as to their efficacy. Inderal is not an approved medication for social phobia.

We previously mentioned Paxil (paroxetine), an SSRI antidepressant; this has recently been approved by the Food and Drug Administration (FDA) for the treatment of social phobia. A concern is that relapse is common once drug treatment is stopped. Additionally, any medications will treat the symptoms but not the underlying problems and the causes. Preliminary data also indicate that, in some instances, the class of antidepressants known as *Monoamine Oxidase Inhibitors (MAOIs)* is effective in treating social phobia (Bezchlibnyk-Butler & Jeffries, 2002). Bezchlibnyk-Butler & Jeffries (2002) do make the point that the data remain contradictory as to MAOIs' efficacy in treating social phobia.

Prognosis

Robert's prognosis is listed as "good." He made excellent progress in therapy and demonstrated good insight from the start of treatment. He realized how "silly many of my behaviors were," and he was highly motivated to "get better. I really did not have any choice in the matter." At last contact, Robert had made the plane trip with some difficulty but "I managed it. I had a lot of seltzers and nearly broke Fran's hand a few times I squeezed so hard. I am flying again, albeit I am still not that steady about it. I'm doing so gradually, gradually easing back into the routine. I'm getting there." He and Fran are discussing having another child but "Fran is still at me about the job. Now she's gone back to work full-time, so she can't say much now, can she? I can't travel like this and have another child. But I'm doing well. I hope I'll be totally back to normal in a few months." Robert was making excellent progress, and we told him our doors were always open should he need our services again.

Review and Study Questions

Paula

1. What, if anything, would you have done differently in Paula's treatment?
2. How important was the absence of Paula's mother from therapy?
3. Discuss your views on the use of medications in Paula's treatment.
4. The helping professions believe that the most effective treatments for some disorders is a combination of medications and therapy. What do you believe?
5. How would you handle a suicidal patient?
6. How would you work on Paula's issues with her mother?

Robert

1. How typical a patient is Robert? After all, he is highly motivated and insightful.
2. Is Robert's insight related to his disorder? Why or why not?
3. Discuss your interpretation of Robert's flying phobia.
4. How do you think Robert's phobias affected his son?
5. Discuss why you would or would not "force" Fran into therapy with Robert.

Terms to Know

Panic Disorder With Agoraphobia

National Institute of Mental Health (NIMH)

blunted affect

Phobic Disorders

agoraphobia

echocardiogram

congestive heart failure

Panic Disorder

unstructured diagnostic interview

psychiatric evaluation

structured diagnostic interview

panic attacks

allergy pill/antihistamine

suicidal thoughts and tendencies

suicidal behaviors

Contac

initial intake assessment

theoretical etiologies

id

ego

defense mechanisms

psyche

classical conditioning

operant (instrumental) conditioning

arachnophobia

negative reinforcement

prepared conditioning

Rational Emotive Therapy (RET)

amniocentesis (amnio)

GABA system

benzodiazepines

antidepressant medications

individual therapy

family therapy

group therapy

arrhythmia

spontaneous remission

Mood Disorders

Zoloft (sertraline)

Paxil (paroxetine)

Tofranil (imipramine)

clitoral priaprism

interactionist or integrated approach

hypnotherapy

progressive muscle relaxation techniques

cognitive restructuring

gradual exposure technique

tricyclic antidepressant

libido

anticholinergic side effects

antihistamine effects

Selective Serotonin Reuptake Inhibitors (SSRIs)

anxiolytics (antianxiety medications)

Xanax (alprazolam)

Valium (diazepam)

detail rep

psychiatric evaluation

phobias

claustrophobia

specific phobia, situational type

case conference

anxiolytics

Rule Out (R/O)

Darwinists

systematic desensitization techniques

diathesis

progressive muscle relaxation techniques

irrational

cognitive-behavioral

cognitive

Ativan (lorazepam)

withdrawal symptoms

behavioral

central nervous system impairment

Beta Blockers

Inderal (propranolol)

Monoamine Oxidase Inhibitors (MAOIs)

nonverbal behavior

Chapter 2

Anxiety Disorders II

Of all the anxiety disorders in psychology, we consider the two discussed in this chapter to be the most fascinating. *Posttraumatic Stress Disorder (PTSD)* affects about 8% of the adult population in the United States (APA, 2000). This is a surprisingly large percentage. PTSD takes on added importance in the wake of the terrorist attacks on September 11, 2001. Anecdotal accounts have noted that the incidence of PTSD has increased significantly since the attacks, especially for residents of New York City and Washington, DC. Self-help groups and workshops have arisen to aid in PTSD treatment, and this author has received many flyers and emails urging him to participate in PTSD training sessions. APA, in conjunction with the *Discovery/Health Channel,* has produced a program called "Aftermath: The Road to Resilience." This program is for public use and is designed to teach *resilience* in the face of trauma aftermaths. One of the areas involved is PTSD. Based on the world situation as of this writing, PTSD will not soon depart from the vernacular.

This is even more intriguing because until relatively recently PTSD was not considered to be a psychiatric disorder. In fact, some professionals and others called PTSD *shellshock,* referring to battle-weary soldiers returning home who were "shocked" by seeing active combat. They would have numerous flashbacks to the battlefields and would usually be prescribed *antianxiety medications* to treat their problems.

Obsessive-Compulsive Disorder (OCD) is also quite interesting. OCD affects about 2.5% of the adult United States population (APA, 2000); thus, it is relatively rare. However, its rarity by no means reflects how debilitating this disorder can be. The film *As Good as it Gets,* with Jack Nicholson, gives a decent portrayal of someone suffering from OCD. Like all motion pictures, things are "adjusted" somewhat to make the movie more marketable. Lady Macbeth is another example of someone who suffered from OCD, and Felix Ungar (of "Odd Couple" fame) can also be viewed in this light.

We will first examine Sarah, whose story you may wish to read twice, since at first glance it seems fantastic. We will conclude with Fannie, who has a classic case of OCD. Fannie is an excellent example of an individual who knows she has a problem but can do little to control her symptoms.

Posttraumatic Stress Disorder (PTSD)
The Case of Sarah:
The Horror of Childhood Sexual Abuse

Presenting Problem

Sarah is a 14-year-old white female who is in the eighth grade at a local public junior high school. Sarah has an 18-year-old stepbrother from her father's second wife. "My dad divorced when I was very young, 6 years old. My mom was an alcoholic, a really really bad drunk. My dad is 38 and is as straight as they come. He finally divorced her and he got custody. My mom's on welfare and couldn't take care of me. I have no relationship at all with my mom. I tolerate my stepmother. I only listen to my dad, and he's very strict with me. It pisses me off."

Sarah had a hardened look to her. She had a blunted affect and rarely smiled. Her demeanor was not depressive; rather it was angry. Sarah was short (5'1"), had long blonde curly hair, and wore a short skirt and "my Go-Go boots" to the first session. She wore bracelets on both wrists and wore an oversized watch on her right wrist. Sarah wore a lot of makeup on her face, including blue eye shadow. She made fair eye contact. Sarah never cried during any of the sessions and appeared angry most of the time. Regardless, she was candid with us.

Sarah's grades are okay in school. She's getting low Cs but does not seem too concerned about it. "What are grades anyway? I ain't going to college, so as long as I graduate, it's cool. I like to hang and stuff. School doesn't interest me much. I do like history though, but the rest, no way."

Sarah's guidance counselor first referred Sarah to the *school social worker*. He was concerned that Sarah was falling asleep in class more often lately. Her guidance counselor was **not** overly concerned about Sarah's grades since they remained consistent throughout her junior high school years. A rule of thumb: If a child's behavior changes suddenly, or his/her grades drop significantly, investigate the possibility of *alcohol/substance abuse*. Do you think that will be the case here? Keep reading.

Sarah's school social worker had a few sessions with Sarah, at which time he discussed her case with the school principal. He noted that Sarah had been cutting many classes and on many days had not come in at all. Her father had been notified and was not "too concerned," according to

Sarah. "My dad always worries about me, but the most important thing for him is his work. I forged the absence notes and no one knew a thing. Dad is cool as long as I call and tell him where I am. If I'm spending the night at a friend's house he's okay with that. He's very careful with me as I said, but he really doesn't pry into my life a lot. He's a strict, yet non-prying dad."

We called the principal since he was the one who referred Sarah to us. He noted as well that she was missing a lot of classes and they could not figure out why her father was unconcerned. He verified that her grades had indeed remained stable this year. Sarah's teacher was more concerned with her falling asleep in class so often. Sarah told them she has a job after school, but they discovered this was not true. They figured that she was out all night long, or staying up with friends. Sarah's eyes were also quite red a number of times during the past month in school (she appeared like this twice in the clinic). The principal was not sure if this was because Sarah was so tired, or was due to something else such as substance abuse (he presumed she was smoking marijuana).

Background Information

The principal met with Sarah and her father before she was referred to us; Sarah related the conversation. "So Mr. Adler told us that I had to come in to this clinic to get psychobabbled or something. Like there's something wrong with me. I'm just a 14-year-old girl who's having fun. Give me a d$#@ break here. But it was either come here or get suspended, so guess which one I chose? Mr. Adler was worried about my ditching classes and school. Well, my grades are okay, so what's the diff what I do? Look at me: Is this college? But my dad will throw me out or put me in foster care or something if I get suspended or expelled."

Sarah's father came in with her to the second session. Sarah was clearly uncomfortable with this but she agreed to his presence. We asked Sarah a few questions and she looked at the floor and responded with one word answers. When we asked open-ended questions, she would tell us she did not know the answers. It appeared as though Sarah was withholding information while her father was present.

He was curious as to what might be occurring with Sarah. We explained to him that he was more than welcome to stay if we saw the need for his presence (and if Sarah agreed), and we praised him for being so concerned. However, we asked him to remain in the waiting room while Sarah spoke to us. We also explained that even though Sarah was a minor, she still had confidentiality rights. He was upset by this but understood.

Sarah then became more candid once he left the room, and we began to learn the reasons behind her recent actions as the sessions progressed. "I guess I've been spending too much time out the past few months, so I'm really wiped in the morning. My dad doesn't know any of this . . . you won't tell him, will you? (We said we would not, without her permission, unless we legally **had** to violate confidentiality.) He'd get really pissed at me if he found any of this stuff out. Well, one of the reasons I've been blowing off school and stuff is that I've been out partying with friends a lot this year. I met these cool people from the private high school. We get together, sometimes go to raves, and sometimes just hang. We drink and stuff. I like vodka and beer. Sometimes I pass out at Joe's place, sometimes on the street. But I'm always safe. Someone's always watching over me. Are you okay hearing this? I feel comfortable here, so I can spill."

So far it seems like we have some key information. Sarah may have an alcohol abuse problem that is causing all of these other problems to occur. It makes sense, since she claims that her mother is an alcoholic and alcohol dependence seems to have a familial component. We asked Sarah some more questions.

"One thing I do want to fix is my sleep problems. I keep having these nightmares that won't stop, and I need you to tell me what's up. They are so wrong. You guys do the dream stuff . . . I read about it. That's one reason I fall asleep in class so much, as I'm not able to sleep much. I keep getting the nightmares and when I wake up I'm afraid to fall asleep again. They seem so real. So okay, that is a problem." Alcohol abusers sometimes have sleep problems. However, when someone is drunk to the point of passing out, *REM sleep* (the dream stage) does **not** occur.

We then brought Sarah's father back in and told him that the clinic wished to see him alone for a few sessions. Sarah was then asked to leave and she agreed, heading to the waiting room. He complained about the cost and about us taping Sarah's sessions but agreed to let Sarah continue. He told us that he was friendly with some of the police, and they told him that on at least four occasions they found Sarah asleep on the street or in the gutter. She appears to be drunk and possibly stoned or high. He was very worried about this and wanted some answers. However, he did not wish to confront Sarah since he feared she might run away "and she's the only child I'll ever have. I have a physical problem that makes producing another child impossible." We asked him to join Sarah in the next session, hoping that he would be candid with her. At that point the session ended.

Thought Questions

1. What is going on with Sarah? Do you have enough information yet?
2. Sarah's father was not being honest with her. Discuss your views on this. What would you do in that situation?

3. Discuss some of the possible causes of Sarah's nightmares.
4. Should Sarah be seen individually or together with her father? Justify your answer.

Assessment and Evaluation

Sarah was assessed with an *unstructured diagnostic interview,* a *psychiatric evaluation,* and a *consultation* with her junior high school. Sarah met with us two times before she saw the psychiatrist. The clinic still had the intention of working with Sarah's father, but we needed more information regarding Sarah's present situation before we could proceed. When Sarah returned, we asked more questions and received some very interesting replies. It should be noted that Sarah's father always brought her to the clinic since she was too young to drive and public transportation was unreliable. He remained in the waiting room, at times pacing nervously. Usually he would read one of the magazines or *USA Today.*

We focused more on Sarah's sleep troubles, specifically her nightmares. The fact that intrigued us was that the nightmares always had the same theme and/or people in them. "I'm usually being chased in the nightmares, but the past 3 or 4 months I've been on a swing in a park. I'm pushing myself and going really fast. Suddenly a person comes up behind me and starts to push me. Then the person starts to put their hands on me and starts touching things they shouldn't. The person grabs my breasts and squeezes my butt hard. I get really scared but I can't scream because nothing comes out of my mouth. I also can't see the person's face but I guess it's a guy. Then I get so scared I wake up in a sweat. It all seems so real, I don't know what's going on."

One of the goals was to figure out what was happening in the dream, and who the faceless person was. We asked Sarah more questions, since we began to get an idea what might be happening. "I started drinking when I was 12. It helps me feel good, and helps me to escape. I chill out when I'm drunk, forget all my troubles. My dad doesn't give me much money for booze and smokes, so I quickly found out that I could make money by trading sex. I'm not a prostitute; I just trade sex for favors like booze, smokes, and cash. It works. Sex has no meaning for me; I'm just a physical substitute. I don't do it a lot, just when I'm really tapped out. Older guys like young girls. But it's all about the booze."

As we heard this we became extremely concerned. Not only was Sarah drinking and ending up on the street at night, she was also selling her body for alcohol and other things. We were unsure whether the latter part was true and we had no way to confirm or disprove these statements. We thus used caution regarding these allegations. We consulted with the clinic's supervisor and he decided to wait and monitor Sarah. We also presented this concern at a staff meeting. The clinic also decided to wait and see what occurred with Sarah. She was aware of her actions and their possible consequences and "I take care; someone's always with me. This is not a Sarah's all alone kind of thing."

We did want to know where Sarah's casual attitude toward sex came from, and how she could detach herself from it like this. In the fifth session we asked Sarah more questions about her background. See if you can assess where we were headed with this.

"My mom? She was a bad drunk. What my dad didn't tell you is why he got custody. Sure, a drunk mom is not a good mom, but she's still my mom. Once my dad left, my mom brought her boyfriend in to live with us. He was a sleaze, an ass. He was in his early 40s, which for a 36-year-old mom is too old. One night he came in to my room and kissed me goodnight, but it was a bad kiss, a deep tongue kiss. I almost puked. I was afraid of him after that, but he would come in every night and do more stuff to me. I knew this was wrong. He told me he'd kill me if I told my mom. I had to tell my mom. How did my f*&^%$#@ mom react? She called ME a liar and said I was seducing him. How can a 5-year-old seduce a man? Ask me that. She said she'd never believe anything I ever said again, and of course he kept on coming in."

"I had to tell my dad and he went ballistic. He threatened to kill her boyfriend and told his lawyer. My mom and dad were separated at the time, and my dad hoped to get back together for my sake. That didn't work. The only reason I'm with my dad is because of his money. He can raise me, and she's passed out all the time. So my mom had an evil boyfriend. Now you know why I really can't stand my mom. She never did anything to help me in this situation. It went on for about a year."

Do you now see where the line of questioning was headed? We suspected that Sarah may have been sexually molested as a child and was *repressing* the memories. What is unusual is that Sarah came out with this information early on in therapy. We suspected that she wanted to disclose this information and wanted help resolving her trauma. Freud would say that the defense mechanisms are not working and this trauma has now moved to her conscious mind. It is best to let patients reveal sensitive information such as this instead of haranguing them until it comes out. Once we learned this information, many of Sarah's behaviors began to make sense. Can you guess which behaviors those are?

We asked Sarah, in a *behavioral homework assignment*, to record her nightmares for the next two weeks and bring the notes to the sessions. When she arrived, she told us she had four nightmares the past 2 weeks, but the last one was the most interesting. "The face of the man . . . yes, it's a man, came out last night. It was my mom's boyfriend, the one who molested me and had sex with me. I should have known! All this time and I had no damned idea. I feel like a jerk. No wonder he's chasing me. I guess I'm still haunted by this bastard. I still wonder what I did to cause this, if I did something like my mom said."

This was a major revelation and breakthrough for Sarah. Once she disclosed this information, we offered to transfer her to a female therapist because we were now dealing with a case of sexual molestation. Good protocol calls for sex abuse victims to use same-sex therapists. Oddly, Sarah did not wish to be transferred. We asked the female therapist to come in and talk to Sarah, but Sarah preferred to remain with us, which was surprising. However, Sarah was always a surprising girl.

All of Sarah's behaviors now began to make more sense. As we continued to question her, she told us that she was unable to concentrate even when sober. She drank so much and traded sex because she didn't see herself "living past 30. I have no future, so let's live it up right now. Who would marry me? I'll never amount to anything. I can totally detach myself from sex. How many people can say they lost their virginity at 5 years old? How sick is that?"

We also asked Sarah about her relationships. "I really don't have any true friends. I hang with people, but that's really it. There's no one I can really talk to, so it's kind of okay I'm here now. I can't talk to anyone in school; who would want to listen to me, and who would believe me anyhow? I really am all alone, except for my dad. It's hard at times." We detected little emotion in Sarah, and her affect remained blunted.

We now had a good idea as to what Sarah was experiencing, and why. We also told Sarah that we needed to bring her father in for some sessions so he could work on these issues with her. Sarah did not wish for that to occur, but Sarah did tell us "it's okay to tell my dad that all of the sex stuff is true. Don't tell him about the trading of sex, but the other he knows." Sarah's father joined her in the next session, and he reacted to the revelations.

"I figured that Sarah was truthful, but it's all so unbelievable that I really was not sure. You trust your daughter, but you read so much of people making things up, and Sarah can manipulate her dad. I'm actually somewhat relieved that it seems to be true. She would wake up screaming at night sometimes. Maybe that's why she doesn't come home and is with friends. She might be afraid I'll do something, or that Sam will come over her and do something." (Sam is her mother's ex-boyfriend.) At this point her father began to cry, and he prematurely ended the session.

Sarah was presented at a staff meeting to get further suggestions. The staff decided to tell the school little except to let them know she was in treatment and was working on some issues. The clinic took risks here, since Sarah was involved in behaviors that could be perceived as being a threat to herself, a legal mandate to violate confidentiality. We mentioned previously how the director and the clinic staff thought we should wait and see what happened with Sarah and her father before breaking confidentiality. Sarah was also referred to the psychiatrist for an evaluation, and the clinic staff also decided to discuss contraception with Sarah through its health educator.

The psychiatrist saw Sarah and had this to say in his case notes, "Sarah is a troubled 14-year-old girl who has a significant *alcohol abuse* problem caused by posttraumatic stress and a family history of alcoholism. Sarah's nightmares and lack of school attendance are related to her being molested as a 5-year-old. *Depression* is mild to moderate, not cause of sleep problems. Emotional detachment and promiscuity are concerns. Rec. (Recommend) once a week family with father; individual with Sarah to work on PTSD, evaluate for meds after one month."

The psychiatrist's diagnoses agreed with the clinic's staff's:

Posttraumatic Stress Disorder, Chronic, With Delayed Onset	309.81
Dysthymic Disorder, Early Onset	300.4
Alcohol Abuse	305.00

Theoretical Etiologies

We can safely say that PTSD is caused specifically because the individual experiences a traumatic event. The key question here is why do some people who are exposed (or who experience) trauma develop PTSD, and some do not? There are some hypothesized factors to be considered. See if any of these factors apply to Sarah.

The intensity of the traumatic event may be related to the development of PTSD (Foy, Resnick, Sipprelle, & Carroll, 1987). Additionally, some people appear to be more vulnerable to developing PTSD than do others. For example, if the individual has a family history of anxiety disorders, s/he appears to be at greater risk for developing PTSD (Foy et al, 1987). It also seems possible that an individual may place themselves in situations where experiencing trauma is more likely. Foy et al (1987) also noted that family instability is another potential etiological factor. Individuals who come from unstable family backgrounds seem to be at greater risk to develop PTSD if they experience a traumatic event.

Social and cultural factors also come into play. Much research has shown that if the person experiences a traumatic event **and** they have a good support system (family and friends), they will be less likely to develop PTSD. It also seems that attempting to cope with the situation (not through avoidance) instead of becoming angry and blaming others also helps to avoid developing PTSD.

Finally, some interesting research has examined memory disruption and memory loss. It seems that PTSD victims have short-term memory disruptions and are unable to recall certain events well if at all (Vasterling, Brailey, Constans, & Sotker, 1998). It has been hypothesized that PTSD victims suffer from chronic brain arousal due to the presence of stress-related hormones (specifically *cortisol*). Because of this, brain damage, specifically to the *hippocampus*, can occur. The hippocampus is involved with memory functions and learning. This might explain why PTSD victims have problems recalling their trauma.

Treatment Plan

We had multiple treatment goals for Sarah. First, we decided, by using *individual treatment*, to work with Sarah's PTSD. Sarah was having *flashbacks* and *nightmares* because of her history of sexual abuse and molestation, and we needed to work with her on these issues. We thus concentrated on her past history and used some *psychodynamic techniques* of *Freud*. Specifically, we focused on her *repression* of her molestation and worked with the information that arose in her nightmares.

We spent a lot of time working on Sarah's past memories and on her nightmares. One goal was to get the nightmares and flashbacks to cease so she could get a decent night's sleep. "It's not easy to discuss things in my past. I still feel so guilty that I did something to bring these things on. The guilt is horrible. It detaches me from so much. My mom is also to blame here, since she still thinks I made this all up. I'll never forgive her for that. My dad is really my hero with this situation. I think I would've killed Sam if my dad didn't get me out of there." Interestingly, a car backfires outside at this point and Sarah jumps and screams. "Sorry, but I've been doing that. I'm always edgy." She appears to be shaking a bit.

We decided to use *exposure therapy* to treat Sarah's PTSD and her nightmares. This is similar to *systematic desensitization*; a gradual procedure where the patient remains relaxed while being gradually exposed to more stressful stimuli. We used *relaxation techniques* with Sarah as we discussed her molestation, and we also had her gradually work herself up until she was able to re-experience one of the episodes in her imagination while she was relaxed. The goal was for Sarah to re-experience the event in a safe, relaxed setting free of all negative consequences. If this occurs successfully, *extinction* is expected to occur.

Sarah was quite frightened of this at first. "I don't really know if I can go through with this. It's scary. I have to deal with this at night, so why do I have to deal with this during the afternoon? Is this some kind of psychobabble torture?" We gradually led her through her experiences until she faced the actual event itself. We began outside of her house and eventually got upstairs to her bedroom. Sarah was sweating profusely as the exposures got more intense and closer to the actual situation but she stayed with the treatment. Eventually she managed to see herself in the situation and she let out a big "AHHHH" while she was relaxed in the office.

"That last bit was intense. It really felt like I was there. It's like a weight has started to be lifted from my stomach and my butt. I don't know if I can go back there." We continued to work on her trauma by using these techniques.

We asked Sarah a bit more about her drinking. "I like to drink and it's not easy to give it up, but I'm staying sober to show you I can. You don't think I can do this, do you? I fool all adults. I don't like the meetings either, but if they'll help me get some good sleep I'll go. At least they're free." Sarah is referring to *Alcoholics Anonymous (AA)* meetings, which the clinic required all patients who had alcohol problems to attend. AA now has meetings especially for young children and teenagers, and AA can be quite effective. It takes more than one or two meetings to work, however.

As the sessions progressed, Sarah opened up more about her past and about her promiscuity. "I feel like I'm just not accepted by anyone, especially my mom and guys. I never had any guy interested in me before I starting boozing and playing around, and now everyone wants me. They know I'm available, fun, and hot. I haven't been sleeping around for a long time, just recently." Her school-related problems began around the time that these behaviors began, as well as when the nightmares increased. We offered Sarah support and *empathy* in therapy, and we encouraged her to express her feelings and to let out whatever was inside (this is known as *catharsis*). Sarah also demonstrated *transference,* as she became very open and candid with us and saw us "as knowing a lot, giving me direction, like a parent or a father should do."

Sarah also realized "that I've done some really dumb things that I hope I can live down. How can I ever tell anyone that I traded my body for booze? No one would believe that. I also realize that Sam is very very sick, and now I see that none of this was my fault. My mom? She's just a stupid drunk, a lush, a bum. We'll never be close, even after I'm done here."

After one month, Sarah returned to the psychiatrist for an evaluation. He felt that medications were not necessary and asked us to reevaluate her at 3 months. This did not occur, and you will see why shortly.

As the sessions entered the third month, Sarah began sleeping much better. "I still get the nightmares but not as much now. I sleep . . . oh, about five nights good a week. Damn, that's better! I do have more energy in school and you know what? I really like English! The books we're reading are really great, and they're teaching me some things about myself. Maybe school isn't so bad. I'll try some more."

At this point we were happy with Sarah's progress. However, we realized that with PTSD a relapse was possible. In Sarah's case, because her past was so traumatic, we feared that this was a likely occurrence. At the psychiatrist's request, we had Sarah's father come back in for a session alone. He was sent to a different therapist who asked him about Sarah.

"Well, I'm pleased that she's sleeping better at night and not waking up screaming. I still need to know what's going on in these sessions. Sarah says things at times that I think are lies. My ex-wife's boyfriend molested her, you know. I saved her from that. She's not real grateful, let me tell you. She doesn't try at all with my second wife. They think she drinks, the school principal. Her mom is an alcoholic, so it makes sense. That was a real bad situation."

Her father was asked why he needed to know what was occurring in these sessions. "Well, heck, I'm paying for them! Am I wasting my money? I see her getting a bit better, but she still sasses me and my wife, still stays out late, and I don't see major grade improvement. I don't want to see results five years from now. She's almost 15. She should get over her past and move on. I bring her here because the principal said it was either here or suspension. That's no choice for a dad to make. But she's my daughter and I'll do what it takes. I won't pull her out yet." We had a feeling that Sarah was not getting a lot of support at home.

Finally, we used *Rational Emotive Therapy (RET),* which is a form of *cognitive restructuring,* to get Sarah to think clearly and rationally about the molestation, and about her present situation. In effect, she was asked to realize that her thoughts were self-defeating and self-destructive. These techniques would also, we hoped, help her sleep better, and might reduce her drinking. We also expected her *self-esteem* to increase. We hoped that her depression *(dysthymia)* would begin to lift once her self-esteem grew. Sadly, some of these things did not occur.

Just before Sarah's *reevaluation* with us and with the psychiatrist, her father called and asked to come in alone. We were not pleased with what he told his therapist and us: "I'm stopping Sarah's therapy as of today. She's sleeping better and is going to school. She still stays out too late, but that will stop soon, I'll see to that. Her principal and teacher are satisfied, so why should I keep doling out the bucks? She won't tell me what's going on in here and neither will you. That's like buying a book for someone, giving it to them, and them not telling you a thing about the book. I won't stand for this anymore. Thanks for your help, Sarah is much better now." And with that statement, he left the clinic. That was our last physical contact with Sarah. Does any of this surprise you, especially since Sarah was beginning to make some nice progress? Was there anything that we could have done, or done differently?

About 6 weeks later we received a phone call from Sarah. She apologized for her father's behavior and told us that when she turned 18 she was moving as "far away as I can from this place. I need to start over." Sarah was drinking again, but told us she now had a boyfriend and was no longer "fooling around; he wouldn't put up with that. I wish I could have stayed with you longer, since you really made me realize some things. I'm not a bad or a sick person, I've just had a bad life. That doesn't make someone bad or evil. People still don't understand."

There are a number of medications that **could** be used to treat PTSD. We will briefly examine each class and explain the positive and negative aspects of each. First, antidepressants, specifically the SSRIs such as Prozac and Paxil, have been successful in treating PTSD. They can help to reduce Sarah's depressive symptoms, and they seem to help alleviate the anxiety and panic attacks that can occur with PTSD.

Barbiturates (sleeping pills) can be used to help Sarah sleep. An advantage is that these drugs "knock out" the REM stage of sleep, thus suppressing dreams. For Sarah, that would be a positive. However, these drugs are addictive and are also lethal when combined with alcohol. Barbiturate withdrawal can be harmful and lethal. They are also designed for infrequent, short-term use. These drugs usually cause more harm than good and therefore it would not have been prudent to have prescribed these to Sarah.

Finally, psychiatrists can prescribe *anxiolytics*, or antianxiety medications such as *Ativan (lorazepam)* and *Valium (diazepam)*. These drugs would relax Sarah and alleviate her anxiety. They would also help her to sleep better. However, these drugs are also highly addictive and are lethal when combined with alcohol. Anxiolytic withdrawal is particularly difficult.

There are related problems with using medications to treat PTSD. Many patients will relapse once the medications are withdrawn. Patients might see the drugs as a crutch and claim the drugs caused the "cure," not the patient or the therapy. The patient would thus terminate prematurely, risking a relapse. All in all, medication use for PTSD may be warranted, but caution is advised. There are more effective ways to presently treat PTSD, and using medications is not the primary (or perhaps even the secondary) method of choice.

Prognosis

Sarah's prognosis is listed as "guarded." Were we being reasonable here? Let us examine the reasons for this prognosis. Sarah was still drinking, which led to many problems. Since there is a history of alcoholism in her family, the fact that her drinking behavior relapsed is a cause for concern. Sarah has a good chance of becoming alcohol dependent if she is not there already. Sarah made some nice progress in therapy, but because she terminated (or was terminated by her father) prematurely, we were not sure how much progress she would have made. Sarah stopped being promiscuous, but what will occur once she needs to boost her self-esteem? Finally, because PTSD can recur, we must list Sarah as guarded. We cannot say with certainty that her PTSD is in *remission;* we can only hope so. Sarah is a prime candidate to re-enter therapy with us, or with someone else once she leaves home.

Obsessive-Compulsive Disorder (OCD)

The Case of Fannie:
Lady Macbeth of Course

Presenting Problem

Fannie is a 26-year-old single Hispanic female who has lived in the United States her entire life. Her parents were born in Puerto Rico and came to the United States shortly after they were married. Fannie has no children and is employed as an administrative assistant for a major consulting firm. She is, as she says, quite good at her job and is in line for a promotion, which would include free schooling.

Fannie presented with an appropriate affect, and she was rather nervous in the intake session. She kept on jiggling her right leg and at times she would clench her fists. Fannie is 5'8" tall and about 30 pounds overweight. She has brown hair, a fair complexion and speaks with a slight accent. Fannie was dressed in jeans and a blouse when she first came to see us. She also had latex gloves on, which she refused to remove. She did not shake our hand when we first met and she kept a small bottle of antibacterial lotion in her hands.

Fannie's mother works as a cook in a large restaurant "and is a darn good cook. That's why my family has a bit of a weight problem, because her meals are so yummy." Fannie's father is a police officer who is close to retirement. "My dad ran with the wrong crowd in Puerto Rico, but my grandfather made sure to head off trouble. He laid down the law when he got in trouble and made sure my dad graduated high school. My dad learned a lot of lessons from his father and sees it as his duty to give something back to the community. He likes being seen as a role model. We always worry about him but he has no fears. His faith keeps him safe, he says."

Fannie told us that she was having odd thoughts that had become more frequent lately; this is what brought her in to see us. "I am really afraid of getting AIDS or another disease, so that may be a problem when it comes to meeting a good guy. I'm also afraid that I may say weird things in public and embarrass my family and myself. I'm really afraid of this happening at work, since it might get me fired. Sometimes I don't go in because of this fear. The arranging thing is really important for me. All of my things at home and at work have to be in the set order before I can continue. It takes awhile but it needs to get done. I also have to be clean always. It takes a long time each day to get to that point. The weird thing is, I know this stuff makes little sense. Everyone does these things, but my mom and friends tell me I do it to excess. The thing is I can't help myself. It's like an itch you know you shouldn't scratch, but you have to, no matter what."

Fannie's parents got worried as her behaviors continued and got worse. Fannie's boss was also concerned about her tardiness at work and told her she needed to seek help for her "issues." "I listened to them and I know these things need to stop. My hands are sore, and I may lose my job, or not move up. And I hate to disappoint my parents. They have no other kids. So I need to stop these thoughts, and hopefully you can help me."

Background Information

Fannie reached all of her developmental milestones at their age-appropriate times and reported no history of mental illness in her family. "At least none that is spoken about. My mom has frequent *migraine headaches*, but that really doesn't matter." Fannie is an only child "but not by choice. My parents wanted another child or two, but my dad had a low sperm count. Eventually they got older and nothing was happening, so my dad had a *vasectomy* to make sure they didn't get pregnant. I always wanted a little sister to hang with. My mom is upset, but they have me. (Laughs) My mom says I'm enough for two kids."

Fannie began to realize that something was different about her when she was a child. "I liked to always make sure my clothes and toys were lined up in a certain way, and I told my Mom I could not go out or to school unless I was sure. I would check things a lot. I also looked under my bed for dust balls; no dust in my room ever! My parents thought I was just being a neat child, you know, anal. They figured that this was normal, since I was a girl, a real girly girl. I was always dressed up, never getting dirty and stuff."

Fannie did well in school, graduating high school with a B-plus/A-minus average. "I really did well in languages, Spanish of course. I got the medal for Spanish. My parents were really proud of me. I studied a lot. Just because you're a native speaker does not mean you speak properly. When my grandma heard, she was so happy that I'm keeping up the tradition."

Fannie presently does not have a boyfriend "but not by choice. I really miss the company. I was with a neat guy for a while recently, but he left me because he couldn't deal with my 'behaviors.' I had an idea what he meant, but I wasn't too sure. Since then I've been too busy at work and at home to find the right guy. My dad also doesn't like me to date outside of the race, but I like to, so that's a problem." Fannie's first sexual experience occurred when she was 18 "and it was not pleasant. It was uncomfortable and messy, and I was miserable afterwards. I needed to try it, but since then I haven't done it much at all. All those germs and dirt."

Fannie told us that her "problems" became much more noticeable when she was a teenager. "I had a normal life, managed to do everything, but I always had to check for dirt and dust everywhere in the house, in my locker. My mom told me that I would always check the locks on the house to make sure they were closed. I would check the windows to make sure they were shut, and I would always check the stove. She and my dad thought I was being careful so they didn't do anything. They were happy I acted so safe, especially because our neighborhood had a bit of a crime problem. They thought I was being normal, like anyone who lives in the city."

When Fannie graduated from high school, she took her present job and moved to a studio apartment 10 minutes from her parents. "I wanted to be on my own; I needed privacy. But I was close enough so I saw my folks almost every day, and of course I wouldn't miss Sunday dinner! My friends told me that I would always check the locks on the car because I was afraid of someone breaking in and raping me, or jacking the car. That makes sense, right? A young attractive single woman needs to be alert in the city." As you continue to gather information, remember that when we make diagnoses, we must keep the patient's cultural background and environmental circumstances in mind.

Things became more troublesome for Fannie as she got older. "Well, they were worried about me at work. I started to worry about everything in the apartment, and it took me awhile before I could leave the house. Everything had to be safe and turned off. I would get to the train and run home because I was sure there was an electrical fire in the kitchen. Then I would check the bathroom for floods, and then I would head out again. Many times I would be in the office building and I would run home to make sure nothing was burning. You do that, don't you? I mean, not as much, but you do these things."

"They got angry with me at work because I was always coming in late. I just had to be sure. I also had to be clean for work, because of so many germs and bad things there. No one is clean at work. I have these alcohol swabs for my computer. No one touches it except me, and if they sneak in and do it, I'll wipe everything clean. Co-workers didn't make much of this, but one day my boss told me she was concerned about my being late all the time. I told her I always stayed late to make up for it, and she told me this was okay. She was also concerned because I was in the bathroom a lot." What Fannie's boss discovered is that Fannie was always washing her hands, something she did a lot at home.

"My hands got raw at times because I just could never get them clean enough. I would see a speck of dirt on them, or under a nail, and I'd wash them again. A few times I would use Brillo (steel wool) to make sure they got clean. That hurt, but at least they were clean so I could go out. I found a better soap and used that, since the Brillo really slashed up my hands. That company should pay me money; I go through about one bottle a day of that, and I have one in my desk at work. There are so many germs and diseases out there today that one needs to be safe." We mentioned previously that Fannie came to us wearing latex gloves, and we asked her about that.

"Well, I don't know you, and there are many germs in your office. Psychologists like to shake hands and touch you, so I'm being safe. I do this a lot, just to be sure, especially when my hands hurt too much to wash. Like I said, can't be too safe in today's world can you? But I will say that not everyone does this." Do they? Donald Trump will avoid shaking hands with people he meets, because he has a stated fear of contracting disease from them and picking up germs. It **is** a fact that many germs and diseases are spread from the hands, especially when you rub your eyes or nose. Is Fannie taking this too far?

Thought Questions

1. What is going on with Fannie?
2. How "normal" is Fannie's behavior? (Recall that she lives in a large city.) Does it become more typical once you take her cultural and environmental background into consideration?
3. What would cause someone to wash their hands with steel wool, even after they are rubbed raw?
4. Fannie seems to have had a normal upbringing. What in your view went wrong, if anything?
5. How typical is it for someone like Fannie to realize that his or her behaviors are unusual?
6. Are Fannie's behaviors a product of today's (germ-phobic) society? Why or why not?

Assessment and Evaluation

Fannie was assessed with an *unstructured diagnostic interview* and with a *psychiatric evaluation.* Fannie came to the clinic with her mother, but she wanted to be alone in the *initial intake interview.* We were able to gather more information on Fannie's condition and situation as we spoke further.

We first asked her about her checking and handwashing behaviors. These are compulsions. *Compulsions* are thoughts or actions that provide relief; they are used to suppress the obsessions. Compulsions can be seen as behaviors whose purpose is to get rid of obsessions. *Obsessions* are intrusive or recurring thoughts, ideas, or behaviors that the person tries to eliminate or resist. It seems impossible for the person to control the obsessions. Compulsions usually fall into two categories: checking behaviors and cleaning *rituals.* Checking behaviors can be annoying; cleaning rituals can be hazardous. You will receive proof in a moment.

"Well, as I got older, things got a lot more complicated. I spent more and more time checking the locks and washing my hands. I even spent a lot of time worrying whether I should do these things again! So a lot of time was spent on this, and they noticed at work and at home. My parents really began to freak. They thought I was bulimic or suicidal because I spent so much time in the bathroom. I was washing my hands, because their soap isn't strong enough to kill the germs. It took them awhile, but they finally made the really strong soap that I need. How long do I do these things each day? Well, I spend about 2 hours every day at least washing up and if my hands need more, I'll be there longer. It is exhausting, so I'm tired a lot."

We asked Fannie again about her interpersonal relationships, and how she found time for men if she was so busy with the washing and checking. "Oh, the checking. I spend a lot of time on that also, because one can never be too safe, especially in today's world. I didn't check the locks as often when I lived at home, but my dad had a gun at home, so there was less of a need. Well, no need to spend a lot of time making sure everything was safe. I still did it a lot anyway, but not as much as in the past. We were safe with his gun. I did often make sure it was put safely away and that the safety was on. I also began to make sure it was loaded before we went to bed. That would take awhile."

"I don't have much guy time. I work hard and late, since my boss lets me stay late when I'm late arriving. Guys also don't want to be with me. They see the gloves and think I've got *leprosy* or something. I really don't have time for guys. Besides, it might eventually lead to intercourse, and sperm is so dirty and germ-filled, I can't have that."

We asked Fannie what happened when she tried to control her compulsions. "Well, I really can't do that. My mom asked me the same thing. As I said, I know a lot of what I do makes no sense and when I do these things, I do them to an extreme. I don't really know anyone who washes his or her hands like I do. I know it's weird, but the problem gets worse when I try to control these things. I can't control them but the few times I've tried to, I've felt a lot worse, you know, more anxious." What usually happens here are that the compulsions get even worse. Compulsions, some feel, seem to relieve the anxiety that obsessions cause.

For example, Fannie's hand washing may lead her to feel more at ease with the fact that this behavior will make her less likely to have germs on her hands. Anxiety may also occur if the compulsions are **not** followed through, as Fannie has explained. Is Fannie's situation becoming clearer to you yet?

Before we continue, we need to note that many "normal" people have occasional obsessions and compulsions, especially children who tend to be creatures of habit. The key difference is that these rituals/compulsions do **not** interfere with these peoples' daily lives and do **not** cause these people to stress out. These are key diagnostic criteria for most of the disorders covered in this book and in your class. When something causes a tremendous amount of everyday stress and interferes with a person's life, then that person likely has a mental disorder. Alcohol abuse is a good example.

Most people who drink do so in moderation. When that moderate drinking causes someone problems in their daily living, then the alcohol is a problem and we can say the person is drinking abusively. The same holds true for compulsions. Who has not recently checked the door locks to their house or car? This alleviates anxiety and gives us structure. (Do you have lunch at the same time each day? Is that a compulsion?) People in Fannie's situation are different of course. Their compulsions are something they cannot change or avoid and if they try to, their distress gets worse.

We now had enough information to present Fannie at a case conference. We also wanted to get other opinions on involving Fannie's family in family therapy. The clinic staff then discussed Fannie's case and decided that Fannie would indeed benefit from family therapy. If this was not possible, then Fannie was recommended to start individual therapy. We presented this to Fannie. "Well, I would like my Mom to join us, since she can give you some more information, because I really want to get well here. Forget about my dad. Puerto Rican men do NOT do headshrinking, no way. Especially one who's a cop. 'This is a woman's problem, not a man's' is what he would say. We already discussed it. He wants the best for me, but he deals with problems by toughing them out." Fannie smiled and the session ended at that point.

Fannie's family had only one car due to financial constraints. Her mother would usually drive her to the sessions while someone would cover for her at the restaurant. At the next session, Fannie's mother came in and we asked her about Fannie's present situation.

"My daughter has gotten worse the past few years. She spends more and more time with us because we're so worried about her. We noticed that Fannie has to check everything in the house and goes nuts when things are not set up a certain way, like at the dinner table. My husband is out a lot so he really doesn't see a lot of this, but he's worried also. Fannie's always washing her hands. The last time she was over, she bled all over the sink because she washed so hard. There was a time when she never changed her clothes because these things like the washing took up the whole morning. She's a sweet, decent woman. What is going on here? Is she possessed?" Oddly enough, many people years ago (and some to this day) equated compulsions with *demonic possession*.

We asked Fannie one more question before we referred her to the psychiatrist for her evaluation. We wanted to know what Fannie wanted out of therapy, and if she had any idea what was occurring. "I want to get better, doc! That's the first thing. I think something's either wrong with my brain or my body chemistry, you know, like Roseanne (the comedienne) has. I want to stop the washing, or at the least control it somehow. If I can't stop it at all I may eventually kill myself. The anxiety is killing me, and I need my hands to work. I'll lose my job, my family, and never get married. There's too much to lose. So fix this for me."

The clinic staff felt as though we had enough information to make an accurate diagnosis. Fannie's case was presented again with this additional information. The clinic went ahead and assigned a diagnosis to Fannie even before she met with the psychiatrist. If the psychiatrist disagreed with our diagnosis, we would discuss it with her and make the most logical, accurate choice. No diagnosis is permanent.

Obsessive-Compulsive Disorder (OCD) 300.3

Theoretical Etiologies

There are some specific etiological explanations for the development of OCD. The primary factor is developing, and expressing, anxiety about having recurrent obsessions. Let us presume that Fannie has a thought (say, about sex) that keeps on entering her consciousness. It is impossible to avoid the thought, and due to her upbringing she believes that thinking about sex is dirty or immoral. She tries to block the thought through suppression or through distraction (like defense mechanisms, in a way). Eventually these methods become compulsions. The interesting aspect is that the compulsions will fail because they actually **increase** the frequency of these bad thoughts. Avoidance behaviors, as we have discussed in Chapter 1, only seems to make anxiety and, in this case obsessions, worse.

Freudians would see obsessions as unconscious id impulses entering the conscious mind and compulsions as acts or attempts by the ego to keep them repressed. Obsessions about dirt and contamination (similar to

Fannie's) would be seen as related to the anal stage. In fact, regression could be applied. The individual may have unconscious desires (again, the id impulses) to play with feces and thus create a mess. The cleanliness compulsion is designed to keep these impulses and thoughts repressed. Perhaps Freud would say this is a true anal expulsive using *reaction formation* to stay clean. As you might expect, this explanation is not supported by research and is thus hypothetical.

Learning theorists such as Skinner would say that compulsions are negatively reinforced by the anxiety relief they provide to the obsessions. This becomes a stimulus-response cycle that continues and is strengthened because the compulsions are reinforced by the anxiety reduction. Cognitive theorists such as Ellis would see these individuals as exaggerating risk factors and misinterpreting cues. In other words, they are alarmists and overreacting to situations. Since they expect horrible things to occur to **them,** they use these compulsions to prevent the trauma and of course the anxiety and the obsessions. These can also be seen as irrational beliefs, where Fannie must be as clean as possible because "it only takes one germ to make me sick!" Perfectionists fit into this explanation.

Begley (1998) reviewed some research that examined an area of the brain that signals danger to the individual. Begley reported that some researchers hypothesize that this area of the brain is **constantly** sending alarm signals; these signals tell the individual to attend to the alarm immediately. This can lead to OCD. It is also hypothesized that the brain is dysfunctional in reducing repetitive behaviors. The motor strip has also been hypothesized to be dysfunctional; the motor strip controls movement. This may help to explain the handwashing and checking behaviors, since the motor strip may be unable to stop these behaviors, or may be inducing them through its dysfunction.

Treatment Plan

The goals in treating OCD are straightforward and simple. The main goals are to alleviate or eliminate the obsessions and compulsions. By eliminating the obsessions, the compulsions will also be alleviated and/or eliminated. There are two accepted methods for this. The first method involves medication, so for that Fannie saw our psychiatrist.

The psychiatrist agreed with our diagnosis for Fannie and decided to prescribe medication for her, in addition to recommending that she attend weekly family therapy sessions. The psychiatrist prescribed *Prozac (fluoxetine).* Prozac is an *antidepressant* that is a *Selective Serotonin Reuptake Inhibitor (SSRI).* Prozac and other SSRIs such as *Zoloft (sertraline)* and *Paxil (paroxetine)* seem to work well in reducing the obsessions, although we are not sure why. About 60% of individuals who have OCD benefit from taking SSRIs. Some theories hypothesize that OCD may have something to do with *serotonin* deficiencies (Greist, 1990; Bezchlibnyk-Butler & Jeffries, 2002). Some patients do not respond to any SSRI. As we have mentioned, these drugs may produce side effects that can be quite uncomfortable. It generally takes anywhere from three to four months before the obsessions diminish or vanish while using these medications. Relapse is common for those who go off of their medications (Bezchlibnyk-Butler & Jeffries, 2002).

The other method used to treat OCD is *exposure with response prevention*. First Fannie would be deliberately exposed to a situation that would set off obsessive thoughts. This might be leaving the house or touching someone or something. Response prevention refers to Fannie physically preventing the compulsion (response) from occurring. The idea here is that eventually Fannie would be able to handle the anxiety brought about by her touching someone while at the same time being prevented from acting on the compulsion triggered by that anxiety. Eventually, the anxiety response to the threatening situation would become *extinct*. We used techniques similar to the exposure techniques used with Sarah and in Chapter 1. In this instance Fannie had her mother and her best friend George's help. Fannie relayed her feelings about this.

"Lemme tell you, this was a bear! It is SO hard to stop these things from getting into my little head. You know, it's like a small fire. You put one out and the son of a b&^%$ starts two more. It doesn't stop. It feels like someone is forcing me to do these things; I have so little control. You can't imagine how hard it is to deliberately be put in these situations. But I keep on doing it." Was either of these treatments successful for Fannie? Keep on reading.

We also provided an *empathic* environment for Fannie, giving her a lot of comfort and support. We discussed how we understood that she was unable to stop her obsessions and compulsions and how she was a decent person who had a lot to offer. Fannie was a very kind and likeable woman and we emphasized this. We educated Fannie and used *bibliotherapy* (suggesting books on OCD, giving her pamphlets to read, and web sites to investigate) to help her understand her disorder.

We also gained more insight from Fannie's mother. We discovered that Fannie's mother would always make sure that the table was set the same way and that everything in her house was in the same place before Fannie came over for dinner. "I really feel guilty for what happened to Fannie. No one in my family or Edmundo's (Fannie's father) family has any mental illness, so it must have been something I did during pregnancy. Maybe that's why we have only one child, that something is wrong with me. It's not Fannie's fault." We included her mother when we provided education about OCD, and we worked on her guilt feelings, which had little basis in reality.

We also used some *reality therapy* techniques, where Fannie had to take responsibility for following through with her medications, with her sessions, and with her education about OCD. We were quite pleased that she did everything she was asked. As the sessions progressed over the next few months and she continued taking her medication and using the exposure therapy techniques, Fannie noticed that her obsessions had decreased. We were not sure whether this was due to the medications, therapy, or the adjuncts to the therapy (bibliotherapy and such). Regardless, Fannie's compulsions had decreased to the point where she was able to go back to work with few problems. "I was on extended medical leave from work after I started coming here. Of course they couldn't fire me because I was getting treatment for a mental condition. I've gone back, and my boss has been great. I started part-time to not get too stressed. My boss told me they were going to hold off on putting me through school until I was in better shape, and I agreed totally. School would weird me out right now; I can't take the pressure."

Fannie was allowed to come in late to work, but she had to stay late as in the past. A doctor treated her hands and the cuts and abrasions had greatly diminished, although they were still there. "I still wash my hands, but not for hours during the day. It's so hard to completely get rid of these nutty thoughts. I wish I could get inside of my brain and shut certain things off."

Fannie's mother also realized that she had nothing to do with her daughter's condition. "I still don't totally believe it. I must have done **something** to cause this. It doesn't just happen. Someone or something has to be blamed here." We did tell her that there might be a *genetic component* to OCD but if so, this was completely out of her control. We explained how, other than that, she raised Fannie the best she could. There was no evidence that her mother did anything "wrong" during her pregnancy or while raising Fannie. We took her word on what she told us in the sessions.

Fannie saw us for seven months after she began her medication. At the end of treatment, her symptoms were controllable but not extinguished. We felt that she was self-sufficient and stable enough to discharge her. At that time, Fannie had begun to date again and had met someone nice in her mother's restaurant. "It was a set-up. I always eat dinner in the restaurant on Saturdays, and there was this cute guy who would sit alone at the counter. My mom kept talking about me and showed him a photo, and wouldn't you know that one night when I'm there for dinner so is this guy! Well, we hit it off and we've been together for one month now. I hope it lasts." Fannie and her mother thanked us and promised to keep in touch when they came by to see the psychiatrist for a *medication reevaluation*.

Research has demonstrated that the most effective medications for treating OCD are the SSRIs (Bezchlibnyk-Butler & Jeffries, 2002). These medications were mentioned previously. We will briefly examine one other option that has proven clinically effective, *Anafranil (clomipramine),* a *tricyclic antidepressant.* Even though Anafranil has about a 60% efficacy rate with OCD, like all tricyclic antidepressants, it has significant and unpleasant side effects (Bezchlibnyk-Butler & Jeffries, 2002). Patients may develop dry mouth, *anticholinergic side effects,* and constipation. Many professionals call these *antihistamine-like effects,* since they resemble the effects of such drugs as *Contac.* When Anafranil is removed, patients tend to have a high relapse rate (Maxmen & Ward, 1995; Bezchlibnyk-Butler & Jeffries, 2002). Anafranil does, however, treat obsessions and compulsions. As research into this disorder continues, the helping professions remain hopeful that more medication options will be discovered.

Prognosis

Fannie's prognosis is listed as "fair." Again, see if you agree with the reasons for this. Even though Fannie has made nice progress in therapy and continues to take Prozac, there is always the risk of relapse, especially if she discontinues her Prozac. Additionally, for reasons unknown, certain medications (or classes of medications) can lose their effectiveness after a while. We cannot guarantee that this will not occur with Fannie.

There are other concerns. Fannie's life is going well right now, but how will she handle a crisis or a stressful event? Many people with mental disorders do not handle stress well, and during these stressful times relapse is more likely. While Fannie was in therapy she suffered no significant setbacks, so we are not sure how she handles stress.

Finally, even with the most successful individuals, significant symptoms may remain. This is quite stressful, especially when the patient realizes that they have made as much progress as can be expected. The end result **could** be similar to the person who loses 200 pounds on a diet. It is really going well, and they stick to the diet, but they *plateau* and are unable to lose any more weight. They get upset, give up, go off of the diet, eat more and thus gain a lot of weight.

We stayed in touch with Fannie for 18 months following her discharge from therapy. She reported that she was still taking Prozac and was still seeing the psychiatrist. She was getting ready to go home to Puerto Rico for two months to see family and have a nice break. She was not too worried about relapsing, especially since her mother was there. She had gone through two boyfriends since we last saw her and was anxiously looking to find a new one. She was optimistic about her future and was told to return to us if she needed to.

We waited for four months and realized that Fannie had missed two psychiatric appointments. We called her apartment and left three messages, none of which was returned. We had no luck re-establishing contact with her. We never heard from Fannie again.

Review and Study Questions

Sarah

1. How accurate were the therapists with Sarah's diagnoses?
2. Cite some reasons why Sarah's father terminated her treatment.
3. Cite some additional reasons that could explain Sarah's promiscuity.
4. How concerned, if at all, would you be about Sarah's drinking?
5. Sarah seems to have a paradoxical relationship with her father. What else could be going on with this relationship?
6. Sarah's father felt that since he was paying for the sessions he had the right to know what was going on in the sessions. Discuss your views on this.
7. Give your views on the idea of bringing Sarah's mother into family therapy.
8. Give your views on Sarah being seen by a male therapist.

Fannie

1. What were the reasons, in your opinion, for Fannie not returning to the clinic?
2. Discuss the possible cause(s) of Fannie's behaviors.
3. What are your views on using medications to treat Fannie, especially knowing about some of the side effects?
4. Suppose that Fannie's obsessions and compulsions were accepted in her culture, but you were treating her in the United States. What would you do, and why?
5. What is your opinion on Fannie's boss, who allowed her to keep her job?
6. Fannie remained in therapy for a long period of time, given her condition. Explain why this might be unusual.
7. What do you **hypothesize** as the reason(s) for Fannie being unable to control her compulsions?

Terms To Know

Posttraumatic Stress Disorder (PTSD)
shellshock
antianxiety medications
alcohol/substance abuse
REM sleep
depression
unstructured diagnostic interview

psychiatric evaluation
consultation
resilience
case conference
alcohol abuse
Alcoholics Anonymous (AA)
Dysthymic Disorder, Early Onset

individual treatment

flashbacks

nightmares

psychodynamic techniques

Freud

repression

reaction formation

empathy

catharsis

transference

exposure therapy

systematic desensitization

relaxation techniques

extinction

Rational Emotive Therapy (RET)

cognitive restructuring

self-esteem

barbiturates

anxiolytics

Ativan (lorazepam)

Valium (diazepam)

reevaluation

unstructured diagnostic interview

psychiatric evaluation

migraine headaches

initial intake interview

rituals

compulsions

obsessions

vasectomy

Prozac (fluoxetine)

antidepressant

Selective Serotonin Reuptake Inhibitors (SSRIs)

serotonin

Zoloft (sertraline)

Paxil (paroxetine)

exposure with response prevention

reality therapy

Anafranil (clomipramine)

tricyclic antidepressant

anticholinergic side effects

antihistamine-like effects

school social worker

cortisol

hippocampus

dysthymia

demonic possession

empathic

bibliotherapy

Contac

plateau

Obsessive-Compulsive Disorder (OCD)

behavioral homework assignment

remission

leprosy

extinct

genetic component

medication reevaluation

Chapter 3

Mood Disorders

After Substance Use Disorders, *Mood Disorders* (previously known as *affective disorders*) are the most prevalent mental health concern in the United States. Each year millions of dollars are spent treating mood disorders. *Prozac (fluoxetine)* and *Zoloft (sertraline)* have entered the vernacular. Some of the most prominent people in the United States suffer from mood disorders: Mike Wallace of "60 Minutes," Colin Powell's wife Alma, and perhaps Jim Carrey the movie actor. Oddly enough, Ms. Powell's depression may have prevented Colin, according to sources, from running for President in 2000. According to some reports (and to moviegoers), Jim Carrey's hypothesized mood disorder has been quite lucrative. He has translated his "manic energy" into a broad type of comedy, similar to what Robin Williams does. However, Jim Carrey's mood disorder has also led to relationship problems. Mood disorders affect at least 31 million people in the United States but we still do not know as much as we should about these devastating problems. Do you know the signs and symptoms of depression? What about *Bipolar Disorder?* Let's look at two different cases and see how mood disorders affected their lives and the lives of their loved ones.

Major Depressive Disorder
The Case of Allison: Singing the Blues

Presenting Problem

Allison is a 43-year-old white female who has been married for 12 years and has one child, a 10-year-old girl. Allison (or Ally as she prefers to be called) is an engineer and works as a consultant for a major firm in the United States. Ally grew up in Europe and was actually born in England. Her parents escaped Hungary during the Holocaust. Ally is 5'8" tall and weighs 160 pounds. She has a younger brother whom she does not often see due to geographical distance. She has lived in the United States for approximately 36 years.

When Ally first came in to see us, she was casually dressed in an oversized blouse and baggy slacks. She wore sandals and had polished toes with no toe rings. Her hair was short; she wore glasses and a wedding ring. She had a depressed affect and smiled infrequently. Her eyes were red and swollen as though she had been crying before she came in to see us. She made fair eye contact and when she did, her depressed affect was more evident.

Ally's mother is a homemaker and her father is a contractor and builder. "My family will often talk about the Holocaust and it's obvious that it really affected them; how could it not? It also affected me significantly. But those tales are for later."

What led Ally to seek therapy? "Things have been weird for me lately. I was angry, sad, and run down shortly after Rose was born but my doctor told me this was typical and was not postpartum depression as my husband Roy thought. This mood lifted after about 3 weeks. Things began to get much worse during the past year or so. I'm sleeping more or sometimes waking a lot in the middle of the night and unable to go back to sleep, my appetite has gone down (which is good since I need to lose some pounds) my sex drive *(libido)* has decreased and I have felt sad a lot. I feel empty and hopeless, like life is not worth the constant hassle and effort. My energy level is totally drained. I thought that working and taking care of Rose was the issue, but I'm not sure. Have you ever seen each and every day as blah, gray, no matter what the weather? It's gorgeous outside today, but to me I only see grays. I'm not a lot of fun to be with and Roy knows it. Is this early *menopause?* I don't know. So I came in to see what was going on."

Background Information

Ally's developmental history is unremarkable; she reached all of her developmental milestones at the appropriate ages. Ally graduated high school with a C average and graduated university with a similar average. "I was okay in school but I never spent ALL my time studying. We had fun. I'm a hard worker but grades were never that important to me."

"I never had any major problems in high school or in university. I was teased somewhat in high school because I had very curly hair and wore thick glasses. I was also a bit overweight then but nothing significant. I got back at everyone by withdrawing and getting into reading. It was a great escape. At university I didn't study that hard but I didn't party that hard either. I hung out with my friends and didn't date that much. I was not promiscuous and that worked for me."

After graduating Ally got her first job at a telecommunications company and stayed there for 8 years. She met her husband "on a blind date. I was not having a lot of luck in the dating department so my best friend Linda set me up. We hit it off very quickly. As luck would have it Roy was transferred to New York with a huge promotion (he's a medical doctor and a research scientist). If he went I would have to follow him or else it would've been a long distance romance. He proposed shortly before he left and of course I quit and followed him to New York. I then got a job as a consultant; we got married and had Rose two years later. We were doing well financially, all of my dreams had been realized with marriage and Rose, and everything was going well."

Ally has some physical problems that need to be noted. "When I was 16 I slipped a disc in my back. It was a bulging disc and it slipped slightly out of place. The pain was excruciating. I had to miss 6 weeks of school until the physical therapy could correct it. I still feel pain from time to time but nothing like it was. My family has a history of back problems and they've either dealt with the pain or used aspirin and *ibuprofen* (*Advil*) to handle it. At times it really flairs up. I've read about chronic pain victims and that includes me. I guess I got my family's backs, so to speak."

"I was also considered to be a high-risk pregnancy because of my back condition and my age. I wasn't 35 or older when I gave birth but my doctor watched me carefully nonetheless. There were no complications except that I was tired all of the time. And of course my back ached more as the pregnancy progressed. That did not make me happy. Roy was also concerned, but never let your doctor husband look after you. They are always on top of you! It's awful." Ally managed a weak smile but it almost seemed forced. She did not look at us as she continued to relate her background.

Ally reported no problems with alcohol and denied ever using or trying drugs. "Absolutely not. I'm not a dope fiend. My university was not a typical liberal institution. If you were ever caught possessing any kind of illegal substances you were expelled. I was paying a lot for school and I had no intention of getting tossed out. I also don't like putting foreign and dangerous substances into my body. I do have a drink on occasion but nothing major. It's never gotten me into trouble." So far there seems to be nothing unusual or "alarming" about Ally's background. Clinicians will look for key incidents and pieces of information to help them form diagnoses. In Ally's case we next need to look at her physical symptoms and see what they might indicate.

"I'm concerned about my sleep patterns. The past 7 months I've been more tired and thus have been unable to concentrate at work. It's really odd. I will be quite tired and sleep a LOT on the weekends . . . at least 12 to 14 hours a day. There are many times when I will wake up at 3 or 4 A.M. and be unable to fall back asleep, which makes no sense. I just lie there thinking about things and the world's problems and our problems. It's crazy because that's never really happened to me before. Roy gets upset also, especially when he's working late and goes to bed late. I'll be tossing and turning and he can't sleep. It's affected our lives tremendously."

Sleep disorders are not uncommon in the United States, especially in today's stressful times. Indeed, sleeping pills (*barbiturates;* also called *sedatives* or *hypnotics*) tend to be overprescribed and in fact they are not that effective. They will work for the short term but in the long term they lose their effectiveness and are extremely addictive (Bezchlibnyk-Butler & Jeffries, 2002). Sleep problems alone are a concern but we need more information to arrive at a diagnosis.

Ally's libido has also decreased. We will investigate this shortly but for now when this symptom arises it needs to be examined. A decreased libido can be caused by many factors: anxiety, stress, a mood disorder, relationship problem, alcohol or substance abuse, or a physiological problem. We noted this and asked Ally to explain.

"Roy has certainly complained about my decreased sex drive. We just don't have sex much lately. He's tired from work, I'm tired from work and Rose . . . but it never used to be like this. I would be tired but I would still want sex, but now I just don't have the desire. It's like even if we try it's no fun. The effort is not worth it. I still love Roy and want to show him this love, but even kissing and foreplay has become an effort. The energy I have, which is not great, is not worth expending on this. He's concerned about that because I used to be wild in bed, almost insatiable. That's what's so weird. You couldn't pull me off of Roy, day or night. And now. . ." She became teary-eyed at this point.

"It's really because of these concerns and the fact that I can't really enjoy life at all lately that I came to see you. I need to get to the bottom of this before I lose my marriage, job and daughter. I have no energy for her and she's about to become an adolescent. I'm worried. It took a lot to come in here psychologically and physically since I'm so exhausted all of the time. I'm sick and tired of feeling sick and tired."

Thus Ally came to us looking for answers for her physical symptoms. This is not that unusual. Psychologists need to be alert to the fact that many psychological problems have physical symptoms, and many physical disorders mimic psychological problems. Ally came to see us with Roy. We initially saw her alone and then she asked if Roy could come in, as he wanted to participate as much as possible and get answers for himself.

Thought Questions

1. Cite evidence as to what could be occurring with Ally. Does she have a physical problem? Cite evidence to support or refute your views.
2. Females statistically suffer from depression more so than males. Cite evidence supporting or refuting this statement.
3. Depression may have a familial component; that component is not completely agreed upon. Based on this do you suspect that Ally's parents or grandparents suffer from depression?
4. How might Rose be affected by Ally's concerns? What would you recommend for her?
5. Her doctor ruled out postpartum depression. Do you see any evidence that might indicate she had this subtype of depression?

Assessment and Evaluation

Ally was initially assessed individually using an *unstructured diagnostic interview* and the *Beck Depression Inventory-II (BDI-II)*. In addition she was sent for a psychiatric evaluation. The BDI-II is a paper and pencil self-report measure developed by Dr. Aaron Beck and his colleagues. The original items came from observing and formulating into questions the typical attitudes and symptoms of depressed psychiatric inpatients. The BDI-II is designed to assess the cognitions associated with depression for psychiatric patients and for "normal" (i.e., non-psychiatric) people. The higher the score on the BDI-II, the more depressed the individual. Some clinicians fill out the BDI-II with the patient; others have the patient fill it out on his/her own. Any self-report measure is prone to bias and thus the results need to be used cautiously.

Ally told us that she had feelings of depression ever since she was 13. "My periods started late and when they did I gained some weight. I was teased because I hadn't filled out at 11 or 12 like the other girls did. Needless to say this brought me down. I managed to deal with this by withdrawing more and there were days when I didn't want to get out of bed. My mom was very accommodating and didn't force me to go to school. My parents suspected something was up but they attributed it to 'teenage blues' or 'hormonal rages.' I always thought it might be more than that but my parents didn't believe in therapy and our school did not have an onsite psychologist or social worker so I never saw anyone about this. I knew then that feeling gray all the time was not the teenage blues. My parents had no way of knowing. They thought they were in touch but they were ignorant immigrants. Europeans don't believe in any depressions and things."

Ally's case is not atypical. Adolescent depression (if that is what was occurring with Ally) affects anywhere from 8% to 20% of adolescents surveyed (Hammen, 1997). One problem is that in the past adolescent depression was not diagnosed or properly diagnosed and so the depression worsened as the adolescent reached adulthood. Note also that many studies produce results inconsistent with other studies. Today more health professionals know what to look for and early identification of adolescent depression is becoming more prevalent. Treatment is becoming more accepted for this age group as well.

Thus it seems that Ally had, at the very least, symptoms of mild depression when she was younger. We questioned her further and we received some crucial pieces of information as the sessions progressed. "My mother has suffered from depression as long as I can remember. She used *Elavil (amitriptyline)* and that seemed to help her but I rarely recall her not taking it. It made her drowsy at times but it also kept her moodiness at bay. She attributed her depression to being a Holocaust survivor, which made sense. How could anyone come out of that situation and be expected to act and be normal?" Elavil is a *tricyclic antidepressant (TCA)* that was commonly prescribed for depression. This was one of the earlier medications to come on the market and was used successfully for many years until Prozac (fluoxetine) was formulated and released for usage.

"My mom, being at home, was able to hide her depression from us. She would stay in bed a lot but we attributed that to her being an insomniac or being tired from raising us and taking care of the house. She lacked energy and focus, like I do at times. It was hard for her to stay on target. There were times when she would start to cook a meal and then stop for no reason. We would be ready for dinner and it was incomplete. Mom would shrug her shoulders, apologize, and then go off to her room crying. We figured she had cancer or something since this happened a lot. We had no idea what was causing this and she never told us."

"My mom to this day will reluctantly admit that she suffers from depression. Of course I figured this out. It makes sense. My family is not one to admit a weakness or mistakes. We like to blame others for our problems. My mom went to many doctors and all they did was prescribe sleeping pills! That only made things worse." Again this scenario is not unusual. Why is that?

There are several reasons. First, some doctors (even today) do not know the signs and symptoms of mood disorders. Sleep problems are one possible symptom and when presented with such, some doctors will mistakenly prescribe sleeping pills to treat this symptom. Some doctors also do not want to pry into their patients' mental health histories out of privacy concerns.

"I went to our family physician when I was having these weird feelings and she also said they were normal for an adolescent. She never prescribed anything except for more exercise, but I always thought that was a subtle attempt to tell me about my weight. At least she didn't prescribe sleeping pills. In my family, therapy was NEVER considered an option because we didn't believe in it. We believed that if you had a problem you would handle it or grow out of it. Thus my coming here today is a major step for me. I still can't understand how, when telling a doctor you see gray and have no energy, this is normal and they imply that this is due to weight."

We also needed some clarification of Ally's moods, specifically her feeling "gray" all of the time. "What does that mean? Hmmm . . . hard to describe. It's like on a sunny day I only see gray or black. If you were to ask me to draw a picture the sun would be black, and not because of an eclipse. I get little or no joy out of life or things that I used to love, like swimming, reading, or playing video games. I get very little joy from Rose. I see everything as bad or negative no matter what is going on. Beyond that the only way to describe this is to experience it." People suffering from mood disorders will often see life like this. I use the analogy of people feeling like "Charlie Brown" in "Peanuts": Life is always failure waiting to happen no matter what you do. Charlie Brown was never allowed by Charles Schulz to be happy except for one notable incident (he hit a home run to win a baseball game). Ironically, Schulz suffered from depression and moodiness as well. We have heard patients say "It's like I am not allowed, or allowing myself, to be happy because I don't deserve it. And if it happened I wouldn't know how to react, it's that foreign to me."

Ally continued, "I often think I'm a horrible person, the Devil at times. I'm failing as a wife and as a mother and I just can't live up to my husband's accomplishments and standards. At times I think about ending it all to ease this constant pain and grayness in my life. I would not be surprised if someone in my family wanted me dead. I'm a lousy mother to Rose since I do not have the energy to be with her at night. It's a major task getting the energy to go into work. Thank God for my carpool, or else I would have to get myself there and home."

We then discussed Ally's decreased libido. Sexual desire problems can be a symptom of physiological problems (i.e., hormonal issues, colds, the flu, seasonal allergies, or sleep disorders) or other psychological problems (sexual disorders, anxiety disorders, and so on.). "As I said I've always had an almost insatiable desire for sex. We would have sex about five times a week no matter how tired we were. It occurred so often I was afraid we would have a whole brood of kids! (She laughs here and makes good eye contact). We are certainly compatible that way. Roy began to think something was wrong with him when I gradually began to lose the desire for sex. At first I figured it was a hormonal problem but after this continued for 3 months I thought it might be something else. It took me another month before I had the nerve to go see a doctor about this. It's not easy to discuss this with anyone; it makes it seem like you are really nuts and frigid. My doctor told me that he could see nothing physically wrong with me and in fact encouraged me to see a psychologist. Of course I didn't listen or believe him initially so I saw another OB/Gyn . . . and he said the same things. How could I possibly lose interest in sex? Even if I just lay there I thought I could get something out of it, but no, not a thing. I was once one of the horniest people I knew, and now it's like someone turned my switch off. I have no idea how to turn it on again." As Ally related this issue we thought she might cry. We looked directly at her and her eyes were moist but her reaction did not progress beyond that point.

We were beginning to see a pattern develop. We next decided to focus on Ally's appetite issues. "I haven't had a great appetite for awhile but I thought it might be related to my sleeping too much and my decreased sex drive. When I was 'hornier' I had a much greater appetite. I'm losing weight because my appetite has decreased and I'm really not eating as much. Being gray all the time does have its advantages. Food has little interest to me, and Hungarians make the best pastries in the world. I am able to resist chocolate pastries all the time. In the past when we visited my parents I would always gain weight since my mom knew what I liked. Now, forget it. The pastries produce nothing. I would almost prefer that I puke when I see them just to get some kind of reaction. (She smiles weakly at this point and looks at us.) Rose likes this because that means she gets more of the pastries. Roy is not happy about this. When he saw this occurring he then knew something might be seriously wrong. How about that?

My sex drive and lack of energy he attributes to hormones and things, but if Ally doesn't want cakes, then I'm nuts." A decrease in appetite and weight loss is one possible symptom of a major depressive episode (APA, 2000).

So far it appears that Ally may have a mood disorder, most likely some type of *depression*. Let us see if we can gather some more data before we arrive at a diagnosis for Ally. Ally's BDI-II score was 25 indicating that she is moderately depressed. Scores of 30 or higher indicate a severe level of depression. Ally's score is high enough to make a diagnosis of some type of depression more likely although as stated earlier, any self-report results must be used with caution.

Once we were done talking to Ally, Roy came in. He agreed with everything Ally told us and said he thought she might be depressed but felt helpless in helping out. "Here I am with all of these years of practicing medicine and seeing literally thousands of patients in the hospital and I can't do anything here. What really gets me upset is when she tells me she is evil because of her low moods, that she is the Devil. That made no sense and was not the Ally I knew. When I heard that the second time I demanded that she see our doctor. Of course Rose was also hurt by her behavior so I told her 'it's not mom's fault, she just has an illness and she still loves both of us very much.' After all of that I told Ally I wanted her to seek some help for this. Fortunately she was thinking the same way and so here we are."

Based on all of her symptoms and the **duration** of her symptoms, we arrived at the following diagnosis for Ally. See if you agree:

Major Depressive Disorder, Recurrent, Moderate,
    Chronic, With Melancholic Features   296.32

Theoretical Etiologies

If we attempted to cover all of the possible etiologies of mood disorders in this chapter we would have a chapter in itself! We will discuss some etiologies that have significant research support. First, stress appears to play a key role in the development of mood disorders, specifically depression. Stressful events include unemployment, relationship problems, physical illness, and economic troubles. People may also develop depression when they believe that they are responsible for bad things occurring in life, such as unemployment, bad grades, and relationship problems. Of course this can go in both directions. Stress in one's life can lead to depression and mood disorders, and mood disorders and depression can lead to stress. Is it necessary to know which comes first, stress or depression?

One way to make it less likely that a person develops a mental illness is to make sure that person has a strong social support system (Karel, 1997). Certain people are better at resisting stress than others, just as certain people can recover better from losses and trauma. Some survivors of the terrorist attacks in New York on September 11, 2001 committed suicide, while others remain depressed. Some have gone on with their lives after entering therapy, and some have done so without therapy. Psychologists generally agree that the lack of a good social support system makes it harder for someone to succeed in treatment. You may have read that marriage is a good way to ward off depression. One study found that divorced or separated people are twice as likely to commit suicide as married people (Weissman, Bruce, Leaf, Florio, & Holzer, 1990). Of course this presumes that the married people are happily married.

Freud and his followers believed that depression is simply anger turned inward instead of outward and towards individuals and significant others. The anger arises from a threatened or real loss of a significant other. *Pathological mourning* will occur in individuals who have ambivalent feelings towards the loss of a significant other, whether through death, separation, divorce, leaving home for good, etc. The pathology arises from this ambivalence towards the significant other: They love **and** feel anger towards the individual. This leads to depression. Thus the individual is angry with the significant other for leaving and the anger gets to the point where it is uncontrollable. However, the guilt that arises (from the super-ego) prevents the individual from releasing that anger. Thus, it stays inside and becomes self-hatred, which then becomes depression. There is little support for this concept with one exception: Some research has shown that the loss of significant others can lead to depression (Paykel, 1982). Freud's concepts do raise one important point: Feelings that are kept inside tend to "snowball" and cause more problems. It is the role of the therapist to help the patient release these feelings in a safe, supportive atmosphere.

Learning theories look at the environment, specifically the lack or loss of positive reinforcement, to explain the onset of depression. Simply put, depression can occur when an individual's behavior does not get enough positive or negative reinforcement from his or her environment. (Lewinsohn, 1974). For example, if you put in overtime each week for a year in the hope of a promotion and you are always passed over, this lack of reinforcement (or punishment) will lead to depression and anger. Family members can also contribute to the individual's depression. They may try and help the individual, cheer him/her up, and so on. This takes away the individual's responsibilities, makes him/her more lethargic and thus exacerbates the depression. Lifestyle changes such as financial instability and chronic or sudden illness can also disrupt the flow of positive reinforcement. This concept has research support, but it remains unclear which comes first: depression or the reinforcement disruptions.

Coyne (1976) explains depression's etiology through his *interactional theory*. Specifically, living with a depressed individual becomes so stressful and depressing that the other individuals become less reinforcing towards the depressed person. The depressed individual might react to this "rejection" by placing more demands on the other people and thus driving them further away. The end result is that the depressed individual becomes more depressed, and the depression becomes more ingrained.

Beck's Cognitive Perspective warrants a special mention because of its influence. Depression develops because of negative or distorted cognitions or thoughts. Beck calls his model the *cognitive triad of depression.* Beck outlined this as follows: The person has a negative view of him/herself ("I'm evil, the Devil, no good"). The person also has a negative view of the environment ("This job rots; school is terrible; this town is impossible to live in"), and finally the person has a negative view of the future and sees things as hopeless ("No matter what I do things will always turn out bad for me"). Individuals who follow this triad in their thinking behaviors are at a greater risk of developing depression if they face stress or disappointment. In other words, they are setting themselves up for failure and perhaps depression by adopting these cognitive *schemes.*

Beck sees these cognitive schemes developing early on in life in response to early learning experiences. Children may discover that no matter what they do it is not good enough to please their parents, teachers, or peers. As a result they may end up seeing themselves as unable to succeed and as incompetent. More importantly, they may see their chances of future success as limited or nonexistent. What occurs later in life is the most important aspect of his theory. These individuals as adults become more sensitized to viewing and perceiving any failure as a reflection that something is inherently wrong with them. Therefore small disappointments ("I was yelled at today by my boss") become major catastrophes, which can lead to depression. Basically the person misinterprets environmental situations and sees any disappointment as being a major disaster and any hope of succeeding in the future as being impossible. The self-doubt does not help matters either. Beck calls these errors *cognitive distortions.* Beck's theory and his concept of the cognitive triad have significant research support. Once again we cannot say which comes first, the cognitive distortions and negative thoughts, or the depression itself. Therefore, it remains to be seen if in fact negative thoughts and thought distortions are a cause of depression.

Seligman (1975) also poses an interesting concept known as *learned helplessness.* This is easy to understand. Individuals develop depression because they see themselves as helpless to control the reinforcers in their environment (and thus the environment itself), and they remain helpless to make positive changes in their lives. Thus, people see themselves as helpless to change their lives; they are a prisoner of their environment and of their situation. Seligman's theory does not account for the reasons why depressed individuals have low self-esteem and it does not explain why some individuals' depressions are more resistant to treatment.

In light of these issues, Seligman and his colleagues revised this theory and called it the *reformulated helplessness theory*. Seligman explains that people who develop depression do so because they link the causes of negative events to three types of attributions: internal factors, global factors, and stable factors. Internal factors are beliefs that their failures reflect personal inadequacies. Global factors are related to flaws in the individual's personality. Stable factors are beliefs that failures reflect fixed personality factors. Research is more supportive of this theory revision but it still does not explain whether attribution errors cause, or are a result, of depression.

Finally, before we decide the best treatment options for Ally, we will examine some biological perspectives. As stated, mood disorders seem to have a familial component and may run in families. Research also seems to point out that the more in common genetically an individual has with a family member who already has major depression the more likely that individual will develop major depression. The same holds true for bipolar disorder (Vincent, Masellis, Lawrence, Choi, Gurling, Sagar, & Kennedy, 1999). Kendler and Prescott (1999) and others believe that genes and heredity play a key role in the development of depression. Kendler and Prescott (1999) also believe that environmental factors play an equal and perhaps larger role in determining the risk of developing depression. What is most interesting is that genes play a larger role in determining who is at risk for developing bipolar disorder. *Dysthymic disorder,* a milder version of major depression, seems to be influenced less so by genetic etiological factors than major depression or bipolar disorder.

Treatment Plan

The most important initial aspect is to investigate Ally's suicidal thoughts. These warrant immediate attention for a number of reasons. First, if suicidal thoughts (which tend to be common in depressions) are not properly checked they might lead to suicidal behaviors, which might include suicide attempts. If Ally was assessed as being *actively suicidal* and considered to be an immediate danger to herself or to others, immediate inpatient psychiatric hospitalization is the most prudent option. The person should be hospitalized for observation and evaluation, and it then becomes the hospital's task to determine if the individual needs to remain in the hospital. We determined that Ally's suicidal thoughts were thoughts upon which she had no intention to act. How did we determine this? We used a two pronged approach, if you will.

The most common way is through the diagnostic interview. Clinicians ask the patient to describe the thoughts, ask how often they have occurred, and when they last occurred, among other questions. They then ask, "Do you have a plan?" The answer here is crucial. We asked Ally about her suicidal thoughts. "I've had these thoughts off and on for the past few years but they've really only been thoughts. I get tired of being blue and tired of the pain I've caused everyone and then I think, 'Boy, it'd be nice if I could ease everyone's pain including myself. Maybe I should kill myself.' I think about it for awhile and I realize that if I do that I won't be able to see Rose grow up, get married . . . (long period of silence) . . . then the thoughts go away. They're present but I don't want to miss all of these things. Do I have a plan? I really don't. I guess if I followed through I'd do the typical, slit my wrists or take sleeping pills. To be honest I never got that far, to have a plan. I guess I'd be spontaneous."

As you can see, Ally did NOT have a detailed plan (does what she said constitute a plan to you?), which is a key diagnostic *criterion* for determining suicidal intent. If someone has a detailed plan to kill himself or herself, many clinicians would then assess the seriousness of the plan and the seriousness of the potential attempt. The more detailed the plan the greater the possibility of a successful suicide attempt. Because Ally's plan is not detailed, the clinic staff concluded that her thoughts were dangerous but not lethal AT THE PRESENT TIME. She PRESENTLY has no access to sleeping pills. We thus can conclude: Suicidal thoughts need to be constantly assessed and monitored, and Ally's thoughts are no exception.

The delusions, if they are active and are indeed delusions, would also warrant hospitalization. Note that there are differences between *irrational thoughts* and *delusions* (a misinterpretation of reality that cannot be shaken or disrupted despite strong and clear evidence to the contrary). Mental illnesses usually include irrational thoughts. These become a concern when a person solidly believes that these thoughts are true and behaves in accordance with them. That is, the thoughts occur frequently and control the individual's life. Roy was quite concerned about her thoughts as you might expect.

The origin of irrational thoughts in mental illness also needs to be considered. Ally told us, "I consider myself to be evil at times because of the pain I have caused Roy, Rose, and myself and the rest of my family members. It's not deliberate so it must be something evil that is causing me to act like this. My family is the most important . . . (Ally begins to cry). . . . I would never do anything to hurt them. Thus it seems like I'm evil because of this." Contrast this with someone who is depressed saying, "I am the Devil and I am evil and I need to be punished, I need to die. I can't take this because I am so awful and horrible, so kill me." Do you see the difference?

At this time we sent Ally to get a psychiatric evaluation. The clinic staff decided that we would follow her recommendations once the report came in. She had this to say, in summary: "Ally is an interesting somewhat insightful woman who presents a flat affect with poor eye contact. She is oriented times three. Ally appears to have been depressed for many years; this condition has exacerbated itself over the past year or so. Ally has demonstrated suicidal thoughts. These thoughts have been recurrent, approximately once a month or more at times. There is no present evidence of a plan, or intent to formulate a plan. Ally is too ambivalent about her future but she does not desire to truly kill herself. She presents it as a 'way to end the constant grays.' Her thoughts that she is the Devil and is evil are not delusional in nature. There is no paranoid content and no actions have been taken on the basis of these thoughts. No danger to self or to others at present time. No need to hospitalize for evaluation at present time. My initial diagnostic impression agrees with clinic's staff:

> Major Depressive Disorder, Recurrent, Moderate,
>   Chronic, With Melancholic Features   296.32
>
> Recommended Treatment Plan: Individual and couple's therapy,
>   possibility of family therapy with Rose
>
> Prozac 10mg bid (twice a day); reevaluate in one month
>   and on a *prn* (as needed) basis

Once we received the psychiatrist's report, we formulated a treatment plan which involved individual and couple's therapy, eventually with the possibility of *family therapy.* Ally was a very verbal woman in touch with her feelings and fears and we surmised that she would do well individually. "I really like individual treatment. For once I felt like I was the most important person. I gave up a lot for my husband and daughter and I'm not sure they always appreciate it. We really struggled when he was in medical school and we still have the debts to prove it. At least in here you can focus on me and my needs and that makes me feel good and helps a lot."

We set various goals for Ally to attain and wanted her to get more active and out of the house more often. "I didn't realize that I had no real hobbies. I used to love to go to craft fairs and shows and to do needlepoint but once we began to struggle financially, and then when Rose was born, it just dropped out. I always loved to walk in our neighborhood but now I don't do that either. I watch television all day and night and that's basically it." We set up various *homework assignments* (they are exactly what they sound like: homework) each week; they initially focused on her past hobbies. For example, one week Ally would take a 20-minute walk every night after dinner with Roy and/or Rose. The goal here is to get her more active and to get her to focus on the fun things in her life, not the negatives. As per Beck's Cognitive Triad theory, we also wanted her to have positive thoughts, which hopefully will lead her to feeling good about things.

Once individual therapy had progressed we asked Roy to come in, and he and Ally were assigned to another therapist for couples' therapy. Roy told the therapist, "I'm really glad I got involved since I was worried about Ally and feared for our daughter and our marriage. I wasn't sure she would be able to pull out of this and I felt helpless, which was awful. I also learned a lot about myself, how I need to be more open with Ally. It's been quite a learning experience." The psychologists focused specifically on communication issues since this is often a significant problem with couples, more so at times than money or sex (although these can be issues as well, as they were with Ally and Roy). The goal is to create an open forum where each member can express their views and issues without fear of reprisal or condemnation from the other member or the therapists.

We then attempted to get Rose to come in so we could do family therapy. Ally told us the results of this request. "Rose told us that she has no desire to go to therapy. She is busy with her friends and she sees this as our problem, not hers. I'm not sure if that's good or not. Rose has withdrawn a lot lately and that worries me. I guess it's somewhat typical but I'm still concerned." Actually some of these things ARE typical. It is difficult to begin, and to maintain, family therapy. Children may not be able to imagine why they need to be involved with therapy when they see the problem(s) as belonging to their parent(s). In fact, there are situations when the child is identified as the primary patient even though they refuse to attend therapy.

It is also hard to be in a situation where your parents are seen as having problems and weaknesses, something children may outwardly enjoy but inwardly deeply fear and deny. Ally and Roy made two attempts to get Rose involved and both times she said no. You cannot force someone into therapy and if you do, in many cases they will not continue, or they will not do any work in the sessions. Ally told us, "Sure we're disappointed, but in the end it's my depression that needs to be considered here. We'll watch out for Rose and hope for the best. I suspect once I begin to get better Rose will open up more. I certainly hope so."

We offered Ally a lot of support and compassion in therapy and encouraged her to read up on depression. We asked her to keep a notebook where she would write down any situations that would cause her stress. We focused on her relationship with Roy and discovered some interesting information. "I noticed that the situations that cause me the most stress and really 'gray me out' are always the same. They relate to work and to Rose, and at times to Roy as well. I feel like I need to always be a sex bomb and I'm not and cannot. Rose is always asking me to do things, work causes me pressure, and there's Roy again, doing his thing, standing by offering support but not really. He'll go to his room and not talk about things. I threatened him to make sure he came in to these sessions and he finally agreed. It's amazing but the sessions really helped him and us."

Ally made some nice progress in individual and couple's therapy. She gained more insight into her condition and learned how to reconceptualize stressful and negative situations. She learned that she does not need to be perfect and that she is not a bad person when bad things occur such as Rose not talking to her. Roy was also taught to praise Ally more and to be more aware of her needs.

Ally was discharged after 10 months of individual and 6 months of couple's therapy. "I'm sleeping better now, eating normally, and my relationship with Roy is better as well. I almost feel reborn in a sense. It's the greatest feeling, waking up in the morning and seeing a nice day and not seeing gray in the sky or anywhere else in my life. It's almost like I'm seeing in color for the first time in a long time and not in black and white. Rose? We're talking a lot more openly these days. She's still angry over my depression but we can discuss it maturely. She's learned a lot about this malady and understands what was happening with me and with Roy. I'm not sure if our relationship will ever be what it was but I'm sure as heck going to try. Therapy opened my eyes. Depression, as you said, is treatable. I believe it's also curable."

We used a treatment modality that worked for Ally and for the clinic. There are other ways to treat depression and, in some cases, some of the following methods have been quite successful at doing so. One method that can be successful but takes a very long time is traditional psychoanalysis. Feelings of anger are worked through, and one goal is to get this anger turned outward instead of leaving it turned inward. The anger is presumed to be caused by unconscious conflicts in the psyche; one goal of analysis is to uncover and resolve these conflicts. This can take years. A more modern approach is called *interpersonal psychotherapy (IPT)*. This is a briefer form of therapy that focuses on interpersonal relationships. The belief here is that depression occurs within relationships and thus relationships need to be focused upon in treatment, usually lasting from 9 to 12 months. The focus here is on current interpersonal relationships, not on early childhood experiences.

Behavioral approaches presume that depressive behaviors are learned and thus, with proper treatment and education, can be unlearned. The goal is to modify the behaviors, not to seek out unconscious conflicts, urges and so on. A nice feature of behavioral therapy for depression is that, if done effectively, it can be quite successful in a shorter period of time (12 to 16 weeks is a good initial goal).

We used cognitive approaches with Ally and we saw significant improvement. As we noted, cognitive theorists such as Beck believe that depression is brought about by distorted thinking. Beck and others would work with Ally to get her to change her distorted and dysfunctional thought processes. Beck would say that Ally spends more time focusing on how bad she feels instead of focusing on the thoughts that are involved with these feelings. The nice feature here, as in behavioral treatments, is that cognitive therapy is designed to work relatively quickly. A benchmark timeframe is usually 16 sessions, or 4 months. Butler and Beck (1995) reported that depressive symptoms often lift within 12 sessions. Much research exists supporting the efficacy of cognitive methods in treating depression. These methods may not be as successful in treating severe depression, but research is still undecided on this matter.

Unlike many of the disorders in this casebook, the mood disorders, especially depressions, have many medication options. We will briefly consider some of the most common options. We first need to discuss some cautions. Until recently research indicated that the BEST treatment modality was a combination of *antidepressant medications* and therapy, specifically *cognitive behavioral*. Recent research, however, has indicated that there is NO significant difference between this combination therapy/medication approach and therapy alone, although this question is still under debate (Craighead, Craighead, & Ilardi, 1998). Note that some clinicians still believe that the medication-therapy combination is still the most viable treatment modality.

Antidepressants have a number of classifications; each *classification* has its own strengths and weaknesses and operates somewhat differently. All antidepressant medications act to decrease depressive symptoms in the individual (such as low libido, altered appetite, gray moods, feelings of hopelessness, etc.). Let us briefly examine each class and a few drugs in each class.

The first type of antidepressant belongs to the class known as tricyclics. Elavil (amitriptyline) belongs to this class, as do *Tofranil (imipramine)* and *Sinequan (doxepin)*. These drugs have to be taken a number of times each day, and it usually takes anywhere from four to six weeks before their effects are realized. This is problematic since many clinicians handle severely depressed patients who wish to get better quickly. Impatience, severe depression, and tricyclics do not make a good match. Additionally, these drugs have many bothersome side effects such as dry mouth, constipation, and blurred vision. These are called *anticholinergic side effects. Antihistamine side effects,* also produced by the tricyclics, include drowsiness, spaciness, and sedation. The tricyclic antidepressants (TCAs) are excellent allergy and cold pills. The side effects (which generally drop out after one to two weeks) are similar to taking a cold pill like Contac.

The TCAs work by evidently increasing the availability of norepinephrine and, to a degree, serotonin in the brain. Norepinephrine is involved with lowering blood pressure and heart rate. Serotonin is involved with, among other aspects, appetite and mood regulation, and sexual behavior. Ally noted that "Elavil really helped my mom but the side effects were brutal. She always seem zombied and out of it. It took a LONG time before things got a bit better for her. Unfortunately Prozac was not available yet."

The next class of antidepressants is called *Monoamine Oxidase Inhibitors (MAOIs).* Drugs such as *Nardil (phenelzine)* fall into this class. The main advantage of MAOIs is that they tend to have fewer anticholinergic side effects and thus the patient will be less uncomfortable while taking them. They tend to have a faster therapeutic onset than TCAs. However, they have two significant side effects that make their use risky. First, the patient needs to be on a *tyramine-free* diet. This means foods containing tyramine need to be avoided: This includes foods such as aged cheeses (Blue, Swiss, and Mozzarella), fava beans, sauerkraut, and some beers, to name a few. The result of consuming any of these while taking an MAOI: Usually severe hypertension or in some cases death. Finally, many other drugs can interact with MAOIs, including cold remedies, stimulants including Nodoz, sleep aids such as Sominex, appetite suppressants, and anti-asthma drugs such as Primatene (Bezchlibnyk-Butler & Jeffries, 2002). MAOIs block the enzyme monoamine oxidase that breaks down neurotransmitters such as serotonin and norepinephrine. The effects are similar to the tricyclics, since more of these neurotransmitters are available in the brain.

Selective Serotonin Reuptake Inhibitors (SSRIs) are one of the newer classes and include the well-known medications Prozac (fluoxetine) and Zoloft (sertraline). These drugs work differently than the others; they inhibit the *serotonin* presynaptic reuptake in a person's brain and also seem to influence the dopamine and norepinephrine systems. Much research has discovered that depression is caused by a diminished amount of activity in the serotonin system in the brain (McKim, 2003). Prozac and the other SSRIs have some major advantages over the other drugs: They have faster therapeutic onset, they have a long half-life (thus missing a dose is not a serious problem), and they have fewer side effects. A big advantage is that it is very difficult to overdose on SSRIs, especially with Prozac. The biggest downside is that some of the side effects are quite unpleasant: sexual dysfunction, lowered sexual desire (this is quite prevalent, occurring in at least 50% of the individuals who take Prozac), insomnia, and upset stomach. Prozac and Zoloft are unique in that they are two of the medicines approved by the Food and Drug Administration for the treatment of bulimia nervosa.

"I really do not want to take any pills but if it will help I'll do it. I've read a lot about Prozac and I saw what Mom went through while taking Elavil, so given a choice I'd want Prozac, especially the longer-lasting version *(Prozac Weekly)*. I'm afraid I might get addicted to it. Is that possible? Are these pills really safe?"

Addiction is highly unlikely with antidepressants so Ally has no need to worry here. Safety is another matter. Oddly enough it is quite easy to overdose on the tricyclic antidepressants and on MAOIs. Since suicidal thoughts and behaviors often go along with depression, clinicians need to be alert to this possibility if drugs from these classifications are used. Antidepressants do not mix well with some other drugs and especially do not go well with alcohol so patients need to be warned about these interactions. Of course when many people get depressed they tend to drink alcohol, which is a central nervous system depressant . . . and they become even more depressed! Finally, patients need to be clear that these drugs do not work magically; they take time to work and they need to be patient. TCAs, MAOIs and SSRIs, according to research, all have the same *efficacy rate* for successful treatment of depression (Bezchlibnyk-Butler & Jeffries, 2002).

In the end Ally was prescribed Prozac and it really seemed to help her a lot. "It was interesting because for so long I waited for something to occur and then one day I began to feel a lot better. I suspect it was the Prozac since I'd only been in therapy for 5 weeks at that time. I know many people hate taking drugs like I do but when you get to the point where suicide seems like a reasonable thing to do, Prozac doesn't seem so terrible."

Prognosis

Ally's prognosis is listed as "guarded". She wants to get better and progressed well in individual and couples' therapy. She has support from her husband and her daughter "still loves me a lot but we're working on communicating and explaining what is going on with me." She has good insight into her condition and knows what she needs to do to get better and to hopefully stay well. At last report Ally was teaching a class in a needlepoint store once a week ("A how to needlepoint, basically") and was enjoying her work as a consultant "more than ever. I have my moments and my days, but life is good now. I never thought I would enjoy my job and enjoy a hobby as well."

We list her as guarded in spite of her progress in therapy. Those who suffer from a major depressive disorder have a tendency to relapse, and this must always be considered when arriving at a prognosis. Ally's depression has been occurring for so long that guarded is the most logical prognosis at this time.

Her family was about to take their first trip to Europe together and she was quite excited about that. At discharge Ally told us "to tell my story someday to show it's okay to have a mental illness and to be depressed. It's more important to realize what the signs are and that it is treatable. I'm glad I realized these things in time."

Bipolar II Disorder

The Case of Ken: Peaks and Valleys

Presenting Problem

Ken is a 37-year-old Asian male who has been married for 6 years and has a 4-year-old Chinese adopted child. Ken stands 5′7″ tall and weighs 210 pounds. Ken's wife is from the United States. Both of their families were somewhat taken aback when they decided to get married. Jacqueline (Jackie is her nickname) is 36 and comes from a white Jewish household. "Everyone has this stereotype of Jews being liberal and accepting. Well that is certainly not true here. My parents were not happy when they met Ken. They loved him and knew he was a great person and all but the Asian thing threw them for a loop." Ken's parents come from Mainland China. His father was born in Shanghai and his mother was born in Shenzen. His family is close to him and to his daughter but "they still treat Jackie somewhat suspiciously and that really hurts me and her. They don't mean to be cruel; it's a cultural thing."

Ken first came to see us dressed in a blue suit with a yellow tie ("A power tie, bro!"). He made decent eye contact and seemed nervous. His voice shook and at times he rambled on without stopping or taking a breath. His face was red as though he had a fever or was overheated. Ken wore glasses and had wiry, prematurely graying hair. He displayed an inappropriate affect at times, laughing and smiling when not appropriate. Ken wore a pager which he initially refused to turn off. "What happens if something goes down at the hotel? No one can do the things I can do. They call me Superman at the hotel. A Chinese Clark Kent!"

Jackie was dressed casually in jeans and a blouse, "just as you might expect for a casual Friday. No need to get dressy." Jackie has a BA in English, "A total waste of time. I was expected to go to school but I really did not want to work. This was the easy way out. The schooling was fun, but what can I do with that kind of degree? Drive a taxi or flip burgers? We figured that to get care for Angela it would cost more than my salary was at the time. I worked for a publishing house." Jackie was 5′2″, wore glasses, and made good eye contact and had an appropriate affect. Jackie was pleasant and smiled often during the sessions. She would often look at Ken when she was speaking to gauge his reactions and perhaps look for approval.

What brought Ken in to see us? "When I was 23 I began graduate school. During this time I noticed I was very moody, blue a lot of the time. I attributed this to graduation and entering graduate school. To be honest I did not want to do grad work but I mainly did so to be with Jackie. Our relationship could not survive if I moved back home to work in the hotel. The sadness was normal (I thought), as did Jackie. But the intensity was not. There were days when I could not get myself out of bed. I did not have energy to engage in conversations with Jackie or anyone else. It seemed like every physical action required so much energy that it would kill me to do it. These moods eventually lifted and then I would go back to being normal. The freaky part happened afterwards."

"I would go from these lows to being stable for awhile. Then suddenly one day this feeling of total euphoria overcame me, like a major rush. I was flying high, on top of the world with no worries. During one of these rushes I ended up spending a lot of money—$2,000 to be exact. But I really didn't care as I felt so good. I cut myself with a knife one evening in the kitchen and Jackie saw this and really got concerned but it didn't really bother me at all. I laughed actually. That was the weird part, that anything painful really did not hurt at all. Nothing could bother me. I had so much energy I told Jackie I was going to re-do the living room, and then I wanted to shampoo the carpet. This was at 3 A.M. I had no desire to sleep, I was wired!" Ken was talking somewhat rapidly at this point, and we had to slow him down so we could take everything down.

Ken then told us specifically why he came to see us. "Because of all of these things I came to see you to try and get some answers. Jackie was the real reason. She encouraged me as well. I'm worried about the lows, but the highs are normal. I'm a high energy type, a live wire."

"Asians do not really believe in going to psychologists unless you're really crazy and even then we question it. We tend to keep everything within our families and rely on them and on ourselves to help deal with things. So you need to know this is a big step for me and I'm not comfortable at all with this. Jackie understands and will join me if it's the best solution. Because my up days are great I don't really know why I'm here. Basically I'm doing this for Jackie, for Angela, and for my family."

Background Information

Ken's parents grew up under Mao's rule and managed to stay in the United States once they arrived. The details of how they got here are not clear and Ken was not willing to discuss those with us at any point during the sessions. "You need to understand that these matters are private and they don't affect me at all as far as coming in here." Ken is an only child as per the one family–one child rule in China. He speaks fluent Mandarin but "I really don't have much chance to use it. I'm teaching our daughter how to speak it but her primary language will be English. Jackie understands some words but she's too busy with Angela to put a lot of time into it."

Ken reports that he had an unremarkable childhood, reaching all of his developmental milestones at the appropriate ages. He struggled somewhat in school because of the language barrier even though he was born in the United States. "My parents speak fair English but we always spoke Mandarin at home. It took me quite awhile to get good at English and I suspect that caused some of the school problems. Regardless of the reasons my parents expected me to do a lot better." Ken graduated with a B-minus average and went on to a large state university. "I figured it would be cheaper and my language problems would be easier to deal with at a large school. I also hoped there would be many Asians there." He joined the International Students Association (ISA) and was president his senior year. Ken majored in computer science and graduated on time with a B average. "I liked school a lot; it allowed me to grow as a person. I was quite shy so I didn't go out a lot. I had many friends in ISA and because of that organization my life totally changed."

"During my last semester I got together with Jackie. I'd always noticed her but we finally started to talk during my junior year and became friends. That developed into a romance during my last semester and I was worried when I graduated that would end things, as she was a year behind me. Fortunately I was accepted to the university's graduate school and so our romance continued. Then she graduated and stayed on for one year until I finished. Once I graduated we got engaged and the rest is history."

"My parents expected me to marry an Asian girl and freaked when they met Jackie. I never expected that kind of reaction. Jackie was so hurt but she kept it inside since she knew how her parents would react. I was furious with my parents. They were acting like idiots. We thought about eloping and I wanted to move far away from them, but I realized how much they sacrificed to put me through school and to raise me in a foreign country. I couldn't do that so we had many talks. Eventually they came to accept Jackie but they would have preferred for her to be Asian. Once Angela came into the family they warmed up to Jackie when they saw what a fantastic mother she was. And Jackie treats my parents with love and respect, which is very important to Asians. We honor our parents and our elders and Jackie knew this. My parents realized this and they appreciated that she is trying to learn Mandarin. When she greets them with "Ni Hao (how are you?)" they always smile and tell me they are so impressed with her."

We noticed at this point that Ken was clenching his fists tightly and it appeared that he had something in them. We asked him to show us, and when he opened his hands we saw a smooth stone in one and a "stress ball" in another. "These help to keep me focused when I need to be focused. Sometimes I have so much energy like now it's hard. I rub my stone and squeeze the ball, take deep breaths, and it helps. I read about this online." We noted these behaviors and continued.

Ken was very candid about the reasons behind their adoption of Angela. "We had been trying for awhile and we had no luck. Jackie's cycles were also irregular. Since we would both be 'older parents' we pursued adoption. We discovered, while waiting for Angela to arrive, that Jackie was unable to bear children. We were devastated when we found this out but both of us suspected that something was not right with one or both of us. Jackie felt like she was not 'a whole woman' and that she was 'damaged goods,' so to speak. Of course this was crazy. Oddly enough neither of our families pressed us as to why we were adopting, which was a pleasant surprise."

"We decided to adopt a Chinese girl since we figured this would not require a long wait and would make more sense for both of us. Jackie had no issues with this at all and of course neither did my parents. Her parents were . . . not thrilled but when they met Angela and saw how she appeared like a fragile doll they were overcome and fell in love with her. Needless to say we made the right decision."

"We haven't yet approached the religion issue with Angela and probably won't for another year or so. I was raised as a Catholic but I'm an atheist and Jackie is Jewish, so we've got an interesting dilemma ahead of us. Our parents have not said anything to us about this nor should they."

Ken works as a consultant for a hotel that is run by family members. "My parents were part of the group of original partners. The hotel eventually grew until it became a large 230-room building. The partners decided to expand and they then decided to build another hotel about 25 miles away. This was a wise decision as both hotels were doing very well. The partners wisely decided to sell the second hotel and the original one is still doing very well. I consult with the partners about Internet and computer issues and advertising. Thus the hotel will stay in the family until the partners sell it, close it, or I leave. Jackie stayed at home to raise Angela until Angela turned 3, and then she went back to work for a publishing house."

It appears like Ken has a stable background and a loving and supportive family. He reports no known history of mental or physical illness in his family. Let us examine his situation more closely. "Once the lows that I told you about stopped I felt relieved. I had a break and then the highs started again. It was such a switch to feel so good that once the high came back I didn't want it to end. I wasn't sleeping because I didn't need to sleep. I got so much work accomplished, I wanted sex more often . . . it was all so wonderful. However, I found out soon enough that these highs didn't last; they were either followed by my stable moods or worse, by the low moods coming back again."

"I thought at first it might have something to do with my being in grad school or the fears about marrying Jackie and how my family would react, but once all of that settled in the moods still occurred. Not all the time but often enough to really begin to bother me. It was like being in fantasy land to crashing to earth and being in an awful reality, like Hell almost. I didn't know what to do and neither did Jackie. We had heard about depression of course and so I finally went to see a psychiatrist and he prescribed Prozac to deal with the lows. He never really worried about the highs, saying that they were a natural after-effect of being so low for so long. To be honest I really minimized the severity of the high moods to him and to myself."

"The Prozac helped for awhile but the highs and shifts in mood kept occurring. Once Jackie graduated and we moved back to my home state the moods eased up quite a bit. I would have the highs and lows but they didn't seem to be as severe as before. This made me feel like I had the problem beaten and indeed it was due to being in grad school. The mood swings came back once we found out Jackie was unable to conceive and they seemed to get worse as the adoption proceeded. They came back again right after Angela entered the family."

"I tried to deal with them as best I could and I went to another psychiatrist who again prescribed Prozac. He did this since it seemed to be successful last time. As in the past it worked in lifting my depression but the highs remained. To be honest I'm not sure if I want to get rid of the highs since they're so much better than being blue. It almost makes up for the lows. The feelings I get while on that high are indescribable. At the same time this is not helping my marriage, my work, or my relationship with Angela. She sees Daddy being all hyper and it scares her."

"The lows have at times caused me to think about suicide, but that comes up more often because of these rapid mood swings. It drives me crazy. The real killer is that I don't want the highs to end and when they do I get so low at times I feel like ending it all. But I think of Angela and Jackie and get out of that mindset." Suicidal thoughts with bipolar disorder patients are common and some patients do indeed take their own lives because of the reasons Ken described.

"Because of all of these things I came to see you to try and get some answers. Jackie encouraged me as well. That's why I'm here and we're here."

Thought Questions

1. How important is it that Ken's mood swings seem to occur when he's under a great deal of stress? Is this something the psychologist should investigate?
2. How appropriate is it for Ken to be taking Prozac?
3. Would you include Jackie in Ken's potential therapeutic treatment? Angela?
4. How affected might Angela be by Ken's behavior?
5. Are highs normal after being depressed? Why or why not?

Assessment and Evaluation

Ken was assessed using an unstructured diagnostic interview, the BDI-II, and by analyzing his past *psychiatric history*. We initially made contact with his psychiatrists to obtain this history and we also decided to obtain a *complete medical history* from Ken. We first sent him to get a complete physical since he had not been to a medical doctor for 5 years. This is standard practice for many psychologists since many physical disorders can mimic psychological ones. We also set up an appointment with our consulting psychiatrist so that he could examine and assess Ken. We will report on these results in a little while.

As we stated previously, depression appears to have a familial component. The closer a person is genetically to a family member who has depression, the greater the risk that individual has in developing depression. The evidence for genetic factors playing a role is even greater for bipolar disorders. Some research states that 80% of the risk of developing bipolar disorder can be accounted for this way (Katz & McGuffin, 1993). This is probably an overestimate but the fact remains: Bipolar disorder has a stronger genetic and familial component than unipolar depressions. This is a crucial piece of information. In many instances *unipolar depression* or another mental illness may become bipolar disorder; in some cases this may take as long as a decade before the bipolar disorder manifests itself (Hammen, 1997). Thus we began by looking into what mental illness(es) if any affected Ken before he developed his present concerns.

"Well, I've always tended to internalize, keep things inside of me and that tends to make me anxious. I'm totally open with Jackie but it's a combination of culture and being a man that leads me to keep a lot bottled up. Asians in general do not openly express anger and other emotions and I fall into that. So yes, that has caused me to be anxious over the years. Jackie has really helped me with this but it still exists. I swallow my anger and other feelings at times."

We then asked Ken to define "anxious" and give us an example. "Okay, my stomach gets all knotted, my blood pressure increases (my heart races so I can tell from that), my face gets red and I tend to sweat a lot. I might even shake a bit. But I control all of this and keep it in. Jackie would prefer to fight than to have me keep this stuff inside."

"The most recent example occurred when I came home one night. It was a bad day at work and when I got home I discovered that Angela had spilled some of her juice on our computer, completely frying it. Well of course I didn't have a recent backup and I was SO angry and tense, but I kept it inside. It was a total accident and I couldn't be mad at Angela. Jackie wanted me to get this out but I didn't and I eventually dealt with it. I ended up with an upset stomach because of this, which is typical."

We wanted to make sure that Ken did not have a substance use disorder so we asked him questions relating to this. It was clinic policy to always ask any patient questions relating to substance and alcohol use (barring certain exceptions, such as very young children and such). "My drinking? Generally not more than a beer or two a week. My family doesn't drink much if at all and neither do I. I just never acquired a big taste for it with the exception of beer. Beer goes well with certain foods so I'll have it from time to time. But never more than one a night." Ken reported having no legal, marital or work problems because of alcohol usage.

"As far as I know there is no history of mental illness in my family. We never discussed such things but it doesn't seem likely, since my family was always open with me about my background. I guess that's because I'm an only child. Once they found out I was married they told me as much as they knew about my ancestors and such. Mental illness was never discussed in Mainland China. What would generally happen if someone were mentally ill is that the government would take him or her away and that was the last anyone saw of him or her. We assumed they were executed. Things are a bit different today of course. So I guess it is possible that there is a family history, but I cannot say for sure."

We then contacted his past psychiatrists and they were somewhat surprised at Ken's mood swings. Ken replied, "Well, as I hinted at I really didn't emphasize the euphoria with them. I told them about it but I didn't spend a lot of time on it and so I suspect they basically were not overly concerned. I guess things would have been different if I'd spoken out more. Jackie said I should but until recently the euphoria was not a constant." The euphoria to which Ken refers is known as *mania,* as *manic episodes,* or as *hypomanic episodes.* This is not surprising since episodes of mania usually do not predate depressions; many clinicians may have problems detecting manic episodes and may attribute them to other factors.

We then asked Ken to have a complete physical to see if anything else might be going on. His results were unremarkable with the exception of high blood pressure. We asked about this. The doctor told us that high blood pressure is common in anxious people and that people get anxious in a doctor's office (do you?). To compensate the doctor will usually retake the person's pressure a bit later during the exam. Ken's remained quite high. This could also explain his anger and anxiety levels being so high, as well as explain his fatigue. But does this explain his mood swings?

"The high blood pressure makes sense. We eat a lot of foods that are high in sodium (smiles at Jackie). That is part of it. High blood pressure also runs in my family. I guess I should look into this." We then sent Ken to a psychiatrist with whom we work closely. After a lengthy time gap Ken returned with Jackie for a follow-up visit. We also had the psychiatrist's evaluation to help us out at this point.

"Well, I'm not surprised what Dr. Jones discovered. Dr. Jones said that it was evident, based on the information you sent him and what I said that I have *Bipolar II Disorder.* I did some reading after our first meeting and some of it clicks, some does not. For Jackie's sake I'm here to follow up. I tell you, I was not going to come back." What exactly did Dr. Jones say? In sum,

"Ken presents with a somewhat inappropriate affect and with fair eye contact. Jackie came in to the evaluation with him initially at his insistence. She was asked to leave shortly after the evaluation began. Pt (Patient) reports high blood pressure, perhaps exacerbated by mood swings. Pt reports mood swings began at age 23. No evidence of mania, but evidence for hypomanic episodes. Pt not actively suicidal, no imminent risk detected. Pt was nervous, jumpy, had hard time staying focused, needed little sleep lately. Still managing to work and function. Pt reports many episodes of depression in past. Oriented times three. Initial diagnostic impressions:

Bipolar II Disorder, Hypomanic, With Rapid Cycling   296.89

R/O Bipolar I Disorder

Treatment Rec: Couples' therapy with Jackie;

Depakene (valproic acid): 250mg bid (bid means twice a day)

Bipolar Disorder is more commonly known as *Manic-Depressive Illness;* the clinical (and correct) term is Bipolar Disorder. Bipolar disorder is evidenced by mood swings between euphoria (the manic episodes as Ken described) and depression. There may or may not be a period of "normalcy"; in Ken's case there was. Bipolar disorder is often masked by other physical and mental conditions which may have caused the lack of proper diagnosing previously.

Jackie was totally supportive. "I'll support Ken through all of this. I suspected something was up with the mood swings. I attributed this to too much caffeine and being overworked by staring at computer screens all day and night." Based on all of the above information, we agreed with Dr. Jones' diagnoses of Ken and designed a treatment plan.

Theoretical Etiologies

In general, bipolar disorder is considered to be biologically based. We have briefly discussed the strong evidence for having inherited the predisposition for bipolar disorder but it bears mentioning again. It is still unclear whether bipolar disorder itself is inherited or the vulnerability (diathesis) is inherited. Stress also appears to be involved in the development of the disorder. Stress can either bring about bipolar disorder, or stress can lead to new bipolar episodes if the disorder has already been developed.

Gene and chromosomal longitudinal studies have found that a number of chromosomes may carry the genetic markers for bipolar disorder. Specifically, chromosomes 4, 12, 16, 21, and even the X chromosome have been identified in various studies (see, for example, Craddock & Jones, 1999). The conclusion here is that several different gene combinations and their interactions may be responsible for the development of bipolar disorder. A more important conclusion is that no **single** gene is responsible for the development of bipolar disorder. These studies also hypothesized that those families who were at high risk for developing bipolar disorder were also a high risk for developing unipolar depression, substance abuse disorders, and anxiety disorders.

Before examining Ken and Jackie's treatment plan, we need to examine the possible psychosocial factors that may contribute to the development of bipolar disorder. These factors can activate new bipolar episodes and can play a role in preventing future recurrences. Environmental stressors have been implicated in setting off episodes of mania. As you saw with Ken, he blamed his mood swings on his circumstances. While he is not totally correct, the stressors in his environment certainly could have played a role. One study discovered that hypomanic episodes seemed to be more likely after events that disrupted an individual's sleep patterns, while depressions were more likely to occur after the individual experienced a loss (Malkoff- Schwartz, Frank, Anderson, Sherrill, Siegel, Patterson, & Kupfer, 1998). More research is needed to discover what the interaction is, if there is any, between stress and genetic vulnerability to bipolar disorder.

Finally, family dysfunction and stress can lead to the development or exacerbation of bipolar disorder. As you have seen with Ken, most people who have bipolar disorder have poor social support systems (Johnson, Winnet, Meyer, Greenhouse, & Miller, 1999). Ken's parents were not thrilled when they met Jackie and discovered he intended to marry her.

This obviously hurt both Jackie and Ken. Jackie and Ken do not have many friends which only exacerbates his condition. "Well, it's hard to go out at times when I'm feeling blue. When I'm on a roll it's easy, but Jackie says my behavior embarrasses her. We've broken a lot of dates with friends, and now they really don't call too much any more." This information is vital because it appears that dysfunctional and negative family interactions, and poor family attitudes, predict bipolar relapse rates (Hooley & Hiller, 2001).

Understandably, bipolar disorder is difficult to live with, especially because family members do not know for sure what will happen next. It would be nice if we could say, "Well, since Ken's depression is lifting we will now prepare for his hypomanic episodes," but that does not happen. Living with this situation can cause tremendous stress for the family and they may develop depression or some other type of mental disorder. Further research is ongoing and is still needed in discovering more information about bipolar disorder.

Treatment Plan

The initial phase of treatment is quite clear: Ken needs to begin his medication to combat the hypomanic episodes. Recall that an individual can function while experiencing these episodes, but Ken was not progressing in therapy. "I made a deal with Jackie that I would do this immediately. I was hesitant about using any kind of medication. I like to believe in a pure body, pure mind kind of thing. No artificial things in my body. What if you guys or Jackie are trying to poison me? (Laughs.) She'd get a big inheritance and I'd be out of her hair! But I'll try it and see what happens. I have to keep seeing Dr. Jones, which is a hassle as well. But let's give it a shot for Jackie."

This is a good start. We decided that Ken needed couples' therapy to aid his communication with Jackie, to educate him and Jackie about bipolar disorder, and to help Jackie (and indirectly their daughter) learn how to interact with Ken. They were also educated about his medication and what to expect from its usage. Role playing and demonstrations of positive feedback and open communication were used.

Ken made significant progress after 2 months; we were somewhat surprised at how hard he worked and how well things were progressing for him. "Well, it's okay to be surprised but I'm not totally. I got the scare of my life. Can you imagine something that might be killing you and you have no idea you've got it? It's like the movie *Alien* where something is inside of you and you really don't know it until it gets you. I'm also learning how to express my feelings to Jackie in a constructive way and to accept my mental illness as something I caught. I'll always be bipolar but it can be controlled."

We gave Ken homework assignments where he had to express his feelings whenever he was feeling anxious. Jackie was instructed to act like a blank slate, letting him express himself without criticism from her. She would then comment once he was done. Ken also had to tell Jackie how he felt during and after these "expression" sessions. Ken told us, "You know I was surprised. I was never really in touch with my feelings before until I got into therapy and these outside assignments you give me. It's scary when I realize what I've been missing."

Jackie benefited as well from the treatment. "I can now understand somewhat what he's going through when he gets hyper. That's not a real problem because of his pills, but in case it does happen again I know how to deal with it. I also think our family's issues surrounding our marriage and adoption contributed to this. We have told them about Ken's condition and of course they blame their son or daughter-in-law (sneers as she says this). What can you do? Being insular and shutting them out is not going to work. We hope that at some point they will understand. We gave them some literature to read hoping this will help somewhat, but we don't have a lot of hope. This is tolerable, because in the end we still have each other and our family."

We can now turn towards medication options, since this is still the primary treatment modality for bipolar I or II disorder. Therapy is useful here but the best way to treat mania and hypomanic episodes is through medications. There are quite a few medication options to use when treating bipolar disorder. Again in the interest of simplicity we will consider each medication briefly and then discuss what Ken is taking.

Lithium (lithium carbonate or lithium citrate; one trade name is *Eskalith)* has been the most common medication used to treat bipolar disorder. Lithium will reduce manic episodes and in some cases will reduce depressive episodes, but the latter is not typical. Note that Ken was still taking Prozac for his depressive episodes when he came to us and Dr. Jones took him off of this.

The biggest risk in using lithium is that it is extremely toxic and so the patient's blood levels need to be monitored closely. Lithium is a naturally occurring salt but the difference between therapeutic effectiveness and lethality is quite small (therapeutically effective levels for lithium are known as the *therapeutic window*). We also do not know why lithium works, so some consider this one of the wonder drugs in mental health.

Lithium alone is not the best treatment for bipolars who have *rapid cycling* (four or more episodes within the past 12 months) because for these patients it may take up to one year (when used alone) to reach therapeutic effectiveness. Some conditions, like diabetes and weight-loss diets, may elevate the levels of lithium in the blood, increasing the risk of toxicity. The most common pharmacological treatment modality today for rapid cycling bipolars usually involves using anticonvulsants.

Anticonvulsants (primarily used to treat *seizure disorder,* formerly known as *epilepsy*) are used to treat bipolar disorder, especially mania and hypomanic episodes. Three major anticonvulsants are *Tegretol (carbamazepine), Klonopin (clonazepam),* and Depakene (valproic acid). These drugs have fewer side effects than Lithium and work faster on reducing the mania. They also tend to reduce depressive symptoms, especially Tegretol.

Dr. Jones decided on two courses of action for Ken. He took him off of Prozac and prescribed Depakene since it tends to work best with bipolar II disorder. Usually the clinical benefits of Depakene are realized within 14 days for mania. It takes between 2 to 3 weeks until the depression is treated effectively. In Ken's case his moods stabilized and he had minimal side effects from the Depakene. Additionally, because Ken was diagnosed with rapid cycling and because his symptoms have been occurring for a few years, Dr. Jones wanted the optimal response from medication usage. Therefore, following recommended practice, he prescribed Lithium along with Depakene. Lithium seems to increase the antidepressive and antimanic effects of Depakene (Bezchlibnyk-Butler & Jeffries, 2002).

"The meds really helped a lot. I was surprised because I initially missed the highs but soon after that the lows began to vanish as well. I felt truly normal for the first time in my life. I don't like the fact that I'm taking these things and that I have to get my blood drawn so often, but Dr. Jones told me I could die if I didn't do this. I can tell you I really miss my highs. They gave me so much energy and I think Jackie appreciated it also. I could go for so long and get so much done! I won't kid you; I get tempted at times to get the highs back. I'm still not so sure they weren't normal stress reactions and not part of this bipolar thing. I'll take your word for it and also Dr. Jones'."

Dr. Jones continued to monitor Ken while he was on Depakene and Lithium. Many patients, if they hope to remain stable, need to be on a medication that treats bipolar disorder for an extended period of time. If the symptoms markedly decrease (specifically the mania or hypomanic episodes), the psychiatrist may wish to take the patient off of the medication. It is recommended that the patient remain on Lithium and Depakene for a minimum of one year. If the individual (like Ken) have had several episodes of mania or hypomania, or have had recurring depression, they should remain on Lithium and Depakene indefinitely. In some instances this may mean for the rest of their lives.

Prognosis

Ken's prognosis is "guarded" to "fair". Do not be surprised at this. Indeed, Ken progressed very well in treatment and at last report was taking his Depakene and Lithium and reporting no complications from this. He reported no thoughts of suicide during his therapy and at last report, his moods had stabilized as well. They have been stable for the past 7 months. Ken remained in therapy for one year, terminating because "I'm better and it's time to move on."

Thus, why is his prognosis only "guarded to fair?" The reasons are simple. There is a significant potential for relapse with bipolar I and II disorder patients. Figures place relapse potential at 20% to 40% of patients on lithium within two years, and at 65% to 90% of those NOT on lithium within 2 years (Maxmen & Ward, 1995). Relapse rates are significantly lower for those taking Depakene and the other anticonvulsants. These must be considered when making a prognosis.

Relapse is also common because patients often "miss" the manic highs they previously had; in effect these are natural euphorias. The risk is the patient stopping the medication(s) in order to re-experience the mania. This, sadly, is quite common, especially if the depression is not lifting. Ken said he did miss the highs at times but would not go off of his medications. What the psychiatrist and psychologist need to decide is how sincere he is. A potential problem is that Ken still seems to believe that the hypomanic episodes are due to stress and are normal reactions. At last report he did not go off of his medications even once (Jackie confirmed this).

Thus Ken has made significant progress but since the potential for relapse is always there (there is no "cure" for bipolar disorder) we must list his prognosis as "guarded to fair."

Review and Study Questions

Allison (Ally)

1. Do you agree with Ally's "guarded" prognosis? Why or why not?

2. What are your views on antidepressant medications? Prozac seemed to really help Ally, but do you think that therapy alone could produce the same results? Why or why not?

3. How important is the support of Ally's husband in her continued success over depression?

4. How important is her daughter's support in this?

5. Cite evidence to confirm or refute the idea that mood disorders may have a familial component.

6. Suppose Ally were in her teens and was depressed. Discuss the positives and negatives about prescribing medications to her.

Ken

1. Do you agree with Ken's prognosis? It does not seem to offer a lot of hope and includes a lot of doubt. Give your views on this.
2. Could Ken's high blood pressure have caused his mood swings? Why or why not?
3. Give your views on why Ken avoided a medical checkup for so many years.
4. What might the reasons be why it took so long for his hypomanic episodes to appear?
5. Angela is quite young. How will she will be affected by all of this?

Terms to Know

Mood Disorders
Affective disorders
Prozac (fluoxetine)
Zoloft (sertraline)
Tegretol (carbamazepine)
serotonin
Klonopin (clonazepam)
Depakene (valproic acid)
Bipolar II Disorder
Beck Depression Inventory-II (BDI-II)
Elavil (amitriptyline)
trycyclic antidepressant (TCA)
barbiturates
sedatives
hypnotics
libido
depression
Data
Pharmacological
Familial Component
actively suicidal
confidentiality
criterion
irrational thoughts
delusions
family therapy
homework assignments

Monoamine Oxidase Inhibitors (MAOIs)
Selective Serotonin Reuptake Inhibitors (SSRIs)
antihistamine side effects
anticholinergic side effects
menopause
ibuprofen (Advil)
unstructured diagnostic interview
cognitive triad of depression
schemes
pathological mourning
interactional theory
cognitive distortions
learned helplessness
antidepressant medications
cognitive behavioral
efficacy rate
classification
psychiatric history
Complete medical history
Prozac Weekly
unipolar depression
Bipolar Disorder
Manic-Depressive Illness
therapeutic window
rapid cycling
anticonvulsants

seizure disorder

epilepsy

tyramine-free

Mania

hypomanic episodes

manic

manic episodes

Lithium (lithium carbonate or lithium citrate)

Eskalith

prn

reformed helplessness theory

dysthymic disorder

interpersonal psychotherapy (IPT)

Tofranil (imipramine)

Sinequan (doxepin)

Nardil (phenelzine)

Chapter 4

Schizophrenic Disorders

Schizophrenia (technically known as *schizophrenic disorders*) is the most debilitating mental illness, affecting about 0.5% to 1.5% of the population in the U.S. (APA, 2000). Schizophrenia appears to know no barriers: It affects people of all races and socioeconomic classes, but not equally. According to the American Psychiatric Association (2000), the risk of "contracting" schizophrenia is increased if the person has one or more of the following characteristics: They are single, they come from a Westernized or Industrialized nation, they come from a lower socioeconomic class (they do not give the parameters), they live in an urban area, they had problems while in utero, they were born during the winter (!), or they had recently experienced some extreme stress (p. 313). Some researchers have discovered that ethnic minorities (African-American and Puerto Rican in the United States) are more likely to be diagnosed with schizophrenia. This may be due to bias and to stereotyping (Lewis, Croft-Jeffreys, & Anthony, 1990). A major problem with schizophrenia is that oftentimes it does not respond well to treatment. We are also not certain as to what causes schizophrenia; thus, finding a highly effective treatment and/or cure has evaded the helping professions.

Before we begin to examine two very different cases of schizophrenia, we need to dispel a few myths:

- Schizophrenia is NOT a split personality (this condition is generally known as *Dissociative Identity Disorder*, previously known as *Multiple Personality Disorder*). The best way to remember this difference is to think of schizophrenia as a break or **split** from reality.
- All schizophrenics are not homicidal maniacs, serial killers, Jason from *Friday the Thirteenth* and so on. In fact, most schizophrenics are more of a danger to themselves than to others. Portraying schizophrenics as raving maniacs is good for television ratings and brings in more moviegoers.
- Schizophrenia does NOT only affect older individuals. In fact the average age of onset occurs between the late teens and early thirties. Thus if someone is diagnosed initially with schizophrenia at age 74, other diagnoses need to be considered first. Therefore schizophrenia can be considered a young person's disease.

- Schizophrenia is not caused SOLELY by any of the following: a bad upbringing, lower socioeconomic status, prenatal brain damage, bad chromosomes, or environmental toxins. In fact many theorists consider ALL of these as being potential *etiological* (causal) factors. A popular line of thinking today is that the schizophrenias are considered to be a series of diseases. Some also believe that schizophrenics may be born with the disease and it takes a long time for it to manifest itself (i.e., come out).

Do any of these myths sound familiar? Do any of the truths about schizophrenia surprise you? Where would someone like Charles Manson, Jeffrey Dahmer, or the fictitious Dr. Hannibal Lecter (*Silence of the Lambs, Red Dragon*) fit in? Let's look at two very different individuals and see if anything about their cases surprises you. These cases will be presented differently than those in the other chapters because in both cases the patients were actively hallucinating when they came to see us. How will that make a difference? Let's see.

Schizophrenia, Disorganized Type

The Case of Henry:
Not the Split That You Think

Presenting Problem

Henry is a 47-year-old white divorced male who is quite slender, weighing 118 pounds and standing 5'9" tall. Henry has no children and was born in a large city in the Eastern United States. Henry's parents came from Eastern Europe. Henry refused to initially supply any details about his father, only stating that when his family immigrated to the United States his father did not accompany them. "I have no idea what happened to him and I don't really care. He left us when I was quite young and I never asked my mom to tell us what happened. Who cares?"

Henry's mother works in a garment factory and she just celebrated her 70th birthday. Henry has an older brother George and a younger sister Clara. George lives in another city and sees Henry about twice a year; Clara lives close by "but she hates me and I hate her; she's a mean witch, mean to me and to her kids. I can't stand her." Henry has no children "and I don't intend to have any. With me being sick and all there's no need to have kids. They couldn't help me any."

Henry has spent the last 18 years in and out of psychiatric hospitals because of his "problems. I came to you because I was told to. The fires in my head started again. I can't get rid of them. And I itch all over. It's like little things are running all over my body. Look at my arms (He shows us his arms, which are scratched raw.) I also have some breathing problems." When Henry first came to us he was sweating profusely even though it was early spring and in the mid 40s. Henry made poor eye contact throughout our sessions, frequently looking at the walls or out the window. Many times he would stare at the radio or at the telephone. He also liked to fix his gaze on a cactus on the desk.

Background Information

Henry reported no problems growing up and told us he reached his developmental milestones at the appropriate ages with one exception. "My mom and the witch Clara said I talked real late, about three and a half, and

I didn't talk much to people. That made some sense but because of our dog not really." We asked Henry to clarify, "Well, our dog was a big part of our family and I have these allergies that make it hard to focus and to live. I think the dog made it hard to learn how to talk at the right time. My mom didn't help either." Henry reported no other problems and told us that no one else in his family suffered from any mental illnesses "but that Clara, who's a witch and a creep; does that count?"

"You know doc, this damned fire in my head . . . it's burning like crazy. I took a shower before coming in because I wanted to smell nice and all, and I hoped that would stop the fire and the itching. It just won't stop. I've also had this buzzing in my head, like a door buzzer or a bee is stuck in my ears. It won't stop either." Some of Henry's statements contradict themselves. Henry was disheveled and in fact looked rather unclean. Dirt was caked under his fingernails and a fine layer of dirt was noticed on his arms. His body gave off a scent that smelled like urine. His hair was unkempt and dirty and his teeth were badly stained, probably from coffee or tobacco. "Yes I smoke, what is that to you? I like a smoke. I make my own to save money ; welfare only gives so much. They're better anyway. Sometimes smoking helps the buzzing."

Do you find anything unusual yet? What do you think of the psychologist's approach so far? What might you do differently? Is Henry suffering from a schizophrenic disorder?

Henry told us that he was sent to us so we asked about this. "Well, you see doc, the cops picked me up for 'wandering.' What the heck is wandering? I was sleeping in my usual place, not bothering no one, and they rassled me up and out, tried to get me to the shelter they did! I ain't going to no shelter to get robbed and stabbed by those people. My spot is safer. It's warm and sunny and nobody bugs me. People bug me. Noise is noise, you know?"

We then decided to gather some more background information on Henry before proceeding. We sent for the police report (this was easier said than done) and his hospital records. Henry helped out by telling us where he was "rassled" and he knew the name of his most recent hospital. The records from both sources helped significantly in piecing together Henry's past. Once we gained the information we needed we asked Henry to come back (after repeated contact attempts) and we continued our initial interview.

"Okay, yes, I was in the hospital for 2 years and they finally released me because I got better. They thought I could manage by seeing shrinks and doctors outside of the hospital and I can. It's just that the hospital did not do a lot once I got ready to leave. You can also fake being better to get out of there and I'd had enough. My girlfriend was waiting for me and I needed to see the sun and eat some fruit." The records indicated that Henry was not hallucinating and was doing as well as could be expected and the doctors saw no need to keep him hospitalized. They determined that he was not a threat to himself or to others and thus discharged him.

The police found Henry on the street, reeking from not having bathed for awhile and shouting unintelligible things to passersby. They tried to reason with him and then realized that this did not work. He refused to go to a shelter and so they had no choice but to put him in jail. Henry was also standing in the middle of the street with his pants halfway down. The police determined that he was not a threat to harm anyone but instead that he needed psychiatric help. Henry told them that he was ordered by his doctors to see someone on an outpatient basis and the police took him to us.

Thought Questions

1. How sensible was it for the psychologist to try to assess Henry while he seemed to be actively hallucinating?
2. Are you surprised that Henry returned to us for a second visit? Why or why not?
3. You don't yet know a lot about Henry but are you surprised by anything that you have read so far? If so, what and why?
4. Discuss your views about the psychiatric hospital's decision to release Henry.
5. Might Henry's hallucinations (if they are indeed that) have been caused by something else? If so, what might those things be?
6. How important will Henry's background information be when trying to accurately diagnose him?

Assessment and Evaluation

Henry was assessed through an *unstructured diagnostic interview* and a *psychiatric evaluation*. Henry met with the psychologist three times before he was sent to our psychiatrist, Dr. Sung (not the psychiatrist's real name). Henry appeared to like Dr. Sung, since he was quite talkative with him and smiled often when he met with him.

As we spent more time with Henry's hospital records a more complete picture arose. Henry's mother was treated for depression when she was in her late 30s; this information was gathered from her and from George. (We contacted George and Henry's mother Goldie and they both willingly and graciously came in to our office to provide additional information.) George appeared neatly dressed, wearing slacks that were about one size too big, since they slipped down below his waist. He displayed an appropriate affect and made fair eye contact during our interviews. George wore glasses, was about 20 pounds overweight, and was 5'6" tall. He had not shaved for at least one day as stubble was evident. George fidgeted a lot during the interviews; "I've never really done this before, so I'm a bit tense. My family has always been nervous."

Goldie was dressed conservatively, and she first appeared to us wearing a wide brimmed hat and carrying a very large handbag. She smiled a lot during the sessions and made good eye contact. She would always sit in the chair closest to us and would begin and end each session by grasping our hands and squeezing lightly. Goldie was 5'3" tall, was neither overweight nor underweight, and had piercing hazel eyes. She showed us a picture when she was a young woman and she was extremely attractive. She walked somewhat slowly but was always pleasant to us.

George was described by his mother as "a bit odd, an eccentric. When my granddaughter was born he always bought her dolls and cute clothes. But he insisted on delivering them himself, taking the train (a 2-hour trip) to drop them off with me. Can you imagine anyone doing this? He is harmless but a bit odd I guess." George provided some information on his mother.

"She suffered from depression for a few years and no one did anything about it. She still managed to run the house but she rarely got out. Cooking was her life and boy is she a good cook! We got used to the circles under her eyes and figured it was from cooking all day long. She slept a lot but always seemed to wake up very early. She also had to watch three kids on her own which was rough. She never told us why Dad left. We suspect it was for another woman or that he would be caught for something once he came over."

"Henry was a high school graduate who did okay. He went to an all-boys school and never really was interested in women until he got out. He then worked in the family business with me while his wife stayed home with Mom and took care of the house. They never wanted kids. We knew something was not right with Henry when he stopped bathing and taking care of himself. He would have these horrible scratches on his arms that we thought were due to a rash or to the heat. It slowly became harder to communicate with Henry until there were times when he made no sense at all. He told us about his head and brain being on fire. We had no idea what was going on."

The question of drug and alcohol use was posed to George and Goldie. George said, "Henry rarely if ever drank and he didn't use drugs, had no use for them and no money. Henry worked in a meat packing plant and didn't make enough for that stuff. Booze never really interested him and no one in our family really drinks anyway." Goldie corroborated this information. "My son may have problems but booze and drugs are not them. Not many people have asked about this but you're only the second. "

We asked Henry about his usage and a somewhat different story emerged. "I drink but only when I'm on the street. I do it to stop the burning in my head and the itching and the voices. The voices always seem to be whispering things to me. I know I'm not good but the voices say that also. They're quiet, almost giggling when they speak. Sometimes the alcohol shuts them up . . . quiet!" At this point Henry began giggling a lot and we had to take a brief break so he could regain his composure.

Henry's usage of alcohol to quiet the voices and his other hallucinations is typical of *outpatient* schizophrenics. For reasons we shall soon see, many outpatient schizophrenics will stop taking their medications because of the side effects, which can be severe at times. Once they stop taking them, the voices (if they are having *auditory hallucinations*) generally return. Thus they have made a trade-off. Many schizophrenics who have been discharged from the hospital will often turn to alcohol to quiet the voices and such. Alcohol produces its own side effects of course but it has some significant advantages: It is readily available, it is legal if you are of age, and it is cheap. Many of the homeless in the United States consist of psychiatric outpatients who use alcohol or illicit substances to alleviate their symptoms. According to an earlier report by Dugger (1995), the homeless who can be classified as deinstitutionalized psychiatric patients (their disabilities may include schizophrenia) may try to alleviate their symptoms by using illicit substances such as crack cocaine. According to Henry and the police reports, Henry himself seems to fall into this category.

We tried to assess the onset of Henry's problems with the help of his family. Henry said things "got really bad when I was 23. My wife left me for another man, we were having troubles you know? She never did like my job none and we never did have a lot of relations. My mom liked her but you know, they're hard to figure out sometimes. She said I talked too much and was crazy. Do you think I'm crazy?"

Goldie and George gave us some additional insight. Goldie told us, "Henry started to hear and react to voices when he was 23 or so, right during the break-up with his wife. He really got stressed about it but he wasn't acting like himself for about 4 years once he graduated high school. Henry stopped taking care of himself and started that blasted scratching. He also told us that sometimes he would get messages from God and that God only chose to communicate with him. We were a little concerned but not overly so. I figured it was a part of his growing up and the fears that come with that. Henry was also never overly bright so I also figured that he might be misinterpreting things. The voices and scratching really got bad once she walked out on him. We tried to calm him down but we had no luck. I was never hospitalized but I knew what had to be done. We called an ambulance and they took Henry away with what we were later told was a *psychotic break* (a sudden break from reality). They explained that Henry had a sickness called schizophrenia that would require lengthy hospitalization and medication and intensive treatment."

She continued. "Well this shocked us! I'd been sad for a long period of time but this schizophrenia in one of my kids threw me for a loop! I didn't think he had a split personality but then the doctors told me what this meant. I didn't feel much better but they told me there was a good chance his problems would respond well to treatment so I told them to go for it. I missed having Henry around but I knew where he needed to be."

"Henry didn't really have many problems as a child. He kept to himself and was generally friendly. He talked late but seemed to catch up rather fast with the others. School didn't interest him that much; he would often seem lost in his own world and get very involved with solitary activities. He was not into sports and wasn't really good at them. Henry went to the prom alone since he was too shy to ask a girl and girls were not crazy about him since he was tall and thin. But we never really saw anything to tell us that he was crazy like this."

So far does there seem to be anything remarkable in Henry's history that might have caused him to "contract" some type of schizophrenia? Let's see if some more information might help. We continued to question Goldie.

"I didn't have any problems while carrying Henry and none of my other kids have any problems so to speak. I told you about my sadness problem but that seems to have gone away. I got better as Henry got worse. I think Henry's dad (my husband) might have had some kinds of problems. He didn't come over with us to New York City and that must have affected Henry. My husband said he heard things at times and would ask me if I heard them and I always said I didn't. In fact there was silence most of the times he asked. He could never stay focused on one thing and that included our marriage. He also tended to make up words at times so it wasn't always easy to understand him. Of course in Eastern Europe mental illness or problems were never discussed. If they knew, you would be sent to prison for life or executed. So we kept quiet about it."

"When Henry was born he seemed to snap. He began to look for wires in our house and pulled up the floorboards. The voices became more frequent. He just couldn't take it anymore. We finally had enough money to go to the United States and he ran away 1 month before we were supposed to leave. I never tried to find him. Henry was 4 at the time and he really didn't understand what was happening. So I guess he got stuck from both of us."

We then returned to talking with Henry. "So what do you think? The weather's nice today no? Good weather for the worms to come out and eat the grass . . . do you like fishing? I love it." We asked Henry if he knew what was happening to him, "I'm sick or so they told me in the hospital. See these itches? They make me scratch. That causes me to hurt a lot. I feel like things are crawling on me, blech. I hate that. And the fire, the buzzing . . . it hurts a lot. They said I had schizzy or something. But they said it could be controlled." At this point Henry began to laugh out loud and roll his eyes towards the ceiling. We asked him about his laughter, "Well, all this crawly stuff really creeps me out, you know? And Clara the witch causes my eyes to twitch." We also noticed a slight facial tic in his right eye.

Henry's speech patterns, and their content, are not surprising for someone who has *schizophrenia, disorganized type.* His speech is often illogical, and Henry will go from topic to topic, each topic having little or no relevance to the preceding topic. We have seen evidence of *tangentiality* in Henry's speech. He will go off on tangents instead of answering specific questions. It becomes difficult to interpret and understand a schizophrenic's speech. Psychologists are often not sure if the patient did not understand the questions, if they were unable to focus on the questions or on the task(s) at hand, or just found the question(s) too difficult to answer. The latter refers to answering personal questions that might cause emotional duress. Of course more than this is needed to diagnose someone, since many "normal" people have a tendency to do this.

We told Henry that he needed to be seen by our psychiatrist which he agreed to. The psychiatrist, Harry, had this to report:

"Henry is suffering from schizophrenia, disorganized type. He has hallucinations, in his case auditory, and *delusions.* His thoughts are disorganized and his *affect* is inappropriate. He knows where he is but he does not know the month or the year. His appearance is disheveled and his hygiene is poor. The hospital reports that 'he was on *Prolixin (fluphenazine)* and was expected to report to us to get his bi-weekly injection. He responded fairly well to Prolixin and was able to function well enough to leave the hospital. He has an appointment at the clinic on Monday at noon and we expect Henry to follow up. His mother will drive him to the clinic to ensure this.' Henry also uses alcohol to quiet the burning in his head and the auditory hallucinations. He is using the alcohol to self-medicate. I see no signs of alcohol or substance dependence, as tolerance and withdrawal symptoms are not present at this time. Based on this and on my impressions I have the following diagnoses for Henry:

Schizophrenia, Disorganized Type, Continuous	295.10
Alcohol Abuse	305.00

Theoretical Etiologies

Not surprisingly, entire volumes have been written about the etiologies of schizophrenia. For many clinicians, schizophrenic disorders are among the most fascinating mental disorders. In the interest of space we will summarize some of the key findings and etiological information.

No discussion of schizophrenia's etiologies can begin without considering genetic influences. First, researchers generally agree that no one single gene is responsible for producing schizophrenia. Instead, they hypothesize that multiple genes are responsible for producing a vulnerability to contracting schizophrenia. Many researchers can state with authority that genes somehow play a role in making certain people vulnerable to contracting schizophrenia. The research is just too strong to discount this possibility (for example, Bassett, Chow, Waterworth, & Brzustowicz, 2001).

Kallmann (1938) produced a landmark study on the families of individuals with schizophrenia. He examined over one thousand family members of people with schizophrenia and the patients themselves. He discovered two important points. First, the more severe the schizophrenia of the parent, the more likely the children of the parent would develop schizophrenia. More important was this discovery: Kallmann hypothesized and concluded that individuals do not inherit a genetic predisposition for the various subtypes of schizophrenia. Instead, the genetic predisposition is inherited for the schizophrenic disorders, which may manifest themselves differently from that of the parent(s). Other studies have pointed to familial components related to the etiology of the schizophrenic disorders (Kendler, McGuire, Gruenberg, O'Hare, Spellman, & Walsh, 1993). Gottesman (1991) concluded that the more genes an individual shares with someone who has a schizophrenic disorder, the more likely that individual will also contract it. For example, you have about a 50% chance of contracting a schizophrenic disorder if your identical (known as a *monozygotic (MZ)*) twin also has it. Genetically, MZ twins share 100% of their genetic information. MZ twins come from one fertilized egg.

Twin and adoption studies are used in research because it is impossible to separate out environmental influence, which certainly has a role in schizophrenia's etiology. Most twin studies conclude that the environment has a role, perhaps as much as 50%, in determining the vulnerability of contracting schizophrenia. The famous Genain quadruplets provide more "food for thought." These four sisters provided a genetic rarity—four identical sisters. All four were brought up in the same household, all four contracted schizophrenia, yet all of them had different familial interactions and different environmental influences. The Genains were a classic example of how important the environment is in regards to schizophrenia.

However, their father may have had schizophrenia; we do know that his brother, mother and paternal uncle all had nervous breakdowns. Thus, is it the environment or is it genetics?

Adoption studies attempt to provide further insight. These studies by nature need to be longitudinal to provide the most conclusive evidence. Researchers in Denmark discovered that 3 out of 39 *high-risk adoptees* (referring to children who had at least one biological parent with schizophrenia) had schizophrenia, which amounts to 8% (Rosenthal, Wender, Kety, Schulsinger, Welner, & Reider, 1975). The conclusions one can make from this and similar studies are that familial influences in schizophrenia involve shared genes, not necessarily shared environments. Thus, genes from at least one schizophrenic parent can be considered a major risk factor in offspring contracting schizophrenia.

We will now briefly examine possible biological and prenatal causal factors. Some studies have noted that pregnant women who had influenza (the flu) during the **second trimester** were more likely to produce a child who had schizophrenia. Neural development is a key factor during the second trimester, and it seems that the flu interferes with proper neural development, and thus may produce a vulnerability to schizophrenia later in life. Other stressors experienced by pregnant women during the second trimester (extreme emotional trauma) also seem to increase the vulnerability to contracting schizophrenia. Once again the second trimester is crucial (Huttunen & Niskanen, 1978).

The dopamine hypothesis provides a fascinating perspective. The condensed version of this theory sounds simple: Too much dopamine buildup at some synapses in the brain is responsible for causing schizophrenia. This is supported by the effectiveness of the typical antipsychotic medications in reducing schizophrenic hallucinations by blocking postsynaptic dopamine receptors. In other words, these medications are effective, in part, because they decrease the dopamine buildup in the brain.

There are some problems with this theory. First, there are schizophrenic individuals who do not respond to typical antipsychotic drugs that will decrease dopamine levels. Second, the dopamine hypothesis is too simplistic and cannot explain why all antipsychotic medications work. The drugs will work quickly when used properly, but any behavior change will occur over time. Logically, this effect refutes the dopamine hypothesis, since we would expect rapid change in the schizophrenic since these medications act quickly.

Before we examine the *diathesis-stress model*, we need to examine one more biological viewpoint. Due to the availability of sophisticated brain scan techniques (like the PET scan), researchers discovered that some schizophrenics have enlarged ventricles in their brains. Ventricles are gaps or crevasses in the brain that contain cerebrospinal fluid. In other words, there is more fluid in a schizophrenic's brain than one would expect when compared to a "normal" individual. There are problems with this etiological viewpoint as well.

First, ventricles enlarge naturally with age. Enlarged ventricles can also be seen in other conditions such as traumatic brain injuries (TBI) and alcohol dependence. We also do not know if the ventricles enlarge because of the schizophrenia, or if the enlarged ventricles are a causal factor. Finally, enlarged ventricles occur in about one-third of schizophrenic individuals.

Finally, the diathesis-stress model of schizophrenia is accepted by many psychologists today. *Diathesis* refers to having a genetic predisposition to developing a disorder, in this case a schizophrenic disorder. The simplicity of this theory is brilliant. The individual is born with this diathesis to contract schizophrenia, this genetic vulnerability. However, it does not mean that they **will** contract schizophrenia. The second part of the equation is thus: They will contract schizophrenia if they experience some type of stress so severe that they are unable to cope (Zubin & Spring, 1977). Such stressors may include extreme trauma (like the terrorist attacks on September 11, 2001), interpersonal conflicts, marital problems, the loss of a loved one (death of a child perhaps), or a total loss of income and savings. If the individual can handle the stress, the schizophrenia, **(even though they have the genetic predisposition [diathesis]),** may never develop. Many accept this etiological perspective since evidence exists to support the interaction of environmental and interpersonal stress as being a causal factor in schizophrenia.

Treatment Plan

The most effective approach towards treating schizophrenia seems to be a combination of pharmaceutical, behavioral, cognitive, and family therapy. Even though many psychologists and others agree that these approaches tend to be more effective, none of them, alone or in combination, can be said to cure schizophrenia. Effective treatments will work on the hallucinations, delusions, and disorganized aspects of behavior and attempt to lessen these aspects. An additional concern is that many schizophrenic patients will relapse, even if their treatment is continuous. Needless to say this can frustrate the patients and the clinicians.

The first aspect to be determined is whether or not Henry needed to be rehospitalized. Harry and we decided to try the Prolixin clinic first and see what happened with that. We also talked to Goldie who did not want

Henry returned to the hospital. "We feel like he's running out of chances here and if he goes back he may never get out. You can talk to Henry and help him but he must be taking his pills. Otherwise it's hopeless. I hope you'll give him a chance." We were concerned that Henry would not follow through with his appointments and made a *behavioral contract* with him and his mother. Specifically we told them that if Henry missed an appointment, refused to take his medication (Prolixin is administered by injection given by a medical professional), or was picked up again by the police we would hospitalize him. Henry understood this and promised to follow through. Do you think he did?

Before we answer that, Henry was required by us to get a complete physical. As we have mentioned in previous chapters, many physical illnesses and symptoms can mimic psychological disorders. We wanted to be certain that Henry was not suffering from some type of neurological disorder or seizure disorder before we began treatment. Nothing had been reported in his past records so we felt confident that little had changed since his discharge. The results of his physical indeed confirmed that Henry was in good health physically; thus we were able to initiate our treatment plan.

Henry was scheduled for our Prolixin clinic, which required a biweekly visit to get his Prolixin injection. This was supervised by the psychiatrist and administered by a visiting psychiatric nurse. Henry was also scheduled for individual, group and *occupational therapy*. Occupational therapy consists of tasks like cooking, cleaning, and arts and crafts. It is designed to get the patient active and to teach (or have them relearn) skills they may have forgotten while hospitalized. You would be surprised how many psychiatric outpatients who have spent a lot of time in hospitals do not know how to make change or use a telephone.

After 6 weeks, Henry returned to individual therapy and we noticed some changes in him. "The burning in my head has really stopped now and so have the voices. I'm scared . . . scared that they will come back. I want this to stop. The shots really hurt but they help me. I don't need the beers any more. The itching is still there. That's a hard one to stop, you know?" In fact it was determined that Henry had *Eczema*, a type of skin condition that worsens when a person gets nervous. The fact that Henry is a very nervous person who also has *tactile hallucinations* (e.g., he imagines that things are crawling on him) only worsened his eczema. Henry was prescribed a *cortisone ointment* to help this condition.

Once Henry's hallucinations quieted down, he began to talk a lot in individual therapy. Group therapy did not work out nearly as well. Henry is a quiet, reserved individual who "does not like to speak in public, especially because I'm sick. Something is wrong with me. I know the name but

I don't know why, you know? Why me?" We asked Henry about his father, "Well, I missed having a dad. He didn't come with us and I never really knew him. Now my mom tells me he might be responsible for my sickness and I feel farther away than ever before."

We then decided to ask Goldie and George to join Henry for *family therapy*. Henry was making decent progress, was able to live with his mother, and stay on his Prolixin and other medications. Goldie was willing to come in but George was unable to because of the travel involved. He did express a desire to know how Henry was progressing. We asked Henry about his divorce. "I guess I loved her but she didn't love me, you know? We weren't married for very long. She couldn't put up with me being sick I guess. I also didn't make a lot of money but what did she expect? We got married too young. Do I think the divorce made me sicker? Well, it really hurt me, you know? I was dumped by my dad and now I was dumped by her, then I got dumped by everyone into the hospital. My mom was always there for me, however. George was sort of . . . not that Clara. She's a witch and always will be."

Goldie then responded, "I can see how my husband and Henry's wife leaving so quickly could upset him. I never saw the connection. I think Henry needs to talk about these things and realize that he is wanted, is a good person and is loved by his entire family including Clara. Clara just doesn't understand what this schizophrenia is."

We focused on the issues of loss and abandonment for Henry in family therapy and encouraged Henry to continue with his carpentry (He was extraordinarily skilled with his hands.) Henry was also involved with a day clinic where he would spend the day doing crafts, chores, and occupational therapy. He won second prize for one of his wood creations at the clinic's monthly contest. Henry was encouraged to come to terms with these losses and to properly grieve in our sessions. Goldie soon dropped out of treatment at Henry's request "I'm the one with schizophrenia, not mom! I want this to be about me and only me for once." Goldie would often call to check on Henry's progress but Henry rescinded the confidentiality waiver he had signed, so we were unable to describe what occurred.

Henry remained in outpatient treatment for 4 months at which time he disappeared. Six weeks later we received a call from the local psychiatric hospital that he had been readmitted due to a relapse. He did not show at the Prolixin clinic and was on no medication when he was hospitalized. The police found him wandering aimlessly on the streets with a blank look in his eyes. He was actively hallucinating and yelling incoherently at strangers. At the present time he is still hospitalized with no discharge date in sight.

The amount and variety of medications available to treat schizophrenia are numerous, to say the least. Each type has its benefits and side effects. Again, for the sake of simplicity we will cover each type briefly, since a thorough examination is beyond the scope of this text. We also need to briefly note the term *neuroleptic,* which when defined refers to the side effects of the antipsychotic medications, specifically the *Parkinsonian-like symptoms* they can produce. Many professionals are turning away from the term neuroleptic and only using the term antipsychotic, so we will follow this trend for consistency.

We also need to discuss the changing of terminology when discussing antipsychotic chemical classes. In the past antipsychotics were divided into typical and atypical classes. "Typical" were dopamine antagonists and include the earlier medications such as *Thorazine (chlorpromazine).* "Atypical" were the newer antipsychotic medications that were more effective at alleviating *positive symptoms* and also appeared to work on serotonin levels as well. Drugs in this class include *Clozaril (clozapine).* Because the distinction between "typical" and "atypical" is not clear to some, some authors now use the terms "Second Generation" to refer to the newer medications (formerly "atypical") and "Conventional" to refer to the older medications (formerly "typical") (Bezchlibnyk-Butler & Jeffries, 2002). This can be quite confusing, so for the sake of simplicity, and since most texts still use the former terms, we will stay consistent.

Most helping professionals believe that using antipsychotic medications is the best and only way to treat actively hallucinating schizophrenic individuals (APA, 2000). Henry was taking Thorazine while in the hospital; some professionals classify Thorazine as a *typical antipsychotic.* Typical antipsychotics seem to be *dopamine agonists,* i.e., they increase the dopamine activity in a person's brain. Some of the other medications in this group include *Mellaril (thioridazine)* and *Stelazine (trifluroperazine).* These drugs have short half-lives, which means that they must be taken daily. Typical antipsychotics will work much better on the so-called positive symptoms (such as hallucinations) rather than on the *negative symptoms* (such as inappropriate or blunted affect). It is also virtually impossible to become addicted to these medications. Oddly enough, it seems that those medications that have a very low addiction potential also seem to have the most serious side effects. They are cheap and generally used more on an inpatient basis where compliance is easier and it is easier to monitor side effects.

We have spoken about side effects; unfortunately, the antipsychotics tend to produce some of the most severe side effects in some patients. The patient (if possible) and his/her family, or the hospital if neither of these is possible, must decide if the trade-off is worth the possible side effects. So what are these side effects? Some of the most common are drowsiness, dizziness, dry mouth, and constipation. These side effects (known as *anticholinergic side effects*) are similar to the effects produced by *antihistamines,* or cold and allergy pills like *Benadryl* and *Contac.* So far these do not sound so bad, and we have come across these side effects before when discussing *tricyclic antidepressants.* However, things can get worse.

The more serious side effects are known as *Extrapyramidal Side Effects (EPS).* These include *Parkinsonism* (Parkinson's Disease-like side effects such as tremors, shaking, rigidity, drooling), *Tardive Dyskinesia (TD)* (involuntary face, trunk, and limb movements), and *seizures.* TD is incurable for many patients; Parkinsonism is treatable by adjusting or changing the medication or adding *Symmetrel (amantadine).* EPS are treatable by prescribing medications such as *Artane (trihexyphenidyl)* or *Cogentin (benztropine).* These drugs of course have their own side effects such as dry mouth, urinary hesitancy, nausea, and insomnia.

Thus it is no surprise that many patients (including Henry) do their best to not take their antipsychotics when they are prescribed. This is the main reason that many schizophrenics turn to alcohol or other drugs when their hallucinations return. Of course these drugs have their own side effects but generally speaking they are not as severe as the antipsychotics' side effects. There are, fortunately, other options for the *pharmacological* (medical) treatment of schizophrenia.

Depot antipsychotics are medications that have a very long half-life, lasting about 2 to 4 weeks. They are injected and are ideal for patients who have poor or inconsistence compliance with drug therapy like Henry. Drugs in this category include *Prolixin (fluphenazine)* and *Haldol (haloperidol).* The biggest advantage is that professionals can be sure that the medication is inside of the patient. These medications have a lower relapse rate and the patient does not need to remember to take pills every day (and of course s/he cannot avoid taking depot medications once they are inside of him or her). The biggest disadvantage? Side effects again. If a patient has a bad side effect reaction, they will have to cope with them as long as the medication is active which can be as long as four weeks, a very long time indeed. They also take longer to reach *maintenance levels* and for the schizophrenic to stabilize while on them compared to 3 to 7 days for oral antipsychotics.

Henry was prescribed Prolixin because of his noncompliance with his Thorazine once he was discharged from the inpatient psychiatric unit at the hospital. This way his hallucinations could be kept under control. As you saw, he managed to go off of his Prolixin by vanishing and not returning to the clinic or to any type of treatment until he was picked up and rehospitalized. This is not uncommon. Fortunately there are some other, newer medications available to treat schizophrenia. They are more effective and have fewer EPS side effects. However they are much more expensive and they are harder to get prescribed.

This newer type of antipsychotic includes Clozaril (clozapine) and *Risperdal (risperidone);* these are sometimes known as *atypical antipsychotics.* These are the newer types of medications to treat schizophrenia and they have markedly fewer side effects. For example, Clozaril evidently does not cause TD and other muscular problems, while Risperdal apparently does not cause EPS and has a much lower TD risk (Maxmen & Ward, 1995). Clozaril and Risperdal also seem to treat the negative symptoms of schizophrenia (inappropriate and/or flat affect, etc.). However, Clozaril may cause *agranulocytosis,* which is, simply, a drastic lowering of the individual's white blood cell count to the point where a minor cut or cold could kill. The only way to treat this condition once it is discovered is to stop Clozaril treatment. Additionally, these medications are much more expensive than the typical antipsychotics such as Thorazine. Some of the other atypical antipsychotics that have appeared recently include *Zyprexa (olanzapine), Seroquel (quetiapine),* and *Geodon (ziprasidone).* (Bezchlibnyk-Butler & Jeffries, 2002).

There are many other medications in the fields of psychiatry and psychology that have been, and can be, used to treat schizophrenia. What has just been discussed is a small fraction of those medications. If you have further interest, an excellent text is *Drugs and Behavior: An Introduction to Behavioral Pharmacology* by McKim (2003).

Prognosis

Henry's prognosis is listed as "poor." There are several reasons for this. First, Henry has had many relapses throughout the duration of his illness, which is not a positive sign. Generally speaking, the more often a patient with schizophrenia relapses the less likely s/he will be able to get the symptoms under control. Disorganized schizophrenia does not respond well to treatment, which is another factor to consider. Pharmacotherapy results in about one-third of the patients NOT responding to medications at all, which is a very high number. Henry has not been willing to stay on his prescribed medications, which also leads to this prognosis. When Henry was on Prolixin, he displayed some insight into his illness, which is helpful. Additionally, Goldie and George are both very supportive of Henry, which is very important. Many schizophrenic individuals have poor or no social and familial support systems, which does not help the individual's chances for improvement. At last report Henry was still in the hospital and was responding well to his medication. The hospital reported that Henry will remain there "until his symptoms subside and he displays marked improvement; at this time the chances of that occurring are marginal." Based on Henry's past history and present condition, the only prognosis suitable for him, unfortunately, is "poor."

Schizophrenia, Paranoid Type

The Case of Ian:
"They're After Me!"

Presenting Problem

Ian is a 35-year-old white male who was divorced for the second time 5 years ago. His first marriage lasted 3 years and his second marriage lasted 11 months. Ian's second marriage produced his daughter Sarrah ("I always did like unusual spellings."). Ian is 6'3" tall, weighs 210 pounds and "has a bit of a gut that I need to work off if I get the chance." Ian comes from a varied background. His mother was born in Edinburgh, Scotland and his father was born in Quebec City, Quebec. Ian speaks fluent French but speaks English without an accent.

Ian presented with an angry suspicious demeanor during the sessions. His eyes often had a piercing glare, and he rarely smiled. He was very serious as well during the sessions, speaking with a lot of emotion in his voice. He would always be looking around the office, scanning everything. If we forgot to block incoming phone calls and the phone rang, he would always demand to know who was calling.

Ian would never remove his outerwear (coat, wool cap) when he was in the sessions "just in case I need to book it fast." His face had a ruddy complexion and he was losing his hair. He wore glasses and would always appear wearing a pair of earmuffs regardless of the weather. "The muffs help me keep alert as to who's watching and what's going on."

One of the reasons that Ian came to us is that he was picked up for Driving While Intoxicated. His Blood Alcohol Concentration when he was picked up was .14, which equals about seven drinks per hour. This was his first offense, so he was sentenced to take *alcohol awareness classes* and to have a psychological and psychiatric evaluation. According to the police report he fell asleep at the wheel and ran into the side of a convenience store. His record was clean otherwise and Ian was assigned to Phoebe, a probation officer.

We checked with Phoebe and she told us that Ian had no prior hospitalizations for mental or physical illnesses; in fact he seemed to be in good health overall. The arresting officer's report noted that "Mr. Ian xx" kept on talking about how we and others were after him, spying on him, and out to get him. He was speaking clearly but making no sense. We held him at county for the night to sober him up and the next morning Officer Caulfield reported that he was continuing with this line of talk but was completely sober according to the Alcasensor. We sent him home on an ROR (Released on his Own Recognizance; this means that he is responsible for all future appearances in court, with probation officers and so on) with a court date set for . . . ."

Once Ian was released he received his sentence. During his Alcohol Awareness Training one of the trainers noted his high BAC. BACs higher than .10 (for this particular school) required an automatic referral for a psychological and alcohol evaluation. Ian would have been referred regardless since Phoebe's cases are all alcohol-related and she automatically refers new clients. We were also initially told by many sources that Ian's "paranoid" behavior was new and had not occurred previously. This raised additional questions which we were determined to try to answer.

Background Information

Ian graduated from high school with a C average. He concentrated more on sports and "girls . . . yeah, I was a lady's man when I was in high school so I didn't take it too serious." In college Ian majored in Biology "although I don't know why; it just seemed like the thing to do at the time." with a minor in Chemistry. Ian graduated college with a C average and shortly after that enrolled in Officer's Training in the military. He completed his training and took a desk job at a recruiting office "before I was honorably discharged. They were not happy with some of my behavior and ideas but I knew. I knew the government was monitoring us, just like the "X-Files" says. I watch that show all the time and I've had some of those experiences. Not the ET ones but where everyone is out to destroy you. The military was like that. I heard things . . . in the bathroom, in the mess hall, on MP duty. I would call these in but no one believed me. They thought I was nuts but I heard people . . . two or three . . . talking about attacking the base and the country. They were gonna nuke us. So I needed to be prepared." Ian's eyes fixed on ours as he related this information to us.

Since Ian was honorably discharged he managed to obtain a job at the local power company. He went from initially restoring fallen power lines to becoming a shift supervisor. "I'm responsible for making sure the lights in this here office stay lit. How does that make you feel?" When Ian came to see us he was on a "leave of absence because of my issues as they call them. Maybe you can help me figure out what they mean. I think someone else wants to see me fired from my job. It's because I know things. I know about the plot to kill the people and spread plague. It's through the rats and the roaches. They've got the nukes. They're worried about me because I know, man."

Ian spoke freely about his marriages. "Okay, the first one, we really loved each other. I met her in training school and we didn't hit it off right away. I was 24 at the time and she was 21, very bright, pretty, graduated early. She was seeing someone else at the time and didn't want to go out with me so I waited. I kept on courting her, figuring I'd eventually win out. Sure enough she got sick of it and went out with me just so I'd stop asking her. She surprised herself because she had a nice time. We went out for one year, got engaged and got married a year later. Shortly after that my wife started acting a bit nutty, telling me that she didn't believe that the government and the military just to keep us honest were watching us. They do that to all ex-officers because of all the spies that are out there. She got fed up with my ideas and me and filed for divorce. We still speak but we're really not too friendly to each other. I suspect she was brainwashed by them and she might even be working for them to watch me. It got to where I couldn't trust her. The voices plotting told me she was a traitor and she'd been turned. Makes sense."

Ian's second marriage is somewhat more intriguing. "We met at the power plant lunch room. I'm a supervisor, she's a receptionist. I'd noticed her before and we'd smile, that kind of stuff. One day at lunch she asked ME out . . . can you believe that?? Well, we fell in love quick and had a fast marriage at the courthouse and discovered shortly afterwards that she was pregnant with Sarrah. Sarrah was born and three months later she filed for divorce. What is up with that? I still love her and see Sarrah once a month. The court decided that 'I'm not very stable for more frequent visits.' That really pisses me off. I'm stable. I'm one of the few who knows the truth and is willing to speak about it. It was a quick marriage but when you know you're in love you go for it. I guess because we met so soon after my first ex filed for divorce you could say I was on the rebound but I don't think so.'

"Sarrah's a good girl; she's 6 now and is doing well in school. My second ex is much brighter than my first, so Sarrah gets that from both of us. Someday soon I'll tell Sarrah about all of the cover-ups and the system so she'll be ready for it when she becomes a teenager. She also likes her sports and really loves to watch baseball and hockey."

Ian was not as willing to extensively discuss his parents or his background. After being asked twice he told us that he reached all of his developmental milestones at the appropriate ages and told us he had no physical problems while growing up. "My parents did not have a good marriage. They divorced when I was 11 and it really hit me hard. I lived with my mom and she raised me. I'm an only child so it was us against the world. She worked two jobs to put me through college and I'll always appreciate that until I die. No one else has done anything like that for me since."

"My dad used to hit my mom and me a lot. I saw him hit her many times and he hit me, but not as much. Growing up in a military family I was told that this is normal. Well I never hit anyone, even when they really deserved it. Never ever hit my kid or my ex-wives. My mom eventually had enough and we both left. She divorced him and he had no desire to ever see me again, and since that day I never have seen him again. My dad drank a lot so maybe he was drunk when he hit us. I don't know and I really don't care. I don't drink if you're asking, don't do drugs. That's just what they want to ruin this country, get us all stoned, high and trashed. Then they take over."

"Well, I made a mistake . . . one mistake! Of course it happened after I dropped off Sarrah. My ex and I got into a bad fight and I had to get out of there. I lost count of the drinks. I rarely drink so to drink anything was off for me. I drove and I shouldn't have. I had to keep drinking because I KNOW someone said, 'Look out for Ian. He works for them and he has information. He has the plans. He knows about the plot. He's a rat bastard, a lying rat bastard. No one cares if he lives or dies.'

Ian was perspiring profusely as he continued to relate this episode. "Well I had to not stand out so I stayed in the bar to let this play out but someone was on to me. They kept talking to me, three of them this time, 'We're gonna poison that traitorous bastard's food, he'll never know. He uses capsules for headaches. Remember the Tylenol poisonings? We'll do that to him. The f***** is too dumb to figure this out."

"Finally I didn't hear anything anymore so I left. Dumb thing to do. They put the cops on me. I hurt no one; I could have driven home if they didn't show up." Again we noticed the piercing glare of his eyes. He appeared to be reliving the entire episode, emotions and all.

We gathered some more information to fill in the blanks, as it were, on Ian since there were some inconsistencies in his story. As you can see, Ian has some unusual thought processes, in this case known as *delusions of persecution*. For those who are not very knowledgeable they would immediately say that Ian suffers from schizophrenia based on these symptoms. However, you are smarter than the average individual. After reading many chapters (and there are more to follow), you are wise enough to know that much more information is needed before we can come to that conclusion. Let us see what else we learned about Ian.

We asked Ian about a family history of mental illness before we focused back on his history. "As I told you, my Dad drank, at times too much. Does that count? My mom was sad a lot but nothing big time. I didn't know that much about my grandparents. My mom's dad died before I was born, and I don't keep in touch with the others. My mom's mom is in a home because she has Alzheimer's. That is really bad. It affects my mom but what can you do? It's a good way to kill off old people . . . once people get old in this country all they do is suck up the Social Security so Alzheimer's takes care of many of them . . . that's what the government wants. Doesn't matter who's President; why haven't they made any progress with Alzheimer's, tell me that. Sounds fishy to me."

Thought Questions

1. You now have some data but perhaps not enough . . . yet. Regardless, what is going on with Ian?
2. What else could cause or contribute to Ian's "paranoid" ideas?
3. How significant is the fact that Ian was beaten by his father?
4. Based on what you know, tell why or why not Ian is being truthful about his drinking based on the information given above.
5. Ian certainly seems to be having a regular discussion with us. Thus, how could he possibly suffer from schizophrenia?
6. Did the County make the correct choice in releasing Ian ROR?

Assessment and Evaluation

Ian was assessed using an unstructured diagnostic interview and a psychiatric evaluation. Ian met with us twice before he was sent to meet with our psychiatrist. Again this is standard procedure when you may be dealing with someone who could be actively hallucinating.

As we expected, a more complete picture of Ian and his history emerged with further interviewing. Ian told us that "they have been spying on me for about 12 years; it started when I turned 23. It happened the time I was almost finished with Officer's Training, so it wasn't a coincidence. I used this foil (he pulls out a piece of tin foil from underneath his wool cap) to block their signals. I'd put it in my cap and under my pillow in my rack (cot) at night and it worked for a while. I found that the signals got stronger and they managed to bypass the tin foil. They were clever! I heard their discussions how they were going to poison me and kill my family. They thought they could put it over on me! But I was a lot smarter. I used Saran Wrap and then I got some lead paint and put a bit on the inside of my cap which really helped. Of course their thoughts and brainwashes attacked me when I was in the shower or in the can or when I was forced to take my cap off."

"Their thoughts and conversations were very loud at first; then as I got older they got quieter, like whispers. My wives never believed me; they were obviously brainwashed by them. And no, I did no drugs at any time in my life. Okay I did drink but never to excess with that one big exception."

We then tried to determine what if anything might have caused Ian's initial *psychotic break*. We asked him if anything dramatic happened to him while in college or during training. "It depends what you mean by dramatic. A good friend of mine in college committed suicide but that thing happens. They probably got to him, drove him over the edge to try and get me to crack. In Basic Training, I did get into two bad fights with a jerk guy. I was telling him about the grand plan to convert all of us and how I had this inside info and he got in my face and wouldn't back down. He began talking smack so I hit him good, right in the eye. He wigged out and we went at it. We were both sent to the brig for the night but we weren't charged with anything. Well, when we got out he started calling me looney tunes, nutso, wacko Ian, stuff like that. I could only take so much before I cracked him again. This time we were told if that happened again we would both be dishonorably discharged, so we stopped."

This provided some more information but we felt we still needed more. We again focused on his family background to see if that would provide any additional clues. We asked him to tell us more about his father. "I really hated him and feared him. I got hit often. I'd come home from school; I'd stay out as late as I could because I knew he would come home and beat me. I was always looking out for him because you never knew when he'd hit you. It didn't happen every day but often enough. If I got bad grades—beat me up. If he had a bad day and I said something—beat me up. Other times he was so sweet and loving towards me. He'd take me to baseball games, shopping, to get ice cream. We'd go to many games each year. You know, it made no sense. He would be loving and hitting me. What is that about? So I hate the bastard. I never want to see him again. I never told him I have a child. He should never see Sarrah. I knew then that there was a plot to break me, to convert me. My dad knew that I knew about the plans so he beat me to make sure I told no one. My mom knows, my ex-wives know, Sarrah will know. Soon everyone important will know."

"One thing people got to learn is not to cross me. I'm big and strong and I work for the power company. You see these metal floors in your offices? I can electrocute all of you if I want; I have the power. So don't cross me or I'll go to work and pull the switch. I mean it, I'll do it. I'm ready. I'm not going out alone when the time comes; I'll take some people with me."

We never really felt threatened by Ian but needed him to have a psychiatric evaluation regardless. The psychiatrist reported, "Ian suffers from delusions of persecution and auditory hallucinations typical of a *paranoid schizophrenic*. His delusional set has been stable over time and hard to disprove. He has violent tendencies but is not likely to act upon them. He learned what happens when he does act on these tendencies. He seems to have a problem with alcohol based on his BAC at the time of his arrest and this should be investigated. Until discharge Ian must remain sober. Ian communicates well and is *oriented times three (i.e., time, manner and place).* (NOTE: This means that Ian knows who he is and who the clinicians are, where he is, what year, time of year, time, month it is and so on). He also has *delusions of grandeur* in that he believes he is superior to everyone else and he has this inside information about conspiracies. His affect is appropriate and guarded, and he appears suspicious of others, always looking around everywhere. He is somewhat agitated, unable to remain in his seat during the interview. He is functioning decently and it is determined that he is presently not a threat to himself or to others. He needs to be carefully monitored. However he must be placed on medication and Clozaril is recommended. The following diagnoses can be applied to Ian:

Schizophrenia, Paranoid Type, Continuous	295.30
Alcohol Abuse	305.00

A complete physical examination is also recommended before a treatment plan is implemented."

Theoretical Etiologies

We examined many etiological explanations for schizophrenia in the case of Henry. We deliberately omitted one other possible etiological explanation since it seemed to fit Ian better. This is the *double bind theory of schizophrenia.* The individual contracts schizophrenia because s/he receives *mixed messages* at home. For example, "I love you more than anything Ian," while his father beats him to a pulp. (This is an extreme example.) The theory states that the individual has a psychotic break because the mixed messages confuse them (Bateson, 1959). They don't know what the truth (or reality) is and they have a break from reality. This theory is no longer supported and in fact if used can be extremely damaging, especially if family therapy is used as a treatment modality. The parent(s) or caregiver(s) of the schizophrenic patient, upon hearing this theory, will perhaps feel extreme guilt that the schizophrenia was contracted by their child because of their mistakes in parenting, causing them to feel very guilty. This theory is best left to its place in history and not used in treatment settings.

An interesting adjunct to the double bind theory is that of the *schizophrenogenic mother* (Fromm-Reichmann, 1948). Based on the date alone you should expect that this theory, before reading further, is archaic, and indeed it is. The schizophrenogenic mother is cold, dominant, rejecting—

like a refrigerator mother, cold with no feelings. This type of mother was believed to cause schizophrenia in her child(ren). Of course this could be generalized to fathers. Regardless, this concept would probably cause extreme guilt and is not supported by research. It too should be left to its place in history.

Treatment Plan

We used a variety of treatment modalities for Ian. Ideally we would have preferred family therapy but in Ian's situation this was not possible. We decided to supplement his pharmacotherapy with individual therapy. We went along with the psychiatrist's recommendation that Ian not be hospitalized until he was tried on Clozaril to see if his symptoms abated. We decided to wait one month with constant monitoring and then determine if hospitalization was necessary.

Ian's physical noted that he was in good health but his blood pressure was high. This is not surprising since he was always on guard and paranoid. Nothing else that would be considered remarkable showed up, so we went ahead with our plans.

In individual therapy we focused on Ian's marriages, Sarrah, and especially his relationship with his parents. Ian loves his mother but "I blame her for not doing anything about my dad. She knew what was going on but did nothing to stop him from hitting me. She should have spoken up." We focused on this theme and also on the themes of abandonment by his father and ex-wives. Ian has a poor support structure and we intended to put him in group therapy to counteract this issue. We also focused on building up his self-esteem.

Unfortunately we were not very successful. Ian complied with his Clozaril treatment and did well. The voices telling him about "the plan" were quieted and he continued to function well in individual therapy, discussing issues surrounding his family and his father. However his delusions of persecution continued and he had several angry outbursts during individual sessions. We never felt threatened by him but Ian was told that no further outbursts would be tolerated. Phoebe was also informed of these outbursts and she told him he would be sent back to jail if they continued. Ian continued to believe that the government was after him and was trying to brainwash him. One example of such an outburst:

"G-damn it, I keep hearing these conversations telling me to shut up, telling me I'm s**t for being here. How would you like it if you were always told you were like the dogs*** on the sidewalk, huh? I'm sick of this. Once I blow look out, I'll get those bastards that are saying these things. My daughter's safety is my priority." Ian was so agitated at this point that saliva was flying out of his mouth while he was talking.

Ian stayed sober throughout the duration of treatment and was generally cooperative save for his outbursts. We did not want to send him back to jail because we felt that would be counterproductive. Jails generally do not rehabilitate. We had Ian sign a treatment contract that if he had one more outburst he would be hospitalized. He agreed to this and did well in treatment for awhile. However he decided that the Clozaril was part of the overall plot and stopped taking it. Three weeks after that he had a bad outburst while meeting with the psychiatrist and was committed to the psychiatric hospital directly after this episode. Ian tried to smash the radio in the psychiatrist's office and appeared to making a dash for the window when security guards intervened.

Ian was taken away in handcuffs and appeared remorseful. "I didn't mean it. I had no choice. The voices keep at me, and it's so loud in my head, in my ears. I don't know what to do. I'm trapped. I can't handle the insults anymore." He was crying at this point. We explained to him that this was the best way to quiet the voices and that he could return to treatment with us once he was discharged.

Phoebe was informed of this and we worked closely with her and the court to try to make sure Ian did not go back to jail. She accepted our clinical judgment and went along with our hospitalization plan. As we saw with Henry relapses are not uncommon with schizophrenia. Paranoid schizophrenia is different in many ways than the other types, as you may have already noticed. The individual's speech is clear although it is not logical, i.e., you can have a conversation with them but their ideas are bizarre. Their affect is usually appropriate. Their delusions usually are of persecution or of grandeur. They tend to be more of a threat to themselves or to others. In fact when you hear about "out-of-control mental patients" going on a rampage on the news, they tend to be paranoid schizophrenics. Note that this is much more the **exception** rather than the norm.

Ian remained hospitalized for three months. He was put on Clozaril and again responded quite well to it. He became one of the "leaders" on his unit, always speaking out a lot in his group and participating. Sarrah visited him once in the hospital and Ian told her to wait until he got out so they could see each other again. At last report Ian was still hospitalized and was still delusional, although the delusions were occurring much less frequently. The hospital planned to release him within one month back to our clinic to restart outpatient therapy. It was also recommended that he be placed in the Prolixin clinic once he was released.

The medications that are appropriate for Ian are exactly the same as those for Henry, i.e., the atypical antipsychotics. Ian responded well to Clozaril and displayed none of the side effects we discussed previously. Other possible medications might be *antidepressants, Lithium,* and *anticonvulsants.* However, when a particular medication is working well it makes little sense to try something else. Thus Clozaril seems to be the best choice for Ian right now.

Prognosis

Ian's prognosis is "poor" for a number of reasons. First, Ian is seeking his first treatment since his schizophrenic outbreak at a somewhat late age. Like all illnesses, the sooner they are treated the more likely they are to respond positively to treatment. Of all of the schizophrenias, paranoid type responds the most favorably to treatment because negative symptoms are lacking. Ian's delusions did not disappear while in the hospital and while in outpatient treatment he went off of Clozaril. Noncompliance is always a concern with schizophrenic treatment. Ian also lacks a good support structure. Sarrah loves him and visits him often, but beyond that he really has no one.

There are reasons to remain optimistic. Ian managed to maintain a job in a supervisory capacity (this was factual, as we checked. He was granted a medical leave of absence and can return at any time to the power plant). In effect, Ian managed to graduate Officer's Training, get married twice and live a "normal" life while he was delusional. Again for paranoid schizophrenics this is not that unusual; regardless, this is a positive sign.

However, because his delusions were not under control and because he was still hospitalized, Ian's prognosis must be listed as poor. Once he is discharged we can change his prognosis to "guarded."

Review and Study Questions

Henry

1. Do you agree with Henry's prognosis, based on all of the presented information? Why or why not?

2. How important will Henry's support system (Goldie and George) be in his recovery?

3. Did Goldie's "depression" contribute to Henry's schizophrenia? Why or why not?

4. Is Henry an alcoholic? Is he an alcohol abuser? Why or why not?

5. Based on what you know about insanity, is Henry insane? Why or why not?

Ian

1. Do you agree with Ian's prognosis? Why or why not?

2. Discuss the decision to hospitalize Ian.

3. Discuss possible etiologies for Ian's schizophrenia.

4. How significant is Ian's being hit by his father regarding his psychotic break?

5. Give your views on Ian having visitation rights for Sarrah.

6. Would Ian have had greater outpatient success if he had been put in group therapy? Why or why not?

For Both

1. After reading both cases, tell whether you think you would be able to do therapy with schizophrenics, either on an outpatient or an inpatient basis.
2. Give your views on prescribing medication to schizophrenics.
3. Do you agree that a reasonable percentage of homeless individuals are schizophrenics? Why or why not?
4. Discuss the reasons why we have yet to discover a very effective treatment method, and a cure, for schizophrenia.

Terms to Know

schizophrenic disorders

auditory hallucinations

delusions

outpatient

Dissociative Identity Disorder

Multiple Personality Disorder

psychiatric evaluation

schizophrenia, disorganized type

psychotic break

Prolixin (fluphenazine)

behavioral contract

occupational therapy

tactile hallucinations

Eczema

Thorazine (chlorpromazine)

neuroleptic

dopamine agonists

Mellaril (thioridazine)

Stelazine (trifluroperazine)

positive symptoms

negative symptoms

anticholinergic side effects

antihistamines

Benadryl

Contac

tricyclic antidepressants

Extrapyramidal Side Effects (EPS)

Parkinsonism

Tardive Dyskinesia (TD)

seizures

Symmetrel (amantadine)

Artane (trihexyphenidyl)

Cogentin (benztropine)

pharmacological

depot antipsychotics

Prolixin (fluphenazine)

Haldol (haloperidol)

maintenance levels

Clozaril (clozapine)

Risperdal (risperidone)

atypical antipsychotics

agranulocytosis

typical antipsychotic

alcohol awareness classes

delusions of persecution

mixed messages

double bind theory of schizophrenia

paranoid schizophrenic

oriented times three (i.e., time, manner and place)

etiological

tangentiality

delusions of grandeur

antidepressants

Lithium

anticonvulsants

unstructured diagnostic interview

monozygotic (MZ)

high-risk adoptees

diathesis-stress model

diathesis

cortisone ointment

family therapy

Parkinsonian-like symptoms

Zyprexa (olanzapine)

Seroquel (quetiapine)

Geodon (ziprasidone)

psychotic break

schizophrenogenic mother

Chapter 5

Substance-Related Disorders

Alcohol dependence (alcoholism) and *alcohol abuse* are two of the most prevalent health problems in the United States. Approximately one in ten people in the United States suffers from alcohol dependence and about 50% have had an alcohol-related problem in their lives (*Driving While Intoxicated (DWI)*, missing work because of alcohol dependence, fights due to drinking, and so on) (Morrison, 1995). Every family has an alcoholic* in it, but in many cases you need to search a bit, and check second and third degree relatives to find them. Even President Bush seems to suffer from alcohol-related problems as he no longer drinks. The same cannot be said of his daughter Jenna who has had brushes with the law regarding her drinking. What does it mean to have problems with alcohol? Let us examine the following cases and see if we can arrive at any answers to these questions.

---

*The term "alcoholic" refers to someone who is alcohol dependent. Since Alcoholics Anonymous (and many alcohol dependent) individuals use this term, we will do so as well, even though the term is considered to be pejorative by some.

Alcohol Dependence

The Case of Rudy:
"I thought all alcoholics were street people!"

Presenting Problem

Rudy is a 53-year-old black male who was born in Georgia. He moved north when he was 17 years old to find work and to escape "Southern attitudes." Rudy has been married for 20 years and has two sons ages 17 and 14. "They're good boys and they have no choice about going on to college; they're going! I work hard and we've been saving up for their schooling. They'll be the first in my family to attend college." Rudy is 6'1" tall and weighs 190 pounds. He also has a slight tremor in his right hand "from a work accident, I think." Rudy works in a factory as a line supervisor, and his wife works at the local superstore. Rudy oftentimes works at night for a while then switches to day shifts, so sometimes his sleep patterns are disrupted. "I deal with it. It's not easy. Sometimes I'll take a sip to help me to sleep. Nothing more than that however."

Rudy's probation officer Mary sent him to us for an alcohol evaluation. She was concerned about his high *Blood Alcohol Concentration (BAC)* and the fact that he had two DWIs within a 3-year period. In examining his driving record, Rudy also had two moving violations and had gotten into one other accident causing significant damage to a Yield sign. Mary wanted to find out if "Rudy was indeed an alcoholic" as she suspected. Once that determination was made, treatment options would be explored with Mary and Rudy.

This is not unusual. The best probation officers want to see their clients get the help that they need. They see their clients as having criminal violations but not necessarily as "bad" people. Mary saw Rudy as a good individual whose possible alcohol problems caused him problems at home. Remarkably, his work did not appear to suffer. Thus Rudy came to us seeking a court-ordered evaluation, wanting his license back and also expecting to not get referred for any kind of therapy.

Background Information

Rudy's developmental history is unremarkable. He noted that he was "a bit of a terror in elementary school; I liked to cause trouble. They said that I also was a slow learner but nothing ever came out to prove that. I think it was because I was a troublemaker. School never interested me. And no . . . I know what you're going to ask . . . I never needed glasses or had a hearing problem. I'm way ahead of you doc!" Rudy smiled frequently during the initial intake, making good eye contact. His eyes often were bloodshot and had big bags under them. He attributed this to a lack of sleep. He talked often and openly in the early sessions, and he had an answer for every question, if not an explanation.

His posture, however, was defensive: his legs and arms were crossed. Rudy held onto his right hand at times in order to control the tremor. "I'm not sure what the problem is; I can't get it to stop sometimes." Initially, his nonverbal behavior did not match up with his verbal behavior.

Rudy had his first sexual experience at 14 years old and noted "that I had some wild times there as well before I settled down. I wasn't a Lothario but I wasn't prim and proper either. I had my thrills. I met my wife at a church function, a dinner for the community. It was one of those love at first sight things. We got married 18 months later. We wanted to wait to make sure this was the right thing to do. I guess it was, since 20 years later here we are. We've had problems and fights but so has everyone else." Rudy was smiling at this point.

Rudy has had some legal troubles, which was his initial reason for coming in to see us. He explained his Driving While Intoxicated citations (DWIs): "Okay, here's the story. I messed up in the first one. I left work and had some with the guys and then I drove home and hit a tree on the way. No damage to me but totaled my car. The tree was fine. I was knocked out and when I woke up the cops were there. They made me blow into their machine, asked me to walk a straight line, all that stuff. I really blew it that time." According to the police and probation officers' reports, Rudy's BAC was .28. This is roughly equivalent to having 14 drinks, or 14 twelve-ounce cans of beer, in one hour.

"So what happened is I was arrested, and my wife had to come and get me. I lost my license for 90 days and had to attend a drunk driving class. I did the crime so I deserved the time. Not much else to say about that. I learned my lesson though," he said with a shrug.

It seems that Rudy did not learn his lesson, for 26 months later he was re-arrested for his second DWI. This time his BAC was listed at .22. "Okay, I was set up on this one. I was at the bar after work and yeah I had a few . . . but I learned from before and I spaced my drinks out. I left at about 1 A.M. and was on my way home when I saw the flashing lights. Of course I pulled over. I was confident because I knew how many I had. The officer said I was weaving all over the place and asked me to step out and walk that line. I thought I did it perfectly but he disagreed and then gave me the *Breathalyzer*. Once it registered he arrested me on the spot and called in my license. Of course the past DWI came up and I was sunk."

"Why was I set up? I was not weaving, I felt fine, and I didn't have an accident. Yeah I was drinking . . why does anyone go to a bar with friends after work? But I didn't have as many as the machine said. 11 drinks in an hour? Come on! I'm married, a hard worker and I've got two teenagers. Why would I booze like that?"

The results here were not pleasant for Rudy. He spent the night in jail because his wife refused to post bail. His marriage suffered tremendously since this was the second time he got stopped. His sons were ashamed of his behavior and could not understand it. Rudy received a break from the judge in this case. Because of his strong family background and his work record (he only missed 4 days in the past 6 years), he received 5 years probation, a revocation of his driver's license (he can reapply for it in one year), mandatory alcohol counseling, and time served in jail.

"That really peed me off. I don't need counseling. That makes it seem like I'm a damned drunk. I can control my drinking and stop whenever I want. Only nuts go into counseling. I'm not an alcoholic; besides, all alcoholics are street people. I'm a hard working family man who goes to church, never cheated on my wife, never beat her, and always provided the best I could for my family. I know I have to be here to meet with you but I don't have an alcohol problem."

Rudy began drinking at age 14 and stayed with beer, his drink of choice. "I never really liked the stuff but all of my friends did it. Boy did it have a nasty taste at first! But eventually I got to like it. Never liked the hard stuff though. Always stayed with the beer." He didn't really notice any change in his drinking habits until he reached his thirties when "it took more beers to get the slight buzz I was used to. Only a slight buzz, never falling down sloppy drunk, vomiting, that type. What was funny though is that I noticed a few times when I'd leave the bar at night I could not remember where I parked my car! The guys thought it was funny and I know that's typical for one who drinks only beer . . . something about the hops and barley does that to your mind . . . I read that somewhere. That only happened a few times and I didn't make too much of that. I would always count my drinks when I was driving and I'd never lose control . . . well, not that often. Like anyone else I had times I went overboard. But that's normal. What do you think?" At this point Rudy leaned forward and looked concerned as his eyes narrowed.

Rudy has just described *blackouts;* these are memory lapses caused by heavy alcohol consumption. Contrary to myths, the person does **not** "pass out" from drinking. Instead, the individual is unable to remember anything that occurred during a period of particularly heavy alcohol usage. In other words, this can be called alcohol-related amnesia. One possible explanation of blackouts is that the high amount of alcohol consumed prevents new memories from being created (McKim, 2003). Blackouts are not considered to be a DSM-IV-TR diagnostic criterion for alcohol dependence. However, it must be noted that these experiences are not considered to be "normal."

Rudy continued to drink like this periodically and never thought about cutting down or stopping. The DWIs bothered him but he saw them as mistakes or as being set up and nothing more. Rudy did mention that "there have been times when I needed to get home early because of work the next day and I ended up closing down the bar. I never intend for that to happen but I get carried away with friends, sports, pool, you name it. A hard working guy needs to unwind at times." Rudy then sat back and crossed his arms, attempting to physically distance himself from us.

Thought Questions

1. Discuss the evidence in Rudy's history that would lead you to diagnose him with a substance use disorder, specifically alcohol dependence. If the evidence presented does not indicate an alcohol abuse disorder in your view, discuss this.
2. What **should** a BAC of .24 do to most people?
3. Discuss your views on alcohol-related blackouts and the possible causes.
4. If Rudy is indeed an alcoholic, how does he manage to retain his job and family?
5. What is indicated by the fact that Rudy now needs more beer to get the same "buzz" he always gets?

Assessment and Evaluation

Rudy's probation officer Mary performed the initial assessment. Mary had an *alcohol-specific caseload,* i.e., she only worked with people whose arrests involved alcohol. Mary was not a substance abuse specialist but she had extensive training in substance abuse diagnoses. Mary suspected that Rudy had an alcohol problem for two reasons: his two DWIs within three years and the BACs recorded for the two DWIs. A person of average weight and height will be able to handle one drink per hour, presuming good health and no involvement of other drugs, medications or other mind-altering substances. This will generally result in a BAC of .02. Rudy's

BACs were both above .20 and yet he was able to operate a motor vehicle, which sent warning signals to Mary.

Rudy was given an *unstructured diagnostic interview* to assess whether he was suffering from alcohol abuse or dependence. During our initial interview some key information emerged, allowing us to form a more accurate and complete picture of Rudy's situation.

Rudy grew up in an alcoholic household. His father was an alcoholic and he routinely beat Rudy's mother when he was drunk. "I remember all of that clearly. I would have done something but my mom always told me that in spite of this, my dad loved her and his kids dearly. She told us that he drank too much at times. He never hit me, to my recollection. But he couldn't handle the stuff at all. No one else in my family drinks because of what we all saw. I'm the only one." Rudy teared up at this point and paused. He pulled out a handkerchief, dried his eyes, blew his nose and then composed himself. His right leg was jiggling at this point.

"My paternal grandmother also drank too much at times. She liked the wine, but she'd just drink it and pass out. She never hurt anyone. My grandfather was out working most of the time so he didn't really know what was going on. Oh . . . I forbid my kids to drink because of the DWI problems I have. They don't need to be seeing you and Mary like I am, no sir."

These facts are important because it is generally accepted that alcohol dependence (sometimes known as alcoholism; this term is not used as often because of its negative connotations, because it is imprecise, and because in the helping professions it is considered to be pejorative) runs in families (APA, 2000). Some consider a family history to be the best predictor of alcohol problems occurring in adulthood. Why might this be?

There are two hypotheses. First, the adults who have alcohol-related problems serve as models for their children. The children see the adults drinking, do not see them punished, and may actually see the adults rewarded for excessive drinking (loud parties, many friends, everyone smiling, and so on). It is also believed by treatment professionals that the relatives of those who have alcohol problems may inherit a genetic predisposition to develop alcohol-related problems.

What psychologists **can** say is that we know certain premorbid criteria but we don't know the exact causes of many mental illnesses. We also know the best ways to treat many mental illnesses without knowing the exact causes! Other mental illnesses, such as personality disorders, also tend to be comorbid with alcohol dependence.

The next criterion that was discussed was *tolerance*. Specifically, if someone is dependent on alcohol, it will eventually take more alcohol to achieve the same effect. Later on, if physiological damage has occurred, it may take **less** alcohol to achieve the same effect. Once the latter occurs, then hospitalization for *detoxification* is usually necessary. Rudy was asked if it now takes a lot more beer to get the same buzz as fewer beers produced previously,

"Okay, I'll admit, it does take about five to six more beers to get that buzz. I'm just good at holding my beer is all that means. I noticed my limit gradually going up as I went out with the guys but I never made anything of that. Just the body getting used to it is all."

Loss of control was also investigated. This simply means that once the alcohol dependent person begins to drink s/he has great difficulty stopping. In other words, s/he intends to have one or two and ends up closing down the bar, regardless of other responsibilities. Rudy was asked if this situation ever happened to him.

"Yeah, I've closed down a few bars in my time (Rudy stood up at this point). Again nothing unusual. Gee whiz Doc, haven't you ever had such a good time that you lost track of the time and kept on drinking? That doesn't always happen to me, but the wife was not happy when it did happen, let me tell you! I heard it for sure." Rudy was then asked if he could stop drinking whenever he wanted to, and if he could never drink alcohol (beer specifically) again starting today.

"Well, that's a tough one. I like the taste! It's perfect with pizza or during the summer. I tried the non-alcoholic beer before and that was horrible! It's like drinking decaf. It's just not the same. But if I had to I could stop anytime I wanted to, no problem. I did after the first DWI. Are you and Mary demanding this?"

In fact a condition of Rudy's probation was that he stay *sober* (alcohol-free) while on probation. If he violated this condition for any reason he would go back to the judge and probably get jail time. This condition is not surprising. The standard practice of some substance abuse specialists is that their clients remain sober (alcohol-free) for the duration of their treatment.

This condition has come under review recently since some professionals believe that *controlled drinking* is a viable treatment alternative. This means that the client will only have a set number of drinks that s/he decides beforehand and then stops. Why is this controversial? Let's examine the reasons.

Some treatment professionals continue to believe that alcohol dependence is a *disease*; it runs a specific course, attacks all races and genders, and is incurable right now. The symptoms are the same for all people. A key component of alcohol dependence is the probability of *relapse*. This means that the sober alcoholic will return to alcoholic drinking patterns at some point during sobriety. Professionals expect that this might occur and know how to handle it. Since relapse is so common, some professionals believe that it is unwise to "tempt fate" by agreeing to controlled drinking. Some alcoholics will tell you the same thing; they expect to return to alcoholic drinking if they drink in a controlled fashion. That is why alcohol dependence is called an *addiction* and this also defines loss of control. We will examine a bit later whether Rudy would be a viable candidate for a controlled drinking program.

Thus it seems like Rudy might be an alcoholic, but let's provide some more data before we arrive at a diagnosis. Later stage alcoholics suffer from *withdrawal symptoms.* These refer to physiological reactions when the alcoholic removes alcohol from his/her body. In other words, the individual will suffer symptoms such as profuse sweating, shakes, visual hallucinations, and possibly seizures. The reason for this? The body is now **physiologically** dependent on alcohol. The body is used to alcohol being in the system; the cells are used to its presence. Once it is removed, the cells and the body react as though something familiar and necessary is missing. To avoid these withdrawal symptoms, the alcoholic will continue to drink. What happened to Rudy?

"I never suffered from things like that. Sure I might sweat at night but it never happened after drinking. I never had seizures; I'm not an epileptic. Shakes and hallucinations? Never had those either. Well . . . wait . . . I did have hallucinations when I had a very high fever from the flu." Based on his report, we can initially say that Rudy has not suffered withdrawal symptoms.

The next criterion to examine is *denial* (denial that the patient has a problem with alcohol). It must be initially noted that denial is NOT a DSM-IV-TR *diagnostic* criterion, but many alcohol dependents (and abusers) evidence denial. Professionals note that once denial is broken, the hardest part of the battle to effectively treat alcohol dependence has been won. "You see, I don't think I've got an alcohol problem. I've got a driving problem and in some ways a stupidity problem. I didn't learn from my last mistake, and I got into some accidents while drinking. But I wasn't drunk when they happened! I just messed up and didn't pay attention for a moment. As I told you, the second time I got set up. So I can stop whenever I want, and I just need to take some driving lessons and some lessons in being smarter." Does this sound like denial?

Finally let us examine Rudy's blackouts. As stated, blackouts are NOT a DSM-IV-TR diagnostic criterion; however, it seems that people who, at the least, can be classified as *alcohol abusers* (more on this later) might suffer from them. See what you think:

"I had a few times when I'd forget where I'd parked my car after going to the bar, but that didn't happen too much. I've heard stories though.

Waking up in bed next to someone and having no idea who that person was or how you got there. Of course there's the Urban Legend. Person drinks a lot, has a blackout, then comes out of it and is either across country . . . or even better, is buried alive. But we laugh about stuff like that. Some of the guys have blackouts; just means that they can't hold their beer well is all."

What is more important here is the following: For most people, having one blackout would scare them so much that they would do their best to avoid repeating them. For many alcoholics, they take them in stride, assuming that they are normal for many people. Like Rudy said, ". . . they can't hold their beer well." Thus, have you decided on Rudy's diagnosis?

Based on the above information, Rudy was initially diagnosed with the following:

Alcohol Dependence, With Physiological Dependence   303.90

Theoretical Etiologies

There are a variety of theories to explain the etiology of alcohol dependence. As in other chapters, we will only cover some of the perspectives. One of the more widely accepted viewpoints is the disease model which, as stated, sees alcohol dependence as a medical condition. The disease model falls under the biological viewpoint. In the disease model's perspective, the only successful way to ensure successful treatment is for the dependent person to totally abstain from alcohol use. This may seem overly harsh and difficult to attain. However, some professionals believe that this will remove temptation and make it less likely that the dependent person will drink alcohol again. In other words, the less likely you are to use something (such as cigarettes, for example), the less likely, over time, you will miss it. The cravings will still appear, and this is acceptable. But the disease model does not provide temptation for the dependent individual. Psychology and the helping professions look at the most logical aspect of the disease model: If something you use causes significant problems in your life, your life will be less complicated and less troublesome if you do not use the particular substance at all.

Alcoholics Anonymous (AA) also adopts the disease model, but AA is **not** a treatment modality. It has been very difficult to conduct statistically significant research on AA since attendance is voluntary (and attendance is sporadic for many members) and participants attend anonymously (Miller & McCrady, 1993).

Let's examine AA. Two alcoholics founded it over 70 years ago. The only requirement is a desire to stop drinking. There are no fees and no age limits, and everything is anonymous. AA has meetings all over the world and is quite effective in helping alcoholics remain sober one day at a time. AA is NOT therapy but is a *self-help group* run by its members. It is NOT only for "hard core drunks and street people" as many people believe. AA does have spiritual overtones but it has no religious affiliations.

The biological approach involves many etiological concepts. Let us examine a few of these. First, evidence is increasing that a genetic predisposition exists for alcohol dependence (McGue, 1999). Substance abuse counselors have suspected this for a few years. Identical male twins in an alcoholic family are more likely to "inherit" alcohol dependence than would fraternal twins. People who have a family history of alcohol dependence are about four times as likely to develop alcohol abuse or dependence as those whose families do not suffer from these problems (APA, 2000).

Additionally, how the body metabolizes alcohol also appears to have a genetic component. In other words, the ability to "hold your liquor," is determined somewhat by genes. If one examines Asians, many Asians tend to be overly sensitive to alcohol use. If they drink they may evidence facial flushing (redness), and increased heart rate and rapid breathing. This may be one reason why Asians, in general, do not have significant substance dependence problems.

Of course this viewpoint is somewhat simplistic. If you have emphysema because of excessive cigarette use, logically you would stop smoking completely. However, this does not mean that life suddenly becomes problem free. This is one problem with the disease concept.

The Cognitive-Behavioral approach sees temptation acting as a trigger towards using alcohol. Once the alcohol dependent drinks, the initial pleasant effects are reinforcing, thus leading the person to continue drinking. Other reinforcing aspects of alcohol usage include wider acceptance among friends (Rudy's more fun when he's had a few), reducing anxiety and tension through drinking, and through modeling. In other words, the alcoholic may see peoples' anxiety reduced because they are drinking, or their problems might be solved because they were drinking (meeting a woman or a man in a bar while drunk, for example). Drinking could also relieve tension in the alcohol dependent person.

Cognitively, alcohol may produce an expectancy set; that is, the alcoholic expects good things and feelings to occur while drinking, even though the results may not be good at all. This expectancy will lead the person to keep on drinking. An expectancy set is a very powerful molder of behavior. An important problem occurs with expectancies and positive reinforcement. The alcohol dependent person will often see and hear of celebrities, sports stars, and so on who have significant alcohol problems yet seemingly never get punished for their behaviors. Indeed, Ozzy Osbourne, who is oftentimes incoherent because of his long-term usage of alcohol and illicit substances, has become so famous that he was a guest of President Bush at the White House! Ozzy has said that his behavior should not be modeled by others, but how many people would listen to that? Unfortunately Ozzy's son Jack may have modeled his behavior after his father's. Jack ended up in rehabilitation because of his alcohol and substance abuse problems. Does this mean that alcohol dependence runs in Ozzy's family?

Finally, we need to briefly consider the psychodynamic viewpoint. The psychoanalyst would see alcohol dependence as a result of anxiety, repressed emotions, and as a way to boost self-esteem. In effect, alcohol usage could be seen as working like a defense mechanism, the goal being to deny or distort reality and reduce anxiety. Additionally, alcohol dependents can be viewed as having an *oral fixation.* Oral traits such as dependence, depression, and the refusal to grow up (regression, if you will) occur due to a fixation in the oral stage. The use of alcohol displays a return to the fixation point to attain anxiety reduction and need gratification. The individual thus has an oral personality, which is associated with babies and young toddlers. Which etiological perspective do you embrace?

Treatment Plan

There are many different treatment perspectives and options when treating someone who suffers from alcohol dependence; we will cover only a few of these. Many people who have alcohol and drug dependence do not want to discontinue their use. These patients rarely come into treatment voluntarily or on their own; usually legal reasons brings them into our offices. As noted by McLellan, Arndt, Metzger, Woody, and O'Brien (1993), relapse is really the key concern in treatment settings. Treatment settings, Alcoholics Anonymous, and other treatment programs preach abstinence and reward it. The real world sees things differently. How can one avoid alcohol? Even in a closed or restrictive society, alcohol can be found (If not physically present, it can be found on the Internet and through satellite television.) We will first focus on the disease model's perspective, which has a simple initial treatment goal: Rudy must stop using alcohol completely. If that is not possible, then he will need to be sent to an *inpatient treatment facility* where he can receive more intensive treatment. There he could expect to have daily therapy sessions, activities, informational sessions, and much more intensive therapy than could be had in an outpatient setting. Most inpatient treatments for alcohol dependence last about 21 days but may be longer if needed.

If need be Rudy could also go in for detoxification, the medical removal and medical withdrawal of alcohol from his system. This is a procedure where Rudy would receive vitamins, nutrients, and antianxiety medications to prevent serious withdrawal complications. This usually lasts anywhere from a few days to one week, depending on the severity of the dependence. In Rudy's case this does not seem necessary at the moment.

A somewhat controversial treatment approach is the controlled drinking approach, first posited by the Sobells (1973). The idea is simple: Alcohol dependents (and abusers) can have one or two drinks and then stop. In other words, the loss of control concept does not apply. Controlled drinking can be seen in many treatment programs that have a cognitive basis. The patient is taught to notice cues and *antecedents* that may lead to excessive drinking, they are taught how to cope so as not to drink too much, and they are taught to note the consequences when they either ignore the antecedents or drink too much. If the patient has a relapse or *a slip*, it is not seen as something that is out of the patient's control. Instead, the relapse is seen as offering a choice: either the patient returns to drinking abusively or dependently, or the patient can use the relapse to continue on the road to recovery.

Needless to say, this perspective, which has been around for decades, was (and remains) quite controversial. Some research has discovered that controlled drinking works the best with younger alcohol abusers or those in the very early stages of alcohol dependence (In these early stages, withdrawal symptoms are usually not a significant issue) (Sobell & Sobell, 1993). They key argument for controlled drinking: It is very difficult to remain abstinent for the rest of one's life, and in some cases it may not even be necessary! The research has still not been conclusive enough for some professionals to espouse controlled drinking, and more detailed, longitudinal research is needed.

Relapse prevention training is a relatively new treatment modality (Daley & Marlatt, 1992). The goal is to teach the patient how to handle relapses or slips, and to notice the antecedents—or high-risk situations—so that they can successfully cope with the stresses in these situations. Examples of such situations might include situations that create anxiety, stress, or tension (exams, argument with a significant other), economic troubles, and in today's environment, the fear of another terrorist attack, or having been near one or having survived one. These are called *negative mood states*, and they oftentimes lead to ineffective or harmful coping strategies. Relapse prevention assumes that the patient can control his or her behavior as long as they continue in treatment and as long as they make an effort to change.

Concurrent with relapse prevention is a concept called *abstinence violation effects (AVE)*. Patients are taught that a slip is not the end of the world or a sign of weakness, and they are taught how to interpret slips. They are not to feel guilt or shame because they had a slip, but instead they attribute it to something temporary, such as a bad grade or a fight at home. These techniques seem promising, but again more conclusive research is needed.

Rudy is not a viable candidate for the controlled drinking approach since he has been drinking dependently for many years, and because he has developed a high tolerance for alcohol. We know this based on his BAC level. Most individuals with a .28 BAC could not drive, much less stay conscious. Rudy also has not learned from his past mistakes (DWIs) and is still in a state of denial. Asking him to attempt to control his drinking would be unethical and unprofessional.

There are not many viable options for the use of medications to treat alcohol dependence. The use of *antianxiety medications* would be extremely hazardous, since one would be treating alcohol dependence with medications that work on the *Central Nervous System (CNS)*. In fact these medications have effects similar to alcohol: muscle relaxation, feelings of calmness for many people, and they are extremely addictive. Additionally, when these medications are used with alcohol, the medications' effects are significantly increased. The combination may eventually lead to death.

Antidepressants are more problematic, since some patients may need to use them if they have a dual/multiple diagnosis. Antidepressants (specifically the *tricyclics* and *monoamine oxidase inhibitors*) are not addictive; however, they have a very low overdose threshold. This means that if the patient wishes to attempt suicide, they do not need to swallow many antidepressants for the attempt to be effective. If you add alcohol, the combination may become lethal. The psychiatrist needs to use caution when prescribing these medications. This is one advantage of using *Selective Serotonin Reuptake Inhibitors (SSRIs):* It is very difficult if not impossible to overdose on them (Bezchlibnyk-Butler & Jeffries, 2002). This class includes drugs such as *Prozac (fluoxetine)* and *Zoloft (sertraline)*. This may be one reason why psychiatrists prefer this class of antidepressants.

Many alcoholics will have sleep disruptions and they will go to the doctor mentioning this. Unfortunately even today a lot of physicians will not investigate alcohol or drug usage and will prescribe sleeping pills. The combination of sleeping pills (barbiturates) and alcohol is perhaps the deadliest drug combination, since both are CNS depressants. Mixing the two can (and often does) lead to a CNS shutdown and the person dies.

There is one medication that has proven somewhat useful in treating alcoholics and that medication is *Antabuse* (generically known as *disulfiram*). Antabuse is not really a frontline treatment for alcohol dependence but instead it is used as a treatment adjunct. How does it work?

The patient must take Antabuse regularly. If taken regularly and if the alcoholic remains sober and **totally alcohol-free,** nothing occurs. However, as soon as alcohol enters the person's system the patient can become violently ill. The idea here is that the alcoholic will associate becoming violently ill with drinking and will thus get nauseated even when they only think about alcohol, for example. Thus the alcoholic will remain sober. This sounds wonderful in principle but how effective is this in practice? Let us examine some of the problems here.

First and most obviously, the patient needs to be motivated enough to take Antabuse regularly and thus must be motivated to remain sober. Of course if the alcoholic "plans" a slip they can go off of their Antabuse before they have their "slip." Second, the reaction once the alcoholic drinks while they are on Antabuse could lead to death, although this is not common. The alcoholic needs to be aware of this before they agree to this treatment regimen. If the alcoholic is suicidal or psychotic, Antabuse is not recommended. Finally, Antabuse is only a treatment adjunct and is no substitute for therapy and Alcoholics Anonymous (AA). Once on Antabuse the alcoholic might discontinue treatment, believing that Antabuse treatment is enough.

Rudy did not want to use Antabuse and was not a candidate for any other medications. "I like the idea but I don't like the idea of taking a pill every day. And I don't like the idea that if I happen to eat something that has a trace of alcohol in it like a cake or something I could become very sick. I don't need that."

Once it was established that Rudy could stay sober on his own, outpatient treatment moved forward. Rudy was not happy that he was recommended for treatment with us. "But it's better than going to jail and losing my job and my family. I do need to find out what the heck is going on with me. I thought I had answers. Maybe I'm not so smart." The clinic decided that Rudy would benefit from individual and group therapy.

Denial and the *disease model of alcoholism* were discussed individually and in group. Rudy's denial seemed to have weakened after it was decided that he needed treatment. "I guess if all of these 'experts' think that something is wrong with me, I may as well find out if they are right. I don't think so but I'm willing to look into it."

In the disease model, treatment is the responsibility of the client, but contracting the disease is NOT. Thus, alcohol dependence is NOT seen as a moral problem, as a character flaw, or as a weakness. Finally, this model states that there is no such thing as a "cured" or recovered alcoholic; the person is constantly in *recovery* while sober. Through this concept the person will hopefully realize that it is not in their best interests to drink again.

"I have a lot of fences to mend. My wife remains pissed at me but the therapy is helping us to communicate. I'm not a big fan of the group. I like to talk but I don't have a lot in common with the other members. I prefer individual therapy. I'm not comfortable talking about my past with others yet. I'm not even that comfortable individually!" Communication and responsibility were some of the themes in Rudy's therapy.

Rudy managed to remain sober (with one relapse) throughout the year of treatment. "I had a slip shortly after my dad died. It was a lengthy illness—non-Hodgkin's Lymphoma—and the doctors were never honest with us about the severity of his condition. When he died after spending the summer in the hospital, it tore me up. My family was very supportive as was everyone at the clinic, but I still slipped. It was like the alcohol was there and I needed to block the pain. But I know now the world didn't end and that this is common in recovery. I'm not happy but I'm not going to beat myself up over this."

Rudy was discharged at the end of one year and he fulfilled all of his probation conditions. "I learned a lot in therapy and really came to appreciate myself, my problems and Alcoholics Anonymous (AA). I'll continue to go to my meetings and do my best to remain sober a day at a time. It's almost like I've been reborn. I can now see the world through non-alcoholic eyes. It's bad to be an alcoholic but it's not a death sentence unless you let it become that." When we last heard from Rudy he was still together with his wife, and his youngest had just been accepted into his first choice university. Rudy reported that he was still sober and encouraged us to share his story with others so "they could learn how something as simple as beer could potentially destroy everything you value."

Prognosis

Rudy's prognosis is "good." He has decent insight into his alcohol problem and seems to know what he needs to do to keep it in remission. Rudy has good support from his wife and his children. He is willing to learn and to accept his limitations and he realizes that his disease is not his fault, but he also realizes what he stands to lose if he does not follow through with treatment. At last report Rudy's sobriety continued, he was still employed at the same position and was still happily married. Rudy knew that the possibility of relapse existed but "I won't let that rule my life. I can control this problem. My family means too much to me to screw up again." It seems as though Rudy has a good start on keeping his alcohol dependence in remission.

Alcohol Abuse

The Case of Chantal:
"I only gulp drinks once in awhile."

Presenting Problem

Chantal is a 20-year-old college sophomore who is half Native American and half white. She is an only child and has always enjoyed being the center of her parents' attention. Chantal's father is a computer engineer and her mother is a homemaker. Chantal grew up in British Columbia (BC), a province in Canada. She came to the United States to attend college "to get away from home and from my parents, who are very over-protective of me. I also wanted to see a new place." Chantal is 5'8" tall, weighs 155 pounds and is "a bit too fat. I work out but the fat seems to stay. My freshman 15 became a sophomore 30 I guess. But I also eat a lot of junk." Chantal was wearing loose fitting clothes and a pair of baggy shorts when she first came in.

Chantal was referred to us because of her drinking. Her grades began dropping in her classes and an astute professor had a long talk with her one day. "My psychology professor—of course—spoke to me after class. I'd just bombed my second exam, I was missing classes and he wanted to know if everything was all right with me. He wasn't being nosy but I was pulling an A in class up until I began to miss and he was concerned. I had him last semester so he knew what I should be producing. So we spoke for awhile."

Chantal's psychology professor referred her to us for an evaluation but she also came on her own "since I don't want something that could be an issue become even more serious. I know there's nothing crazy about me but I may as well find out before I get too old to do something about it."

Background Information

Chantal's developmental history was unremarkable except for the fact that she was reading fluently in English by age 3 and in French by age 4. Chantal is bilingual, which is typical for people schooled in Canada. "My mom and dad really emphasized reading and thus I learned to read early. I became a voracious reader. It's funny that I didn't do that well in school. I got boy crazy as a teenager and that didn't help. I also really didn't intend on going to university but my dad gave me no choice in the matter. I'm glad he pushed me."

Chantal's parents have an interesting background. "Okay, you want to know about the Indian part. My dad was born in BC and lived there all his life. His family lived on protected land but they experienced racism just like in the United States. Indians are not well liked and rarely get a chance to advance. My dad's family struggled but they were never dirt poor. He graduated high school and then decided to enter the military. The recruiter came to his high school and made a big impact on him. They offered him direction, a steady paycheck and security, so he took it. He refused to end up like a lot of his friends in dead end jobs. Once he was in the military for a while they saw promise and encouraged him to go to college. He eventually got his degree in communications and graduated with honors. In college he met my mother, they fell in love fast and that was that! They've been married for 23 years." Chantal spoke rapidly and made fair eye contact during the initial intake session. She smiled appropriately but looked down when faced with a difficult question or when discussing her family.

Chantal did reasonably well in high school, averaging Bs and Cs and ending up with a B-minus average. She noted, "In Canada our schools go to the thirteenth grade, so that explains why I'm an older sophomore. It's not because I blew off classes or anything like that." Chantal is presently considering majoring in history but is not sure. "I don't know, history or computer science, whichever leads me to having a better career. I intend to work when I get married and if I make more than my husband all the better." Chantal's college is a small liberal arts college so the choice of her potential major led to more questions.

"I wanted a small school. The universities in Canada tend to be large and I hate being a number. This school appealed to me and I loved the location. It's far from home but not too far. Since my dad is helping out financially I also needed to find a cheap school that met my needs and this one does. This school also has a great reputation and I need to get a good job once I graduate. Besides, I want to get a good education; nothing in life is more important than that."

Chantal was partying quite often lately and it turned out that she was becoming a *binge drinker*. For a male, this means that they will consume five or more drinks in a row on at least one occasion during the preceding 2-week period; for a female, four or more (Wechsler, Lee, Kuo, & Lee, 2000). This is becoming more and more prevalent on college campuses in the United States. Wechsler et al (2000) discovered that binge drinking occurred frequently (28.1 percent of the time) on college campuses. Do you know which students were most and least likely to binge drink? The most likely, according to the study, were fraternity and sorority students; the least likely were students who were married, students 24 and older, and African and Asian American students. Binge drinking is a serious problem and it can sometimes lead to death.

"Well, I do like to party. Why be serious when I haven't yet declared my major? I recently broke up with my boyfriend (3 months ago) and that really hurt. My friends have tried to cheer me up so we've been going out a bit more lately. Yeah, there are times when I gulp my drinks, but I only do that once in awhile. I don't need the alcohol and I don't see pink elephants when I do drink. I have no DWIs and no legal problems. Who doesn't have fun once in awhile? Do I have an alcohol problem? No, not a chance." Chantal was wringing her hands at this point and her eyes averted ours. We also noticed that she began to play with her hair.

Chantal was asked about any family history of mental illness including alcohol and drug problems. "Well, yes. My father was counseled in his early days in the military because he used alcohol too much and would get sloppy drunk. His Commanding Officer (CO) noticed it and initially said nothing, as is typical. One day he didn't show up for detail and he was found passed out in his bunk. His CO thought that he might have had a heart attack or something and when they found out he was drunk they were not happy. But can you believe they didn't put him on report? Instead they mandated counseling. He was SO scared that after that day he's never had a drop. 'I saw my career going down the drain. Thank goodness they helped me,' he told me. So I guess he had some problems with alcohol. My mom very rarely drinks. She can't hold her liquor anyway. She's afraid that if it's in the house my dad will use it and more problems will occur. She also doesn't want alcohol around her only child which is nuts. What is university all about if you're not wasted from time to time?" Chantal looked at us expectantly for a reaction to this last statement.

"I haven't been going out a lot until Bob and I broke up but since then it's been more frequent. I have missed a couple of days at my campus job because I got in too late the night before. And my grades have gone down a bit this semester. I don't think it's related to my partying too much."

Thought Questions

1. What information would you cite from above to indicate that Chantal has an alcohol problem?
2. Explain why Chantal's drinking may have caused problems in her work and school lives. Use the information given to support your answers.
3. Chantal's father got into trouble in the military because of his alcohol use. What implications if any does this have for Chantal?

4. Chantal says that her increased partying is a result of her breakup with her boyfriend. Discuss the likelihood, based on the information given, that this might be so.

Assessment and Evaluation

Chantal was assessed using an unstructured diagnostic interview. We were looking for any signs of alcohol abuse and perhaps dependence, which we were hoping to *rule out*. To rule out a diagnosis means that you feel, initially, a specific diagnosis does NOT apply to the individual based on current information. Many clinicians arrive at a diagnosis once they have ruled out all other possibilities. Thus clinicians often diagnose by the process of elimination. (Sherlock Holmes often worked the same way!)

Medical doctors do this as well. They will prescribe a medication and if it does not work, they will rule out conditions until they find the proper medication for the patient. Once the condition responds to the particular medication, the doctor can then make a more certain diagnosis. This practice by medical doctors is quite controversial.

Chantal mentioned previously that her father had a history of alcohol-related problems. "My dad actually got in trouble more than once in the military. He was intoxicated while on duty (only once) in addition to the other time I mentioned. This happened before he got caught the second time. The MP who caught him was his friend and he told my dad that he would keep this quiet. My dad rarely mentioned this because he could have been bounced out of the military. One incident can be overlooked but two, no way. I always wondered why he didn't stop drinking once he got caught the first time."

Chantal knew of no other history of alcohol-related problems in her family. "I told you about my mom. The rest of my relatives also have no problems. However we know very little about my paternal grandfather. He left the family when my dad was 2 years old. My dad was raised by his mother and by her mother. I suspect there might be some things in his family's past that we don't know about. I know that Native Americans tend to have alcohol problems. I don't think I do but perhaps if I DO have a problem it's because of my background."

Chantal also, after much questioning, admitted that she had some legal issues herself. "I hit a mailbox on the way home from a party one night. Yeah, I'd had too much to drink. I really did some damage to my car. I was so scared I left and didn't tell anyone about it until now. It's like the mailbox jumped out at me." She grinned widely at this point.

We also asked Chantal about her drinking patterns and history. "Okay. I don't drink to get drunk. My thing is that I'll stay away from partying and then when the weekend comes watch out! I like to drink fast to keep up with my friends and to show the guys I can hold my beer. I guess you could call me a gulper. But I'll go for weeks at a time without partying at all."

Chantal denied any tolerance or withdrawal to alcohol and denied losing control of her drinking. However, "I have had two blackouts which really scared me. I'm not sure what is going on there. I was with my girl-friends both times. They told me that I seemed totally normal and that I was having a very lively conversation but later on I didn't remember any-thing that I said. That really freaked me out. Then a month later it hap-pened again. My friends told me that when they gulp their drinks they tend to have blackouts too. They did scare me."

We thus had to determine what if anything was going on with Chantal. Based on her information we believed that she was suffering from alcohol abuse. Before we examine why this might be so, ask yourself, "Do you think she should be diagnosed as having alcohol abuse?"

Substance/Alcohol Abuse can be seen as a category for individuals who do not fit the criteria for Substance/Alcohol Dependence in the <u>DSM-IV-TR</u>. Specifically the individual does NOT have tolerance or withdrawal symptoms. Put simply, alcohol is causing problems in the person's life, be it school, work or home life. In effect, physiological dependence is not present. Let us then look at some of the criteria and see if (and how) they do or do not fit Chantal. Note that a person only needs to fulfill at least one of the following criteria to receive the diagnosis of substance (in this case alcohol) abuse (APA, 2000).

First, has Chantal continued to drink despite social or interpersonal problems such as fights or loss of friends? "My friends have always been there for me and my drinking has done nothing to change that. We have fights like everyone but it's rarely due to alcohol."

Next, is Chantal **not** fulfilling her obligations at school, work and home? Her grades have dropped and she has had problems missing work because of her late night partying. Both of these situations are "unique for me; I've always been great at being at my job and I've never had school problems." So it seems like she fits this criterion.

Does Chantal use alcohol when it is physically dangerous to do so? Ac-cording to her, she does. She has had blackouts, which are not normal oc-currences. They MAY be a sign of an alcohol problem or dependence but we are still unsure. She also continues to "party" even though she dam-aged her car when she hit a mailbox. Thus she seems to fit this criterion as well.

Finally, does Chantal continue to use alcohol in spite of recurring legal problems such as DWIs? Based on her account she has had no legal issues but could have been arrested when she hit the mailbox. She would also be guilty (presumably) of leaving the scene of an accident. After this accident "I continued to party. As I said I made a mistake. I also was not really paying attention when I hit the mailbox. I had no problems driving and was in control of my car." She does not seem to fit this criterion.

Since we have ruled out alcohol dependence, and since alcohol seems to have caused problems in Chantal's life, we arrived at the following diagnosis:

Alcohol Abuse   305.00

Theoretical Etiologies

We examined some of the key etiological theories on alcohol dependence with Rudy. There is really little else that needs to be said for alcohol or substance abuse. One important aspect is how ethnicity may be related to the likelihood of becoming an abuser or a dependent. Chantal herself touches on this issue, and we examine it below.

"I also know that certain ethnic groups have a higher degree of alcohol dependence and unfortunately Native American is one of them. I always heard about the stereotypes and it is, to a degree. But I did some reading and it seems to be more prevalent, so I got hit that way as well."

According to some research, Native Americans (Chantal uses the term "Indian" at times, which is confusing and can be considered pejorative) and Irish Americans have the highest rates of alcohol dependence in the United States (Moncher, Holden, & Trimble, 1990). Native Americans have suffered greatly and have very high rates of psychopathology, including alcohol dependence. Poverty and a disruption of their culture and heritage have contributed to these concerns. Native Americans also tend to suffer from high unemployment, and suffer from poor or little education. All of these factors are seen as contributing to the high incidence of alcohol dependence.

Alcohol use is widely accepted among Irish Americans, many of whom are immigrants. Pub life is a part of Irish culture, as is alcohol usage. Many Irish do not have a lot of money and also do not live in large houses. The pub is seen as a place to relax, to catch up on the news, and to socialize, all with alcohol included. A person would "stick out" if they did not have anything to drink. Perhaps it is the cultural acceptance of alcohol as a socializer, and the acceptance of using it excessively at times, that may contribute to the high incidence.

Research has also discovered that Jewish Americans seem to have a low incidence of alcohol dependence. One widely accepted explanation for this is that Jews use alcohol in religious rituals and condemn excessive and underage use of alcohol.

African Americans are less likely to develop alcohol abuse or dependence, but they are more likely to develop physiological problems related to alcohol abuse or dependence. There may be several reasons for this. One commonly accepted reason is that, because African Americans suffer from high unemployment and from poverty, they do not have access to good health care. Problems that are untreated will usually become much worse. Of course this does not mean that all alcohol dependent people will be Irish, or that you will never see a Jewish person who has an alcohol problem. Chantal told us how important this is to her. "I need to be alert once I have kids. They're more prone to developing alcohol problems. I can't change my heritage and why would I? I just need to be careful here."

Treatment Plan

The same treatment options exist for those diagnosed with alcohol abuse as for those diagnosed with alcohol dependence. In Chantal's case we decided to perform individual therapy first and then see if a *beginner's group* would be appropriate. In a beginner's group, Chantal would be placed with others who have never been involved with therapy before. All of the individuals in her possible group have diagnoses of alcohol abuse. Some clinicians like to mix alcoholics with abusers in the same group. We do that, but we also had some groups only for abusers. The group is not only a therapy group but is also an *educational group.*

A focus of most educational groups is the disease model of alcoholism. Chantal learned in this group that alcohol dependence is a progressive disease; thus alcohol abuse CAN lead to alcohol dependence. "I never knew that. I guess it's similar to smoking leading to lung cancer." Not exactly, but this is important because once alcohol abuse is diagnosed, the chances that it will become alcohol dependence are increased if the abusive drinking continues.

Chantal also appears to be a good candidate for a controlled drinking program, and/or a relapse prevention program. As previously stated, a controlled drinking program might work well for Chantal, since her drinking is abusive at the least, and she appears to have sought help in its early stages. Marlatt, Larimer, Baer, & Quigley (1993) found that women tend to have more success in controlled drinking programs. The clinic did not believe in using the controlled drinking method for a variety of reasons. In sum, the clinic director and the university believed in the disease model, and both felt that using the controlled drinking perspective (even as an option instead of total abstinence) was not well supported by research and would lead to relapse and lawsuits. Chantal was informed that she could search for a treatment facility that used the controlled drinking approach, but she chose to stay with us.

"Well, first of all, my student fees will pay for any treatment. If I want to leave, I'm only out the time spent. Besides, based on what has happened to me and what I know, I think trying to stay alcohol free would be the best procedure for me right now. I'll also save some money and I may lose some weight since alcohol has so many empty calories."

Chantal did well in individual therapy as she began to gain insight into her usage. After 12 weeks we decided to place her in the beginner's group because she was making nice progress and would be a good influence on the younger members. "I never realized how much I was messing with my future until I started looking at myself and getting through this denial. I now see how I picked up some of my dad's behaviors. We both didn't learn from our mistakes when we were younger but we didn't suffer too much because of good fortune. Actually that good fortune led to the continuation of problems." In the addictions field this is known as *enabling*, (i.e., enabling the user to continue drinking). When you think you're helping them by overlooking these behaviors, in fact you are enabling them to continue drinking.

Chantal did well in the group and eventually terminated treatment after 24 weeks. She decided to try to remain sober but felt that this would be "hard because of peer pressure and such. At the least, I will not drink as much and never drink and drive again. The blackouts scare me but I can't decide if I should (and will) remain sober." Chantal managed to remain sober throughout treatment and "told friends that it was the doctor's orders that I not drink . . . for health reasons." Not all clinicians believe in this treatment requirement but it seems to work well and removes temptation from the patient.

Chantal also attended Alcoholics Anonymous (AA) meetings to gain more insight into her issues. "That was a trip. I thought they'd be filled with drunken old men and sailors smoking like chimneys . . . you know, rummies. But all types and all ages were there. I enjoyed it but it was too spiritual for me."

AA has two types of meetings: open and closed. Open meetings are open to anyone who wishes to attend. Sometimes they are regular meetings, and sometimes they will have speakers. Anyone who wishes to find out about AA or who thinks s/he has a problem with alcohol is welcome. Closed meetings are only for alcoholics and for those who think they have a problem with alcohol. Closed meetings tend to be somewhat more intense than open meetings.

Chantal went to open AA meetings, looked in on a closed one and "ran out. I got scared and felt like I didn't belong in that group. But I tried." She was encouraged to continue attending AA and to continue her sobriety. She made good progress, broke through a lot of her denial and had some insight into her potential problem.

Antabuse was never really considered for Chantal. Generally medications are not used when a "minor" case of alcohol abuse exists. Chantal reported having no problems staying sober and never showed up under the influence to any sessions (The clinicians had a *breathalyzer* available; this is a machine that measures the blood alcohol concentration of an individual through a breath sample.) Chantal did not appear to have any other psychiatric or medical concerns; therefore no medications were prescribed to her.

Prognosis

Chantal's prognosis is "good." She remained sober throughout treatment and was genuinely motivated and interested to learn about how her alcohol use was affecting her life. Chantal reported that her grades were back up to where she expected them to be once she began treatment and remained sober. "I guess there is a connection between the two but I might try to strike a balance between studying, working, and partying. If I have problems again I'll call . . . and probably stop the partying." She decided to switch her major to Social Work because "I liked the therapy, believe it or not! I got to know myself better and I like the idea that I can make a difference in a mixed up kid's life someday." At last report Chantal was well on her way to graduating "perhaps with honors if I can keep up my good work." She has a new boyfriend, still goes out and would not say if she's staying sober or not. "But I'm staying out of trouble, and that is what counts."

Review and Study Questions

Rudy

1. What is **your** prognosis for Rudy? After all, he relapsed while in treatment and really likes his beer. Do you expect him to remain sober?

2. Would you give Rudy any additional <u>DSM-IV-TR</u> diagnoses? Justify your response.

3. Are you surprised that Rudy is alcohol dependent? After all he is educated, a good family man, and a hard worker. Why or why not?

4. Discuss your views, based on the information given, about the desire of the clinicians to prescribe Antabuse to Rudy, especially considering the side effects it can produce.

5. Based on your knowledge, discuss whether or not you think alcohol dependence is controllable and not curable. Use information from this book and class to support your response.

6. Some might say that Rudy has a character flaw because he is an alcoholic.

Indicate any data in his case to support or refute this assertion.

7. Give your views on the disease model of alcohol dependence

Chantal

1. Point out any data that would lead you to assess Chantal as having an alcohol problem, or any information that does not support this view.

2. Why do data indicate that certain racial, ethnic, and religious groups have more (or fewer) alcohol problems?

3. Discuss your opinions on Alcoholics Anonymous. Discuss whether or not you would attend an open meeting.

4. Cite data and give some reasons why Alcoholics Anonymous appears to be so successful.

5. Chantal is a binge drinker. As she said, everyone on college and university campuses does this today. Give your views on binge drinking.

6. Rudy and Chantal experienced blackouts. What could cause them to occur? What might this be a sign of?

7. What is your prognosis for Chantal?

Key Terms to Know

alcoholism

alcohol dependence

alcohol abuse

Antabuse (disulfiram)

Blood Alcohol Concentration (BAC)

Driving While Intoxicated (DWI)

tolerance

withdrawal symptoms

Breathalyzer

blackouts

detoxification

loss of control

controlled drinking

addiction

denial

inpatient treatment facility

alcohol abusers

sober

disease

relapse

disease model of alcoholism

Central Nervous System (CNS)

Prozac (fluoxetine)

Zoloft (sertraline)

binge drinker

alcohol-specific caseload

unstructured diagnostic interview

diagnostic

self-help group

oral fixation

antecedents

slip

relapse prevention training

negative mood states

abstinence violation effects (AVE)

antianxiety medications

antidepressants

tricyclics

monoamine oxidase inhibitors

Selective Serotonin Reuptake Inhibitors (SSRIs)

recovery

rule out

enabling

beginner's group

educational group

Chapter 6

Eating Disorders

Eating disorders appear to be on the increase in the United States and in other developed countries (Wicks-Nelson & Israel, 2000; Steiner & Lock, 1998). One recent study found that as many as one out of one hundred girls ages 16 to 18 may have an eating disorder (Goldstein, 1999). The "drive for thinness" affects Hollywood actresses and actors, athletes (gymnasts and cheerleaders are especially susceptible), models, and royalty (the late Princess Diana). Jamie-Lynn Sigler ("Meadow" on "The Sopranos") and Tracey Gold have battled anorexia nervosa, while Calista Flockhart ("Ally McBeal") has been rumored for years to also suffer from anorexia. It seems like every month or so, *People Magazine* has an article detailing the horrors of *bulimia nervosa* and *anorexia nervosa* and how they affect the general population. The "drive for thinness" in Hollywood has received a tremendous amount of popular press lately. What causes these disorders which primarily affect women? Let us examine two case examples and see how complex the behavioral and thought patterns of afflicted individuals are.

Bulimia Nervosa

The Case of Molly:
I Wanna Be Like Princess Di

Presenting Problem

Molly is a 23-year-old 5'11" sophomore at a state university who is a Social Work major. Molly weighs 134 pounds and is white. Molly has aspirations of becoming a therapist and attaining her masters in social work. When Molly first came in it was summer and quite hot and humid. Molly was wearing tight jeans, a long sleeved sweater and had her black hair pulled back through a baseball cap. It had her school's logo on the front of the cap. Molly's eyes were sunken into her head and they had big black circles surrounding them. Molly made fair eye contact and had a *flat affect*. In our first interview she never smiled; indeed, she never displayed any emotion (this is what is meant by flat affect). Molly would often speak in a whisper and we would have to ask her to speak up. She yawned frequently and looked at her watch.

Molly was referred to us by her aunt, who had known about Molly's "issues" for awhile. Molly had a history of psychiatric difficulties beginning at age 11. "My aunt was concerned that my life was getting out of control again. She saw that I was eating in secret and that I was not working. I needed to take some time off from school but I could not go home, so I went to live with her. She saw stuff, I guess (she shrugs here) and here I am. I don't want to be here, but my aunt told me to show up—she's outside—or else she'd kick my sorry butt out of her house. What can I do? I need a place to live, I don't want to work, and I have no energy."

Background Information

Molly grew up in a small rural town where everyone really did know everybody else and everyone else's business. She had a relatively normal childhood and an unremarkable developmental history, walking and talking at the appropriate ages and maintained average grades (a few Bs, many Cs, and some Ds and Fs) in school. Molly was not a behavioral problem in school and "got along well with most kids. I had some friends, but not an awful lot." She reported that she often felt embarrassed to bring friends home because of "issues" involving her parents, especially her father. Molly's face tightened here and she raised her voice, evidently in anger. Her eyes narrowed and she stared out the window as she continued to speak.

"My dad's had an alcohol problem as long as I can remember. He's got to be an alcoholic. My mom also has a serious alcohol problem; I don't think she is an alcoholic though. She never really pushes the drinking issue with him. My dad is also very fat. He has the worst diet imaginable and never eats properly. It's always junk food and fried foods. I'm so worried he'll have an attack or a stroke. And he smokes like a fiend! I don't know what to do."

Molly is the oldest of three children; her sister is 19, and her brother is 9. Molly's father works for the electric company, and her mother is an elementary school teacher. Molly's parents have been married for 26 years, are white, and are Irish-Catholic. Her family is rather devout and attends church regularly. Molly did attend church on a regular basis but stopped going three years ago.

Molly first began menstruating at age 11 and was never more than 25 pounds overweight at any time during her life. However, once she hit puberty, "my appetite really increased and so did my weight. I gained 25 pounds so fast I was stunned. Kids at school looked at me like I was a hippo. I hated them and I hated ME. I had to do something about the weight. I hated being FAT."

At the age of 12 Molly had her first major life-altering event. Molly came home with a bad report card from school and was told she needed to show it to her father. When he came home he erupted and sent Molly to her room for the evening without dinner. He never hit nor abused Molly and this time was no exception. What was also typical is that "when he got really upset he'd drink until he passed out and many times my mom would join him and do the same. When I needed parents they were drunk." Molly was so upset by her low grades and more so by her father's reaction that she attempted suicide by swallowing a bottle of multivitamins. She was rushed to the Emergency Room and the attempt was unsuccessful.

"I really had no intention of killing myself; I just wanted to punish myself and my parents for treating me like s . . . for so long. It was always about my brother or how beautiful my sister was and was never about me. And when I needed them, they're drunk."

Molly was in a psychiatric hospital for two months and participated in counseling sessions which seemed to help her. She realized that she wanted to live and that she did "a really dumb thing by trying to kill myself." Molly had a renewed energy and self-esteem once she was discharged, but some things did not change, and other things became worse.

Once Molly returned to junior high school she discovered through peers at school another way to help control her emotions and hurt feelings. She realized that if she could "control my weight by binging and purging, I could take control of my life AND eat what I wanted while putting on no weight! Actors and supermodels do it all the time. All my friends at school were doing it. Why not?"

Molly discovered how easy it was to use this method to "control" her weight. What she did not realize was how addictive this behavior was. She needed to *purge* (throw up) in secret, and it was also becoming impossible for her to eat a lot *(binge)* in public, with friends, or at home. Molly had heard about bulimia nervosa but she did not think much of it. "I eat; I don't starve myself and I don't use laxatives to get rid of what I do eat. It didn't sound like bulimia to me at the time."

Molly began to develop other problems. She became quite depressed and began to have serious sleep problems. She was on edge constantly, always arguing with her parents. Her grades in school began to slide. But all the time she was popular and constantly praised about how good and thin she looked. Many boys were interested in her, and she had her first sexual experience at age 13. Molly began to "sleep around," telling me that she enjoyed this and it made her feel even prettier and thinner.

Molly eventually graduated with a C-plus average and decided to attend a state university. Molly's bulimic behaviors had continued unnoticed (she thought) by her family and friends, and her promiscuity continued as well. Molly also adopted another detrimental behavior while in college: She began to drink heavily on the weekends and would get drunk quite often. This caused her problems because when she would get drunk she would *black out* (she would have memory loss while she was drunk). This led Molly into compromising situations; for example, a number of times she would wake up in the morning and have no idea how she got into the bed, or who the guy was sleeping next to her. Initially she was not too upset about this but when it occurred often she decided to seek help.

The campus counseling center was most concerned about her bulimic behaviors and focused on those. When it became clear that the counseling sessions were not productive because her bulimic behaviors continued, her therapist urged her to seek inpatient psychiatric treatment. Molly was not willing to go back to the hospital and became so upset with the recommendation that she dropped out of school and went to live with a boyfriend in a major urban city.

Molly found a job as a waitress and said that at first she was quite happy, especially because she was far away from her parents. However, the bulimia and drinking continued while she lived with this boyfriend;

eventually he managed to convince her that she needed some help. She saw a counselor and once again inpatient hospitalization was suggested. The reasons for this were simple. Molly's behaviors were not improving while she was in counseling, and her behaviors were of such a self-destructive nature that the need for hospitalization was mandatory. Molly agreed and, while in the hospital, decided to end her relationship and return home to her family once she completed treatment. She was then referred to another counselor but really did not "connect" with her, and so Molly ended treatment.

In the meantime, Molly returned to school and soon "rediscovered" her bulimic and drinking behaviors. Her promiscuous ways also returned. Her grades significantly declined and she realized that she needed to continue in therapy. This decision was made in May, at which time she was referred to me for therapy.

Thought Questions

1. Is Molly too young to have the classic symptoms of bulimia nervosa (binging and purging)? Cite data and evidence to support your response.
2. Did Molly's condition warrant her being sent to an inpatient psychiatric hospital?
3. How important is a family's history of mental illness as you try to diagnose Molly?
4. Molly reported that she was never more than 25 pounds (11 kilograms) overweight but she said she was like a hippo and needed to lose weight. What could be the reason(s) that she sees herself as being so overweight?

Assessment and Evaluation

Molly was assessed and evaluated by many mental health professionals: a psychologist, social worker, psychiatrist, medical doctor and a nurse. We used a standard, *unstructured diagnostic interview* with Molly, the *Eating Disorder Inventory-2 (EDI-2)* and the *Beck Depression Inventory II (BDI-II)*.

Molly was asked about an early experience with drinking alcohol to the point of drunkenness. She replied that this indeed did occur. However, she also noted that she vomited soon afterwards and that it "felt good, like a release" once she had finished vomiting. We then asked her if these feelings were similar to those when she vomited during a purging episode; "Yes, in fact I got addicted to that release of tension."

Her BDI-II score was 35 which indicates severe depression. The BDI-II is a paper and pencil inventory that can be filled out by either the patient alone, or by the clinician asking the patient for his/her replies.

Molly's EDI-2 profile was also interesting. She was preoccupied with being thin and dissatisfied with her body. She stated on the EDI-2 that her ideal weight would be 110 pounds, which for a woman of 5'11" is considered to be underweight. She was overly concerned with reaching this ideal weight. Once reached, she felt that her problems would be over. For Molly, the key issue was not only reaching this weight but also maintaining it. Some of her subscale scores on the EDI-2 were elevated, possibly signifying that Molly has bulimia nervosa.

Her Drive for Thinness (DT) subscale score was 15; most individuals who have bulimia nervosa will score in this range. Her Bulimia (B) subscale score was 16, indicating that binge eating is a problem for Molly. Molly's Body Dissatisfaction (BD) subscale score was 11, considered a moderate elevation. Extreme dieters will score in this range. Bulimic women are dissatisfied with their bodies, but not as much as anorectic women. Finally, her subscale score on the Ineffectiveness (I) scale was 4, indicating moderate to severe feelings of insecurity, worthlessness, emptiness, general inadequacy, and of a lack of control over life's events. These feelings are typical for those who have an eating disorder.

Next, Molly fulfilled all of the <u>DSM-IV-TR</u> diagnostic criteria for a major depressive episode during the initial interview. Her appearance was disheveled; her eyes had huge circles under them, and she appeared emotionless (a flat affect). Molly was sleeping about 16 hours a day, was crying virtually every day without provocation, was not eating much at all, and had very little energy. Additionally, she felt that her life was hopeless since she could not control her bulimia anymore ("It was controlling me, which is NOT what I want"), and her *libido* was significantly diminished (i.e., her sex drive or desire to have sex). "I can't remember the last time I wanted to have intercourse, much less kiss a guy." Additionally, her replies to my *open-ended* questions were of the one- to five-word variety.

Molly teared up a bit but did not cry as she continued. "I know that something else is wrong with me besides bulimia but I'm not sure what it is. It's become so hard to even get myself out of bed, and it was hard to get up the energy to come in today, even though I've been looking forward to trying to get things fixed. It also sucks that my binging and purging have gotten worse in the past few weeks. I now do it . . . oh . . . about four or five times a day every day. I think that's too much. I hope we can find out what is wrong with me in these individual sessions. Am I going crazy?"

Molly is not "going crazy" but is suffering from depression and bulimia. How do we know that she is bulimic? She was *binging* and *purging* about five times per day for at least four months. Molly's binges consisted of gorging herself on high caloric, high carbohydrate foods and junk foods such as chips, cheese puffs, ice cream, and doughnuts. She said a binge for her would consist of, on average, about three to five thousand calories at one sitting. She felt that she had no control over her eating, much like an addiction. Once she began to binge she felt like she could not stop.

She would then purge, or get rid of the food that she had just eaten. Molly always purged and did so by vomiting, which is the most common method. Molly had gotten to the point where she could make herself vomit on cue; if she ever had difficulty doing so, she would stick a toothbrush down her throat to induce vomiting. The goal was to prevent weight gain since Molly saw herself as "very very fat."

From our perspective, Molly's depression was severe, and her bulimia was out of control. Anorexia was ruled out since Molly was menstruating, was a normal weight for her height (134 pounds), and was eating. Many times anorexia and bulimia appear to be similar, but there are some striking differences between the two disorders as we shall soon see.

Based on these symptoms, the clinic staff determined in a case conference that Molly was not considered initially appropriate for outpatient therapy. She was clinically depressed and we were worried that things would continue to worsen and that she might eventually try and take her life again soon. Her bulimia had worsened significantly during the past 3 weeks. Her vomiting had increased and she was losing weight. Molly also told us that her vomit "was now having a weird color, a bit reddish-brown. It's never really been like that before." Since I was not a medical doctor, and since this might have meant that she was vomiting blood, I became concerned about her safety and the harm she was already doing to herself. Thus, based on my clinical judgment, inpatient treatment was recommended to her. She agreed to discuss this with her mother first, and she gave me permission to contact the psychiatrist she worked with at the hospital. We reviewed Molly's case and he also agreed that inpatient treatment at this time would be the most beneficial for Molly.

Molly's mother came in and agreed that Molly should go to an inpatient setting "since I am really worried about her. She rarely gets out of bed, looks real bad, and she keeps on vomiting. I'm afraid she'll try something silly again, and soon. I'll take some time from work to be there as much as possible during the first week or so."

After hearing the professional opinions, and listening to her mother's views, Molly finally agreed to go, albeit reluctantly. Her mother was going to drive her to the hospital and call us once Molly was settled on the ward. Molly also made a *behavioral contract* with us that, once she was discharged, she would call us and we would then begin outpatient treatment.

When someone's mental illness gets worse and the therapist feels that medication and once a week sessions (or more) would not be enough to help the patient overcome his/her situation, inpatient treatment may be a viable option. This is not done as a punishment, or as a way to avoid working with "undesirable patients," as it might seem. The goal is to make the patient as self-sufficient as possible so that they can be somewhat stable between outpatient sessions. Since Molly appeared to be a threat to herself (based on a past history of suicidal attempts), and based on the fact that she might be vomiting blood, and because her depression seemed to be worsening, inpatient treatment was recommended.

Molly was in the hospital for 28 days before discharge. She was seen by the entire treatment team in the hospital, received vitamin and nutrient therapy, nutrition counseling, individual and group therapy, and attended self-help groups. At discharge we received the following diagnoses for Molly from the hospital:

Major Depressive Disorder, Single Episode, Severe, Without Psychotic Features	296.23
Bulimia Nervosa, Purging Type	307.51
Alcohol Abuse	305.00

Theoretical Etiologies

There are many possible causes of bulimia nervosa. Like many other mental illnesses, the causes are often multiple and varied. A key causal factor of bulimia nervosa (as well as anorexia nervosa) is the United States' society's emphasis on a woman's weight and appearance. "Thin is in, and fat ain't where it's at," goes the cliché. Women in the United States get tremendous pressure to be unrealistically thin, such as from the media, peers, coaches, and so on. Women who read *Vogue* and see Giselle Bundchen, Naomi Campbell or Cindy Crawford view these supermodels as having ideal shapes and thus aspire to be like them. It does not help that after having two children Cindy Crawford really does not look that different. The same can be said for actresses who have had children yet show no visible signs of this.

Research supports this sociocultural etiology. Stice (1994) discovered that eating disorders are uncommon in non-Western countries such as in parts of Asia and Africa. Indeed, Stice found that eating disorders are also rare in Japan, which can be seen as the most technologically advanced country on earth and also one where United States television and movies are extremely popular.

Some cultures value women who are not thin and in some cases "Plus" size. Women who are "chunky" are often seen as having enough money to eat properly and are seen as being good child producers because of their fat stores. In certain cultures, thin implies that you do not have enough money to get food, or that you have to severely ration what you have.

White American female adolescents tend to have the highest rates of eating disorders. In one study, the randomized subject pool consisted only of white female volunteers (Getzfeld, 1992). The study was open to all, but the researcher was unable to attract any ethnic or racial variation. This is not to say that African Americans and other racial and ethnic groups remain unaffected. Research has also discovered that eating disorders may increase in the future in developing countries, particularly as they get exposed to United States media and female ideal body image depictions. Kate Dillon, a plus size model, has stated that she would starve herself in order to not lose out on modeling jobs. The result: She would faint quite often because she would not eat much if anything for days, and when she did eat, she would throw it up.

Let us now examine some possible psychosocial etiologies. One thing women suffering from bulimia nervosa have in common is that most have a history of extreme or very rigid dieting (Patton, Selzer, Coffey, Carlin, & Wolfe, 1999; Hunicutt & Newman, 1983). In addition, they tend to exercise very often, and they tend to be extremely restrictive as to what they actually eat. In some instances these women will not eat much in public; binging almost always occurs in private if possible, as does purging.

Female athletes, especially in sports where weight gain is considered a reason to be thrown off of a team or squad, are much more susceptible to eating disorders such as bulimia nervosa. Ballet dancers are particularly at risk, where gaining as little as five pounds can be considered a career ending situation (Abraham, 1996; Garner, Garfinkel, Rockert, & Olmsted, 1987). An interesting view is that ballet requires precise control, and an eating disorder usually involves control issues.

An important symptom that many bulimics and anorectics have in common is body dissatisfaction, which may lead to bulimia and/or anorexia (Fairburn, Welch, Doll, Davies, & O'Connor, 1997; Getzfeld, 1992). A woman may attempt extreme measures to obtain the perfect shape or figure. What is most interesting is that women with eating disorders do not see their bodies realistically. If you ask them to look in a mirror (no easy task) and to describe their bodies, most will say they are fat (Getzfeld, 1992). A key difference is that bulimic women will have a more accurate perception of themselves than anorectic women and will be more likely to reveal their abnormal eating behaviors. (In some instances they need to be persuaded to reveal such information.) Many bulimic women are indeed a bit overweight, just like Molly, before they begin to develop bulimia.

Cognitive factors have been touched on briefly. Bulimic women tend to be perfectionists and to never go off of their "diets;" if they do and they gain even one pound, they see themselves as total failures and will often try even harder to control their eating. Bulimic women also exaggerate and distort the consequences if they do gain any weight. They are obsessed with weight gain and can easily tell you how many calories they consumed at a given meal. Women who manifest eating disorders like Molly tend to have very low self-esteem and a lack of self-confidence. To paraphrase a psychiatrist with whom I worked, a bulimic woman's thoughts are illogical, meaning that they make no sense. Many of these women come from high achieving, middle to upper middle class backgrounds.

Behaviorists have a very logical explanation for bulimia: Purging is reinforced by the extreme fear of gaining weight. As weight is lost through purging techniques, the likelihood increases that purging behaviors will continue. Purging also leads to relief, and to anxiety reduction, as Molly will demonstrate shortly. The anxiety reduction and "numbing out," as Molly will tell us, reinforces the purging behavior.

Some research has discovered that eating disorders may have a familial component, especially among females (Strober, Freeman, Lampert, Diamond, & Kaye, 2000). Some researchers believe that women who develop eating disorders do so to punish their families for being too harsh, too demanding, or too cold and distant. What can be said with some certainty is that bulimic and anorectic women generally have issues with their parents and families, and their families have a significant amount of intrafamilial conflicts (Getzfeld, 1992; Fairburn et al., 1997). The plus size model Emme (Aronson) has stated that her father used to draw a line around her waist with a black marker and would verbally abuse her every time the line expanded.

We will next examine some personality and psychological factors relating to the etiology of bulimia nervosa. A key criterion of bulimic women is that they seem to have other psychological disorders in addition to bulimia nervosa (Fairburn et al, 1997). Common disorders among bulimic women include alcohol dependence, mood disorders, and anxiety disorders. Bulimia can be viewed as a type of self-medication to cope with these disorders. Bulimia can also be seen as a way to cope with childhood physical and sexual abuse, although this view is not universally held.

Finally, have researchers identified any biological etiologies for bulimia nervosa? Low levels of serotonin activity have been linked to bulimia nervosa, especially to binge eating, specifically carbohydrates. Low serotonin levels have also been associated with impulsive behavior, of which binging and purging should be included. Some researchers have posited a link between bulimia nervosa and depressive or mood disorders, but they are unsure which one comes first (Getzfeld, 1992). This link can be substantiated by the fact that some antidepressants, which work to increase serotonin activity in the brain will, in many instances, reduce and/or eliminate bulimic symptoms (Getzfeld, 1992). Which etiological viewpoint do you embrace?

Treatment Plan

Standard practice when treating bulimia nervosa suggests using the treatment modalities of individual and family therapy (see Eisler, Dare, Russell, Szmukler, le Grange, & Dodge, 1997 for example). According to her hospital's discharge summary (and to Molly), individual therapy provided Molly with the most insight, then family therapy, and finally group therapy. Based on this, we decided to follow the hospital's and Molly's suggestions initially and keep an eye on how successful this would be.

Once it was decided that Molly would be involved with individual and family therapy, the next step was to formulate the treatment plan. We decided to focus on the bulimia first, since this was the primary presenting problem. Additionally, one of the main goals was to get Molly more active and thus try to combat her depression. Much research sees *comorbidity* (a link) between bulimia and major depressive disorder, and this situation did not seem to differ. What is not agreed upon is which comes first. Hopefully by treating the bulimia as the primary diagnosis the depression would also lift. Can you anticipate what occurred?

Molly was asked to keep an *eating diary* noting what she ate each day and when, and if she binged or purged. The time of day was crucial, since we were looking for possible situational cues that might set off a binge/purge cycle. Molly was also asked to weigh herself, initially at least once a week. We understood how traumatic this might be, but we needed to find out how much her weight was fluctuating (if at all) and also wanted her to get more in touch with her body and her actual weight. Molly did not have a problem completing either of these assignments.

Typically a behavioral approach will look for stimuli that set off behaviors. This approach will also give homework assignments. The assignments are easy to do and generally are not designed to be too threatening. So what did her eating diary produce?

Molly noted that most of her binges (which had decreased to about two times per week when treatment began) occurred in the evening, after dinner. She was able to be alone and to hide what she was doing. She "had a major energy drop in the evenings and I'm not sure why. Perhaps it has something to do with the sun going down, or perhaps it's the pressure of going out and not knowing what will happen that night. I'm not sure." Most of her binges consisted of junk food and ice cream and other high carbohydrate foods. This is typical for most bulimics.

Molly weighed herself initially on Tuesday mornings because "I never go out Monday nights, and by then anything bad I did should be out of my system by then. What's weird is that my weight has not really changed much at all. It's frustrating because I know I can be thinner, but I also know that my way of doing it is not healthy. I still feel this 'pull' towards binging and purging."

We discussed various ways for Molly to get her energy "up" again in the evenings. She had no hobbies, so exercise, like a brisk after-dinner walk, was suggested. She started doing that and found that her head cleared and her energy increased. This also gave her a sense of control in that she was now able to boost her energy on her own. Bulimics typically will have major issues involving control; indeed, controlling their eating and weight is oftentimes the only thing in their life they feel they can control.

We also used a cognitive treatment modality, focusing on teaching Molly ways to resist the binge/purge impulses and notice the warning signs, and we also mentioned that she should not be alone after eating so as to forestall any binging/purging behaviors. We discussed dieting and how binging and purging do not lead to successful weight control. We contacted a dentist in the area who sent over some literature to Molly. It described the physical consequences of bulimia nervosa and even supplied some photos of teeth badly damaged by binging/purging. Molly was shocked to see this, especially since she always had difficulty "looking in the mirror, even if it's not full length. My fat face disgusts me."

Going along with a cognitive plan first described by Fairburn (1985), a major researcher in the field of bulimia we, in conjunction with Molly's psychiatrist, set up an eating plan where she would have many small meals a day, with no more than three hours between any meal. What purpose does this serve? Fairburn (1985) notes that this planned eating schedule will eliminate the bouncing back and forth between periods of overeating and purging (or restriction) that occur with bulimia nervosa.

Typically psychodynamic therapy is not used in the treatment of bulimia nervosa. This modality poses a number of problems. It takes awhile before progress is made and requires a long-term commitment on the patient's part. While waiting for progress, the binging/purging may still be occurring. What some professionals will do is to combine psychoanalysis with behavioral therapy to look for repressed material while attempting to disrupt the binge/purge cycle.

As treatment progressed, Molly gradually noticed a connection between the timing of her binges and purges and family dinners, the only time the entire family was together. "I guess my family is partly the cause of my bulimia. For some reason I get so uptight during and right after dinner and I need to escape and 'numb out,' so I do my stupid stuff. It does help to get my mind off of all of my family nonsense."

While in the sessions some other key information arose. Molly's maternal family has a history of mental illness. An uncle was "either mentally retarded or schizophrenic; I don't know which. And my mom's mother was schizophrenic." Additionally, her sister has "an alcohol problem which is never mentioned. Often she'll end up sleeping on the street because she's afraid to come home at 5 A.M., after the bars close. Gee whiz, the only normal one is my brother!" She slapped her forehead lightly at this point and looked to the sky. Molly also noted that this was the first time she had a male as a psychologist and, interestingly, she felt she could be more open.

Molly also volunteered a crucial piece of information once she began to feel comfortable in individual therapy. "My uncle repeatedly sexually molested my younger sister and me when we were both 12 years old. My grandmother never believed me and for a long time neither did my mother. I only mentioned this with my therapists when I was hospitalized; my sister never spoke about this to anyone with the exception of me." Molly spoke haltingly while describing her uncle. Her eyes teared up as well. Initially Molly did not realize how significant the impact of these incidents was on her and on her sister, even though she seemed quite upset when describing them.

Based on this, the next approach was twofold. Molly was referred to a local psychiatrist for an evaluation and for possible medications. Additionally, Molly's family was contacted in an attempt to begin family therapy. Not surprisingly they were all willing to come in with one notable exception: her sister. Usually a family will be eager to begin therapy but once actual issues surface and it appears that the family is affected and/or may be partially responsible for the patient's problems, the family will usually drop out of treatment. What do you think occurred?

Molly's father was a gregarious man, smiling a lot and talking loudly. He would dominate the sessions at times, not letting his wife speak. He was obese and had a large belly. He appeared to have difficulty breathing since he was wheezing a lot during the sessions and in the waiting room. He attributed this to "working too hard." Molly's mother was very quiet at first, perhaps intimidated by her husband into not speaking too much. She smiled infrequently and seemed very tired during the initial sessions, yawning a lot and looking glassy eyed. She opened up and spoke more as the sessions progressed. Molly's brother made poor eye contact and rarely looked at us. He always sat next to his father and would twiddle his thumbs during the sessions. He never said a lot in any of the sessions he attended. It seemed evident after awhile that he had no interest in attending or participating.

Her family was "very eager to participate in the first three sessions," but when Molly began to focus on her parents' drinking and other problems, they became very defensive and her mother told her that her bulimia was "selfish. It's really all your fault and your problem. Did we complain when you clogged up all the drains with vomit? We never even said anything! We've helped you financially and been there for you emotionally and you tell us we're not there, that we're alcoholics?"

After this Molly's brother began to question why he was in family therapy since "she's the one with the throwing-up and guy problems. I don't need this stuff." He proceeded to drop out after the third session.

Molly's father was the next to drop out. He was the focus of her attention during the sessions, especially his drinking and diet. He refused to change either of these behaviors and instead insisted on focusing on Molly and "the fact that you never finish anything. We spend all this money on school, the hospital, psychologists . . . and you never follow through. I just don't understand that." Her father dropped out after the fifth session "since I don't see the purpose in this and I won't come here to hear how horrible I am."

Finally, Molly's mother stayed until Molly was transferred to another psychologist. The two of them spoke about Molly's depression and bulimia, her problems with guys, and her seeming inability to finish things she starts. Her mother admitted that "we handled the abuse situation incorrectly and I apologized for that. "We'll also cut back or give up on the drinking, whatever it takes to get you over this. Dear, you're killing yourself, and that's killing us."

Molly made some nice progress in individual therapy as well. She realized that her bulimia and drinking behaviors were physically and psychologically harming her. She found a night job which "I hate, but I need the bucks. I also moved in with my aunt, which is really a lifesaver. I love my parents but I can't do this treatment and live at home. It's like I can never get away from these problems. I can now come and go as I please, and I finally feel independent."

Molly also "met a nice guy who wants me to come visit, to spend the weekend with him and his family. We haven't had sex yet, which is really a first for me. I don't want to ruin this one. In the past as soon as I slept with guys I broke up with them. I would almost always sleep with them right after we met. I was so upset when they saw me naked, my fat body. I couldn't stand to be with them after that."

Molly realized that most of her difficulties occurred shortly after she began to menstruate and her body changed rapidly. The fact that Molly was sexually molested by her uncle only made things worse. It needs to be noted that in spite of what the media say, childhood sexual molestation is

NOT **always** linked to an individual becoming bulimic. In Molly's situation it was just one of many contributing factors.

Molly also established a decent relationship with her psychiatrist. He prescribed *Prozac (fluoxetine)*, a *selective serotonin reuptake inhibitor (SSRI)* antidepressant approved by the Food and Drug Administration (FDA) for the treatment of bulimia. Once it took effect she was "amazed at how much better I feel. I have more energy and the urge to binge has really decreased. I'm sure that the therapy and insight has helped a lot, but this drug has really done wonderful things for me. I feel like a new woman."

Molly gained much insight into her difficulties. She realized that alcohol seemed to create problems in her life but "it's hard for me to give up everything, all these addictions, at once. It would be like giving up smoking, drinking, chewing sugarless gum, and my bulimia. One thing at a time! But yes, my drinking is lately causing many many problems for me." For example, Molly has *blackouts* which she thought initially were normal results of getting drunk. They frightened her but in therapy she realized that they might be a sign of a possible serious alcohol problem. She also discovered in therapy that alcohol also caused her problems with men, specifically that "I sleep around too much. It makes me feel thin and pretty when guys all want to have sex with me. Getting drunk makes it easier for me to be naked with them. Unfortunately once they see me naked I never see them again. Even though I usually do the breaking up, I'm sure they're repulsed by how fat I am."

Molly remained in individual therapy for four months. At the end of this period of time, she had not binged or purged for 10 weeks and remained in a steady relationship for about 8 weeks. She was steadily employed (although she did not like the job), was living on her own and responsible for her own bills, and planned on returning to university in the fall, continuing her social work major. Her symptoms of depression had cleared up significantly. She was not sleeping nearly as much, felt better about herself and about her life, her desire for sex had returned in earnest, and her energy level had markedly increased. She reported no thoughts of suicide while in therapy.

Unfortunately her relationship with her parents remained strained at discharge. She still had issues with her father which most likely would not be resolved until he returned to treatment. Her issues with her mother had lessened once she had moved out. "I really can't see getting along with my sister since we're so different. She's a solid partier and I've never been like that."

Molly was looking forward to continuing therapy with her new psychologist and would continue seeing her psychiatrist. For the first time she openly discussed her past history of sexual molestation and realized she needed to work on these issues. Molly was being transferred because I was moving out of town to take a new position. During the final session Molly was sad but was happy, a "feeling I have not had in so long. I forgot what happiness was . . . I forgot what feeling anything was. Life just seemed blank and dark, endless sad."

We will now turn our attention to medications which may be used in treating bulimia nervosa. Let us first look at which medications would **not** be appropriate for bulimia nervosa. *Antipsychotic medications* would not work since bulimia is not a *schizophrenic disorder* and does not include in its symptoms delusions and hallucinations. *Antianxiety medications* (such as Valium (diazepam) and *Xanax (alprazolam)*) also do not seem to be well-suited for treatment. These medications are highly addictive and should only be used on a short-term basis for anxiety disorder treatment. They also, in general, do not work on serotonin extensively; serotonin seems to be linked to the manifestation and exacerbation of bulimia.

Molly was taking Prozac, an antidepressant. Research has discovered that antidepressants oftentimes are quite effective in reducing bulimic symptoms. These can be Prozac or other SSRIs (such as *Zoloft (sertraline)* and *Paxil (paroxetine)*), or standard *tricyclic antidepressants* (such as *Norpramin (desipramine)*. Other types, such as *Monoamine Oxidase Inhibitors (MAOIs; Nardil (phenelzine)* and *Parnate (tranylcypromine)*, for example), have also proven somewhat effective. However, anyone on MAOIs needs to be on a *tyramine*-free diet. This means that they need to avoid foods that contain tyramine such as aged cheeses, some beers, fava beans, and sauerkraut. It is difficult to tell a bulimic to watch what they eat while they are binging. One possible side effect of being on MAOIs while ingesting tyramine foods is death.

Antidepressants such as Prozac alter the brain's chemistry; in this case, serotonin activity is presumed to be diminished in the person's brain. SSRIs inhibit the reuptake of serotonin, leading to a buildup of serotonin at neuronal synapses in the brain. Simply, more *serotonin* is available. Why is this important? Serotonin is involved in the regulation of appetite, mood, sleep and sex drive. All of these are disrupted in bulimic individuals as well as depressed individuals. Because antidepressants are quite effective in reducing bulimic symptoms, there is a hypothesized relationship between bulimia and depression. The unanswered question remains: Is bulimia an "outgrowth" of depression, or vice-versa? Future research must answer this and other questions.

Prognosis

Molly's prognosis is "guarded." She shows decent insight into her bulimic behavior and into her depression, but lacks sufficient insight into her alcohol problem. If she continues to drink, it is likely that trouble will eventually follow. It is also a sad fact that many individuals with eating disorders relapse. Molly has already done so twice within the past 5 years and psychologists need to constantly be aware of this possibility. She has never been able to control her bulimic behaviors for more than one year without binging and purging. She wants to get better and has the motivation, but until her bulimic behaviors remain under control, and more importantly until she shows more insight into her drinking behavior, her prognosis must remained guarded.

Anorexia Nervosa

The Case of Florence: Disappearing Act

Presenting Problem

Florence is a 30-year-old never married single white female who comes from a Protestant background. (Keep reading to discover her height and weight during our initial intake interview.) She lives in a major urban area and is a graduate student in English. She has no children and has an older married brother, 34, who has two children and lives 30 miles away from her. She sees him somewhat often and talks to him about two to three times per week.

Florence comes from a family of high achievers. Her father is the director of a statewide bank and her mother is a registered nurse. Florence's brother is a criminal attorney who is well known and well respected in his field. As for Florence? She decided to return to school to "find herself; I really did not like managing a supermarket chain. I needed to find something more fulfilling and being an English major seemed to be it."

Florence had previously been in treatment for anorexia nervosa. She received inpatient hospital treatment as well as outpatient and "did well, if you ask me. As I'll tell you, things took some bad turns in my life and so I'm back, trying to find out what went wrong and where and put a stop to this."

Florence made poor eye contact when we first saw her. Her eyes appeared hollowed out, and her hair was stringy. Our office thermostat was set at 73 degrees Fahrenheit but she was shivering. We noticed a very fine coat of hair on her arms when she briefly rolled up her sleeves. She was wearing long pants and a long-sleeved top and spoke very softly. Her affect was flat, but she was very pleasant during the initial intake.

Florence was feeling more and more pressure from being promoted at the supermarket chain and from her family and "I just seemed to snap right back into this nonsense. My boss found out that something was happening, since he saw how little energy I had and how good I looked. I think he was jealous, but he always said I was getting too thin. I think I look hot if you ask me. I'm a fox."

Florence's boss was getting very concerned and he consulted his supervisor who told him that Florence was endangering herself with her behavior. Florence's boss at the supermarket chain's regional headquarters finally gave her an ultimatum: Get some treatment or lose the job. Florence initially went along with the ultimatum because she did not want to lose her job. She telephoned us since she had heard through a friend that we specialized in the treatment of eating disorders and we set up an appointment for an initial evaluation.

Background Information

Florence had a rather unremarkable childhood, reaching all of her developmental milestones at the age-appropriate times in her life. Florence graduated with a B/B-minus average from high school and had a G.P.A. of 2.8 out of 4.0 from her undergraduate school. She majored in business as an undergraduate and took off six years to work in the supermarket chain, where she worked her way up to regional manager in a short period of time. Florence and her family had no history of alcohol or drug problems and no prior history of mental illness.

Florence first began to notice a change in her physical appearance at age 13. She began to gain weight, started to menstruate, and noticed that her voice began to drop. She also developed "curves, and breasts. I was tall—5 feet 8 inches—so I did not have large breasts. The boys would mock me for this, calling me flat; that really hurt. They also said I was fat, which hurt even more." In fact she was not considered overweight at all; she was 125 pounds at age 13. Her weight slowly increased as she got older and she did her best to control it, but it was to no avail. At the same time her grades began to slip somewhat. Where she had previously gotten all A's and A-minuses, she was now getting B's and B-minuses. "I also began to get a big butt, even though I exercised every day. My family had a sweet tooth and so did I. I was eating too many sweets, which is not good when you're an adolescent and the hormones are raging. I also began to start noticing the boys."

Florence, in reaction to her weight, began to cut out sweets. That was easier said than done. "I felt like the cravings at times would kill me. I was really addicted to these things. However, when I did give up the sweets, I noticed that I was not as hungry and more importantly, how my weight began to drop." Florence, like many other teenage girls in the United States, also admired actresses and models. "Karen Carpenter, Gia, Ally Sheedy, Suzanne Somers, they all stay so thin. How? I needed to find out and I wanted to be like them. I really liked the way they looked. To me they were very healthy, beautiful people. I was tall and wanted to get rid of my butt and breasts. I thought it would be easy."

So Florence exercised more and more, eventually peaking at 3 hours a day. Her grades remained at a B-minus level but the boys still did not seem to be interested. She was also eating less and less and realizing that she was losing weight faster this way. "I can't really say if, at the time, I was starving myself. I would rarely eat in front of people and I would tell my family that I was too tired from school to eat dinner. 'I'll eat later,' I would say, which was always a lie. But this technique really worked. My breasts decreased a lot, my curves vanished and my butt was gone! I was really pleased. Now I knew the boys would like me and all of the girls that hated me would now be so jealous of how great I looked."

Florence had a boyfriend at age 14 and she told me "that I'm sure he hooked up with me because I'd lost the weight. I now really looked womanly and he noticed. We really hit it off and it lasted for about one year until he broke up with me. I'm sure the reason was because I got fat again. Exercise and portion control just did not do it. So I tried something else that I'd heard about from a friend at school. She basically did not eat. She smoked cigarettes which helped to keep her weight down but I'm allergic to smoke, so I decided to try this other method. She kept a strict calorie count and would eat only on certain days and at certain times. She eventually got herself down to 90 pounds, which sounded like a good goal. I felt fat at 97 pounds."

Florence tried this starvation method and had success with it. She continued to lose weight until she reached 93 pounds. "But it was hell. Imagine going to all these parties and seeing chocolate, Cheetos, chips, burgers . . . and I really wanted to gobble all that down. I knew I couldn't because I'd really balloon up again. So I would resist and drink water all night. On occasion I would sneak a celery stick and eat that in private. No one was allowed to see me eating."

Florence also began to notice some physical changes at this lower weight. She stopped menstruating which scared her at first but eventually she began to like this idea. "It meant that once I had sex I could not get pregnant. Menstruation was also messy so I didn't have to deal with that now." Her cheeks began to hollow out similar to a chipmunk's or a squirrel's. Her eyes looked sunken, like they had moved further back in her head. She was always cold.

"That part was really weird. Here it was late May and I was wearing layers! I hated that because I wanted to really show off my figure but I was so cold I had no choice. I took my temperature because I thought at first I had a high fever!" In fact this is typical for anorectics. Because they lose so much body fat and weight, they don't retain body heat and they get chilled easily. There is a saying among some eating disorder specialists: If you see young women wearing sweaters and many layers during the summer heat, most likely they have an eating disorder.

Florence also noticed some other disturbing signs. Her hair began thinning and some of it fell out in small clumps. Her breath was quite bad. She also seemed to get a fine coat of hair on her arms and on her face. It was not noticeable unless you got really close to her and being blond and fair skinned helped to hide this. Florence also had a scary moment when she was 15.

"I was in school one day; at the time I weighed 103 pounds. I felt good but fat. I knew I needed to lose more but I wanted to do well on this next exam so I concentrated on that. I went to the bathroom and as I got up to leave I felt woozy. I figured that I got up too fast so I went ahead and headed out. I then fainted. When I came to a girl was standing over me tapping my face asking me if I was okay. I had never fainted before and it spooked me. But I threw some cold water on my face and went off to my exam." This was not the last time Florence fainted. When she fainted in front of her house she bruised her head and it bled for awhile. She then began to think something was not right.

"I had to explain the cut to my parents who were obviously worried. They had suspected that I did not eat enough and that I was too thin but they did not want to invade my space. They also figured that I was going through an adolescent girl phase and that I would snap out of it. I guess I didn't." Florence eventually went into therapy and she was then told that she suffered from anorexia nervosa. Her therapist referred her to an inpatient hospital program where she could receive proper medical care for her condition. She also was in intensive therapy in the hospital.

When she was discharged and re-entered outpatient therapy, Florence realized that she had a problem. "I had no idea who I was but whoever I was I hated it. I hated my body and my life. How the heck could I be a success when compared with my family? I'll never amount to much . . ." Florence said that therapy was successful for her and she eventually left to go to college. She did not continue with therapy there because her problem was "cured and under control. Sure I got urges to not eat and I still didn't like the way my body looked, but it was no big deal."

Florence's anorexia stayed under control until crises occurred in her life. Usually the crises centered on work or men. She had few relationships in college, preferring to study and exercise instead. The relationships she did have usually did not last too long. It was very difficult for her to eat around others, and "this did not make for good first dates. Going out to dinner, getting a pizza late at night, I couldn't deal with those things. It was not fair to constantly tempt me with these things, these evil foods that pack on the pounds." Florence had already gained 20 pounds (the "traditional freshman 15") and was horrified. "I did not stop eating. However, I instead increased my exercise regimen and worked hard to take off the weight. It was tempting to smoke or to make myself vomit, but both of those things repulsed me."

Once Florence graduated and got a job with a supermarket chain, she quickly moved into higher and higher positions. The chain came on campus for interviews and they liked the fact that Florence was very studious, quiet, and "no-nonsense." The chain wanted to expand and test some new regional product lines and Florence seemed like the perfect candidate for the position. Her research led the chain's stores in her region to post yearly profit increases and they were so pleased with her that they made her regional sales manager.

"How ironic is this? I graduate with a business degree, and a supermarket chain wants me! Food has caused me so many problems in my life and where do I end up? How nuts is that?" Interestingly, those who suffer from addictions and eating disorders will very often be employed in places where food or alcohol is central such as in a restaurant, supermarket, bar or liquor store, or a hospital. Can you guess why this might be?

Florence's anorexia problems returned once she entered graduate school. She attended school part-time due to her job and things went well at first. Soon the pressures of maintaining good grades in school and working full-time caused her to put on some more weight. The strain of the added pounds, work and school pressures, and turning 30 caused her to relapse. Her weight dropped to 93 pounds, her periods once again stopped (*amennorhea*) and all of the previous symptoms had returned. Co-workers and friends were very concerned about her.

"People had no idea what was going on. I looked fabulous again and here they thought I was very sick or I had AIDS. Wrong! I was on a great weight-loss and weight-control program that worked before."

Thought Questions

1. Cite reasons why those who have addictions and eating disorders will very often be employed in places where food is central, such as a restaurant.
2. Florence noted that she still ate and decided to "exercise her pounds off." Because of this, cite evidence why she might be suffering from anorexia nervosa. Might she be suffering from something else?
3. Most anorectics tend to be white females in developed countries such as the United States and Canada. Lately anorexia and bulimia have been seen as increasing in those countries where it was previously nonexistent. What might be the explanation(s) for this increase?
4. Florence seems to be preoccupied with her body's shape and weight. Based on this, how often does anorexia "strike" men? Discuss the reasons behind the discrepancy between men and women.

5. Based on her story and the evidence presented so far, discuss how Florence will progress in treatment.

Assessment and Evaluation

Florence came to us because of the ultimatum posed by her boss: Get help or get fired. This is illegal, but Florence decided not to press charges since her boss was "looking out for my best interests. Besides, once I'm diagnosed and in treatment, they can't touch me anyway."

Florence was initially assessed with an unstructured diagnostic interview, the EDI-2, the BDI-II, the *Thematic Apperception Test (TAT),* and was also sent to a medical doctor for a complete physical. Florence was assessed for depression and other mood disorders since lack of eating can be a symptom of such.

The TAT is what is known as a *projective test.* The psychologist Henry Murray developed it. Like other projectives, the goal is simple. The patient responds to a black and white picture that is shown to them and they must tell a story about what they see in the sketch. The psychologist will later score the results and will look for themes, such as who the hero in their story is and so on. The notion here is that the patient will *project* his/her unconscious wishes, thoughts and desires (which are assumed to be *repressed* or blocked by *ego defense mechanisms*) onto the card. The *Rorschach Inkblot Test* is another example of a projective. Projectives are helpful, especially when dealing with resistant patients or those who are in denial, typical for eating disorders.

Some interesting information arose in the interview. Florence felt like she needed to control everything in her life since she was 10 years old. She had issues with food since that time and felt that her friends and family overemphasized its importance. Family meals were always a big occasion, especially since it was somewhat rare when both parents were home for dinner at the same time. Her parents always made sure that she cleared her plate and that she stayed around for desert, which was "always a big deal. My mom loved to bake and would always have something fresh for us. It was considered rude if you refused to eat it so of course I never refused." Florence began to notice that the control issues were becoming more extreme and that she needed to somehow regain her life.

Florence's BDI-II score was 10, which indicates minimal to mild evidence of depression. Some symptoms might be there, but they are nothing to make a professional alarmed. The EDI-2 revealed more information. She was obsessed with being thin and thoughts of food occupied her daily life to the point of these thoughts becoming obsessive. Her ideal weight was initially listed as "less than what I weigh now." After discussion, she listed her ideal weight at 87 pounds; "this way I'll be as pretty and as sexy as I can be and all of my friends will be so jealous. By then the fat will finally be gone."

The next step was to see which if any disorders Florence had according to the DSM-IV-TR. Florence presented the following symptoms. See if you think they fit your image of an anorectic woman. Florence refused to maintain her minimally normal body weight for her age and height. She still denied how serious her low body weight was and continued to see herself as fat. She had not menstruated for at least four months; however, this did not disturb her. She did not purge but did, on rare occasions, binge. Does this surprise you? After all, anorectics are known for not eating at all, but Florence said that she did go on eating binges. About 50% of all anorectics binge **and** purge (APA, 2000).

One interesting feature of anorexia nervosa is that many of the people afflicted with it will keep a very close eye on their actual weights, unlike many bulimics who are petrified of stepping on the scale. Anorectics may weigh themselves often; Florence did so just before she **initially** came to my office and proudly reported a weight of **91 pounds** "which is okay, but I could still afford to lose some more. Still, not bad for a 5'9" chick." The clinician must keep as accurate a weight record as possible when dealing with eating disorders.

Does this sound like anorexia to you? All of these are DSM-IV-TR diagnostic criteria for anorexia nervosa but we still have some more information to consider such as the TAT results. Florence's stories displayed a sense of aloneness and abandonment. Her stories often told of families fighting and putting too much pressure on their children to succeed. The sun was rarely out and most tellingly, the women in her stories were never happy, either with their lives, their appearance, or their weight. Communication was poor among all people in her stories. The young women were always trying to control everything in the stories, especially their weight.

Any ideas yet as to what might be occurring with Florence? Let us look at the results of her medical doctor visit. She was asked to return to me for a follow-up visit afterwards. The doctor confirmed her weight at 92 pounds which upset Florence since she had gained another pound. Florence had a body temperature of 96.3 degrees Fahrenheit, had cold intolerance, had cold extremities (hands and feet), reported fatigue and episodes of dizziness, constipation, periodic vomiting, and shortness of breath. Her hair was thinning, and a coating of fine body hair was noticed on her extremities (known as *lanugo*). The doctor diagnosed her as having anorexia nervosa since these are all physical symptoms of this disorder and recommended hospitalization for her. Florence reluctantly agreed and called me from the doctor's office to tell me that he was checking her in immediately. Note that in today's medical situations getting a bed rapidly is not an easy task. Fortunately the doctor was able to convey the urgency of her situation and she was hospitalized that afternoon.

Florence was not happy with the results but realized that her job depended on it. "The doc also really scared me for the first time in my life. He mentioned that I was dangerously underweight and that if I did not get immediate medical assistance I might go into cardiac arrest. I'm not sure if I believe that, but is having the perfect body worth dying for? I don't really think so. . . ."

It is standard practice for some clinicians to make sure that their patients have a complete physical before treatment commences for a number of reasons. First, psychological problems can at times mimic, or mask, physical problems. Second, most clinicians are not qualified to make medical diagnoses; if they are, they may not possess the proper equipment to confirm hypotheses. Third, if a physical condition is present and needs immediate treatment, it is unethical (and dangerous) for a clinician to proceed with therapy while a condition remains untreated. There is a risk that once discharged from the hospital the patient may decide not to return to therapy. This is of course their choice, but this is also a risk inherent in a referral.

In sum, Florence received the following <u>DSM-IV-TR</u> diagnosis upon admission to the hospital:

Anorexia Nervosa, Restricting Type   307.1

Theoretical Etiologies

Before we begin to examine some possible etiologies, researchers agree that the specific causes of anorexia nervosa are not yet known. We do know that cognitive factors, personality factors, and environmental factors all seem to contribute to anorexia nervosa. One common trait among anorectics is that they tend to be perfectionistic and have obsessive-compulsive tendencies. They tend to strive for high achievement and come from high achieving backgrounds. Research has also discovered that anorectic women tend to also suffer from depression, although this may not be a function of the anorexia itself since depression seems to dissipate once the woman is in recovery and is making progress.

Control issues also seem to be prevalent among anorectics. The lack of eating (perhaps this is a type of highly restrictive diet) can be viewed as a way to gain control over their lives and as a way to gain a sense of independence. The anorectic may feel that her weight, and thus her appearance, is the only thing that she can control without parental or other outside influence or interference.

Body dissatisfaction is a key factor in both bulimia nervosa and anorexia nervosa. However, the anorectic is much more concerned with her appearance and is totally dissatisfied with her body shape to point of pathology. In other words, she will continue to starve herself even when her weight is dangerously low "just to lose a bit more" and to appear ever thinner. This can also be seen as culture specific, since most Westernized countries (like the United States) place a very high value on a reed thin body. It has come to the point where Hollywood and fashion designers consider a size 8 to be too large.

Psychodynamic perspectives on anorexia tend to be antiquated but still warrant mention. Hilda Bruch (2001), a well-known author who examined anorexia nervosa, states that girls with anorexia nervosa may have problems separating from their families, and they also may have difficulty establishing an identity separate from their family. An interesting perspective views anorexia as the girl's desire to remain just that—a prepubescent girl. Once the weight loss becomes severe, the girl may stop menstruating. Her breast size will decrease (since breasts are mainly fat tissue), as will her hips. Psychodynamic theorists may see these girls as avoiding adulthood and its responsibilities and independence through anorexia nervosa. One researcher hypothesized that anorectic girls may be engaged in a slow form of suicide, slowly disappearing and wasting away (Getzfeld, 1999). The desire to remain a child appears to be strong, according to this viewpoint.

Learning theorists view anorexia nervosa in a simpler fashion. The chronic weight loss is reinforced by society's demands for reedy women and young girls. If an anorectic is complemented on her thin appearance, this will reinforce her starvation and the cycle will continue. She is "punished" by society when she gains weight and is not noticed, or is criticized by significant others for her weight (including her family and friends and, of course, herself). Anorexia can be viewed as a weight phobia in this respect.

Finally, we will examine familial factors. Like many of the disorders in this casebook, eating disorders tend to run in families and thus **may** have a genetic component (Strober, Freeman, Lampert, Diamond, & Kaye, 2000; Hudson, Pope, Jonas, & Yurgelun-Todd, 1983). Female relatives are affected more so than are male relatives. Hsu (1990) hypothesizes that certain traits such as poor impulse control and emotional instability might be inherited. In other words, the tendency to react poorly to stressful situations and having poor coping skills might be inherited, thus leading to poor coping mechanisms such as an eating disorder. The vulnerability is inherited.

In sum, anorexia nervosa's cause(s) remain somewhat of a mystery for the research community and more research is needed before we can definitively state what these cause(s) might be.

Treatment Plan

The initial goal here should be evident: Florence needed to be hospitalized so that she could return to a safe weight. The medical doctor and I agreed on this point; fortunately, Florence also agreed to voluntarily go to the hospital. She had been hospitalized as an inpatient before and the results were successful but "I need to learn how to keep this under control for good, and how to deal with stress. I know now that my anorexia cannot be cured," she stated in our first session after hospitalization. So we have now established that Florence needs to be hospitalized. What happens when an anorectic goes into inpatient treatment?

The first goal is to restore Florence's weight and normalize her eating patterns, which should lead to the return and normalization of menstruation and ovulation. A healthy goal weight is often linked to the return of normal menstruation and ovulation (APA, 2000). The weight gain needs to be gradual (about two to three pounds per week) for a number of reasons. First, rapid weight gain could backfire and the anorectic might drop out of inpatient. The body, in general, also cannot physically tolerate rapid weight gain when it is significantly underweight. For example, constipation, bloating and abdominal pain might occur as the weight returns (APA, 2000). Finally, rapid refeeding can lead to cardiac arrest. In some instances the *denial* is so strong that the anorectic needs to be "force-fed." Experts in eating disorders do not have reliable data on how long an anorectic should remain hospitalized. In Florence's case 28 days had not been successful in the past. This time she remained for 30 days before discharge, at which time she weighed 116 pounds and was eating normally.

From this point on (once she is out of any extreme physical danger) treatment becomes "multimodal," i.e, many different approaches are used. We have already used the medical approach. Florence was placed on a specialized weight gain program. Many times this is paired with behavioral treatment where rewards are contingent on staying on the refeeding and weight gain program. This is most effective in an inpatient hospital setting. The rewards might be visits from family and friends, social rewards (television, games and such), or perhaps a day pass to go out of the hospital.

Cognitive interventions focus on replacing the negative thoughts that continue the anorexia nervosa. For example, the anorectic might think, "I can still lose more weight. Look at me, I'm repulsively fat." The psychologist would attempt to replace these thoughts with positive thoughts that emphasize health, healthy eating, and a positive outlook. For example, "Let's look at what would constitute a healthy dinner that would not lead to excessive weight gain." The psychologist would also attempt to get the patient to focus on the non-physical aspects of herself and to emphasize those aspects.

As you will soon read, family therapy appears to be one of the more successful treatment modalities for anorexia nervosa. Family therapy seems to be most successful with young girls who have not had anorexia nervosa for a lengthy period of time. Mealtimes and thoughts about food and weight are presumed to be dysfunctional within the anorectic's family and are focused upon in treatment. Family attitudes towards body shape are also discussed. Any underlying conflicts will be discussed as well.

Florence was involved in group and family therapy while in the hospital, as well as daily individual therapy. "I was therapied out! The hardest part was going to the groups and doing the family things. You think of how bad your behaviors are and then you hear the other girls . . . it really opens your eyes." Her family was surprisingly cooperative and came to all of the family sessions.

Florence's parents also realized how much pressure they placed on her. They had always hoped that she would become an attorney or a doctor, and when she made great strides in her workplace, they were proud but subdued, like "they were disappointed in me." Her father was quite proud but was never sure how to express this. "My mom seemed to favor my brother because he was married and was a professional. She didn't have a lot to say in some of the sessions, which led me to believe that I was right." Her father "told me for the first time how proud he was of me to go back to school, become a regional manager, and most of all to admit that I have a problem that needs to be taken care of. That made me cry . . . and him too." One of the goals of family therapy is to open up communication among family members no matter how painful this might be. Communication problems are often at the root of many interpersonal problems and this was the case here as well. Typically anorectics will have poor interpersonal relationships, in part because food issues rule and control their lives.

Group treatment for anorectics has a mixed success rate. Anorectics are secretive and placing them in a group therapy situation with other anorectics is risky. They may not say anything, they may be jealous when they see other women who are thinner and thus may drop out of treatment. Florence said she felt threatened in the group because her family was coming to sessions while some of the other families were not. She also felt self-conscious because she was one of the heavier women in the group and "it made me look at myself more, questioning why I'm here."

Florence reported the most progress with individual treatment. "I liked the one-on-one idea, I felt the most comfortable and I could open up without fear of being criticized." Some important information arose here as well. Florence never wanted to be an attorney or a doctor. She also did not have a desire right now to get married and especially to have children. The idea of children scared her and, to a degree, so did men. "I guess I've always been afraid of relationships, letting myself go, falling in love and stuff. It's scary to let someone else into your life and head. I can control food and my weight, although it's now at the point where it controls me, which is not good. At times I wanted to revert back to being a little girl when life was not so complex; at other times I just wanted to vanish . . . but not die! Just be invisible for awhile, you know?"

Freud and others would say that there is a reason many anorectics do not want to have children. In effect they are *regressing* once they contract anorexia. They lose weight and thus lose their curves and breasts, amennorhea occurs and in effect they physically appear, and physiologically become, pre-pubescent. Freud might also say that anorectic women have unresolved *Electra Complexes*, leading to disruptive relationships with their fathers. Indeed, Florence's father was always pressuring her, leading her to "shut him out" and not listen to him. "He tried to control my life, career and social life; I needed to control something before I could move out. I couldn't run away, so I turned to food for comfort and then for control."

Once Florence's weight and eating stabilized, she was discharged from the hospital with diagnoses identical to those at admission. She then called me back and we began individual therapy. We examined control issues, identity issues, and interpersonal concerns. Florence was not only afraid of men, she was afraid of having orgasms either with a man or on her own. "I won't let go, won't give anyone else that control over my life. I always need to be in control."

Eventually Florence returned to a more reasonable 128 pounds. She continued in individual therapy with me and saw her medical doctor once a month for maintenance monitoring. I also sent her to get a psychiatric evaluation to detect the presence of any other mental disorders and to see if the psychiatrist thought she needed any medications. She reported no concerns other than Florence's anorexia, and deemed no medications necessary at the present time.

We discussed family therapy and Florence realized how that needed to continue outside of her hospital stay. She agreed to try this "later on; I need to focus on me and only me right now. I've come too far and realize that I've got a very serious problem."

Florence was also referred to the *American Anorexia Bulimia Association (AABA)* (**http://www.aabcinc.org**), a national nonprofit organization. They offer support groups and information for individuals suffering from eating disorders. Florence liked this referral because "I decide what to do in treatment, not some doctor! Gee whiz, it's the control thing again." Typically many therapists who work with eating disorder patients and substance use disorders will make referrals to self-help groups like AABA and *Alcoholics Anonymous (AA)*. These are not therapy groups but are support groups, run by fellow sufferers. There are no membership fees or costs, and the proceedings are anonymous.

Florence continued in treatment for one year with all of her helping professionals. Finally she felt confident enough to terminate treatment, and all of her therapists agreed. Her weight and eating had remained stable ("I had one relapse but you guys all caught it in time"), she felt more comfortable with her body, and she was now effectively communicating with her family. She returned to work and received a nice bonus and raise at year's end, and had started to date again "but just casually for now." We all told her that if she needed to ever return we would all be available. After her final session, that was the last time any of us had heard from Florence.

Most professionals agree that *psychotropic* medications should not be used in the treatment of anorexia nervosa. There are several reasons for this. First, because anorectics are severely underweight and malnourished, side effects of medications may be more pronounced and this can lead to significant complications and non-compliance. For example, tricyclic antidepressants may lead to heart arrhythmias, which can potentially lead to cardiac arrest. Additionally, many anorectics do not respond much if at all to many psychotropic medications. There is also the possibility that many medications may lead to weight gain. This is of course a desired result, but only for the clinicians, not the anorectic! Thus, she might go off of the medications or drop out of treatment all together. Finally, the research on the usage of psychotropic medications with anorectics points to the relative lack of efficacy of many classes of these drugs.

If medications are prescribed, they are typically prescribed for two reasons: To maintain the weight and normal eating behaviors once these have been restored, and to treat any psychiatric symptoms or conditions **other** than anorexia nervosa. But again, many medications fail to show much success with maintaining the anorectic's weight and/or normal eating behaviors. The general rule of psychotropic medications applies here: If there is little clinical efficacy with certain medications, do not prescribe them, if for no other reason than to eliminate adding side-effect reactions to the other issues involving the patient. Thus, in Florence's case, she was not on any psychotropic medications while she was in treatment with the "treatment team."

Prognosis

Florence's prognosis remains "fair." Why does she not have a more positive prognosis? Let us examine some reasons for this. With any eating disorders, the possibility of relapse is high no matter how successful the treatment, patient's compliance, and lack of denial. Unfortunately we can never say that an eating disorder is cured; we can only say that it is in remission. This means that, similar to cancer, there is always a chance that the condition can recur. Substance dependence is similar. Because of this, Florence always needs to be alert to possible relapses occurring. As you saw, while she was in treatment with us she relapsed once.

Many anorectics have difficulty resolving their control and food issues. Since food is crucial in life as well as in social and in business situations, the temptations to return to anorectic behaviors will be present every day. Control issues also surface every day. Thus, anorectics cannot "hide" from those things that cause them problems. If they are feeling vulnerable, these "cues" can set off their anorectic behaviors.

Finally, if an anorectic has relapsed in the past, in general she is more likely to have another relapse. Once a certain behavior occurs, most people are more likely to repeat it, especially those suffering from mental illnesses. Sadly, Florence falls into this category and a more positive prognosis cannot be given to her at this time.

Review and Study Questions

Molly

1. Review the DSM-IV-TR diagnostic criteria for bulimia nervosa. List some differential diagnoses for Molly.

2. Molly seemed to have a problem with alcohol. Why did the psychologist choose instead to focus on her bulimia and not on her alcohol usage?

3. Discuss the reasons why the psychologist used the technique of "getting her more active" to help Molly deal with some of her issues.

4. Molly was taking Prozac, which proved quite helpful in treating her bulimia. Discuss the positives and negatives of prescribing an antidepressant for the treatment of bulimia nervosa.

5. Discuss the reasons why Molly's family slowly dropped out of therapy.

6. Molly reportedly made a suicide attempt with multivitamins but only intended to "hurt" herself. Do you believe her? Why or why not?

7. Is it unusual that Molly felt more comfortable with a male psychologist than a female, based on her presenting problem(s)?

8. How important is the fact that Molly was sexually molested when she was 12? That is, were these incidents a major reason for her to become bulimic and depressed and if so, why?

Florence

1. Florence had some episodes of binge eating. Explain the reasons, based on the <u>DSM-IV-TR</u> diagnostic criteria and the information supplied, why or why not Florence should (or should not) be diagnosed with bulimia nervosa.

2. Florence comes from a white, upper-class, professional background. Explain whether most anorectics come from this socioeconomic class and racial background or not, and give some possible reasons for this.

3. Eating disorders appear to be as prevalent in other countries around the world (for example, in China, Japan, African countries, Brazil) as in the United States. Cite evidence either supporting or disproving this assertion.

4. Florence talked about models' bodies being ideals. How much does culture contribute to anorexia and bulimia? Genes and biology? Racial background? Ethnic background?

5. Why do anorectics always see themselves as fat even when they are stick thin?

6. Do you agree with the clinicians to NOT use medications with Florence?

Key Terms to Know

eating disorders

bulimia nervosa

binge

purge

Eating Disorder Inventory-2 (EDI-2)

Beck Depression Inventory II (BDI-II)

unstructured diagnostic interview

structured diagnostic interview

Major Depressive Disorder

eating diary

Prozac (fluoxetine)

Selective Serotonin Reuptake Inhibitor (SSRI)

Valium (diazepam)

Xanax (alprazolam)

serotonin

Zoloft (sertraline)

Paxil (paroxetine)

Monoamine Oxidase Inhibitors (MAOIs)

Nardil (phenelzine)

Parnate (tranylcypromine)

tyramine

amennorhea

anorexia nervosa

lanugo

Thematic Apperception Test (TAT)

projective test

projection

regression

repression

ego defense mechanisms

Rorschach Inkblot Test

denial

American Anorexia Bulimia Association (AABA)

Alcoholics Anonymous (AA)

psychotropic

Electra Complex

flat affect

black out

libido

open-ended

binging

purging

behaviorial contract

blackouts

comorbidity

antipsychotic medications

schizophrenic disorder

antianxiety medications

tricyclic antidepressants

Norpramine (desipramine)

Chapter 7

Sexual and Gender Identity Disorders

Sexual disorders confuse many people when they first see the term. Why is that? Many people think that sexual disorders refer only to *male erectile disorder (impotence)*, *premature ejaculation*, or *female orgasmic disorder* (incorrectly known as *female frigidity*). The prevalence rates of Sexual and Gender Identity Disorders range from 3% for those suffering from *male dyspareunia* (painful male intercourse) to 33% for *female hypoactive sexual desire disorder* (This has also been referred to as female frigidity) (APA, 2000). In many cases sexual disorders have psychological origins and are oftentimes best treated by using *behavioral modification techniques*. However, as you will see, it is mandatory for psychologists to ensure that these patients receive a complete physical evaluation before making a definitive diagnosis.

Sexual and Gender Identity Disorders fall into four categories in the <u>DSM-IV-TR</u>: *Sexual Dysfunctions*, whose key characteristic is a disturbance in sexual desire; *Paraphilias*, generally known as *fetishes* (characterized by sexual urges that involve unusual objects or activities); *Gender Identity Disorders*, occurring when the patient is uncomfortable with their assigned sex and; *Sexual Disorder Not Otherwise Specified (NOS)* (APA, 2000, p. 535).

We will first examine Solomon, who exhibits a difficult, yet sadly somewhat common, problem. Read his case carefully before you assess what might be occurring with him. We will conclude with Emily, whose difficulty has created significant problems in her relationships and has led her to contemplate some difficult decisions in her life.

Pedophilia

The Case of Solomon: A Long-Standing Problem

Presenting Problem

Solomon is a 42-year-old black Jamaican male who has been in the United States for 3 years. Solomon was married for 5 years while he lived in Jamaica but "it didn't work out. I left to make some money, she didn't come with me, and so we broke up." Solomon had no children with his ex-wife. When Solomon came to the United States, he quickly found work as a sheet welder. "It pays me good money. I do construction work, but this is good enough. It's what I like to do, but not what I'm best at doing." Solomon worked the morning shift, and on occasion would work the afternoon shift.

Solomon appeared at our clinic one afternoon. Since the clinic's population consisted mainly of *mandatory clients* (those who had to attend sessions), the fact that Solomon, initially, was voluntary surprised us. We soon learned that he was not entirely here of his own volition.

"Okay, here's what happened, so they say. As I told them, I watch Mandy's daughter a lot (Mandy is his girlfriend). We do a lot together. Mandy and I live near each other, about 15 minutes away. Her daughter stays with me a lot; she stays over some nights as well. We play games. I really love her daughter. I have a Playstation, which she really loves. In my apartment building the toilets are in the hall. I always go with her to the toilet because my building is not that safe, especially in the halls for little girls. When she finishes on the toilet I clean her up. I always have done this for her since she was trained, ever since I've known Mandy. The next morning Mandy said that my finger entered her daughter's vagina while I was cleaning her up; she accused me of this! We weren't fighting or anything. What is she, crazy? I have no idea where this came from. This is crap."

"She told the police that morning that this happened, and they came and arrested me. I was charged with child molestation. I have never done anything wrong, ever. I still can't believe all of this. So that is why I am here. Now you know. And I need to know."

Solomon was dressed very casually. He was wearing a gray T-shirt and overalls ("my work uniform"), Timberland boots, a checkered hat, and he had a huge tool belt on when he first appeared at the clinic. Solomon made good eye contact and displayed a somewhat flat affect. He was a very pleasant individual even when he was angry, and freely answered all of our questions. Solomon appeared very nervous at first, constantly playing with his tool belt and exhaling loudly very often. As the sessions progressed he relaxed and sat with a more open posture. Solomon's eyes were very red and we made note of that. (This was not from crying, since his eyes were red in each session.)

Background Information

Solomon's developmental, physical, and psychological histories are unremarkable. He reached all of his milestones at age-appropriate times. More importantly, he had never had any legal difficulties before coming to the clinic. "I have few friends. There are many Jamaicans in the community and I hang with them sometimes but I spend a lot of time alone. It's just me. These guys like to party a lot, do drugs and things. They're also younger than I am. I really don't know anyone close to my age."

Solomon's first sexual experience occurred at age 16. "I really didn't want to, but my friends had all done it, so it was time for me if I wanted to still hang with them. We were really drunk. It was over fast and wasn't enjoyable for either of us. We had sex on the beach, which was the only nice thing about it! We both wanted it over with."

Solomon dropped out of school in the ninth grade to work on job sites in Jamaica. "My dad left us when I was very young, and my mom could not support all of us. I made the choice to stop school and bring in dollars. I could have followed my friends and gotten involved with drugs and crime, but I was raised right by her. I lied about my age and made nice dollars in construction. Jamaica was getting more tourists, so hotels and condos were going up. Someone needed to build them!"

Solomon is the youngest of four children. "My brothers and sisters? Not real good. My oldest brother, Samuel, is 53 and has been in jail for a drug-related murder. My father was around for him and hated him. Samuel was always cursed at, called horrible things. He never got married. One day he was in a deal gone bad. He said he was innocent, but all I know is that someone ended up dead. Samuel was identified and he's still locked up. Thank God he never got married or had kids. My mom still thinks he's innocent but she doubts she'll be alive when he goes free."

"I have two sisters, Sarah and Alison. Sarah is 48 and married, has three kids and is a drunk! She's always wasted! It's really disgusting. She lets her husband do everything; he takes care of everything while she sits at home and drinks rum all day long. She also eats a lot, so she's really fat as well. Her kids have all moved away or to the States, and she hears from them time to time. I don't really know what's going on with them, since I've got my own stuff."

"Now Alison. She's the star. She manages a hotel in Jamaica and got that position quickly. She's the only one of us who finished school, and she's as smart as a whip. She's 44 and is a real doll. Her marriage ended because her husband didn't like to compete with her work. They had no kids. Alison still works today and really has no problems. We talk about once a week or more."

Solomon has been seeing his girlfriend Amanda (Mandy) for two years. "We met at a park near my apartment. I was reading my book, keeping to myself. I saw Mandy and she was gorgeous. I got up the nerve to go over and talk to her. I had seen her in the park for a few weeks and watched to see if she was married or had a boyfriend. She never met any guys there and she was available, so after we talked for awhile I asked her to have coffee with me, then it led to dinner, and shortly after that, 2 years go by! We get along really well, or so I thought. She's a receptionist and really likes her job. Her boss loves her."

Mandy's daughter is 4 years old. "Mandy was never married, but her ex-boyfriend got her pregnant and she kept the baby. Her daughter is a joy and a doll. I take care of her often. I get her at daycare, take her to the park, all kinds of things. She really loves getting Happy Meals with me, and since I get out of work early, we can have a lot of time together before Mandy gets home."

More information will follow in a moment, after this brief pause.

Thought Questions

1. Were you surprised as to why Solomon came to the clinic? Why or why not?
2. Does this seem like a case of pedophilia to you? What would you expect a pedophilia case to entail?
3. How important is Solomon's family history in this situation?
4. What key pieces of information do the psychologists need before they can properly diagnose Solomon?
5. Consider, and justify, why you would or would not bring in Mandy and her daughter.

Assessment and Evaluation

Solomon's assessment had a multifaceted approach. He was referred to our psychiatrist for an evaluation. Additionally, an independent psychiatrist at the state psychiatric prison evaluated Solomon, at his lawyer's request. Solomon's lawyer approved this psychiatrist, and we used his evaluation in our diagnostic and treatment determinations. Finally, we used an *unstructured diagnostic interview* with Solomon.

Solomon's lawyer wanted an evaluation completed and treatment to be ongoing before Solomon's trial date came up. There was a significant additional problem. Because of Solomon's pending court date, we were unable to bring in Mandy or her daughter. This caused considerable problems, since we were missing key pieces of the story. We wanted to get the information firsthand, but Mandy refused to come in and, of course, we could not force her. Regardless, Mandy's lawyer also told her not to contact us and not to speak with us. Solomon's lawyer did not want Mandy to come in, believing that our contact with her would bias our opinions of Solomon and his situation. What would you do in this situation? Is it possible to make an informed decision based on one point of view?

As we continued to speak with Solomon, more information arose. "I was drinking heavily that night, I admit it. It's not something I usually do, but I hurt my back earlier that day at work and I was in major pain. Some co-workers asked me to go out with them and so I did. I drank a lot. I don't really remember how much, but it was quite a lot over a few hours, then I headed home on the bus. I did the usual thing after that with Mandy's daughter. I put her to bed as I usually do on a Thursday night, since Mandy works that night for extra bucks. I have no idea what Mandy's talking about, saying that I sexually assaulted her daughter. What B.S.! My record is clean. I also have a perfect work record: no violations, never late, never out sick. Check it out."

We did indeed check this out with Solomon's boss. We first needed to obtain *a release of information form* from Solomon; this gave us permission to contact his boss. We also obtained a release to talk to the police. What did we discover?

That Solomon indeed was being truthful with us. His boss told us that his work record was exemplary. In fact, "Solomon is one our best and hardest workers. We have to fire many people, but Solomon works very hard every single day. In this day and age that's nice to see, since he doesn't make a ton of money for his work." The police and Solomon's lawyer told us that he has had no prior legal difficulties except for two parking tickets. Solomon also had no past history of psychiatric or psychological treatment. What, then, is going on?

We questioned Solomon further, armed with some new information from these outside sources. See if his responses help to clear up this apparently muddled picture. "My lawyer sent me to this clinic to try to find out what actually occurred that night with Mandy's daughter. Yes, I guess I was drunk, or at least had a lot to drink. My lawyer thought that you should look at me and see if I'm a drunk, which I'm not. He also wanted you to evaluate me, which is fine. I can take that. There is more."

"Mandy was also quite drunk that night; she could barely walk up the stairs and she slurred her words. She later told me that she was 'waiting for a chance to get back at me' for my unfaithfulness. What did that mean? I don't know. Was I unfaithful? Depends who you ask and what you mean by that. Did I have sex with someone else? Not at all. Did I have dinner with other women? Yes, but what's wrong with that? Mandy thinks I'm a gigolo, which is nuts. My pants stayed on the entire time. I only have eyes for her, but I have a few female friends from the island that I chat up. I would never do anything to hurt her daughter. What the hell kind of pleasure would I get doing things to a 4-year-old? Mandy is totally nuts."

During our sessions, Solomon seemed *competent* (aware of the pending charges against him and aware of the consequences of his actions) and was deemed able to progress in therapy. He was totally cooperative and always very pleasant with us. Solomon was sent to see our consulting psychiatrist for an evaluation. His report, in sum: "Solomon has a lot of pent-up anger and emotion to be discussed in therapy. Pt. (Patient) shows signs of alcohol dependence, tolerance, and loss of control. Possible ocular (eye) damage because of alcohol usage. Pt. denies sexually molesting/sexually touching child. Pt. says has been cleaning her this way for 2 years now; she requests it and he wants to watch her in 'dangerous halls in the building.' Finger may have entered vagina or anus of girl by accident in past; pt. unsure and states his memory is unclear on this. Denies sexual thoughts involving girl, children or minors. Denies pleasure from cleaning child while toileting. Preliminary diagnostic impressions:

Alcohol Dependence	303.90
Pedophilia, Sexually Attracted to Females	302.2

Rec (Recommendations): Weekly individual sessions to work on alcohol dependence. Work to R/O (rule out) pedophilia. Re-evaluate prn (as needed).

The psychiatric evaluation was important. The psychiatrist told us that the evidence was unclear as to whether Solomon could be diagnosed with pedophilia. He also told us that it was the clinic's responsibility to rule out pedophilia to the best of our ability, and he mentioned that we needed to gather more information.

When Solomon returned to his next session he made some more interesting statements. He made it clear to us that "I would never harm Mandy or anyone. I'm not that type of guy. I worked too hard and too long to get to where I am, and I would never hurt Mandy. Sure, we've had fights, but nothing physical. But I have fantasized about getting revenge because of what she did here. She's trying to ruin my life."

Solomon agreed to follow all of the treatment protocols deemed necessary by the clinic. This is not surprising since his lawyer specifically told us that if he did not he would have gone to jail until his hearing. Sometimes the fear of incarceration is the best treatment motivator, but treatment might not be taken seriously. The goal of entering and maintaining treatment is to stay out of jail or prison, not to examine issues and to make progress.

Solomon, most importantly, was willing to examine his drinking patterns. He attended *Alcoholics Anonymous (AA)* meetings three times a week and produced an attendance sheet for us. He remained sober the entire time he was in treatment with us. He continued to work since he was not yet convicted of any crime. He stayed away from Mandy and, naturally, still harbored resentment towards her, which was discussed in therapy.

The clinic supervisor was told of Solomon's progress and hard work in therapy. He met with the clinic staff and told them he had "no problem with continuing outpatient treatment at the present time. Solomon's case needs to be evaluated on a constant basis for everyone's protection." Solomon also told us a bit more about his family background, which gave us a clearer picture of his situation.

"I told you my dad left when I was young. I came to the USA to make a living for myself. I send a lot of my money home to my mother, who is quite ill. I want to move her here but it's too expensive for me right now. No one else is helping out like I am right now. My dad gives nothing to my family, nothing. I was hoping to marry Mandy so I'd have a stepdaughter but after this, she's lucky I don't do something terrible to her. I tell you, I never hurt a woman or a child in my life. I see my sisters' kids and I never mistreat them. I don't understand any of this."

We asked Solomon about his use of alcohol and other drugs and got some surprising information. "Yes, there are a few times I drink way too much. I get drunk, but I always take the bus home. You see, I'm worried about my mom and I'm homesick. I miss the island and the people and my friends. It's been awhile since I've gone home, so it's hard on me. I drink to forget, and it's gotten a bit worse lately. Sometimes I can't stop it. The problems with Mandy haven't helped me, like the problems with my mom's health. It's not real good right now, except for work. I never used drugs and never will. First, if I do I'll get deported and fired. Second I'll end up in jail. A Jamaican caught using drugs? You know how that will end up, for sure."

Solomon's situation was discussed extensively in a *case conference* along with the psychiatrist's views. Based on all of the information gathered, we made the following diagnoses which agreed with the clinic's psychiatrist:

Alcohol Dependence	303.90
Pedophilia, Sexually Attracted to Females	302.2

Theoretical Etiologies

In order for someone to be diagnosed with pedophilia, the sexually arousing fantasies (about young boys, girls or both), or sexual behaviors (involving young boys, girls, or both), must be recurrent for at least 6 months. This is not entirely the situation with Solomon and is unclear. Solomon denies that he has any sexual fantasies towards Mandy's daughter. He stated this often in treatment and vehemently denied this to the psychiatrist. His lawyer told us these thoughts never occur to Solomon, and the lawyer's handpicked psychiatrist supported him. However, it is troubling that Solomon still cleans Mandy's 4-year-old daughter after she is finished toileting. All Solomon would tell us is that this is normal for her and has gone on since he has been with Mandy (two years). He also mentioned that his finger may have "accidentally" entered the girl's anus or vagina while cleaning her. We asked Solomon about this statement and he said accidents can happen. "She's a mobile little thing; she won't sit still a lot. Accidents happen. If this is so bad, how come no one said anything before now?"

As you can see, without any refuting evidence, and with only one viewpoint, it is very difficult to state with certainty that Solomon warrants a pedophilia diagnosis. While these incidents are indeed troublesome (if you believe what you have read, and what will follow), this is not enough.

Pedophiles are not the typical "dirty old men in raincoats" who hang around playgrounds and school yards. In fact, they tend to be in their 30s or 40s, tend to not have broken the law, and tend to be respected in their communities and in the workplace. They tend to know their victims, either through friends of the family or through relatives. The behaviors usually begin when the child is young and continue until the pedophile is discovered or until the relationship ends for whatever reason(s). A crucial fact is that not all child molesters have pedophilia.

Tracing and discovering the origins of pedophilia leads to a lot of "dead ends," specifically because we are not certain what causes pedophilia and most of the other paraphilias. One theory that has support is that those with paraphelias do not develop adequate social relationships. These individuals are unable to develop appropriate social relationships with appropriate people. Therefore, they attempt to develop sexual relationships with the same people. Thus, this **seems** to be associated with developing inappropriate sexual relationships (Marshall, 1997).

The behavioral perspective also has some merit and is quite interesting. This perspective states that the nature of the individual's **early** sexual fantasies is involved. For example, if the individual associates sexual arousal with leather or latex, these neutral substances will now take on a reinforcing value if these objects were repeatedly presented while the person was aroused. Researchers have generalized this concept. Early sexual fantasies (sex with little girls) may be paired with the sexual arousal caused by masturbation. Thus, the arousal and possible orgasm is associated with the fantasies, and the arousal and orgasm reinforces the fantasies, so they continue.

David Barlow (2002), the well-known psychopathologist and researcher, has recently posed an interesting etiology. He hypothesizes that many individuals with a paraphelia have an uncommonly high sex drive. For example, some of these men may masturbate as often as four times a day. Based on these data, he hypothesized that this may border on an obsession and may be related to Obsessive-Compulsive Disorder (OCD). Therefore, the act of trying to suppress this obsession may in fact increase their intensity and frequency. This is a relatively new concept that warrants further research.

One final viewpoint sees these men as being sexually abused in childhood, which is not uncommon. The men may now attempt to reverse the situation. Whereas before they felt humiliated and subversive, they now sexually abuse children to achieve this sense of power, dominance, and control.

In sum, what can we say about the etiology of pedophilia and the other paraphilias? Unfortunately, not a lot. Research on the paraphilias is difficult to conduct for many reasons. (As you will soon see, this also leads to problems in finding very effective treatment modalities.) People with paraphilias rarely seek professional help. This is one reason why Solomon's "voluntary" appearance surprised the clinic's staff. Because of this, most of the data we have are based on single case study designs, which have significant methodological flaws. Research performed without control groups or control subjects leads to results that are empirically difficult to support. Generally speaking, the interactionist perspective, seeing the paraphilias as a combination of heredity, biology, and environment, seems to hold the most promise.

Treatment Plan

The treatment goals here are simple. First, the clinic decided to keep Solomon in *individual sessions* to treat his Alcohol Dependence. We also needed to *rule out* the pedophilia diagnosis if possible. First we concentrated on Solomon's alcohol use. He began Alcoholics Anonymous (AA) meetings at his lawyer's request and he liked them. "They're a good group of people at the meetings. I know some of them from work and from the apartment building. The sessions have really made me look at myself and at my drinking. I can see how my drinking led to problems in my life, how it began to control me, how I was headed down a dark road. The meetings are also spiritual, which is something I stopped when I came to the USA. I started going to church to help me find some direction and guidance in my relationships. And as I told you and tell you every week, I haven't touched a drop since the arrest. My lawyer told me and you told me, and I listened. At first I was really mad, treating me like a child. But I'm grateful now. It was causing me bad problems. Bad problems."

Solomon told us that he began his sobriety the day he entered therapy, and he did little in the sessions to disprove this. We trusted him on his assertions; the clinic had a *Breathalyzer* just in case we needed it. Solomon's boss was also asked about his drinking, and he told us that "after work Solomon goes to his meetings or goes home. We're very worried about him, so I have some of the guys keep tabs on him, you know, to make sure he stays straight. He IS a decent guy." We were, quite frankly, amazed at the boss' compassion and concern for Solomon, since he had previously told us that he has fired many workers in the past for minor errors and indiscretions.

Pedophilia was the second concern. The key aspect here was the first DSM-IV-TR (APA, 2000) diagnostic criterion for pedophilia: The behavior must be recurrent over a period of 6 months. Solomon mentioned once that the behaviors in question may have occurred prior to the incident bringing him into the clinic. As to the frequency and the motives behind the other incidents, the clinic staff was uncertain and needed more information. Solomon refused to discuss the incident while his case was pending on his lawyer's advice. Mandy and her daughter were also being questioned by court-appointed psychologists and psychiatrists. We also noted that Solomon and, he said, Mandy, were quite drunk when the incident leading to his arrest occurred.

As the sessions progressed, Solomon's hearing grew closer. Solomon made significant progress in discussing his drinking behavior, his shyness and social isolation, and his bad history with Mandy. Solomon realized that "I need to dump Mandy, for sure. She's bad news and will ruin my life. My mom told me to dump her, as did my sisters. Even my boss told me this. Everyone tells me the same thing, so I'd better do it. She's evil and a liar."

We questioned Solomon extensively about his sexual predilections, and we discovered no aberrations. "I like grown women, and that's it. I don't use pornos, but I do read *Playboy*. Other than that, I'm a very straight, conservative man. I would never lay a finger on any child, ever, sexually or otherwise to hurt her." Solomon's court date grew closer, and his lawyer received some information from Mandy's lawyer regarding her daughter. We will consider this information in a while.

Once the sessions began, Solomon cut all communication with Mandy and her daughter "and I really don't miss it. I miss her daughter, sure, but not Mandy so much. And since I can't see Mandy, I'll lose her daughter. I need to, or else I'm dog meat. I see how angry Mandy got me all of the time. I could only focus on her, and have no female friends. It's hard enough for me in the USA, so I take friends where I can get them."

Solomon's lawyer scheduled a meeting with us before the hearing to go over some new information. The content of that meeting follows: "I met with Mandy's lawyer to see if they were still going to proceed with the case. It turns out that Mandy's daughter had no memory of the specific episode, and it seems like Mandy's memory is unclear as well. Mandy admitted that she was drunk during the reported incident, which further clouded her judgment and harms her credibility. Mandy also verified the fact that Solomon cleans her daughter after toileting, but this is at her daughter's request. Mandy did indicate that it is unusual but her daughter has accidents at times, so Solomon is a big help here. Mandy also told us that Solomon was drunk and has a drinking problem, but he never hit her or her daughter when he was drunk. He would usually come home and pass out."

"Additionally, Mandy's daughter, at both attorneys' requests, was examined by a medical doctor who specializes in child abuse. This doctor was unfamiliar to Mandy and her daughter. The results of this examination were inconclusive. He was also unable to disclose any specifics due to the pending trial. Neither Mandy nor her attorney saw the need to get a second opinion at this time."

Based on all of this information, Mandy's attorney convinced her to drop the charges and the case as long as Mandy and Solomon never contacted each other again. Solomon and Mandy agreed to this ("I had no choice. It was either agree, or go to court and get 20 years. My word against a mother's? Who wins this?"). At Mandy's request, a *restraining order* was issued against Solomon, since she now feared for her life. Solomon did admit to "having a mean streak and a temper. But as I said I would never harm Mandy or her daughter." Solomon learned in therapy that the behaviors he demonstrated towards Mandy's daughter were unacceptable and could be considered criminal, even if Mandy and/or her daughter asked him to perform them. "I realize this now. I was trying to help, be a gentleman, show Mandy and her daughter that I could be a good father. I still think I can be."

Solomon continued in treatment until we left the clinic, at which time he was transferred to another psychologist. At last report Solomon was continuing in AA three times a week and had just celebrated his first year of sobriety. He still came to therapy every week and was transferred to a group where he could discuss many issues including his drinking problems. Solomon continued to work at the same job and his new psychologist reported that he had stayed "clean and sober. He had no more charges of child molestation since that one reported incident. We continue to believe that, if the specific incident in question did occur, it was an aberration and poor judgment, since Solomon demonstrated very poor insight and poor judgment when he first came to see us. The "Pedophilia" diagnosis remains, since we are unable to conclusively rule out at this time. We continue to investigate Solomon and his past behaviors with Mandy, and we continue to see if other incidents with Mandy, or other underage girls, have occurred."

Finally, once he celebrated his first year of sobriety, Solomon became engaged to Andrea. "I've known her for awhile; she works at the factory. I never noticed her at all; she asked me out after work one day! She's really sweet and precious. No kids to worry about and no, she doesn't drink at all. She's very devout. We go to church together, and I've become friendly with her friends. I cannot tell you how happy I am. Sometimes you need a real scare to wake up and get straightened out. That happened here. Once we get married we're moving far away from here. I need a new start."

There are a number of possible treatment modalities for pedophilia and the other paraphilias. The behavioral method generally uses *aversive conditioning,* which has had some success in treating the paraphilias. However, aversive conditioning involves a certain amount of pain, and this has caused controversy in the treatment field. How does this work? The stimulus that leads to sexual arousal in the pedophile (such as a child's underwear or shoes) is paired with an aversive stimulus such as an electric shock. The concept here is that the stimulus will soon acquire aversive properties and will thus be avoided. A problem is that aversive conditioning does not lead to the acquisition of new and/or adaptive behaviors but only leads to avoidance behaviors.

Psychodynamic theorists would use long-term analysis to treat the paraphilias. They would see the paraphilias as a result of unresolved castration anxiety and an unresolved Oedipal Complex in the Phallic Stage. The idea of intercourse—the penis vanishing inside of the vagina—is seen as a type of castration. This occurs unconsciously. The individual will then compensate for this fear by *displacing* his sexual arousal into safer venues: children, animals, leather. This is an interesting concept but the evidence for it generally does not exist.

As was mentioned, the evidence appears strongest for the use of behavioral treatment methods for the paraphilias. The problem, again, is the lack of designs other than case studies, and the lack of studies that have control groups. Additionally, some of the research bases its results on self-reports, which are prone to bias. The final concern is that the paraphilias appear to be chronic, do not respond well to treatment other than aversive conditioning and chemical castration, and may recur often.

What medications could be used for the treatment of pedophilia? Hormonal agents such as *DepoProvera (also available as Provera; medroxyprogesterone)* have been used successfully with **repeat** sex offenders. These medications, generally speaking, reduce *testosterone* levels and also reduce the sex drive. DepoProvera is used when the pedophile's sex drive is uncontrollable and thus dangerous, not the situation with Solomon. *Antiandrogen* agents such as *Androcur (cyproterone)* will reduce sexual desire and sexual fantasy by reducing testosterone levels. However, once the usage is stopped, the sexual fantasies and the sexual arousal return. Androcur is used when "chemical castration" is discussed. Relapse once these medications are discontinued is quite common, so the pedophile needs to be on a long-term administration. Finally, there may be a risk of the pedophile developing liver disease or cancer from long-term usage of these medications (Bezchlibnyk-Butler & Jeffries, 2002).

Prognosis

Solomon's prognosis can be listed as "fair". Does this seem unusually harsh? Let us examine the reasons why. First, the clinic felt that Solomon had poor *impulse control*, i.e., he had anger control problems and his judgment was very poor when he first entered therapy. These issues can be difficult to treat. What would happen once Solomon gets into a bad fight with his fiancé or their future children? Who is to say if his poor judgment has significantly improved over the past year?

Additionally, Solomon suffers from alcohol dependence. Because alcohol dependence, even when in remission, can relapse in stressful situations, we felt that a prognosis of fair was justified.

Solomon's case provides an excellent example of how difficult it is to arrive at a conclusive diagnosis of pedophilia. Solomon's case also illustrates how clinicians often disagree about diagnoses, treatment plans, etc. on the same case. This can cause some confusion when trying to diagnose a case where the diagnostic information is not conclusive, as you have read.

Female Orgasmic Disorder

The Case of Emily: Breaking the Barrier

Presenting Problem

Emily is a 45-year-old white female who grew up in a middle class suburb and recently moved to an urban area. Emily has been married to Joe for 12 years; they have no children. "It's not that we don't want any, but there seem to be reasons why we can't have any." Emily is an only child and was raised by her father. "My mother died when I was 5 years old, and it had a big impact on me. My dad worked hard and raised me, and he eventually remarried when I was 14. However, I never took to my stepmother, so I see it like my dad raised me."

Emily was well dressed in a black business suit, low heels, and a cardigan sweater. She wore no jewelry except for her wedding band and a Movado watch. She was of average build and was 5'5" tall. She did not wear glasses but would squint whenever we asked her to sign a form or to read something. She made good eye contact but her affect was flat. At times her voice would crack during the sessions but she did not cry much.

Emily had not been in therapy for many years, so we were curious as to what brought her to see us. "Well, it's real simple. I have no desire for sex anymore . . . oral or vaginal. It's like it just left me a few years ago . . . two I guess. I still go through the motions because I love Joe so much, but there's no desire in me. I just don't get horny like I used to. Joe knows this, but he's too polite to kick up a fuss. We used to be quite wild when we first got married. Now, I just don't understand it. I went to my OB/GYN and my general practitioner, and both said that physically I was fine. Well that made no sense at all. I know my hormones are whacked out somehow. My OB/GYN suggested that I see a psychologist, since he suspected that this might be a psychological problem. I guess he's a Freudian (laughs)! I read Freud, so I guess it makes sense. Anyway, that's why I'm here, to see if these sex problems are in my head. Joe would like to know also, and we'd both like to see these things fixed." Emily reported this information matter-of-factly, displaying little emotion.

Background Information

Emily has an MBA from a well-known university and is employed as an accountant. "We really get busy during tax time. I put in long weeks then, but that's my job. Joe isn't thrilled, but we need two incomes to keep up our lifestyles." These lifestyles include taking yearly cruises and a trip to Europe every year. "My relatives all live in Europe, so we like to see them whenever we can. My grandma is 90 now; she's a Holocaust survivor and lives in Vienna. We see her more often now since she's gotten forgetful. She's the only relative I'm really close to."

We asked Emily about Joe. "He's a sweetie, but like all men there are things he just does not understand. My needs, for one. My needs for work, privacy, rest, love. Things like that. Joe is an office worker; we work close to each other so we travel to work together each day. It's odd, but we really have not been apart since we got married. Maybe that's part of the problem (laughs)!" Joe has a BA in Literature "and since he said it was useless, he got this job and slowly moved up to the position he has today. He makes good money and is happy."

Emily reported that she was a late talker. "I started talking around 3 years old, which is very late. Look at me now; can't shut me up! I also got very blue after my mom died and I really withdrew from everyone." Her father took her to see a psychologist and a psychiatrist because he was really worried about her. Keep in mind that one of the fastest rising mental disorders in the United States is *childhood depression.* It is a dangerous fallacy to believe that children do not get depressed.

"I was diagnosed with depression at age 6 and was in therapy for 5 years. I still did okay in school, but I had no friends. I would come home, withdraw, and watch TV and go to sleep. I was very thin because I never ate a lot. Because of this I had problems as a teenager I think." Emily reached all of her other developmental milestones at the age-appropriate times.

Emily did indeed do decently in school; her grades in high school were mostly Bs. She did even better at university, graduating Magna Cum Laude and being asked to join Phi Beta Kappa. She was an Economics major, since "I always liked numbers and money."

Emily met Joe at Spring Break in Cancun, Mexico. They went to school in the same area of the United States, and they kept in touch until they graduated. "It was a real long-distance affair, if you will. We saw other people, but we really wanted each other. I was a virgin when I met Joe. I saved myself for marriage. How about that for a shock! My dad raised me very strictly, if you're wondering." After graduation, Emily entered her MBA program and Joe applied for jobs near her university. Once he was hired, they had a "normal, close-distance relationship. Joe said that when I graduated and found a job we could get engaged. He was, and always has been, a man of his word."

Emily's wedding was quite interesting. "My dad of course gave me away. I really didn't want my stepmother there, since I'm not close to her at all. She tried to tell me what to do when I was a teenager, and I really resented that. She'll never replace my mother; she'll never be my mother. Of course my dad would not attend without her, so she sat with the guests and was not in the wedding party. My dad said he understood and even though he was paying for it, this was my decision and I had to live with it. It really did not bother me that much. I just don't like the woman. My dad and stepmother sat together at the reception, and she was in some of the pictures. It was very uncomfortable. Joe stayed out of it, since he did not want a big fuss. That woman always tried to butt into my life."

We asked Emily about having children. "Well, we keep on trying but it's not happening. If it were meant to happen it would. We don't have the bucks to go through adoption, and we want to know about our child's background. Is that cruel? I know of women in their 50s who get pregnant. Joe is 48, so he's not too old. We both want them, but it just hasn't happened. As I said, my body is normal, but something's just not working here. It IS hard since all of our closest friends have kids. I guess they see us as selfish or freaks."

Joe works a normal 40 to 50 hour week, according to Emily. "He'll come home, get dinner ready if I'm not home, and read the paper and watch TV." They both enjoy using the computer and surfing the Internet. They do not spend a lot of time talking to each other once both are home, but they always talk for a while before going to bed. "Usually on the weekends we'll go to a movie or a show, eat out, and then stay in on Sunday. If the weather's nice we'll ride bikes."

So far nothing appears to be really unusual here; however, as is often the case, do not let appearances deceive.

Thought Questions

1. Was Emily depressed after her mother died? Why or why not?
2. Explain your position on whether or not children can get depressed.
3. What would be the next steps you would take if you were Emily's psychologist, and why?
4. Discuss whether or not you believe Emily really wants children.

Assessment and Evaluation

Emily was assessed with an unstructured diagnostic interview, a *psychiatric evaluation,* and a complete physical to gain second opinions. We had a good idea of what was occurring here, but we needed additional information to support these hypotheses. See what you think after reading her replies. We asked Emily if something had changed with her or Joe since she lost her *libido.*

"Well, that depends what you mean. I love Joe dearly, but physically he's let himself go the past few years. He used to exercise a lot but he basically gave up on that. I'm not sure why that happened. As for me, I didn't notice anything unusual happening with me. I just don't have the desire. I don't even have the desire to cheat on Joe, so it has nothing to do with him."

We then asked Emily if she masturbates, or has the desire to masturbate. "Actually, yes to both. I masturbate about four times a week, and I do have the desire often. That is one of the main reasons I came in. This makes no sense. I like to pleasure myself, but I have no desire to get any pleasure from Joe or any other man. I thought I might be bisexual or homosexual, but doing something with a woman has never entered my mind. I have no desire for that at all. I think Joe would like me to, but that will never happen."

Well, this is indeed quite interesting. The puzzle gets more confusing. We asked Emily if she orgasms during masturbation, and if she orgasms during sex. "Well, at times during masturbation I have, but not recently. With Joe, I can't remember the last time I did, if I ever did. I really don't know what it means to have an orgasm. Of course with Joe it's obvious—he ejaculates. I've heard all this stuff about female orgasms, but the earth doesn't move, I don't ejaculate, nothing major happens. So I guess the answer is not recently for when I'm with Joe. By myself, I shiver at times and get a nice rush, but that's it. Is that good enough? It doesn't sound like an orgasm to me."

Hmmm. We now had some important additional information with which to work. The most common sexual complaint for women who seek therapy is the inability to reach orgasm. According to one study, 25% of women studied had significant difficulty reaching orgasm (Heiman, 2000). On the other hand, an earlier study found that 50% of all women orgasm on a regular basis during sexual intercourse (LoPiccolo & Stock, 1987). It seems like Emily fits into the former study's results. However, she may physically be unable to have an orgasm. There is a distinct difference between difficulty achieving and physically never reaching orgasm. If the latter is the case, we need more information. We sent Emily to get a medical opinion.

After her results came back, the situation was the same: Except for high blood pressure, everything else was normal, including hormonally. "I was frustrated when I got the results. I was sure that something physically was causing these problems for me. So what's the next step?" Emily furrowed her brow and looked perplexed.

We then sent her for a psychiatric evaluation, specifically to see if she was depressed. The psychiatrist's report? In sum, "At the most, Emily is suffering from mild depression, which may be a reaction to her inability to orgasm and lack of desire. Based on her physical and psychological evaluations, Emily is diagnosed as having the following conditions:

Hypoactive Sexual Desire Disorder, Acquired Type,
Situational Type, Due to Psychological Factors   302.71

Female Orgasmic Disorder, Acquired Type,
Situational Type, Due to Psychological Factors   302.73

No other psychiatric conditions exist at the present time."

Thus, it seems like the issues are psychological in nature. We then asked Emily some more questions and slowly things cleared up. We first asked her about her upbringing. She closed her eyes as she began to speak, almost as though she were picturing her past, "As I said my dad was strict. I was not allowed to date until I was 16 and if I got caught doing anything—anything—I had to answer to him. I know dads are strict with their daughters but this was crazy. We were also quite devout, and I was taught that a woman's place was in the home, to produce kids. Of course I didn't listen, but I was raised with these ideas. I was taught that it was proper to save yourself for marriage and so I did. I was never serious with the other guys at school. I kissed them but it meant nothing to me."

"I took a Sex Ed class in university, but I cut a lot of the classes. The whole thing was embarrassing for me, especially the anatomy part. Some of the things were silly or lies, especially regarding female anatomy. I knew about the penis, and I know my anatomy. 'Pleasure is not a goal for a woman during sex' is what I learned." Believe it or not, some of the brightest most educated people lack basic knowledge about anatomy and sex. In today's world where self-examination is crucial for the early detection of some physical disorders such as cancers and sexually transmitted diseases, this lack of knowledge is dangerous. We then discussed Emily's workload.

"Well, as I said, we have peaks and valleys. However, the past year or so they've been talking about making me a partner in the company, since I've shown a lot of loyalty. To be honest, they appreciate the long hours and the fact we don't have kids yet; that makes these hours possible. So I'm in line for a big promotion, which could set us up for life. Joe is happy about that but he wants kids, so he's not thrilled with the ramifications of the promotion. It's also hard to give up the lifestyle."

We then asked if Joe was masturbating. "Yes, and I don't mind at all. Men do that regardless. He masturbates to orgasm about three times a week, sometimes in my presence, sometimes not. It seems to be good enough for him. He never says anything to me about the lack of sex. At times I just lie there while he goes at it with me, just to please him. It doesn't do much for me though."

Let us sum up what we have so far. Emily appears to be mildly depressed. She has little or no desire for sex with Joe, but masturbates. She's working very hard, expecting a promotion and thinking that the promotion may be based on her being childless. She is not sure what an orgasm is and reports having a very strict (some would say *sexually repressed*) upbringing. Thus, Emily could be suffering from depression, from a sexual desire disorder, or from an orgasm disorder.

Emily is too young to be going through *menopause;* even if that were the case, her physicians did not mention this, so we can rule out menopause. Her life is very hectic and busy, and she had significant issues when she was a child, lacking a mother/mother figure for a long period of time. Her father was overprotective of Emily, and it seems like she still has not forgotten this. Suffering from childhood depression also contributed to her difficult upbringing.

Joe seems to be very understanding, perhaps too much. He did not wish to participate in therapy, since he is "happy" with his marriage as it stands. Joe told us on the telephone that he just wants "Emily to be happy, so I support her in this. I want children, and Emily says she wants them but this might interfere with a significant promotion in her eyes." She thus may have a fear of becoming pregnant. Any ideas yet as to what might be going on?

We asked Emily about alcohol and drug usage. "I drink once or twice a week, a glass of wine at dinner. We'll have beer on occasion; it goes well with Thai food, which we love. I haven't used drugs since university, when I tried pot a few times. I stick to wine and that's usually it for me."

We felt as though we had enough information to make preliminary diagnoses for Emily. The clinic staff, in a case conference, agreed with the psychiatrist's diagnoses of Emily. They are repeated below. See if you agree and if not, think about the reasons why. Perhaps once you have finished reading, your opinion of Emily's case may change:

Hypoactive Sexual Desire Disorder, Acquired Type,
Situational Type, Due to Psychological Factors   302.71

Female Orgasmic Disorder, Acquired Type,
Situational Type, Due to Psychological Factors   302.73

Theoretical Etiologies

Unlike many of the disorders discussed and to follow, the etiology of sexual dysfunctions is easier to pinpoint. In some instances the cause is attributed to a combination of physiological and psychological factors, but not always. At the least this gives us guidance while we diagnose individuals.

There are many physiological conditions that can lead to a sexual dysfunction, in this case hypoactive sexual desire and female orgasmic disorder. Diseases such as diabetes may cause nerve damage and nerve deadening in the genitalia, thus leading to decreased sensitivity and therefore making it difficult to achieve orgasm. Other disorders such as chronic fatigue syndrome can leave an individual so exhausted that they have little desire for sex (lack of energy) as well as for other things. Chronic illness, such as high blood pressure and cardiac issues can also lead to sexual dysfunction. The individual may be so stressed about getting aroused and/or having an orgasm that it may not occur. They fear that this would lead to a stroke or a heart attack.

Prescription medications can decrease sexual desire and cause additional problems. Antidepressant medications, specifically the SSRIs, can lower sexual desire and cause arousal problems (Bezchlibnyk-Butler & Jeffries, 2002). Tricyclic antidepressants (recall these are the older classification with more significant side effects) may also disrupt desire and arousal. What about alcohol?

Oddly enough, even though alcohol lowers inhibitions and loosens social restraints, it actually interferes with sexual performance since it is a *central nervous system* depressant. That is, you will psychologically desire sex more, but physically be able to perform less. Chronic alcohol dependence can lead to liver and neurological damage, and can also cause fertility problems for both men and women. Fertility problems may be related to the increase of premature ejaculation in alcohol dependent men. Illicit substances such as cocaine and pot have the reputation of increasing performance and desire. While cocaine is an anesthetic and can delay ejaculation, the ability to physically increase desire is questionable.

Psychological factors can also contribute to sexual dysfunction. As we have seen with Emily, she seems uncertain at the least and unwilling at the most, to have children. Unconsciously this may be preventing her from enjoying sex or pursuing it with Joe for fear of getting pregnant. If she enjoyed intercourse, it would be more likely that she would repeat this behavior, and thus become more likely that she would get pregnant. Freudians would focus on unresolved penis envy thus leading to hostility towards Joe. In this case, Emily remains fixated in the phallic stage and is punishing Joe for having a phallus (penis) by not allowing the phallus to bring her pleasure. She has also been unable to overcome penis envy and mature beyond the phallic stage. What happens here is that she cannot transfer erotic feelings from her clitoris (a phallus, if you will) to her vagina, thus preventing orgasm through intercourse (Kaplan, 1974). The analytic viewpoint has little research support, as you might expect.

Performance anxiety can also affect women. The woman might feel un-attractive or "not complete" if she cannot orgasm, thus placing more pres-sure on her to orgasm and increasing her anxiety level. She might also engage in negative thoughts such as "I can't let go like that; I'll look fool-ish." You have heard similar sentiment from Emily when she stated that sex for a woman is only to make babies and is not to be enjoyed.

The cognitive perspective of Albert Ellis is useful in the etiological and treatment perspectives. Ellis states that irrational beliefs and attitudes may lead to sexual dysfunctions. For example, Emily might say to herself, "I am an unfit woman if I do not enjoy sex at all times and always desire my husband. If I am a bit overweight I am as big as a moose," and so on. In other words, by expecting perfection each time, Emily and others guaran-tee failure.

Finally, we will examine cultural and social etiologies. Researchers concur that early sexual traumatic experiences can have a negative impact on later sexual functioning and behavior. For example, if a woman were a victim of forced intercourse, date rape, or had been victimized by a male early in life, she would have a negative viewpoint towards sexual contact later on. A more obvious cause is rather simple: The individual may no longer be physically or emotionally attracted to one's partner. It may not be easy for the affected partner to communicate this, so they may suffer in silence. There may also be communication problems even if the affected partner is still attracted to his/her partner. Joe may have poor sexual skills and thus may not be arousing Emily. Because his skills may be poor, Emily is not getting aroused and therefore she develops a sexual desire disorder.

As we have seen with Emily, the fact that she was raised without a mother/mother figure to love could also lead to problems. Even today women may be raised to believe that sex is dirty and not meant to be en-joyed. They are taught to be submissive, which occurred with Emily. They may desire to somehow gain power back, and so they withhold pleasure and orgasm from themselves, and subsequently from their partner.

Thus, most clinicians view sexual dysfunction as a combination of physical and psychological factors. In a lot of instances the cause(s) are psychological, but clinicians need to rule out any potential physiological causes before they proceed with treatment. Perhaps some people have a bi-ological predisposition to have a sexual dysfunction, and psychological factors interact and bring out the disorder.

Treatment Plan

We followed the proper modality in setting up Emily's treatment plan. We interviewed her and gave her a psychiatric evaluation. We also sent her to get a complete physical to rule out physiological causes. Finally, we assessed her for the presence or absence of any psychopathology, not limited to sexual disorder (Wiegel, Wincze, & Barlow, 2001).

The **ideal** treatment plan would be *couple's therapy*, but since Joe initially refused to come in, we had to resort to other methods. We thus involved Emily in *individual therapy* using *cognitive behavioral methods*, *homework assignments*, and *bibliotherapy*. In other words, a lot of sex education and education in general (Bach, Wincze, & Barlow, 2001). Before we examine Emily's progress and see whether the diagnoses are correct, a few notes are in order.

First, it is preferred by some clinicians that when a female patient has sexual difficulties (especially if she is a victim of sexual abuse), the therapist should be **female.** We asked Emily about this (which is the proper action) and she told us she had no problem discussing "intimate" issues with us. Second, homework assignments, a typical component of some behavioral treatments, are good practice when treating sexual dysfunctions. The goal is to practice techniques, report on feelings and problems, and so on. *Masters and Johnson* (1970) pioneered these techniques as a way to facilitate communication between partners. Imagine having homework where the goal is pleasure!

Bibliotherapy is also used to help treat more issues than ever before. Bibliotherapy is just like it sounds: The psychologist prescribes books for the patient to read on his/her own. This is especially useful with sexual disorders, but one needs to use caution, since many of the books are popular books that are not based on facts, but are designed to sell. Emily was asked to read *The New Male Sexuality* (Zilbergeld, 1999), and *For Yourself: The fulfillment of female sexuality* (Barbach, 2000). Helping professionals consider these books and authors to be some of the best in the field. These authors do not get too "clinical," thus making for easy reading. Some professionals also "prescribe" adult films and sex toys to use; we held off on this, since Emily seemed like this might bother her.

We also asked Emily to keep a diary and note whenever she felt sexual desire, when she masturbated and what she thought about during those times, and when she thought she was having an orgasm. The results were intriguing, to say the least. Emily discussed her homework, and the results of her book assignments, with us.

"It's interesting, because I noticed that when I'm in bed with Joe I do get a bit of a 'tingle,' but it stops quickly. I'm much hornier when I'm by myself in the shower or at night before Joe comes to bed. The desire is always strongest when I'm alone, but I'm happy that something does occur when Joe's in bed with me. Usually I masturbate in the late evening or in the mornings in the shower. I never realized what I thought about before, but I fantasize about the first few months we were married. The sex was unique and amazing. I don't fantasize about other men when I masturbate, just those first few months or so. (Laughs) We were a hot couple, always all over each other! I also fantasize about falling in love with Joe all over again and I get real tingly then too, like shivers and a chill. My body shakes a bit. That seems like an orgasm to me but I don't know."

Based on this information, we focused on Emily's desire, the timing of the desire, and the fact that she appeared to be able to have an orgasm but was stopping herself from experiencing one. We discovered, as the sessions progressed, that she was indeed "petrified of getting pregnant and having kids. I work hard to keep my figure, so that's part of it. I might not get the promotion, and we'd have to change our lifestyles. Also, my friends have told me so many pregnancy horror stories that I don't want to go through with it. I'd be an old mother, and to put up with so much pain and produce a child with *Down syndrome* would put me over the edge. I just really can't deal with all of that. On top of it, I don't want to die early and have my baby go through what I went through."

We worked on these issues with Emily and she came to realize that she did not have to control everything in her life, which was a big part of her troubles. Women who have orgasm difficulties sometimes are afraid to "let go," to give up control, which occurs during orgasm (the muscle contractions are involuntary). She also realized that many of her pregnancy fears were myths and thus were unfounded. Emily decided to discuss these fears with us and with her OB/GYN and, most importantly, with Joe. "Joe really did not care if having a child ruined my promotion. He just wants me to be happy and, to be honest, deep down I want a child." Emily appeared shocked when she admitted this.

We discussed her mother's death and Emily realized how much it still affected her. "I thought I would be over it by now, almost 40 years later, but I guess I'm really not. It's amazing what it takes for a person to realize things like that." Emily told us that her mother had been diagnosed with cancer shortly after she was born, and her father "said it was terminal which, back then, it always was. She was a heavy smoker, so in effect she brought this on herself. If only she had known . . . ." Emily learned not to feel guilty about her mother's death and, more importantly, that it was okay to still grieve but to **not** let the situation control her for the rest of her life.

Finally, we told Emily that the best way to treat her sexual disorder (note the singular here) was to have Joe come in for a few sessions. It took some persuading but Joe finally did come in, and quite reluctantly. At that time Emily's individual therapy was terminated; we also added a *female co-therapist,* which is practiced by some professionals when doing sex therapy. The therapists taught Joe and Emily *sensate focus* techniques, pioneered by Masters and Johnson. Briefly, sensate focus techniques allow the couple to focus on sexually pleasuring each other **without** intercourse; each member must focus on his/her own pleasure, and not on the partner's. Masters and Johnson (and Zilbergeld) believe that focusing primarily on intercourse and orgasms is the primary cause of many sexual dysfunctions. An additional goal is to improve communication, which Joe and Emily needed to work on. Sensate focus techniques are a form of behavioral treatment and last anywhere from eight to twelve sessions.

At the end of these sessions, Emily and Joe communicated very well and decided to continue in therapy as a couple. "We realized that my sex problem was at the core of other things, so we need to stay for a while to work things out." They discussed her fears of getting pregnant, the issues surrounding her promotion, and Joe's not exercising any more. As the sessions progressed and Emily and Joe perfected the sensate focus techniques, Emily learned how to let go and told us at the end of one session about her news.

"I finally had an orgasm! It was like nothing I've ever experienced in my life. Joe was petrified because he's never seen me like that. I was so happy I couldn't stop crying. I felt so much letting go when it happened; it was like a huge weight had been lifted from me. Joe touched me in just the right way, I shut my eyes and got past the shivering for once and it just happened. I can't believe what I was missing all these years. What was really great is that Joe was there to share it with me. This brought us closer than ever, since Joe blamed himself for my predicament."

Joe and Emily continued in couple's therapy and eventually transferred to a couples' group. They still had communication and work-related issues, but they managed to work through most of them while in treatment. Joe and Emily eventually terminated treatment after 2 years and told us of their future plans. "I got the promotion and you know what? Kids or lack thereof, had nothing to do with it. I know because I asked, and my boss told me I was totally nuts. To celebrate, Joe and I decided to go on a cruise and start trying to get pregnant. We have had no luck so far, but we're going to keep on trying. I have a greater appreciation for Joe, and it's amazing he didn't leave me during all of my craziness. I also talk to my dad more often, and I thanked him for doing such a nice job raising me as a single parent. He cried when I told him." As you can see, sometimes there is more to the *presenting problem* than meets the eye.

For the initial disorders evidenced by Emily, there are no typical medications that are used. Mythological *aphrodisiacs* such as *Spanish Fly* have been used in the past to increase arousal in both men and women; however, this substance has no medicinal value and is thus a *placebo*. People have also used alcohol to increase sexual desire and loosen inhibitions. Alcohol, since it is a central nervous system depressant and is in fact a drug, does have the ability to loosen inhibitions by dulling one's reaction time and sense of reasoning. However, it is rarely "prescribed" for the treatment of sexual disorders. Why is that? Contrary to popular belief, alcohol **decreases** one's ability to perform sexually, whether that be maintaining an erection (or getting one) or increasing vaginal lubrication. The person **thinks** that they are more potent when, in fact, the reverse is true!

As stated above, the best forms of treatment for Emily's difficulties remain education, sensate focus, communication techniques, and behavioral modification techniques. Treatments for the sexual dysfunctions tend to have a high success rate, especially if the patient is motivated to succeed and to enter/continue in treatment.

Before we end this section, we should very briefly mention *Viagra (sildenafil citrate)*. Viagra does not directly cause erections, but does positively affect the penis' response to sexual stimulation (Fuller & Sajatovic, 2000). Thus, it does **not** increase a male's desire, but instead works to correct "mechanical" difficulties. A female Viagra, *Viacreme*, is called a natural compound and can be bought over the Internet (**www.herbalo.com/via/**). However, its clinical utility is suspect.

Prognosis

Emily's prognosis is listed as "good." She demonstrates good insight into her difficulties and is willing to work on her issues with herself, her past, and her husband, not easy tasks. Emily refused at first to admit that the problem could be psychological but when this turned out to be the case, she faced her problems and involved Joe in treatment as well. She was able to finally give up some control in her life and made excellent progress in therapy. Finally, Emily has the complete support of Joe, which will make her path to recovery that much easier to maintain. We do not foresee Emily's difficulties resurfacing but if they do, she knows where to turn.

Review and Study Questions

Solomon

1. What are the chances that Solomon's lawyer encouraged the clinic to diagnose Solomon with a substance use disorder, in order to make it less likely that he would get convicted?

2. How would you feel working with someone who was accused of child molestation? Would you be able to remain impartial? Why or why not?

3. Does Solomon appear like the pedophiles on television and in the news? In other words, is this what you might expect a pedophile to appear and act like?

4. Discuss why you would try and gather more information about Solomon's father.

5. How different would the outcome, and therapy, have been if Mandy had been allowed to participate?

6. Discuss why Solomon's incident might recur, or might not.

Emily

1. Is it possible that Emily's desire and inability to orgasm are indeed psychological? Why or why not?

2. Tell why, if Viacreme were clinically proven, you would or would not prescribe it to someone like Emily.

3. How important was Joe's participation to Emily's recovery?

4. What are your views of sensate focus?

5. What impact does the death of a parent at a child's early age have on that child?

6. Is there is a connection between years of schooling and sexual naïveté? Cite any available evidence to support your position.

Terms To Know

sexual disorders

male erectile disorder (impotence)

premature ejaculation

female orgasmic disorder

female frigidity

male dyspareunia

female hypoactive sexual desire disorder

behavioral modification techniques

Sexual Dysfunctions

paraphilias

fetishes

Gender Identity Disorders

Sexual Disorder Not Otherwise Specified (NOS)

competent

release of information form

Alcoholics Anonymous (AA)

individual sessions

rule out

Alcohol Dependence

Pedophilia

restraining order

pedophile

stigma

antiandrogen

DepoProvera (medroxyprogesterone)

Provera (medroxyprogesterone)

childhood depression

unstructured diagnostic interview

BDI-II

psychiatric evaluation

libido

sexually repressed

menopause

couple's therapy

individual therapy

cognitive behavioral methods

homework assignments

bibliotherapy

Masters and Johnson

sensate focus

aphrodisiacs

Spanish Fly

placebo

central nervous system

Viagra (sildenafil citrate)

Viacreme

Down syndrome

mandatory clients

case conference

Breathalyzer

aversive conditioning

displacing

testosterone

female co-therapist

presenting problem

Androcur (cyproterone)

impulse control

Chapter 8

Developmental Disorders I

The two cases we will discuss in this chapter entail very different issues. The first case, Tillie, involves a *Reading Disorder* that is more commonly known as *dyslexia*. In fact, reading disorder is one of many types of *learning disabilities (LD)*. To call someone "learning disabled" is viewed as pejorative. The proper reference is "Someone with a learning disability," or "Having a learning disability." Reading disorder affects about 5% of the United States public school population (APA, 2000). Later statistics point to dyslexia affecting up to 1 in 5 school children (Cuadros, Land, Scully, & Song, 2003, July 28th). Many famous people suffer from Reading Disorder: The short list includes Tom Cruise and Cher. What makes this more remarkable is that both Cruise and Cher are actors who are multimillionaires, and their jobs depend on the ability to read and to comprehend written words and text! Perhaps they have learned how to *compensate* for their reading disorder. Keep this in mind as you read about Tillie.

Mental Retardation (MR) is a very different situation. This disorder has a variety of causes, not the least of which is the disorder known as *Down syndrome*. What makes this disorder different from the rest is that it is possible to assess *prenatal* risk factors for some of the causes of MR. Depending on the definitions and assessment methods, MR affects about 1% of the United States population. A more commonly used estimate is approximately 2%. Suffering from MR is not, contrary to popular belief, a "death sentence." Many individuals with *mild mental retardation* can function in everyday life. Ray Kroc, the late founder of McDonald's, was widely known for employing individuals who had MR in his restaurants. Chris Burke is an actor who has Down syndrome.

Two other factors make this diagnosis unique. First, MR **must be** diagnosed before the age of 18. In other words, if someone comes into your office and tells you that, at age 50, they suddenly contracted MR, that is not, by definition, possible. Second, MR is coded on *Axis II* of the <u>DSM-IV-TR</u>. Generally speaking, Axis II disorders last a lifetime and are not considered by many in the helping professions to be curable. While it can be difficult to work with individuals suffering from MR, there are nice benefits as well. What might those be? You will have to keep on reading to discover them.

Reading Disorder
The Case of Tillie: Special Needs

Presenting Problem

Tillie is a 22-year-old junior at a major state university who transferred from the local community college and decided on a Nursing major. Tillie is the younger of two sisters. Tillie told us that her "26-year-old sister has been 'medically diagnosed' as dyslexic, and my mom is also dyslexic yet she was never medically diagnosed." Tillie has an interesting background. "I consider myself Caucasian/Puerto Rican. My mom is white and my dad is Puerto Rican. I spent 10 years of my life in Puerto Rico and loved it there. I hate the cold weather here! I am bilingual but at home we speak English." Thus, English is listed as Tillie's *primary language.*

Tillie was very well dressed when she first came to see us. She had excellent eye contact and displayed an appropriate affect. Tillie was dressed in a blue warm-up suit that was neatly pressed and looked new. She wore black cross trainers and had a scarf wrapped around her long brown hair. She told us she wore contacts but "I am planning on having the eye surgery to get rid of my glasses and contacts." Tillie is 5'10" and slim; she smiled often during the sessions.

Tillie went to high school in the United States and did not do well. We received an official copy of her high school transcript once Tillie was referred to us, and it revealed 3 Fs in grade 11, with most of her other grades ranging from Bs to Ds. Tillie's overall GPA in high school was 2.3. It should also be noted that she received As in Design and in Honors Spanish. The clinic did not find these grades to be particularly alarming. What do you think?

"I wasn't reading until the second grade, about age seven and one half. The school figured it was because I was bilingual. The school I went to in Puerto Rico was terrible. That's one reason my parents moved us here. I think I needed extra help but the school had no clue at all." We asked Tillie about her writing and she told us "I was writing with no problem in the first grade, age 6 or so. We learned our letters then. The writing was never much of a big problem for me; it's just the reading and understanding." What is interesting already is that, while Tillie seems to have an academic difficulty, nothing was discovered or diagnosed while she was in school. Although this may seem very unusual, it is a lot more common than you might think. Can you figure out the reasons for this?

Tillie also "received tutoring the summer after the eleventh grade for English. That was a sucky summer. I spent the whole time with the tutor. My English is not so good. I can speak it fine, but reading it is a major problem for me. I grew up speaking English and I am fluent in it, but I have a lot of problems reading. I'm not sure what is wrong, but I have a good idea." We then examined Tillie's university transcripts. They revealed a GPA of 2.53 on a 4.0 scale. Most of her grades ranged from Bs to Cs, with two Fs. Tillie told us that she has "difficulty in math, oral and written communication, organization skills, short-term memory, and reading comprehension. You should also know that I study about 4 hours a day. I also teach aerobics about 3 hours a week, sometimes more if I'm subbing for someone. It pays okay and keeps me in shape"

Background Information

Tillie has an interesting family background. Tillie believes that "both my mother and father have learning disabilities. My dad had an academic breakdown at college and had to drop out. My mom dropped out of high school and said she did it to work for her family. My mom works as a maid at a hotel, and my dad works as a superintendent for an apartment complex. He makes the good bucks! My dad was a math major but he never really caught on. It was too hard for him. My dad is a very proud man, so maybe that's why he had his breakdown. My mom is really bright but she never tries to do what she can with her mind. She's happy cleaning rooms right now, which bugs me to no end. It kept me and my sister fed and clothed, but this is beneath her."

Tillie's sister is the "star of the family. She's in medical school right now. She got the brains I missed. It's like she got all of the good genes and I got the table scraps. It's not really fair. She's got a great life, a fiancé, and because she's bilingual, so many hospitals are begging for her to join them. It makes me sick." We pointed out that nurses, especially bilingual ones, are in huge demand. Tillie told us "yeah, I know, but they're not doctors. Nurses always get low pay, all the blame and no credit."

Tillie reached all of her developmental milestones at the appropriate ages with the exception of her not reading until age seven and one-half. Tillie reported no prior psychological or psychiatric treatment, no history of alcohol or drug abuse, and no family history of mental illness. "I'm a bit afraid of coming here and telling you things, because I want to graduate and I don't want my professors knowing I'm here. My family? Forget it. If they found out I was coming to a witchdoctor they'd go nuts. We were taught to keep our problems within the family and that's it. Keep your mouth shut. Sure we have our problems, but no one knows about them." Tillie was talking with her hands at this point, waving her arms in a very animated fashion. We noticed that she was wearing many rings, with a diamond ring on her left hand, fourth finger.

We then asked Tillie about her social life. "I have this boyfriend. He's white and is on one of the teams here. I always like athletic guys. Makes sense since I teach aerobics. We get along okay. My dad hates him, but all dads hate their daughter's boyfriends. I think he hates him because he's not Puerto Rican or Latino. Keep it within the race, you know? Stick with your own. Who cares? I'm not going to marry this guy. He keeps me company until I graduate. Once I get a job I'll look for someone to get serious with. It's hard to meet a good guy these days. I also have a small group of friends, and we go out to the movies, for pizza, and to dance and club on the weekends. I love to dance! It frees my emotions to dance."

So far it **seems** as though Tillie's concerns are typical for a university student. A casual reader might assume that Tillie's concerns stem from her being bilingual and from being "second best" when compared to her sister. However, you are not a casual reader. Let us briefly examine Tillie's medical history before we look at her situation more closely. We asked Tillie, as we do all patients, if she has any significant medical concerns. Tillie's responses proved to be rather interesting. See what you think, and try and guess what they might indicate, if anything.

"I had a history of recurring ear infections as a child, and nearsightedness which developed three years ago. I never had tubes in my ears, since the docs didn't think it was necessary. I took a lot of antibiotics, but my body seemed to be okay with them. My hearing is fine; it's been tested a lot. I also have asthma, which is situational and stress-related, and allergies, which also provoke it. I have a lot of allergies, and I take *Zyrtec* (*cetirizine*) sometimes. My doctor told me that Zyrtec can safely be used to treat allergies in people that have mild to moderate asthma. Still, I rarely use it. I hate to take something that might cause an attack, or worse. Finally, I take *Pepcid* (*famotidine*; this is an *over-the-counter* medication used to reduce and prevent heartburn) and *Carafate* (*sucralfate*; typically prescribed for patients with *duodenal ulcers*). I guess you could say I've got a nervous stomach or something."

Thought Questions

1. What is going on with Tillie?
2. Tillie briefly mentioned that her parents have learning disabilities (so she believes). Discuss the reasons why this information might be important.
3. To what extent might Tillie's medical concerns contribute to her difficulties?

4. How important is the fact that Tillie had many ear infections as a child?
5. Where might Tillie's bilingualism fit into the assessment?

Assessment and Evaluation

Tillie was assessed somewhat differently than the other people we have discussed. In addition to an *unstructured diagnostic interview*, Tillie received a *psychoeducational evaluation*. These are performed when the psychologist suspects the presence of some type of learning disability. Typically these evaluations will consist, minimally, of an *intellectual assessment (IQ test,* usually the *Wechsler)*, a *cognitive measure* (usually the *Woodcock-Johnson)*, a *behavioral observation*, and an achievement test (again, usually the *Woodcock-Johnson)*. The psychologist will administer all of these devices, score them, and then analyze the results. The results are then examined to see if there is a statistically significant difference between aptitude (the IQ results) and achievement (the achievement results, and school grades).

We gathered some additional information about Tillie before we administered the psychoeducational devices. Tillie came to us because one of her professors "realized that I was doing terribly in class. He saw that I was close to failing and suggested that I get a tutor or some outside help. He really took an interest in me, and I thought it was, at first, for the wrong reasons. He asked me how my other classes were going and I told him not that well. I always do well in my art classes, but when I have to read or write something I have problems. This professor saw that in my essays I would confuse or screw up the same letters again and again. He thought that meant something like dyslexia, so he sent me here. I think I need to have my glasses changed." Because we wanted to consider all possibilities, we suggested that Tillie visit her ophthalmologist. She returned the following week.

"Well, it's not my eyes! At least I feel good about that. When your eyes go, what can you do? I guess it's something else. It's your job to find out." Tillie gave us permission to contact the ophthalmologist and we confirmed this. We again asked Tillie about her university performance. "I was told by my advisor that I would be on probation if my grades keep up like this. I'm failing three of my five classes, so I dropped one and it still didn't help me. I thought it might be my eyes or the meds I'm on, but it's obvious that something else is causing this. I'm not depressed or anything. But my grades have tanked this semester. I can't get thrown out. What will I do then? Clean hotel rooms like my MOM?" She was again very animated while she was speaking to us, and she opened her eyes widely.

Tillie gave us permission, and we thus spoke with her medical doctor who told us that, indeed, she does have allergies that can lead to asthma attacks. Tillie has been going to this doctor since her family came to the United States, so he knows her quite well. More importantly, she had an ulcer and is taking the medications to make sure it does not recur. He told us Tillie is very nervous and secretive about things, and he got the feeling that she was holding back information from him. He also told us that stress and psychological issues which may be related to physiological problems such as ulcers, gastritis, and heartburn could exacerbate asthma. He recommended that we pursue counseling with Tillie. Finally, he told us that her medications most likely would not cause academic difficulties, since their side effects do not affect the *central nervous system,* for the most part. Armed with this information, we returned to Tillie.

"I do get stressed, a lot. Who wouldn't if you have to be compared to Suzie cream cheese all the time? No one could match up to her. On top of it she's a real bitch about it. She's always bragging about her life, fiancé, job offers and things. Lay off. I'm good too you know. My dad is so in love with her, it's incestuous. My mom cares about me, but she's so tired at the end of the day she doesn't call me. They hope my sister will get rich and take care of them. As for me, they want to see me graduate. They figure I'll get pregnant, stay at home, and waste my degree."

"I've had an ulcer for about 5 years now. It really started when I went to community college. A professor called me stupid in his office because my writing was so bad. That hurt. I was also stressed because I was SO dumb to go here, while stupid sister is in med school, shining star she is. I had financial aid, so I had to pull good grades to keep getting it. My parents can't give me money, so I teach aerobics to get 'pocket' money. I also didn't have a lot of friends when I was younger, since I didn't fit in. I'm confused as to who I am." Many people think that individuals with learning disabilities (if indeed this is what is occurring with Tillie) only have academic problems. It seems like Tillie is very different. Or is she that different? Keep reading.

Tillie told us about the ear infections she had as a child. "I had at least three that I know of. My mom told me I took antibiotics and they went away; she can't remember what kind. Penicillin I guess. Anyway, I missed school during the last infection, one month almost. It was hard to hear, I remember that. I also felt sick to my stomach a lot. The doctors in Puerto Rico did not want to put tubes in, and neither did my family. They would look ridiculous and hurt."

We then performed the psychoeducational evaluation on Tillie. The testing ran for three sessions, and once the results were tabulated, Tillie came back and we discussed what we found. The report read, in part, "Tillie's results on the *Wechsler Adult Intelligence Scale-Third Edition (WAIS-III)* showed that she had a *Full Scale IQ* (or IQ), of 95." While this sounds wonderful, this places her in the Average range of intellectual functioning. The average IQ for adults falls between 85–115. "Tillie has a deficit in short-term memory skills. These skills are crucial in aiding memorization, a key skill required for nurses." We then examined her achievement test and cognitive test results.

We found that her achievement test and cognitive test results were significantly **lower** than her IQ results. When this occurs, usually a learning disability is present. "Based upon her Woodcock-Johnson results, Tillie would appear to be a better visual learner than an auditory learner, but her learning ability in both of these areas is below average. She has particular difficulty with remembering letters and words that are visually presented in groups instead of one at a time. Tillie's *Serial Learning* results display inefficiency at ordering and organizing incoming information. Seriating, or ordering events which would otherwise need to be learned independently, makes memorization more efficient. As Tillie does not use the sequence of information to help her remember and retrieve information, learning is tedious for her. Reading comprehension, spelling and written language will be impacted by this. These academic areas all involve order and organization of information, whether it is the order of events in a story, the order of letters within a word, or the order of words within sentences, sentences within paragraphs, or paragraphs within a composition."

The report continued. "Of greatest concern is Tillie's deficit in *Paired Associate (PA) Learning* skills. Deficits in PA learning, a skill which is critical in trying to learn foreign language vocabulary, will likely affect her ability in math and language classes (However, Tillie received an "A" in Spanish; this may be due to the fact that she is bilingual in both Spanish and English). It appears that she attempts to learn lists without making associations. Because of this, Tillie may also have difficulty integrating and remembering new and difficult concepts learned in the classroom. Tillie also exhibited some significant deficiencies in problem-solving and concept production skills; this may affect her conceptual reasoning abilities (i.e., *higher order reasoning* skills) in the classroom."

We also asked Tillie to provide a writing sample. The psychologist who scored it noted in part ". . . a lot of letter reversals and lack of comprehension in answering the question. . . ." The treatment team thus determined that Tillie had a learning disability, specifically Reading Disorder.

We need to be clear on some issues here before we continue. A psychoeducational evaluation is a lengthy, complicated procedure. It is not possible to completely describe the procedure in the limited space of this text, so what has been (and will be) presented is a significantly condensed version. You should also note that only psychologists with master's degrees in specialized concentrations (such as School Psychology) or doctorate degrees (also in specialized concentrations such as Clinical and School Psychology, and with proper training) can ethically administer IQ measures. There are some problems with these measures. They may be culturally biased, and bilingual individuals may attain lower Full Scale IQs. All of the devices mentioned have flaws, and the results, while accurate, can be *skewed* by many factors, such as medications, physical and psychological disorders, and attitudes towards the tests. The latter was not a problem for Tillie, since she appeared to be cooperative during each session. She seemed intent upon doing well and scowled whenever she had difficulty with a question over which she struggled. She took each measure seriously and some of the flamboyance, sarcasm, and bravado that were present in the sessions were noticeably absent.

We thus arrived at our diagnoses; once again, see if you agree:

Reading Disorder	315.00
Generalized Anxiety Disorder	300.02
Ulcer, Duodenal, Chronic	532.70

The last diagnosis is **not** a <u>DSM-IV-TR</u> diagnosis but rather an *International Classification of Diseases, 9th Revision, Clinical Modification (ICD-9-CM)* diagnosis. The last diagnosis was provided by her medical doctor. The <u>ICD-9-CM</u> allows us to code and classify certain general medical conditions. These are coded on *Axis III* of the <u>DSM-IV-TR</u>.

Theoretical Etiologies

We are not entirely sure what causes reading disorder (dyslexia). We can hypothesize that a single area of the brain is not solely responsible for learning or reading disorders. Rather, it seems that several brain areas may not "communicate" with one another, and thus the information gathered by each portion is left on its own. These problems may even begin in the womb (Miller & Tallal, 1995). However, research has focused on brain dysfunction and cognitive and perceptual difficulties. As we have seen with Tillie, many children with dyslexia have visual or auditory perceptual problems. For example, dyslexics are unable to copy words correctly or to discriminate between shapes. The words may become blurry or seem to leap off the page, which Tillie described to us. One of the reasons we wanted her vision checked was because the words often seemed blurry to her.

Dyslexia seems to run in families, much more so than other learning disorders. Like the other disorders discussed, it is unlikely that dyslexia itself is inherited. Instead, it is hypothesized that the brain dysfunction (perhaps the communication disruption) itself is inherited; this can lead to a learning disorder (Castles, Datta, Gayan, & Olson, 1999).

Finally, a connection has been established between *Attention Deficit Hyperactivity Disorder (ADHD)* and dyslexia. Some children who have dyslexia have shown short attention spans and/or hyperactivity, which may point to a common link (Purvis & Tannock, 2000). The key here is that ADHD and dyslexia are two separate disorders even though they share characteristics. There are three ways to explain this connection. First, early developmental problems may lead to behavioral problems, which will lead to a learning disorder or to dyslexia. Why is that? The behavioral symptoms disrupt the learning in school and outside of school. Second, learning disorders will lead to anxiety and depression, and thus to frustration and subsequent failure in school and outside of school. Finally, it has been hypothesized that somehow learning disorders and ADHD interact and thus each "strengthens" the other disorder.

In sum, biological and familial factors seem to be key components in the etiology of learning disorders, especially dyslexia.

Treatment Plan

The treatment plan for Tillie will differ from those for the other patients in this book. Two aspects need to be focused upon: Her reading disorder, and her generalized anxiety disorder. Reading disorders, like all of the learning disabilities, have no cure. However, those like Tillie can be taught how to compensate for their disabilities. This perspective is sometimes known as the *medical model.* Disorders in the medical model are categorized together because they all have common symptoms. For example, everyone who contracts alcohol dependence will share some of the same symptoms. Additionally, the medical model takes the viewpoint that someone contracts a mental illness and thus it is not their fault that they become sick. Finally, like in medicine, some disorders are curable and some are not. Where do you stand on these viewpoints?

First, we encouraged Tillie to get involved with individual therapy to work on her anxiety issues. We received a surprising response, "Well, I saw a therapist when I was in the community college, because I was so nervous and depressed. She told me that I was very nervous and depressed and mentioned *Xanax (alprazolam)* as a possibility. My doctor advised against this because of my allergies and asthma. I got something out of seeing her, but I didn't continue because she got into too much of my personal life. I can see the benefits of getting some help with this anxiety; perhaps that's why I have these reading problems." Tillie thus agreed to see us for individual sessions for a while until "my anxiety is manageable. Hope that won't take too long."

Tillie was also encouraged to seek tutorial help and training in paired associate and serial learning techniques. We referred her to the learning center at the university, and mentioned that she should have strategies explained to her, extensively modeled, and taught in a progressive manner, starting off with easy tasks and gradually getting harder. She eagerly embraced this suggestion, and she was automatically eligible because of her reading disorder diagnosis. Many such centers at universities will offer extensive services only to students who have a learning disability. Tillie was anxious to share the center's suggestions with us, and we are anxious to share them with you.

"They told me, first, that I should keep on using my computer's word processing program and the spell-check program to help with my spelling problems. They set me up with a tutor who will also proofread my papers but he won't write them, darn it. They mentioned that I should start to bring a tape recorder to my lectures. This will help me to concentrate only on taking notes and not getting too confused, which happens a lot. I can then play back the tapes and fill in any gaps that may exist. My tutor is also helping me with the learning problems the clinic mentioned to me. He uses flashcards and other things to help me learn. It's slow, but it seems to be working well."

The learning center also used the psychoeducational model which focused on her strengths and preferences. Using the tape recorder is an example, since her auditory abilities are stronger than her visual abilities. Other intervention techniques could also have been used with Tillie. We will focus on the most commonly used ones before we examine what happened in therapy.

The behavioral perspective focuses on direct instruction of techniques to the individual. It uses a stepwise progression, where basic skills are taught first; the assumption is that by learning these skills, the more complex skills will be learned as a result. The cognitive perspective examines how children and adults organize their thoughts while learning material in school. The child is taught to recognize the task at hand, use problem-solving strategies, and then monitor their success or lack of success. One goal is for individuals to monitor their own thought processes. Finally, computer-assisted instruction, as was used with Tillie, is also used quite often. The advantage is that computers seem to hold the attention of children more often than some basic instruction methods (Hall, Hughes, & Filbert, 2000).

Tillie also examined her anxiety and other things in therapy. She realized "that I'm not stupid, I just learn differently than other people. Sure

I'm no Einstein, but I can do the work. It just takes longer, and I have to use different methods. I felt stupid for so long, but now I know better. You know, I have made more friends since I started therapy and the tutoring. These places make you feel human, like it's okay to be different and have problems."

Tillie also "finally came out of my sister's shadow. I know she's special, but so am I, but in a different way. It doesn't make me better or worse, just different. I've talked to her a lot lately, and we have a lot of catching up to do. She suspected I had dyslexia, so she's really happy it was finally discovered. I told this to my parents, and they were happy that I was happy." The concept that learning disabilities have a genetic component is similar to the medical model, since many medical diseases have genetic components as well. What is frustrating is that we professionals (some of us anyway) accept this, but the *genes* or *genetic markers* have yet to be discovered for most of the mental illnesses. That does not mean that effective treatments do not exist, of course.

Tillie's ulcer also remained under control and "I think it went away. I still take my pills, but I don't get the burning pains in my stomach much if ever anymore. I think that since I know what has been happening with me, my anxiety has gone down a lot, and so my stomach is also thanking me. Because my ulcer was bleeding, I still see the doctor often, but he expects me to make a full recovery. I know I'll never be free of all anxiety, but now that I can control it, I'm much happier. And my students in aerobics also see this. I seem less confused in class and happier."

Tillie received her *special education services* for the remainder of her university career. They told her that she did not need these services during her last semester since she had made nice progress, but "I felt like I wanted to continue. I was still not that sure of myself and I had it coming to me. I had a lot of lost time to make up for." Tillie spent 4 months in therapy and also made excellent progress. "My anxiety is under control, I sleep better, my stomach is better, I'm in okay shape. I just need to find a guy now and I'll be set. Oh, yes, and a job." When we last contacted Tillie she was working in a major hospital as a registered nurse and had recently gotten engaged. She also told us, somewhat gleefully, "My sister graduated med school and works in a hospital close to mine. But get this: Her fiancé left her for another woman, so now I'll be getting married before she will! How great is that? I can finally shine on my own. And you know what? She couldn't be happier for me."

As you can see, people that have learning disabilities have their own unique set of issues that usually include psychological concerns. Tillie's university was one of the first in the United States to recognize this, and they set up a well-known program to help students like Tillie who should have been diagnosed in elementary or secondary school but were not.

For the learning disabilities, no specific medications exist for treatment purposes. However, all of the psychiatric medications are available for use to treat any co-existing concerns brought by the patient. In Tillie's case, Xanax (alprazolam) was recommended by her psychologist a few years ago to treat her anxiety. These medications are problematic because, briefly, they are very addictive and are designed really for short-term use. Long-term use can lead to psychological and physiological dependence. Xanax and some of the other *anxiolytics* can also make the user very sleepy and, in some cases, dangerously relaxed. Tillie told us that "I was very sensible in refusing to take it, since I would be sleepy all day and get addicted to it." We did not recommend anxiolytics for Tillie unless her anxiety had become so unmanageable that she needed some help to "get over the hump."

Tillie continued to take Zyrtec, which is one of many new allergy medications. Most of these medications have side effects (like all of the others we have discussed), but since this text focuses on psychological disorders, we will not cover those here. Tillie also remained on Carafate and Pepcid for her ulcer, and she reported no side effects from these medications to us.

What about *Ritalin (methylphenidate)?* Ritalin is typically prescribed for Attention Deficit Hyperactivity Disorder (ADHD), which will be discussed in a separate chapter. Perhaps in the future, someone will develop a medicine that will be able to control, or cure, learning disabilities. The question remains: Would this medication be more effective than teaching those who are afflicted new strategies to learn and cope?

Prognosis

Tillie's prognosis is listed as "good." She continued to get appropriate help while at university and realized that her situation was different than other people. She showed good *insight* into her problems and wanted help for them. She managed to control her anxiety without using medications, and kept her ulcer as quiet as possible. Tillie also became engaged, got a good job, and reconnected with her family and sister. In short, if Tillie continues at her last reported state, she is expected to lead a normal, happy, and healthy life.

Mental Retardation

The Case of Samuel:
Lots of Love to Go Around

Presenting Problem

Samuel is a 17-year-old white male in the tenth grade at a local public high school. Samuel had never received any type of therapy before, but his last school had previously assessed him. Samuel had thus already been diagnosed as having mild mental retardation when he came to us for treatment purposes.

Samuel is an only child. His mother Janice works as a "baby sitter and, when I can get it, as an office temp. It's too hard to work and watch Samuel. There's no one else to help me. After Samuel was born and he had all of these problems, we swore not to try again. We were really scared. We thought he wouldn't even live. But God says we must love all people regardless of their situation. You'll see when you meet him how wonderful Samuel is. He's slow, but he's a good kid."

Samuel had an unsteady *gait*, wore thick glasses, and was short of stature, 5'1" tall, and somewhat overweight. His tongue protruded often from his mouth, and at times his speech was difficult to comprehend. Samuel's eyes also had very thick lids, and he had a rounded face. He wore large coke-bottle lens glasses. Samuel's nose was flattened and he had short stubby fingers. He was wearing a "Bart Simpson Cowabunga" T-shirt with baggy shorts and white sneakers. In his shirt pocket Samuel had a pencil and a pen along with a pocket calculator. His *hand-eye coordination* was poor. He had problems shaking my hand.

Samuel displayed inappropriate affect at times, smiling a lot when we were discussing serious issues. He had a very short attention span and was easily distracted. He had extreme difficulty in sitting still in the office. Samuel brought some baseball cards with him and he held them throughout the sessions, except when he was required to use his hands.

Samuel was sent to us specifically because some of his previous records could not be located. After a lengthy discussion with the school superintendent, Samuel was referred to us for diagnostic and treatment purposes. Note that this is not as unusual as it might sound. When students switch schools, many times their previous records get lost or misplaced, or the student "falls through the cracks." This means that the student is some-how missed by his or her new school and thus does not receive proper treatment. We have seen many students in the latter situation, and it is crit-ical that the new wave of helping professionals do all in their power to pre-vent this from occurring.

Background Information

Samuel talked freely with us, but because of his disability, we gathered most of our information from his mother and his past records (those that we could obtain). We first met with Samuel's mother alone. "The schools helped Samuel, and they helped a lot at first, then not so much. They taught him how to tie his shoes, how to make a phone call, how to clean himself. He potty trained late, at about 4. They told us that these days that's not so odd. Well, if you clean up the mess it is. Samuel just could not seem to learn things. When he would it would take forever. And his sweet tooth! He could live on sweets, even now!" Samuel's mother was dressed in a hooded sweatshirt that was unzipped, shorts, and sneakers. Her hair was in a ponytail and she was well kempt. She smiled weakly and dis-played appropriate affect. At times she would get teary-eyed.

Samuel had received special education services in the *resource room* at his local public elementary and junior high schools. Resource rooms are designed for special needs (also known as *special education*) students. They are self-contained classrooms, sometimes housing students with a wide variety of concerns. In Samuel's case, his past resource rooms contained students who had mental retardation in varying degrees, *cerebral palsy (CP; a neuromuscular disorder)*, and *hearing, visual and language impairments.* Usu-ally these rooms are staffed by at least two special education teachers, *teacher aides* (they help out the special education teachers), and in some in-stances student teachers. The schools try and limit the number of students in each resource room, but this does not always occur. For Samuel, he was one of usually six students in the room.

"Samuel was a difficult pregnancy. I'm an older mother; I had Samuel when I was 40. The doctors told me that I was a high-risk pregnancy, but I wanted to have a child. You see, I don't believe in getting a lot of tests. The tests could kill you, and the results might kill you too. So we had no idea what was occurring with Samuel until he was born."

"When we saw him, we knew something was not exactly right with him. Physically he did not look like we thought he should look. The doc-tors didn't say too much; afraid of getting sued I guess. We had a baby book that told us what Samuel should be doing at what ages, and he never did any of those things. He was very very slow. We had no idea what hap-pened. We knew he looked and acted differently."

"My husband left me shortly after Samuel hit 3. He couldn't take all of the physical problems Samuel had: troubles with his eyes, heart, and stuff. It seemed like we were always going to the doctor. We would get into wicked fights. He blamed me for what happened to Samuel, which is totally bogus. I know I had nothing to do with this. Sure I really didn't get good care while I was pregnant, but I don't drink or smoke or stuff or do drugs. It was bad luck is all."

We asked Janice about her family history, and then about Samuel's history. "My family is fine. No one's crazy in it that I know of. We have our weirdoes, but who doesn't? My ex's family had some wackos though. He had a cousin that was retarded, and another one that was schizo. Of course if you dragged the bum in here he'd deny all of that. He had nothing wrong with him, he was just a bum. Not one bit of support do I get for Samuel. I don't really know where he is. He calls from the road time to time. Did I leave when it got tough?"

We already have a bit of a problem here. First, we do not have a complete set of Samuel's past records, which means that there may be information gaps. Second, because of this, we need to rely on his mother to deliver accurate information. As you can see, she appears to be somewhat biased (which is not unusual). Additionally, Samuel's father is not around to question, and it seems unlikely that we will get him to come in. As you will see, questioning Samuel will not be a terribly fruitful endeavor.

We then asked Janice about Samuel's history. "Samuel had troubles early. His eyes are awful, so he has to wear them coke-bottle glasses, like you see in the waiting room there. He has problems walking. That occurred when he began to walk, which was at about 21 months I think. He talked late also, after 3. The doctors then knew something was wrong. You can see that; look at the poor boy! His face is all wrong." Janice was referring to Samuel's physical features, which are different for those who have mental retardation.

We determined at that point to bring in Samuel and ask him some questions. See if you can guess where Samuel's case is headed as we take a brief pause.

Thought Questions

1. Based on what has been stated above, do any of Samuel's *symptoms* seem familiar to you?
2. Discuss Janice's reactions to Samuel's situation.
3. How valid are Janice's comments and history, i.e., how significant are her biases, if they exist?
4. Give some reasons why Samuel may have a major sweet craving.
5. How significant is Samuel's father's background in making an accurate assessment?

Assessment and Evaluation

Samuel was given a psychoeducational assessment to detect the presence or absence of mental retardation. This assessment will be performed differently than Tillie's. Specifically, to detect the presence of mental retardation, the clinician must demonstrate a significant difference between *aptitude* and *adaptive living skills.* These latter skills are measured using an *adaptive behavior scale,* such as the *Vineland Scales.* These scales are forms filled out by the teacher and caregivers of the individual, and they represent a comprehensive estimate of a child's level of personal and social sufficiency. *Adaptive functioning* is measured by three main domains on the Vineland: *Communication,* which includes *receptive, expressive, and written abilities; Daily Living Skills,* which includes personal, domestic and community skills; and *Socialization,* which includes interpersonal relationships, play and leisure, and coping skills. In brief, the domains measure everyday behaviors and see if the behaviors demonstrated are at an age-appropriate level. Where might Samuel's behaviors be on the Vineland?

We invited Samuel in to the session and asked him some brief questions before we set up a testing appointment. We asked Samuel about school. "I really like it, especially my resource room teacher, Mrs. Smith. She's great. I love her so much. She teaches us how to clean up and how to make things. I want to talk about my friends, my mom, and my pet hamster. Is that okay?" We asked Samuel if he wants to go into a regular classroom. "No, no. I love my class. I learn so much. The kids laugh at me in school, but not in Mrs. Smith's class."

Samuel then told us about his family. "My mom is the bomb, she's phat. No one's mom is better. Did she tell you about my hamster? She let's me play Playstation games, even the adult ones. But I have to do my lessons first and then I can play. She lets me have friends over and things. She works so hard. I want to be like my mom or Mrs. Smith one day. My hamster runs on a wheel. My mom lets me feed him a lot. He's really a bit fat, so he should go on a diet. Do you have any pets? Can you tell me about your mom?" We now had a chance to *self-disclose,* about which there is much disagreement. We discussed the pets I did not have, and we briefly discussed my mother. "Your mom sounds as great as my mom. They must be alike." Of course we had to agree with Samuel here!

Samuel wanted to discuss the latest television shows, and he told us he's a huge Yankees fan. "My mom took me to a baseball game, and I got players to write their names on baseball cards. See? I carry them with me always. Mariano Rivera wrote on this one." Samuel then produced his cards and proudly displayed them. Samuel was smiling during this discussion and he seemed at ease with us.

As you can see, it is sometimes difficult to have a higher-level conversation with someone who has mental retardation. That does not mean that you should avoid discussions like this. They serve a diagnostic purpose and they put Samuel at ease. We then set up the testing appointment and asked Samuel to return with his mother.

The tests took four sessions, since Samuel had a lot of problems staying *on task*, or focused. In addition to the Vineland, Samuel was given the WAIS-III. Even though he was legally not an adult, the school psychology supervisor deemed it appropriate for him to receive the adult version of this test. We scored all devices and came up with the following results:

Samuel's Full Scale IQ was 65, and his *estimated adaptive behavior composite* on the Vineland was an age equivalent of 5 years, 1 month. We saw that on the Arithmetic subtest of the WAIS-III, Samuel pulled out a calculator to help him with the problems. We told Samuel this was not allowed and he became quite upset. This is crucial, because Samuel has learned how to compensate for a difficulty of his. Cheap pocket calculators, spellcheckers, and pocket computers are a huge boon to special education individuals.

Based on the results, we can safely say that the intellectual and adaptive behavior scores are below the norm for Samuel's age. Thus, the previous diagnosis of mild mental retardation was appropriate and accurate. The clinic decided to stick with this diagnosis and saw no reason at this time to change Samuel's treatment, i.e., the resource room.

We explained this to Samuel and to his mother when they returned, and they were not surprised. His mother was more to the point. "I figured that, and it seems like Samuel's time was wasted. Look at him! How could he not be retarded? Look at him, talk to him!" We explained that we were required by the school, and by law, to re-evaluate him. "I'm not upset with you, I'm upset with his school. Four days of tests! What the hell is up with that, huh? School makes no sense. No way should he leave Mrs. Smith. She's taught him, with me, how to survive." While this was occurring, Samuel was drawing a picture and looking at his autographs. The treatment plan for Samuel will soon follow. First, his diagnosis:

Mild Mental Retardation   317

Theoretical Etiologies

We are somewhat more fortunate when looking for possible etiologies of mental retardation, since in many instances biological causes are implicated. Weeks in the classroom can be spent discussing the possible causes of mental retardation; indeed, one study found that there may be over one thousand different **known** biological causes (State, King, & Dykens, 1997). The problem is accounting for the causes of mild mental retardation, similar to Samuel's. Some causes of mental retardation can occur prenatally (in the womb), some can occur at birth (*perinatal*) such as *anoxia* (a lack of oxygen), and some can occur due to traumatic brain injury, meningitis, and other *postnatal* factors.

The most common chromosomal abnormality that leads to mental retardation is Down syndrome, also known as *Trisomy 21*. In Down syndrome, the fetus has three number 21 chromosomes instead of two. Down syndrome occurs in about 1 in 800 live births. Down's victims are identified by unique physical features. They will have a small head, a large tongue protruding from their mouth, broad, square hands, a crooked pinky, and almond-shaped eyes. In some individuals these features are more noticeable than in other individuals. Almost all of these children suffer from mental retardation and other physical problems such as respiratory and cardiac problems. Down's is related to maternal age; as the potential mother gets older, the odds of producing a baby with Down's increases. Chromosomal abnormalities in general also become more likely as potential mothers age.

Recent research has uncovered some fascinating information about Down syndrome. According to Thase (1998), by the time most Down individuals reach their 30s, many of these individuals develop brain pathologies that are similar to those individuals suffering from *Alzheimer's Disease.* Most people with Down's do not live past middle age, but because of modern medical technology, we are seeing more and more individuals with Down syndrome living into their 50s and 60s (Down Syndrome Educational Trust, 2003).

Fragile X Syndrome is the most common cause of inherited mental retardation and is the second most common type of retardation after Down syndrome. This disorder affects between 1 in 1,500 to 2,000 males and affects between 1 in 2,000 to 2,500 females (usually the effects are not as severe). The X chromosome appears fragile; since females have two X chromosomes they seem to be better protected against contracting Fragile X. In many instances males and females carry the Fragile X gene but show no effects of it. They may pass this along to offspring. Retardation is usually mild to moderate; some children may have profound retardation, and some may be totally unaffected.

Phenylketonuria (PKU) is a genetic metabolic disorder affecting about 1 in 10,000 live births. This is a recessive disorder that prevents the metabolism of *phenylalanine,* an amino acid found in many foods. (Take a look at your next can of Diet Coke.) This amino acid accumulates in the body and may eventually lead to brain damage and thus mental retardation and emotional problems. PKU is detected at birth by analyzing the infant's blood or urine. If present, the infant is placed on a special, restricted diet and will receive protein supplements shortly after birth. Recently (Simonoff, Bolton, & Rutter, 1996), women with PKU have begun to have children, thus leading to an unusually high percentage of mental retardation linked to PKU. Simonoff et al recommend that prepregnant women who have PKU be placed on a special diet before getting pregnant to prevent these problems from occurring.

Tay-Sachs disease is worth examining. This is a degenerative central nervous system disease that targets Eastern European Jews and their offspring. One in 25 American Jews is a carrier for Tay-Sachs. Since this is a recessive disorder, both parents need to be carriers before the disease can be expressed. However, this still does not guarantee that the disease will surface. There is still a 75% chance that the child will not have Tay-Sachs. Tay-Sachs leads to loss of muscle control, paralysis, blindness and deafness, and generally death by age 5. Blood tests can detect Tay-Sachs carriers, while *amniocentesis* can detect Down's.

Prenatal factors can also lead to mental retardation. Certain diseases, such as *rubella* (German measles), *syphilis,* and *genital herpes* can cause fetal brain damage. These diseases are, for the most part, preventable either through education, careful sexual contact, or vaccine. Rubella is of greatest concern during the first trimester. If a mother has genital herpes, the fetus, during birth, comes into contact with the lesions while passing through the birth canal. Thus contact may be reduced through a *Caesarian Section (C-Section).*

If a pregnant woman ingests drugs, illicit drugs, or alcohol these may also lead to mental retardation. Some drugs, and alcohol, are able to pass through the placenta and thus reach the fetus. There is no guarantee that if any of these substances are used the fetus will be harmed. However, the chances are increased if these substances are used. A significant cause of mental retardation is *Fetal Alcohol Syndrome (FAS);* this occurs when pregnant mothers drink, in most cases excessively, during pregnancy. FAS affects about 1 in every 1,000 live births in the United States (Centers for Disease Control and Prevention, 1995). The rates are higher among African Americans and significantly higher among Native Americans. FAS leads to central nervous system damage and/or dysfunction, facial abnormalities and growth reduction (i.e., the child is below average in height). Individuals with FAS often have mild mental retardation and deficits that resemble ADHD such as poor impulse control.

Finally, research has examined some possible social and psychological causes of mental retardation. These include an impoverished environment or home, lack of stimulation (intellectual, emotional, or physical) of the infant, or parental neglect or abuse (again, physical, emotional, psychological, and now including sexual). These causes can be easily explained and traced. Children raised in such an environment may lack toys, books, computers, or other resources that aid in development. Their parents may have to work multiple jobs, thus having little time left to spend with their children. These children may be raised by television. It is likely that the parents themselves were raised in poverty, and social activists (and researchers!) have often said that poverty breeds a vicious cycle. These parents may lack the resources and skills necessary to enable their children to escape poverty, and thus the cycle continues. Harry Harlow's experiments focused on the effects of deprivation on Rhesus monkeys, and psychologists have often cited his work to advocate for more "hands-on" parenting to avoid deviant behaviors, and perhaps retardation, from occurring. Programs such as Head Start can effectively combat the effects of cultural and psychological deprivation, so much so that some children may eventually function normally.

In sum, even though we have pinpointed some physiological causal factors for mental retardation, in about 50% of the cases the causes remain unknown. Most of these individuals have the classification of mild mental retardation.

Treatment Plan

The treatment plan for Samuel was quite simple. Since he was making nice progress in Mrs. Smith's resource room, we told the school that he should remain in that setting if possible. We also told them that, if appropriate, he should be *mainstreamed* into some classes. We felt that Samuel was capable of this, especially in art classes. His pictures were wonderful and he got a lot of joy from drawing. We also wanted Samuel to get involved with family therapy and his mother reacted to this suggestion. "No way. I can't take off work to come in here, and Samuel doesn't need that. He's got Down syndrome, not a mental illness! He needs help in school, not with other stuff. Get his father in here, he's the kook." Are you surprised at this reaction? We attempted to get both Samuel and his mother involved in family therapy, but we had no luck. We relayed this to the school, and they accepted her position. Short-term therapy is one of the best ways for a family to handle the issues presented by mental retardation. The role of the parents can be seen as teachers; this role will of course last beyond school. The most practical role for parents would be that of teaching skills and not focusing on reducing problem behaviors (such as anger management).

The school's view was that Samuel had learning issues, not mental health issues. Technically, they could "force" him into therapy, but no one benefits from that. They did tell us that they would use us if they felt the need was there and would send him to the school social worker. It was a shame, because our interactions with Samuel were wonderful.

Samuel's special education teacher spent a lot of time teaching him basic living skills in the resource room. These included skills such as how to shave, how to brush his teeth, and how to get dressed. Typical behavioral approaches such as instruction (both physical and verbal), guidance, and reward (when the behavior or a close approximation is performed) were used in the resource room. These methods are most effective when teaching a simple skill such as brushing one's teeth. Social skills training (how to behave properly in social situations) and anger management were also taught in the resource room. Samuel had some control and boundary issues upon which his special education teacher focused. He would lose his temper rather easily, and would sometimes masturbate in public. Behavioral interventions (teaching basic skills, modifying aberrant behaviors, and strengthening positive behaviors) have been the most effective treatment modality for mental retardation.

Interestingly, one type of treatment modality that should be used more often is that of prevention and early intervention. As we have mentioned, by getting proper and good prenatal care (sometimes easier said than done), the chance of having a child who has mental retardation is decreased. Prenatal genetic tests, amniocentesis, and sonograms are all measures that can help to determine the future of the fetus. Sonograms can detect fetal structural abnormalities which **may** be related to mental retardation. We have previously discussed prenatal screening and amniocentesis. When we speak of prevention, we focus on the expectant mother. She should, as was mentioned, get all of her vaccines before she gets pregnant, avoid alcohol and other drugs, and lead a healthy lifestyle. Early intervention refers to screens for PKU and dietary restrictions if need be (or supplements).

Let us examine Down syndrome a bit further. The amniocentesis (amnio) will be performed from the sixteenth to the twentieth week of pregnancy. A sample of amniotic fluid is taken from the mother's placenta, withdrawn via a needle inserted into her stomach. The procedure is somewhat uncomfortable and is relatively risk-free (there is approximately a 1 to 2% miscarriage risk). It is strongly recommended for all mothers 35 and older, since the risk for Down's increases significantly after that age. Some mothers, like Samuel's, choose not to perform an amnio and will accept whatever state their future baby is in. Some mothers choose the amnio and if the results are not what they desire, they may choose to terminate the pregnancy. You should note that just because a pregnant woman is 35, it does not guarantee that she will produce a child with Down's. Given the overall odds, the chances are still small no matter what the mother's age.

The physical features of Samuel are those of someone who has Down's. The difficulties that Down's causes are counterbalanced by one wonderful aspect. These individuals are some of the most loving, giving individuals you will ever meet. Samuel was very affectionate with us, hugging us, taking our hand whenever we changed rooms, and smiling a lot. Even though his mother had an apparent attitude, you could see how much Samuel loved her. When a psychologist experiences something like this, it makes everyone feel good.

As was previously discussed, no medications exist to treat mental retardation. If the individual has additional psychological problems that warrant medication, they can be considered. Because individuals with mental retardation have a variety of physiological concerns, any medications must be prescribed with caution.

Prognosis

Samuel's prognosis is listed as "fair." See if you agree with the reasons. Samuel was making nice progress in the resource room and he was learning how to compensate for his limitations. We listed him as fair since his mother did not want to get involved with family therapy, and we saw the need to work on some issues, most notably hers. We were concerned that her issues affected Samuel and would hurt his progress in school.

Samuel returned to the resource room and at last report was making progress in his mainstreamed art class. Some of his art was displayed in the halls, and the principal told us that students seemed to not pick on him as much. He met a girl in the resource room and Samuel was happy about that. We received a letter from Samuel 3 months after we last saw him for the diagnostic testing. In it he had enclosed a picture and a Derek Jeter baseball card ". . . because I have two." The card was autographed.

Review and Study Questions

Tillie

1. How unusual is it that Tillie's sister was in medical school, while Tillie had school difficulties?

2. How might Tillie's allergies be related to her reading disorder, if at all?

3. Discuss why you would, or would not, prescribe medication for Tillie.

4. How are Tillie's anxiety disorder and stress related to her reading disorder?

5. Cite some reasons why those with learning disabilities often will also have psychological concerns.

6. What might have contributed to Tillie's ulcer?

Samuel

1. Discuss the most effective way(s) to handle Samuel's mother.
2. What are your views on amniocentesis?
3. Down's syndrome has been around for many decades; we know how to detect it. So why can we still not prevent it or cure it? Discuss these issues.
4. What would you suggest if the need arose for Samuel to be prescribed psychoactive medication?
5. How important is Samuel's father's history?
6. Discuss your views on mainstreaming.

Terms to Know

Reading Disorder

dyslexia

learning disabilities (LD)

compensate

Mental Retardation (MR)

Down syndrome

prenatal

over-the-counter

mild mental retardation

Axis II

primary language

Xanax (alprazolam)

Zyrtec (cetirizine)

Pepcid (famotidine)

Carafate (sucralfate)

duodenal ulcers

psychoeducational evaluation

unstructured diagnostic review

intellectual assessment (IQ test)

Wechsler

cognitive measure

Woodcock-Johnson

behavioral observation

central nervous system

Wechsler Adult Intelligence Scale-Third Edition (WAIS-III)

Full Scale IQ

Serial Learning

Paired Associate (PA) Learning

higher order reasoning

skewed

medical model

genes

genetic markers

special education services

Ritalin (methylphenidate)

Attention Deficit Hyperactivity Disorder (ADHD)

gait

hand-eye coordination

resource room

special education

cerebral palsy (CP)

neuromuscular disorder

hearing, visual and language impairments

teacher aides

aptitude

adaptive living skills

adaptive behavior scale

Vineland Scales

adaptive functioning

Daily Living Skills

Socialization

Communication

receptive, expressive, and written abilities

perinatal

anoxia

postnatal

Trisomy 21

Fragile X Syndrome

Phenylketonuria (PKU)

phenylalanine

Tay-Sachs disease

rubella

syphilis

genital herpes

Caesarian Section (C-Section)

Fetal Alcohol Syndrome (FAS)

amniocentesis

mainstreamed

International Classification of Diseases, 9th Revision, Clinical Modification (ICD-9-CM)

anxiolytics

self-disclose

insight

estimated adaptive behavior composite

symptoms

Alzheimer's Disease

Chapter 9

Developmental Disorders II

The two developmental disorders we are about to discuss involve *behavioral control* or *behavioral disruption* issues. *Conduct Disorder* is rather interesting for a variety of reasons. It tends not to respond too well to treatment interventions and, more importantly, if left untreated may turn into *Antisocial Personality Disorder (ASPD)*. Conduct disorder also seems to be associated with alcohol and drug abuse/dependence in adolescence.

Attention Deficit/Hyperactivity Disorder (ADHD) has received a lot of press the past few years, and with good reason. According to some research, ADHD affects at least two million schoolchildren in the United States, anywhere from 3% to 6% of the school age population (Hill & Schoener, 1996). ADHD is much more common among boys than girls. There seems to be a positive correlation between ADHD and mood disorders, learning disabilities, anxiety disorders, and substance use disorders (Lambert, Hartsough, Sassone, & Sandoval, 1987). Like conduct disorder, ADHD does not respond terribly well to treatment, but like conduct disorder it is treatable.

Our first case, Bernard, is an 8-year-old boy who has behavioral problems. Bernard has some other concerns. See if you can discern them before we give him a diagnosis. Jacqueline is more atypical, since boys suffer from ADHD anywhere from three to nine times more often than do girls (Angier, 1991). However, that does not mean that ADHD cannot affect girls. Jacqueline is a 12-year-old girl who may suffer from ADHD. Like many of our other cases, she may also present additional concerns. Keep in mind that ADHD may be overdiagnosed among school children. We will examine some of the possible reasons for this. Finally, ADHD is often treated with medications, specifically *Ritalin (methylphenidate)*. We will discuss some of the issues involving Ritalin a bit later in this chapter. (NOTE: Because of the ages of the individuals discussed, and because both Bernard and Jacqueline were uncomfortable being taped, this chapter will occur in some sections in a more traditional narrative style. Whenever possible, direct quotes will be used.)

Conduct Disorder
The Case of Bernard: Loss of Control

Presenting Problem

Bernard is an 8-year-old white boy in a local public elementary school. Bernard is in the first grade and is one of the older students in his class. Bernard is an only child. His mother works for the county, and his father is a foreman in a local canning factory. "My dad runs the people who puts all the stuff in cans, stuff like beans and things. He's real good at that. He's the boss! My mommy works also, but I don't know what she does. She types a lot. I saw her at work one time." Bernard's mother decided not to have any more children. The referral noted that his mother "realized that we were going to have major problems with Bernard. Because of that, we decided to stop at one. We can't handle a lot of problems, and we can't afford another child with the extra treatment Bernard gets."

Bernard was quite active during the sessions, always fidgeting with his hands, rubbing his head, waving his arms, and was constantly into everything in our office. He displayed an appropriate affect and would frown a lot during the sessions with narrowed eyes when he made eye contact, which was very infrequent. Bernard was dressed in jeans and a "Limp Bizkit" T-shirt. His sneakers had no laces and his jeans were bunched up around his heels. His mother presented with an appropriate affect, was pleasant, appropriately dressed, but did not smile much. Her eye contact was fair.

Further examination of Bernard's school records revealed some more useful information. Bernard had periods of time when he would behave appropriately, usually in the morning, and by the afternoon he would often *act out* and have emotional outbursts in the classroom. Because of these outbursts, which tended to be violent, the school decided to provide him with a full time aide, Mrs. Q. The school noted, "His behavior has improved somewhat this year due to the presence of an aide. It still needs improvement."

Bernard came to us through his principal, who noted, "His problems appear to be getting worse when he does not have his aide. Along with a proper diagnosis, we need to have continued justification to keep Mrs. Q."

Background Information

Bernard has an extensive and interesting background, complicated by a difficult medical history. Bernard demonstrated developmental delays and emotional problems shortly after turning 1-year-old. He was sent to the local hospital for an evaluation. The hospital kept him and involved Bernard in its early childhood intervention program. He made some progress, but his progress was hampered by his mother, who was "unable to provide for his needs," according to the hospital's report. Bernard was initially raised without a father. "His mother, who has an alcohol problem, got pregnant while drunk. The father disappeared once he discovered she was pregnant. Subsequently, she attempted to raise Bernard on her own and was unsuccessful. Child Welfare was familiar with her case, since the police had picked her up a number of times before and after Bernard's birth, usually for D&D (Drunk and Disorderly). Brenda was eventually deemed to be an unfit mother and, for Bernard's protection, he was placed in foster care.

Bernard was in foster care until the age of 5, at which point a local family adopted him. Bernard's foster parents can be described as being upper-middle class. They have a small mortgage and are warm and caring people. His mother told us, "We knew that Bernard had some problems, but we wanted kids. It has not been easy, but when we saw him we totally fell in love with him. He just won us over. It's hard for many older kids to get adopted, but we were willing. It has been hard though."

Bernard's medical history is troublesome. He wears glasses for *astigmatism* (nearsightedness). According to his records, his prescription was initially misdiagnosed in that his glasses were underprescribed by about 20%. This made it difficult for him to function in class and in the schoolyard. Initially Bernard was perceived to be clumsy and uncoordinated, but once he received the proper prescription, he improved significantly. When he was 5 years old, Bernard had tubes inserted into his ears due to recurring ear infections. Finally, when he was 6 (3 days after his birthday), his appendix ruptured and he had an emergency appendectomy. Needless to say, this little boy has experienced a lot in his short life. "I liked the hospital Mr. Doctor. I got a lot of ice cream, and they gave me balloons and a teddy bear!"

Before we proceed, we need to examine some facts and issues regarding Conduct Disorder. First, Conduct Disorder often occurs (or is *comorbid*) with ADHD. There are differences, and it is the psychologist's job to discern these. Many times a child is simply poorly behaved, lacks discipline, or is a behavioral problem that does **not** qualify for a DSM-IV-TR diagnosis. Teachers, unwilling or unable to handle behavioral problems that are not diagnosable, may attempt to get these children removed from their classrooms. In general, education classes do not adequately prepare teachers for these types of concerns, so their reactions are understandable. Finally, there appear to be certain key causal factors related to the manifestation of conduct disorder. See if you can recall these as we learn more about Bernard.

Thought Questions

1. What is going on with Bernard?
2. How important is Bernard's medical history when assessing his condition?
3. How important is his mother's drinking history?
4. Discuss how typical it is for a child to be removed from his biological parent's house.
5. What would you need to find out about Bernard's biological father?
6. How typical is Bernard's speech for an 8-year-old?

Assessment and Evaluation

Bernard was assessed with an *unstructured diagnostic interview,* an examination of *permanent products* (school and hospital records, and previous reports), a *psychoeducational testing battery* and a *psychological testing battery.* We worked closely with Bernard's school and teachers on this case, since his school was responsible for the referral and for the majority of the treatment. Through these means, we learned a lot of additional, important information about Bernard.

Bernard told us that he had "two mommies. One of them made me, but she was mean to me. My other mommy is very nice to me. I only have one daddy, and he's with the nice mommy. He's the big boss at work!" In examining his records, we discovered that Bernard's biological father beat his mother "with a stick and an electrical cord. He continued to beat her while she was pregnant. Once he discovered her pregnancy, he left and has not been heard from since then. Additionally, his mother has been diagnosed as alcohol dependent. She told us she was drunk when Bernard was conceived. No signs of *Fetal Alcohol Syndrome (FAS)* or *Fetal Alcohol Effects (FAE)* are present in Bernard." We asked Bernard if he remembered what his mother did when he was home. "Before I left for the big boy's house, my mommy would sleep a lot. When she would be up, she would walk funny. She would also talk funny." He was smiling at us while relating this information.

Upon reading this information some aspects became clearer. Even though there were no signs of FAS or FAE with Bernard, it is possible that he may have some type of *learning disability* based on his upbringing. Perhaps as a fetus he suffered some physical trauma due to his mother being beaten, such as *traumatic brain injury (TBI).* We asked Bernard some more questions, hoping to gather some additional key information.

"I fight a lot of kids. They pick on me because I wear glasses and I talk slow. They pick on me because of my two mommies. So I hit them and bite them a lot. They don't pick on me after that. I hit them hard, in the face." We also asked him about how he acts in class. "I am a good boy in class. But if a kid picks on me I hit him. Yesterday a kid knocked my glasses off, so I hit him. I had to see the principal again."

We also interviewed his teachers, who reported similar incidents. Bernard was getting into many fights at school, especially during recess and gym periods in the yard. He would indeed hit kids, even if it seemed like they were not picking on him. Mrs. Q told us that "for some reason, he's okay during the mornings, but something happens in the afternoons. His control worsens and his attention span decreases also. I'm not sure what is happening." We investigated this further by asking Bernard when recess is.

"I play after I eat lunch. I eat lunch here at school. It's yucky a lot. I like the juice. We also get soda sometimes; I really like that. I always play in school after I have lunch." We found this schedule interesting, especially because it meant that Bernard was at recess in the afternoon. Could this be related to his behavioral issues? We discussed this with the teachers and his principal.

Their response? They were unsure, but because of schedule limitations (including having too many students, not enough teachers and aides, and limited funds), Bernard's recess times really could not be changed. We asked the school to do so on a trial basis, just to see what occurred. We also asked them to eliminate soda from his lunches, since caffeine does not help attention deficits. We continued to examine Bernard's hospital records.

We discovered that he had tubes in his ears because of "significant ear infections. His speech development was compromised because of them. Additionally, his birth mother left him alone for long periods of time, and she rarely spoke to him. His 'late talking,' by age three and a half, caused him to have some of the delays he presents. Additionally, he was diagnosed as being farsighted when in fact he has astigmatism and is near-sighted. This took one year to correct and also may have impacted his development."

We also discovered in Bernard's hospital and school records that his biological family, specifically his mother and his maternal side, had a significant history of learning disabilities. Both his biological mother and his mother's sister had been diagnosed with learning disabilities, specifically reading and speech difficulties. Note and recall that learning disabilities may have a familial component and seem to run in families, even though they may skip a generation. For example, *dyslexia,* the most common learning disorder, seems to be associated with genetic factors that cause some type of brain abnormalities (Shaywitz, 1998). Children whose parents have dyslexia are at a higher risk of contracting it (Vogler, DeFries, & Decker, 1985).

This background data is crucial, since we could now point to some of the origins of Bernard's problems. People with learning disabilities also tend to have emotional difficulties as well, and they often tend to suffer from ADHD. Bernard still needed to be officially diagnosed as having a learning disability, and we still needed more information on his behavioral issues.

The school performed the psychoeducational assessment, since they had a *school psychologist* on site and it would be cheaper that way. Bernard's parents needed to *consent* to his being tested, which they did without issue. The results of this assessment were quite interesting. Bernard's test scores pointed to his having a learning disability, specifically in writing and in language. The school psychologist noted that his speech was developmentally appropriate for a 5-year-old, and his writing was at the first grade level. He also had short-term memory (STM) deficits. One advantage is that this diagnosis would allow him to receive special educational services and to retain Mrs. Q. It should be noted that Mrs. Q needed to sit in on two of the three testing sessions to "keep Bernard calm and on task. At one point he threw some of the materials at the examiner, at which point the session ended."

We still needed to focus on Bernard's behavioral issues. We administered a series of *behavioral checklists,* a *sentence completion test,* the *Children's Apperception Test (CAT)*, and a *House-Tree-Person (HTP)*. The last two devices are *projective measures.* We gave the behavioral checklists to his teachers and his adoptive parents. The results substantiated the fact that Bernard was a behavioral problem, prone to violent outbursts, especially during the afternoon. He did not have as many problems at home, so his issues seemed to be confined to school, for the most part. His mother did note, "Bernard is fascinated with fire and flames. He also likes to break glass. He broke three windows in the neighborhood, which he said were accidents."

Some of the themes present in the CAT, sentence completion, and HTP were anger, detachment, rejection, low self-esteem, and alienation. Bernard told us that he would like to be a "lion like the picture, so I could beat up and kill anyone who picks on me. I'd be super strong." He also told us that he "wished I could fly like Superman, away from everyone. I would go to Krypton and leave everyone home. And no one could fight me because my body is the man of steel. I could hurt them with one punch!" In his HTP, the sun was black, and he drew "my two mommies." His adoptive parents were facing forward, and his biological mother was facing backward, away from the front. He also drew his room with no windows. We were impressed with the clarity and sophistication of his drawings and asked Bernard about this. "I love to make pictures with crayons. Mrs. Q will help me a lot with them. I draw a lot. She got me a big big box of crayons!"

At this point, we felt like we had enough information to make a preliminary diagnosis for Bernard. Our diagnosis appears first; the school's diagnoses follow. See if you agree with the diagnoses and if not, think about those reasons:

Conduct Disorder, Childhood-Onset Type	312.81
School's Diagnoses:	
Expressive Language Disorder	315.31
Disorder of Written Expression	315.2

Theoretical Etiologies

We have already examined the origins of learning disorders in Chapter 8, so we will focus on the etiologies of conduct disorder, which is Bernard's primary diagnosis and is the focal point of his treatment plan with us. Children who have conduct disorder are intentionally cruel and deliberately aggressive towards animate and inanimate objects.

Genetic and environmental factors seem to contribute to the development of conduct disorder. Research has found that family environment contributes to the development of conduct disorder, but research has been inconclusive as to whether this is due to the family's environment or to genetics. Some research hypothesizes that there may be two types of conduct disorder: The first type fades out during adolescence, and the more pervasive type persists and does not fade out. The second type seems to be associated with a genetic predisposition to developing conduct disorder, or inheriting a diathesis making the child more vulnerable in times of stress. The type that fades seems to be related more to parenting, the child's peers, and to the environment (Comings, 2000). The genetic link between conduct disorder and ADHD occurring together seems to be stronger, as it does with conduct disorder appearing with substance dependence (Comings, 2000). Finally, antisocial behavior in childhood seems to predict similar behavior in the child's offspring. In other words, deviant behavior seems to have a familial component that may not be environmental.

Familial background is quite important when searching for the etiology of conduct disorder. Studies have concluded that these families may have experienced (or are experiencing) financial hardships, unemployment, severe physical illness, and lack of consistent shelter or location. They have poor support systems and may be at odds with others in their neighborhood. The parents may also lack parenting skills, but poor or lacking parenting skills does not mean that any offspring will develop conduct disorder; it just makes it more likely (McMahon & Estes, 1997). Children may learn coping skills in their family and learn how to use these skills, though deviant, in situations outside of the family.

Not surprisingly, children with conduct disorder have poor peer relationships. What does this mean? They seem to have poor social skills if any; they may also make *attribution errors*. That is, they may inaccurately label other peoples' emotions, and they may attribute hostile intentions to other people. This is especially true when the other peoples' emotions and situations are ambiguous (Dodge, 1993). A classic problem associated with conduct disorder is the concept that such children often respond to problem-solving with aggressive responses. For example, instead of pressing the coin return on a video game or a soda machine, they will kick the machine and attempt to break into the coin box.

Dougherty, Bjork, Marsh, and Moeller (2000) discovered that children with conduct disorder tend to underachieve academically and tend to have reading difficulties and problems staying on task (paying attention). It is possible that these school-related concerns may be due to a brain or neurological malfunction (Toupin, Dery, Pauze, Mercier, & Fortin, 2000).

In sum, most helping professionals take an interactionist view on conduct disorder's etiology. That is, there seems to be a genetic component though as stated, we are not sure whether this component produces the disorder, the characteristics leading to the disorder, or the diathesis for conduct disorder. Familial environment and poor parenting, or lack of parenting skills, as well as significant environmental and social stressors also seems to be key contributory factors.

Treatment Plan

We worked with Bernard's school as we devised the best treatment plan for him. We decided on individual therapy for Bernard, and also decided that, as required, he receive *special education services* in his school. This would involve his being placed in the *resource room* for most of the day, if not all of the day. Bernard's behaviors were deemed too severe to place him in a regular classroom at this time. The resource room also had the advantage of only having eight students in it. Bernard would have Mrs. Q in addition to one teacher and a *teacher's aide*. The individual attention he would receive would help him progress and hopefully come close to reaching his age-appropriate levels in school and in his behaviors.

Conduct Disorder is difficult to treat effectively. However, three therapeutic modalities have been tried with varying degrees of success. We used the Multisystemic Treatment (MST) approach with Bernard (Henggeler, Schoenwald, Borduin, Rowland, & Cunningham, 1998). MST sees all systems having an impact on the child and thus needing to be involved in the child's intervention and treatment. The family, school, and community are included. The antisocial behavior can be triggered or maintained by interactions with any or all of the systems. MST will use other treatment techniques which will be outlined shortly. In effect, all family members, school personnel, and all other individuals in the child's environment are included if possible. We involved Bernard's special education teacher and Mrs. Q. The school wanted us to set up a behavioral system, where good behaviors (and lack of outbursts) were rewarded, and outbursts and aggressive behaviors were punished, usually by a *time-out* or some other form of punishment. We did **not** use *corporal punishment.*

We also used Kazdin's technique of Cognitive Problem-Solving Skills Training (PSST; Kazdin, 1996). Instruction and feedback are incorporated with practice to get the child to discover different ways to handle problematic situations. The key is that the child needs to alter his/her attributions about others' motivations. We taught Bernard to be more sensitive to other children's feelings and to use socially appropriate responses to problems.

We also told Mrs. Q to focus on Bernard's interests and strengths, specifically his drawing. We suggested that she allow at least 30 minutes each day for Bernard to draw, and we also suggested that he have time to draw at home. Bernard liked this. "I really like to draw. I love to use my crayons to make pictures!" We discovered that drawing allowed him to focus his attention and calmed him down. Eventually Bernard was calm while he was drawing, and for about 30 minutes before and after the drawing time. Mrs. Q kept the sessions at the same time in the afternoon so Bernard could look forward to it and exercise better control over his behavior. Emphasizing the positive is another aspect of MST.

The school also eliminated any caffeine and excessive sugar from Bernard's diet. We hoped that this would help to calm Bernard. Bernard was indeed calmer once these diet changes were implemented, but we had no way to be certain if this was due to his diet, or to his drawing times. Bernard was still prone to outbursts during recess times, and the punishments became even more severe. Eventually the principal "had no choice but to remove him from recess. We tried him with older kids and that helped a bit, but he would also fight with them. We decided to remove him from recess and give him time outside alone with Mrs. Q." The school wanted to wait and see if the anger control techniques, and the rewards and punishers, helped Bernard enough to return him to recess.

Bernard worked with the special education teacher and the learning specialist in learning strategies to help him cope with his learning disabilities. As odd as it may seem, getting diagnosed with learning disabilities helped Bernard. He now had his aide, and he had the special education services available as well. He would receive these services for the remainder of his time in school.

We also brought in Bernard's adoptive mother and worked with her on programs and techniques to use at home. She told us, "I'm getting a bit afraid of what Bernard might do. His outbursts have led to broken windows, and we think he also killed a stray neighborhood cat. We're afraid he might do something to us." We discussed various options with Bernard's mother, and she agreed that they have been thinking of putting Bernard into a youth home if the situation did not improve at home and at school. "Of course we don't want to, but things seem to be getting worse." We discussed how Bernard was learning new techniques to manage his behavior and attribution errors, and discussed how she should focus on his drawing at home. The school suggested to her that she keep sweets and caffeine away from Bernard.

We used Parent Management Training (PMT) with Bernard's mother. The goal here is simple: The parent(s) is/are taught to change the child's behavior at home. This is based on the concept that dysfunctional home environments are partially responsible for the antisocial behaviors, and changing the parents' interactions with the child will lead to behavioral change in the child him/herself. We wanted his mother to learn new specific skills, such as communication, monitoring, and supervision. PMT is most effective with children under 12, but its long-term effectiveness is unclear at present (McMahon & Wells, 1998).

Finally, some professionals feel that prevention is the most effective way to treat conduct disorder. Prevention is based on certain assumptions that may or may not be accurate. First, prevention works best when symptoms of conduct disorder are discovered and treated early. That is, it is easier to treat conduct disorder in younger children. Additionally, prevention can focus on the strengths of the child and work to alleviate the risk factors that may lead to antisocial behavior in young children, such as academic and peer-related problems. Prevention, while expensive, will benefit social agencies such as schools and mental health settings, thus saving money and saving lives.

Since Bernard was already demonstrating antisocial behaviors, we included prevention of future problems in his treatment plan. In addition to using PSST and PMT, we spent a lot of time with Mrs. Q and his special education teacher to help them focus on his strengths and eliminate his deficits to avoid future problems. In other words, if caught early, the chance of treatment success is increased.

We spent most of our remaining time with Bernard drawing and using *play therapy*. Bernard loved to play with the dollhouse, and he always had his adoptive mother and father with him in the dollhouse. When we included his biological mother, Bernard would put her "in the bathroom. She was always there. She would sleep in there a lot." Bernard did not include her in any of the activities and would rarely use her. Bernard really wants a "kitty. See? He's in the house with us. He's a boy cat. His name is Benny. He's black with a white stripe." While in our sessions, Bernard played calmly and drew calmly.

Psychoanalysis generally is not efficacious for treating conduct disorder. The pressing goals were to get Bernard to change his behavior. Delving deep into an 8-year-old's past would not be the best way for this to occur. Since the school hired us, they wanted us to work on Bernard's outbursts and to do so quickly. Behavioral techniques were best suited for this.

As time went on in our sessions and in school, major progress was not seen immediately. We continued to work with his mother and taught her about time-out procedures, appropriate punishment, and parenting and communication skills. We discovered that she was not implementing many of the techniques at home since "they seemed cruel to Bernard. I'm not sure if there's any hope anyway. I'm afraid he'll always have this temper. Looking at his background, can you blame him?"

We also taught Mrs. Q and Bernard's mother *progressive muscle relaxation* techniques. The goal here was to ensure that Bernard's mother and Mrs. Q were not as tense when Bernard would have an outburst. They proved to be successful for both women.

Once they learned these techniques, (and once the caffeine and sugar were washed out of Bernard's system, in which the school had a major interest), Mrs. Q and his mother noticed that his outbursts had decreased somewhat. Instead of being on edge the entire afternoon, Bernard would have bad hours. He also learned to put his hands in his pockets, take very deep breaths, and to close his eyes when he felt like he was going to hit someone. "I really don't hit people a lot now. I used to hit girls but I don't do that. I still hit boys sometimes, because they still pick on me. One of my drawings is on the wall in school! It has a gold star on it!"

We worked with Bernard for 5 months until the school year ended. He had to go to summer school and was retained for lack of scholastic progress. Mrs. Q told us that "his outbursts still exist, but they're not nearly as bad as when we first saw you. Whenever he swings at someone he gets a time-out. Bernard knows that he'll get into big trouble with these behaviors, but at times it's like he can't help himself. He feels no regret at what he does. It's really quite sad."

Bernard drew us a picture during our last session. It showed his family, a cat, Mrs. Q, and us. We were all facing forward, and the sun was bright orange now. His biological mother was not in the drawing. Bernard was there, hands in his pockets, and smiling. For treating conduct disorder, even small progress can be considered significant.

We will now examine some possible medications that could be used to treat Conduct Disorder. Some past research states that Ritalin (methylphenidate) may have some utility in treating conduct disorder, specifically the antisocial behaviors associated with the disorder (Abikoff & Klein, 1992). It seems that if ADHD is comorbid with conduct disorder, stimulants such as Ritalin seem to be the most effective. This is best decided on a case-by-case basis (Abikoff & Klein, 1992). Sometimes *antipsychotics* are considered. These may include such medications as *Haldol (haloperidol)* and *Thorazine (chlorpromazine)*. These drugs are often considered when the behavioral outbursts are particularly violent. The major concern here is that the side effects of the antipsychotics can be significant and quite crippling, especially if they are used for a long period of time. There are additional risks in using such medications with very young children. Finally, there is not a high success rate with these medications in treating Conduct Disorder's behavioral symptoms (Bezchlibnyk-Butler & Jeffries, 2002).

Lithium (lithium carbonate) has been used in the past, but like all of the other medications, its efficacy is questionable. Antidepressant usage has been attempted, but the results are similar to all of the other medications described so far: questionable. One other type of medication, *anticonvulsants,* has been tried in the past. Some research has demonstrated that these medications, such as *Tegretol (carbamazepine),* may be effective in reducing behavioral outbursts. However, like everything else, this needs to be decided individually for each child (Bezchlibnyk-Butler & Jeffries, 2002).

Thus, we can conclude, as does the research, that no one type of medication appears to be uniformly accepted, or effective, for the treatment of Conduct Disorder. Cognitive-behavioral techniques, as well as approaches such as MST, PMT and PSST, seem to be the most effective treatment approach, with medications in the background as a possible treatment adjunct. Kazdin and Wassell (1999) made two conclusions in their research on conduct disorder. First, there appears to be no single or combined clearly effective treatment modality. More importantly, they concluded that the degree of success, or failure, depends on the type and severity of the related risk factors (such as social stressors), protective factors (parents with good parenting skills; a supportive and knowledgeable school), and the type and severity of the conduct problem. More research is needed in this area.

Prognosis

Bernard's prognosis can be listed as "guarded." There are several reasons for this. First, all of his conditions do not seem to be responding particularly well to any of the treatment modalities attempted. Additionally, conduct disorder does not respond very well to any type of treatment program, which makes a better prognosis a risk. Bernard also has an unfortunate background to overcome in addition to his presenting learning and behavioral problems. Bernard's parents are considering placement in a youth home (an inpatient, sheltered care facility). Many times these settings exacerbate the problems. Bernard's adoptive father appears to be detached from the present situation.

On the positive side, Bernard has formed a close bond with Mrs. Q and is making slow progress because of her. His school realizes that he needs extensive help and is to be lauded for doing everything they can for him. Bernard also has a very strong creative side to his personality, and the school is encouraging this.

At last report in a follow-up, Bernard finished summer school and was restarting first grade. His outbursts had been limited to about one to two per day, and he was not hitting people nearly as often. His drawing was progressing nicely, so much so that the school was going to try him in an advanced art class. Mrs. Q noted that "his adoptive mom is still supportive of Bernard, and they are not thinking of a group home right now. Unfortunately, his adoptive father is still not that involved, but we will work on that this year. Bernard also grew 2 inches over his summer recess, and his control seems better. His drawing seems to be the key, since his reading and writing have progressed, but not as quickly as we had hoped. We will keep trying until we have exhausted all resources and hope."

Attention Deficit/Hyperactivity Disorder

The Case of Jacqueline:
Easily Distracted

Presenting Problem

Jacqueline (or Jackie) is a 12-year-old black female in the sixth grade in a public elementary school in a small urban city. Jackie is an only child whose mother, age 30, works at a fast food restaurant and also works as often as she can as a cleaning lady for local families. Jackie's mother got divorced when Jackie was 6 years old; she "threw the bum (her husband) out. He was cheating on her and he was bad. He also hit her sometimes. My dad is a creep and a bum. I hate him." Jackie's father was often in trouble with the law. He spent a good part of his life in jail or prison for crimes ranging from breaking and entering to selling crack cocaine. "I could deal with the crime stuff, but not the drug s**t. My dad was a pusher. I don't do no drugs and never will. Bad stuff." Jackie's mother remarried because, her mother told us, "Jackie needed a father, someone who was clean and a decent person for a role model. Sam fit the bill." Sam is a civil servant and has worked in his position for 20 years. Sam is 44 years old "which is old, but I need some stability. I was not going to be a statistic, a single black mother with a child who gets in some kind of trouble. Jackie's been good that way, really great, but the other things have caused her some problems."

Jackie came to see us with her mother. Jackie was dressed in long slacks, a tank top, was 5'6" tall and about 20 pounds overweight. She made good eye contact, had an appropriate affect, and always sat forward in her chair during the sessions. She had a loud voice and when she said something dramatic, she would always look at you to see your reactions. Jackie also carried a large handbag and sometimes wore a baseball cap. Her mother was 5'8" tall, overweight, and had some grey hairs. She wore glasses, smiled frequently and had an appropriate affect. Her mother spoke softly and would always say "Excuse me" whenever she "used a bad word." Jackie would usually look away whenever her mother was speaking, but she would look at us when we were speaking.

Jackie did not perform well at school, which was one reason for her referral to us. She achieved a lot of "Unsatisfactory" grades in school and since the fifth grade, when grades were assigned, she received a lot of Ds and Fs. These were usually based upon her "lack of paying attention in class, and her inability to stay on task," according to her current teacher. Because of her attention problems, Jackie was left back this year and is repeating the sixth grade. "I really don't care about that. I don't like school that much; it bores me and stuff. I like to do sports and video games. No time for guys now. My mom and stepdad won't let me do that." Jackie's mother rolled her eyes.

Jackie was referred to us by her school, specifically her teachers. They were concerned that her progress was regressing and that she would be held back yet again if things continued on the present path. Jackie's past history did not bode well for her, and her teachers agreed. They told us that her behavior has slowly gotten worse as she has gotten older. They had spent more time with her and told us that she is very happy at home with her stepfather. Her teachers were at a loss as to what might have been causing her problems, specifically what might be making them worse. Based on these concerns she was sent to us.

Background Information

Jackie's developmental history was unremarkable; she reached all of her developmental milestones at their age-appropriate times. We asked Jackie's teachers and school social worker if she had ever had any alcohol, drug, or legal issues. Her social worker Sandy told us, "Not really. To our knowledge she's experimented like all of our kids, but we are not overly alarmed at that. This is normal adolescent behavior for us. She may have told you that she's not interested in boys, and that's not entirely true. She IS interested, but she's afraid of what her mother and stepfather would do if she pursued the interests. She keeps those interests under control and secret. Her mother married at a very early age, so we can understand her views. And with her father in legal trouble a lot, it makes even more sense."

Jackie was sent to the school social worker because of her grades. This was before she came to us for an evaluation. Sandy told us that "Jackie wouldn't talk too much in our sessions but when she did, it became clear that she had some unfinished business and other concerns. We felt the need for further evaluation." We then decided to corroborate this information with Jackie.

"Geez, what is with you? I told you I don't do drugs or booze. No way, not after what my dad did. My mother also drinks sometimes. That's how she got pregnant, so I stay away from that. All my friends want me to drink, but I won't! I won't lie, I tried a lot of stuff, but I don't do it now! Look at that over there!"

We then asked her about guys and boyfriends. "Well, Arthur wants to hook up, but he's older and I won't. I won't lie, I like him, but my stepdad and mom would kill me if we got it on, you know? I need to keep peace in my house and stay out of trouble. My mom promised me a car when I graduate, if I stay out of trouble, so I need to do that. That's a nice computer. Does it have games on it? I've got a PS2. Ever play Tekken?"

We questioned Jackie about her problems of paying attention in class. "You must have no memory. I told you school doesn't work for me. Sometimes it's so wrong in there. I like to read and do Playstation and stuff, hang out. Where will school get me? Look at my mom. I can get a job at McDonald's with no schooling. I can get good money doing other things. I won't do what my dad did or what my stepdad does. School is just something to get out of the way before I get married and have kids. Who's that a picture of?"

We had already noticed some slight, but we felt significant, features of Jackie's that needed further investigation. We had some ideas as to how to approach further questioning and, if necessary, further sessions. Before we reveal our ideas, we would like you to consider some questions.

Thought Questions

1. What is going on with Jackie?
2. The psychologist has some ideas as to how to approach Jackie's situation. What questions should he ask?
3. How important are her father's legal problems in relation to Jackie's situation?
4. Her teachers and school social worker consider Jackie's drug and alcohol experimentation normal and typical for a 12-year-old. Discuss your views about this.

Assessment and Evaluation

Jackie was assessed with an *unstructured diagnostic interview* and a *psychiatric evaluation*. The latter was deemed necessary during a *case conference*. We also decided to continue questioning Jackie's mother and, if needed, her teachers and school social worker. We continued to question Jackie further in order to try to make an accurate diagnosis. We returned to the issue of her not paying attention in class.

"Well, school is kind of hard for me sometimes. I don't like it much, but it's hard to get what the teachers say, you know? They also are out to get me. Here I am, phat, and they don't want to accept that. I bet I can do the stuff if they want me to." We then asked specifically which subjects she likes and dislikes.

"Well, I hate all of them, to tell you the truth. I like writing however, since it gives me time to daydream and write my songs. I'm going to be a star when I get older. My teacher told me I've got a great voice and should use it. See what I mean? How many big stars did well in school? Puffy's a criminal and he's a millionaire, so what's up with that? Nothing much else in school does it for me except when I write. So how old are you?"

While our questions were going on, Jackie was often out of her seat and was pacing around the office, looking at books and trying to open file cabinet drawers. We repeatedly had to tell her to stop and to stay seated. She told us she has a lot of "energy that needs to be let out. It really builds up and it gets bad, like a stomachache. I get all jittery and I need to let it out somehow. You know what that's like."

Jackie told us that this "has been occurring for about 5 years in my eyes, but I really don't know. I've had this extra energy for awhile now. I usually get in trouble at school because of stuff, so it may be that long. (She's walking around as she speaks.) It's been happening for a while. I can't tell you more about it, but I hate school. Let me sing, that's my life. Music is it." At this point she continues to pace around the office and now begins to sway back and forth.

We asked Jackie if she had a tendency to lose things. "Oh boy do I! I can never keep my cell phone with me, and I always forget my keys. That puts me in Frances' place a lot (Frances is her friend), since I have to wait until someone gets home to let me in. Cool tie. I forget a lot of things. Tonya's number, my best friend? Don't ask me. I write it on my hand. Birthdays? Can't remember. Am I talking too fast? Who's the dude in the photo?" Jackie was speaking very loudly at this point.

We then spoke briefly with Jackie's mother. We made repeated attempts to bring in Jackie's stepfather, but we had no success. We asked Jackie's mother about her behavior issues. "Well, what can I say? I get called into school all the time. Her teachers are fed up with her and so am I. My thing is, is this typical teenage girl behavior? I don't think so. We tried some other things in the past to deal with Jackie's problems but she didn't respond too well. We may have to try those again. She resented some of the methods, but they seemed to work, when she cooperated with us."

We were curious now so we asked Jackie's mother to clarify her remarks. "Well, Jackie was always a bit of a problem and, as you know, her behavior has gotten a lot worse lately. Her grades have fallen, and my husband and I are concerned that her behavior is getting too extreme. We're worried that she'll be thrown out of school because she's become so disruptive in class. She rarely completes her homework and often comes to class unprepared. She's always losing things or forgetting them. We thought something might be wrong with her brain. Jackie will walk around a lot and will not stay in her seat too often. She has also been argumentative with her teachers, but not in a physical way."

"When she was younger the school social worker, on a referral from her first grade teacher, asked Jackie to see a psychiatrist. He came to the school on a consulting basis and examined Jackie. He decided that she had ADHD and should be prescribed *Cylert (magnesium pemoline).* He also said that she should see the school social worker once a week and, if possible, I should also go in with her. I couldn't at the time, and Jackie refused to go to the sessions after a short time. This occurred towards the end of the school year, and the school told us we should consider another school for Jackie if she continued to refuse treatment. It was a struggle to get her to take her pills. She developed a rash and would often spit them out. We eventually moved, and Jackie ended up in another school anyway. Her new (present) school never got any records with this diagnosis, and her problems got a bit better, so we never pressed the issue. Of course things got a lot worse the past year so here we are."

Now this is interesting. Jackie had already been diagnosed, according to her mother, but her present school has none of her records. This is not that unusual, especially when a student transfers to another school. As was noted in the previous chapter, we call this "falling through the cracks," i.e., the past history gets lost during a transfer. We thus had to diagnose Jackie and decide if she needed to be on any medication. We also contacted her previous school, but they were unable to locate any of her files. A lot of their files had been damaged or destroyed in a flood that occurred when a blizzard hit the town (this was in another state). This was indeed unfortunate but there was nothing that could be done.

We also decided to have Jackie see our psychiatrist, especially because she had been taking Cylert in the past. Additionally, this particular psychiatrist was an expert on ADHD, and we hypothesized that Jackie might need to be taking some kind of medication. Jackie was not happy about this. She protested, began yelling, threw down a pencil she was holding, cursed, and finally stormed out of the office when we told her. Her mother ran after her and the session ended at that point.

We received a call from Jackie's mother later the same day, apologizing for Jackie's behavior. "I had a long talk with Jackie and set the law. I know Jackie has to be in treatment and evaluated, and Jackie now accepts this." We rescheduled an appointment for Jackie to see the psychiatrist, and then to see us. The psychiatrist had some interesting comments about Jackie. In sum:

"She has a lot of problems staying on task and was often pacing around the office. She would answer a question and then quickly change the subject. Patient mentioned that she was on Cylert when she was younger and gave her a rash. Stopped taking it and she got more anxious. Mother worried about patient being expelled, and becoming violent. No signs of alcohol or drug abuse. Preliminary diagnosis:

> Attention-Deficit/Hyperactivity Disorder,
> Predominantly Hyperactive-Impulsive Type   314.01
>
> Treatment Plan: Return after patient presented at case conference; evaluate for medications"

Based on our observations and conversations so far, we were inclined to agree with the psychiatrist, but we needed to present Jackie at a case conference to be certain. Before this occurred, Jackie called up and apologized for her behavior. She was concerned that we saw her as an "obnoxious" teenager who didn't respect adults or authority, and she was concerned that we would report this to the school. Jackie's mother assured us that Jackie would cooperate in therapy once her appointment arrived. Her mother also told us that she would participate if we thought this best.

The case conference's staff concluded that the psychiatrist was correct with Jackie's diagnosis and concurred that medications were warranted, at least initially. The staff suggested that Jackie come in alone and that her mother be included on an as-needed basis. Additionally, they decided that the school should be notified of Jackie's progress in general terms. This would avoid potential complications.

Theoretical Etiologies

As of this writing the causes of ADHD are not yet known. However, as with many of the other disorders discussed, both biological/genetic and environmental factors seem to come into play. We will examine some of the theories and focus briefly on some of the "pop" theories as well. Part of the difficulty is due to the fact that each person diagnoses ADHD differently, i.e., not standardized.

The present research seems to suggest that ADHD is inherited (Tannock, 1998). However, we do not know which specific genes to examine, or the mechanisms that may be at work in ADHD. Some research has implicated the dopamine system, stating that reduced dopamine activity may in fact be related to the behavioral aspects of ADHD. This is important, but we need to keep in mind that most likely several genes are responsible for the behavioral aspects of ADHD, and the other aspects as well.

Pregnancy and birth complications can also be implicated. Low birth weight, brain trauma before and/or after birth, malnutrition, mothers who abused alcohol or other drugs, or who smoked during pregnancy, may be related to ADHD. Excessive alcohol abuse or dependence can lead to Fetal Alcohol Syndrome (FAS), and FAS symptoms may include hyperactivity and impulsivity, and learning and behavioral problems. It is difficult to separate out environmental factors, since it can be assumed that a child who grows up in such a household will not have the most stable living situation. It is not yet known that these factors are specific to the development of ADHD, but it does seem that they tend to increase the chances that a child will have ADHD.

Brain imaging techniques point out some abnormalities in children and adolescents with ADHD. Specifically, areas in the frontal lobe seem to be implicated. These areas are involved with attention, arousal, and inhibition of motor movements. These areas in question seem to suffer from structural abnormalities (they are undersized) or from underactivity. We still need to know why these differences occur.

We will examine family influences before we get to some of the "pop" explanations. The concept that negative family influences lead to ADHD has received little support in research. However, some aspects need to be examined and clarified. First, it is possible that family influences may indeed lead to ADHD; more importantly, it is more likely that negative family influences may lead to an exacerbation of ADHD symptoms. It is also possible that negative family influences may occur because family members do not react well to a child who is impulsive and is a behavioral problem. As stated with Bernard, there is support that family conflicts may be related to the appearance and maintenance of conduct disorder symptoms. This becomes a vicious cycle of ADHD symptoms, the family reacting poorly, and the symptoms exacerbating or becoming more numerous. Lack of parenting skills, lack of a father or father figure, and marital or relationship problems have also been implicated.

We will now look at some theoretical etiologies that do **not** have support in the field or in the literature. Previously, sugar was seen as a major cause of ADHD. Many studies have shown, perhaps conclusively, that sugar is not the cause of ADHD (see, for example, Milich, Wolraich, & Lindgren, 1986). Other theories have posited a connection between diet, allergies, and ADHD, but this correlation has not received a lot of support either. In the 70s and 80s food additives (such as dyes and preservatives) were thought to be connected to ADHD but this too has not received much support. Of course it is possible that if a child has food allergies, those allergies may exacerbate or mimic ADHD symptoms. Lead has also been hypothesized to cause ADHD, but again research has not supported this contention. Other causal factors such as yeast, motion sickness, and television have also been suggested, but the evidence supporting these, like the factors mentioned above, is limited or nonexistent.

Thus, the evidence seems to point to ADHD having a biological cause(s). However, we still do not know what specifically causes ADHD. This is also an area that warrants further research.

Treatment Plan

Treatments for ADHD have varying degrees of effectiveness; a key problem is that no known cure exists yet. Thus we can hope to control the symptoms when they are present. As stated, Jackie was assigned to individual therapy and an additional visit with the psychiatrist. He decided to try Jackie on *Adderall (dextroamphetamine)* since this medicine does not produce a rash as a side effect. She was being carefully monitored by the psychiatrist, since *psychostimulants* such as Adderall have numerous side effects and are also dangerous. Research has demonstrated that approximately 70% of children who take psychostimulants for ADHD respond positively to the medications (Bezchlibnyk-Butler & Jeffries, 2002). These medicines also work quickly, usually within a week of dosing onset.

The psychiatrist also recommended PMT and educational interventions, specifically working with Jackie's teachers to train them how to control her behavior and how to reward positive behaviors or control. While Jackie was involved in therapy, we spent some time on-site at her school working with her teachers to develop effective strategies to manage Jackie's ADHD. We used *response-cost methods,* which can be quite powerful when properly used. We also encouraged her teachers to focus on Jackie's strengths such as her singing (in appropriate settings of course). As you saw with Bernard, a common concern today is that people tend to focus on the weaknesses instead of trying to build up strengths.

Jackie was cooperative in therapy, and she began to look at her behavior and how to control it. She didn't want to get in any more trouble, and she wanted to make her parents "proud of me. I want to graduate soon, and I want to be a success. My dad is a louse. I want to make good bucks and be a good mom to my kids. I want lots of them!" Jackie spent some time talking about her father in our sessions, specifically about his drug usage and selling.

"How could anyone do those things to a mother and her young child? The man has no shame; he's a monster. I hope he gets his in prison. My mom never visits him. He calls sometimes; he knows my great-grandma's number. She tells him where to go. He's bad news and yesterday's news. He never beat me though, I can say that. Some father. When he's out I'll be long gone from this hellhole city. He's not my father. My stepdad is."

As the sessions progressed, Jackie was able to stay focused a lot more often. Her speech slowed down considerably, and it was easier to understand her because she was speaking much more slowly. She told us that she was making "better grades in school. I don't get so anxious and nervous. I can get into reading and things. Hey, I like math! It's fun to do problems on my calculator. It also plays games! But I'm doing better. No As or Bs, forget that. I'm not THAT smart." We corroborated this with her teachers. They told us that, indeed, she was staying in her seat lot more often, was not talking as fast, and remembered to bring school supplies most of the time. She was now producing homework which, while C level, was at least getting done. She also was not arguing with the teachers much anymore, which pleased everyone. Her teachers told us that the response-cost method was quite effective for Jackie, and that she and her teachers had set mutually attainable goals.

Jackie did not like taking the Adderall but "I know I need to. It made me dry. That was not fun. I don't like taking pills. But if it gets me through school and doesn't get me thrown out, I'll do it. I like the doctor, so that helps too. He really understands teenagers." Astute helping professionals will make sure that they have established a good relationship with a psychiatrist, and they should also know someone who specializes in children and teenagers, like we had. As you can see, that can make a difference in compliance.

Jackie's mother would sit in the waiting area while Jackie was in therapy. She wanted Jackie to "be on her own, like on the way to being an adult. I won't be here forever, and she needs to know how to handle future problems. Since her school told me she's getting better, I'll stay outside for now." Jackie also preferred this, since "that was like two adults attacking me at once. One is enough, thank you very much. I answer to my mom at home, so why should I also do it in here? I love her and all but come on."

We did work with Jackie's mother through PMT and Jackie seemed to like this. PMT is not really therapy since the goals are education and the teaching of behavioral management techniques to the parent(s). Jackie's mother came in alone during these sessions, usually when Jackie was in school. She would always bring a notebook and took copious notes during each session. The clinic had some videotapes demonstrating behavioral management techniques, and these really seemed to help Jackie's mother, and eventually Jackie herself. Jackie's mother was also taught progressive muscle relaxation techniques and was encouraged to do more exercise. Both of these techniques were taught to help her reduce her stress.

As Jackie's treatment progressed, she continued to see the psychiatrist for medication monitoring, and saw us individually once a week. In addition, she was now *classified*, so she was able to receive compensation and special education services to help her in school. She was assigned an aide and a tutor and was allowed to go to the resource room when her teacher felt it necessary. Because Jackie's behavior improved so much, her regular teacher tried to avoid using the resource room unless it was necessary. Her teacher told us that "it is nice to have that option now, and to see Jackie doing better. The aide really helps her with her work and behavior."

Jackie continued in therapy for approximately 8 months, at which point she was discharged to the school social worker for further treatment. We never discussed case specifics, but she told us that Jackie spent a lot of time discussing boys, her father and mother, and sexual feelings. Jackie did not discuss her behavior or schoolwork with the social worker, to our knowledge. Jackie had made good progress and was now maintaining high Cs in her classes. She had a few behavioral problems and outbursts, but these were few and not unexpected. She was happier and less nervous now, and she was enjoying math and her calculator. She still had tremendous anger towards her father, but she told us she was discussing this at school. She felt more comfortable discussing these issues with a female. (We offered this option to Jackie and she declined.) Jackie got promoted and would be entering the seventh grade in the fall "and it looks like I might graduate on time. How the heck about that?!" Her mother no longer feared that Jackie would become violent "as long as she takes her Adderall, which does not seem to be an issue right now."

At last report, Jackie was still producing high Cs and was on track to be promoted to the eighth grade. She was reluctant to keep taking Adderall, but told us that she would do so regardless. She was very interested in one young man, but he was in high school and "wanted an older woman." Jackie still loved to sing and wanted to record a CD one day. She's also "into shopping, a lot. I love to do that." Jackie seems to be on track for a "normal" teenage life.

As we mentioned, the most common medications used to treat ADHD are the psychostimulants. They have a very rapid onset and have a short *half-life* which means that they will be cleared out of the system quite rapidly. Because these medications are at their most effective for 2 to 4 hours, the psychiatrist (or school nurse or caregiver) needs to take the time of day into consideration. For example, if the child's problems are exacerbated in the afternoon, it is not wise to give the first pill right before s/he leaves for school (Pelham, 1993). These medications, like all of the *psychotropic drugs*, have significant side effects and need to be administered with caution. Specifically, if the child has a family history of mood disorders (depression or manic episodes), the use of stimulants is not recommended. Some research has found that ADHD-like symptoms in a child with this kind of family history may be a premorbid indicator of Bipolar Disorder (Krehbiel, 2000).

Antidepressants have also been used to treat ADHD, but these are considered only if psychostimulants prove to be ineffective. Because their side effects can be quite severe and significant, these drugs are usually the last choice for psychiatrists. Lithium (lithium carbonate) is also a consideration, but its effectiveness has not been substantially proven (Bezchlibnyk-Butler & Jeffries, 2002).

The real risk in treating ADHD is that parents and schools may rely too heavily on medication usage and thus not be concerned with other treatment modalities. Medications will treat some symptoms, but the concomitant problems need to be addressed as well. Society has also tended to overmedicate children in the past, and this has led to many problems. Psychostimulants are addictive, which is a problem in and of itself. Additionally, their long-term benefits appear to be rather limited. By overmedicating, we are teaching children that all problems have a simple, rapid solution, and we teach them to rely on medication instead of relying on themselves, or using other resources. In some cases medications are under prescribed, which can also lead to significant problems. Even though the use of medications in treating ADHD has helped many children, the position here is that all medications, when children are involved, must be used with caution and foresight.

Prognosis

Jackie's prognosis is listed as "fair." From our perspective, we can change her prognosis to "good" when she completes high school successfully. She has made good progress and has tremendous support from her mother, which is a big advantage. Jackie also wants to get better, and she is aware that her behaviors have caused problems in the past.

We are concerned about the fact that she does not like taking the Adderall, and we see her being at risk for discontinuing its use. Jackie told us that she has no immediate plans beyond high school for continuing her education, but of course she is only 12 and that could change. We are thus cautiously optimistic about Jackie's situation.

Review and Study Questions

Bernard

1. How might Bernard's visual misdiagnosis have affected his development?

2. How might this have affected his behavior?

3. Discuss the reasons why Bernard's history of ear infections, and his having tubes inserted into his ears, is significant.

4. The school told us that they needed a diagnosis for Bernard in order for him to

continue to receive proper special needs services. What are you views on this?

5. Would you give Bernard (or anyone) a viable DSM-IV-TR diagnosis so that they could receive treatment, even if it were not warranted?

6. We used projective drawing techniques with Bernard. What is the validity of these techniques?

Jacqueline

1. Jackie told us that her biological father hit her mother at times. If this occurred while her mother was pregnant, discuss the possible ramifications of this for Jackie.

2. Jackie's mother thought that Jackie's behavior was typical for an adolescent. Your views?

3. Discuss the possibility that Jackie is indeed just not interested in school and would rather sing and play video games.

4. How difficult would it be to differentiate AHDH from someone who is using psychostimulants (such as speed)?

5. Discuss your views on giving psychoactive medication such as Adderall to an adolescent.

6. Discuss Jackie's chances of graduating high school.

Terms to Know

behavioral control
behavioral disruption
Conduct Disorder
Antisocial Personality Disorder (ASPD)
astigmatism
dyslexia
Attention Deficit/Hyperactivity Disorder (ADHD)
act out
comorbid
permanent products
psychological testing battery
Fetal Alcohol Effects (FAE)
traumatic brain injury (TBI)
Fetal Alcohol Syndrome (FAS)
school psychologist
consent
behavioral checklists
sentence completion test
Children's Apperception Test (CAT)

House-Tree-Person (HTP)
projective measures
corporal punishment
time-out
play therapy
Ritalin (methylphenidate)
antipsychotics
progressive muscle relaxation
Haldol (haloperidol)
Thorazine (chlorpromazine)
Lithium (lithium carbonate)
anticonvulsants
Tegretol (carbamazepine)
attribution errors
Cylert (magnesium pemoline)
Adderall (dextroamphetamine)
psychostimulants
response-cost methods
half-life
psychiatric evaluation

case conference

unstructured diagnostic interview

psychoeducational testing battery

psychotropic drugs

learning disability

special education services

teacher's aide

classified

resource room

Chapter 10

Personality Disorders

Personality disorders (sometimes called *character disorders*) affect about 15 million adults in the United States. These disorders, which can be subdivided into three clusters, are very difficult to treat. *Cluster A* includes disorders where the individual is viewed as being odd or eccentric. *Cluster B* includes disorders where the individual is viewed as being overly emotional or erratic in his or her behavior. *Cluster C* includes disorders where the individual appears anxious or fearful. In the eyes of some psychologists, they are impossible to cure. According to the DSM-IV-TR (APA, 2000), a personality disorder is "... an enduring pattern of inner experience and behavior that deviates markedly from the expectations of the individual's culture, is pervasive and inflexible, has an onset in adolescence or early adulthood, is stable over time, and leads to distress or impairment ... The clinician should assess the stability of personality traits over time and across different situations (pp. 685–68)." Personality disorders can be diagnosed when the patient in question displays extreme rigidity in relating to other individuals. Because of this, they cannot make adjustments to other people and/or to the environment and subsequently, their behaviors become self-defeating.

A key characteristic of the personality disorders is that the person must be at least 18 years old before s/he can be diagnosed with one. The two disorders we will examine fall into Cluster B. We will first look at Lisa, who presents a wide variety of symptoms. We will conclude with Adam, who may or may not be what you think.

Borderline Personality Disorder
The Case of Lisa:
Walking the Tightrope

Presenting Problem

Lisa is a 27-year-old single white female who works in a supermarket as a clerk. She has never been married and has no children. Her father is a truck driver and her mother stays at home. "She never did work, but stayed home to take care of the kids. Since my dad's on the road a lot he wanted her to stay at home so they could have lots of time together when he came home." Lisa has a younger brother Christopher whom she sees once a week. He is a senior in high school and is 17.

Lisa was poorly dressed when she first came to see us. She wore an oversized dirty T-shirt that had food and paint stains on it, ripped jeans that were too tight and tattered Nike sneakers. She wore a floppy hat that appeared well-worn, no jewelry, and no watch. Lisa was 5'9" tall, very thin, and wore no makeup. Her brown hair was stringy and evidently needed to be washed. She made good eye contact but had an inappropriate affect. She always appeared angry or suspicious and didn't smile much if at all. We noticed what appeared to be burn marks on her arms. We began by asking about that.

"Oh, those? That's part of an initiation into my club, my clique. We girls want to prove that we can handle stuff, so you get burned with cigarettes by each member. That's why you see those. It hurts but it's not so bad. I'm a big girl, I can stand it." This explanation seemed dubious at best, so we noted these marks and decided we would come back to this issue a bit later.

Lisa's recent history is of particular interest. "I got this supermarket job after I got laid off from a megastore. I came in late too often and they got bummed, so I was let go. I like being a checker. It's a people job and the pay is okay. I won't do this for the rest of my life but it's okay for right now. But you probably want to know why I came in to see you."

"Well, my personal life has been messed up real bad lately. I don't know what it is, but during the past 2 years I've been real moody, lashing out at people one moment and then being quiet the next. It's gotten me into some trouble at the supermarket, but they've been real nice about it. They figure it happens during my cycles and it's a "woman" thing. I don't know if my hormones are messed up or what. I have a bigger concern however. . . ."

I asked Lisa when these problems started. "Well, my mom got sick with *Non-Hodgkin's Lymphoma,* which has a low cure rate. They caught it in time and she responded well to the chemo. She was very lucky. That happened a little over 2 years ago. My dad is rarely home, so here I was, trying to balance school, work and caring for my mom. My stupid brother wasn't much help, but he's in the girl-crazy stage. Shortly after my mom came home from the hospital my moods got weird. It was like everything was too much pressure; everything collapsed at once."

"I've never been in therapy before. I don't want to lie on a couch and have someone tell me I'm nuts. That's what you guys do isn't it? You'll tell me I'm nuts and then put me in the looney bin. But I think, even if that happens, I need to find out why I'm so darned moody lately. My latest boyfriend says I'm like Dr. Jekyll and Mr. Hyde. Nice one minute and horrible the next. He says he's getting ready to leave me as he's had enough. I don't blame him really. And this other concern I have? Well, I sleep around—a lot. Usually this is what I do. I'll meet some guy, either at work or after work at a bar or wherever. If I like him I'll have sex with him any which way. I'm usually careful, but sometimes I'm not. I mean, I don't use drugs and the guys are not gay, so I really can't get AIDS. I may stay with them for 1 or 2 weeks, and then I'll dump them for someone else, or just dump them."

"This happened a few times at first and I thought it was just a state, but now it happens all the time. My boyfriend is ready to leave after 2 weeks because of the mood swings he says I have. Anyways, I'm totally bored with him. We did it about 1 hour after meeting in the stockroom and became boyfriend-girlfriend after that. I cheated on him last week. I met this guy after work and we went near the bridge and had sex a bit later in the night. I felt bad afterwards but I wanted more of this. I called him the next day and he didn't want to see me again. I've had . . . oh . . . about 15 boyfriends the past 6 months. It helps me to know who I am, I think. All these guys wanting to have sex with me makes me feel wanted and attractive."

"I spoke with a good friend of mine who told me that this is crazy and nuts and might get me killed or very sick. I don't agree, but it did make me a little bit suspicious and this friend has been around the block, you know. She's aces, as smart as they come. I trust her judgment. Is this behavior normal? I'm not no dummy, so I figured I should get my head checked out to make sure I'm not crazy. So here I am. Any ideas?"

Background Information

Lisa's developmental history is unremarkable, and she achieved all of her developmental milestones at the appropriate ages. Lisa did reasonably well in school, graduating high school with a C-plus average. Lisa attended a community college for 2 years "because I thought I needed more school stuff, you know? I was hoping to get a better paying job with my Associate's degree. I went for three semesters and then I had to stop. My mom got sick and my money got real tight, so I went on a break for awhile." Lisa achieved Bs and Cs in college, but she also "got a lot of Incompletes. I really was not interested in some of the work. I get bored easily."

Lisa's brother is not performing as well in school. "He's a problem. He acts up all of the time. He's a real pain to my mom and dad. Not so much to me, because I don't see him too much. He gets into trouble at school. He was suspended once for a week for fighting, and when he got back things were not much better. But it's not my problem. He seems to have gotten worse when my mom got sick."

We asked Lisa about any history of mental illness in her family. "My brother seems to be normal, whatever that is for an adolescent boy. My dad . . . well, he does drink too much at times. I only thought about that recently. There have been times when he will start drinking and be unable to stop. He really can't control himself at times. Other than that he seems to be okay. Like I said, I don't know because he's rarely at home, and when he is at home he watches WWF and sports, and he sleeps. My mom gets depressed at times. Nothing really serious though. And nothing else on either side of my family that I know of. We're far from great, but we're basically normal."

We probed a bit further into Lisa's background and discovered some interesting facts. "My sex stuff began a bit earlier than I said originally. I really started having all of these boyfriends when I was about 19 or 20. I was in college and just in my freshman year. I was really bored and moody. I was trying to find myself, my identity and stuff. I felt lost. My mom was never the warmest person around and my dad was never really around much. We were not a loving house. So I lost my virginity at 15 and really enjoyed sex a lot once I turned 18 and got out of the house a lot more. I liked the sex, and I liked dumping the guys. It made me feel good, to cut them off emotionally instead of me."

We then asked Lisa about her alcohol and drug usage. "Well, of course I drink and I smoke pot, but who doesn't? I started drinking when I was 18 and smoking pot about a year later. It makes me feel good. I never really liked any of these boyfriends; most of them were lousy in bed also. They were all mistakes. I would usually be drinking before I would pick up the guys and go home with them. Sometimes I would be smoking pot and sometimes I would not. It depended on how I felt and on whether I had a stash or not. I can stop using these things whenever I want to, but I don't want to right now. It would help me to save some money however."

"I do have to admit that I'm usually on something or boozing when I get a guy, but not always. My drinking has never really been a problem. When I go out, I'll have a beer, maybe two. I'm watching my figure and booze puts on the pounds, you know. I don't smoke pot a lot, maybe four times a month or so. That's not really much. I would probably use it more but I don't have the money. It also gets me too hungry."

We followed up on this theme with some more questions. "Nah, the moodiness seemed to come before I started to drink. I was not that easy growing up. My mom had health problems for a long time, and with my dad away so much it makes things hard. We never had a lot of money, and my mom worked long hours every day. My brother and I were not close, and we're still not that close. No one has a drinking or drug problem in my family, but we all drink from time to time. My mom said I was moody when I was a teenager, but all teenage girls are like that. That is normal, so we never thought nothing about that. Look at my brother, for example. He's hyper and girl crazy, like I'm boy crazy. So that's why I don't see nothing wrong with me, but my friend Lucy is smart, so I came in because of her."

As you can see, we had some difficulty with keeping Lisa to stay on task (focused) and on the topic. She had a tendency to go off on tangents and not answer the questions. We tried again and the following occurred, "You know, I came in here for some answers and all you are doing is asking questions and stuff. I am SO sick of this crap. This time will be it, and I'm never coming back to see you again. What are you, a pervert? Why do you need you know about my drinking and my sex life? Huh?" With that outburst, the session ended and Lisa left the office. Does her behavior make any sense yet? Can you guess what might be going on here?

The next afternoon we received a call from Lisa. She said that she really needed to come back in to try and explain why she acted up. We scheduled the next appointment for her and returned to asking her some more questions to gather more facts. "I'm really sorry about what happened a few days ago. I now see that I really need some help with these moods of mine. Here I am, in a doctor's office, and I'm acting like a jerk. But this has happened a lot. Usually I dump the boyfriend first, but sometimes they do it to me when I explode. I really have some anger problems. I'm really worried about my job. I love what I do and I can become store manager but I've had these temper things at work. My boss deals with it because he likes me, but I can lose a lot if this keeps on happening. I'm worried about that."

Thought Questions

1. What is going on with Lisa?
2. Do you agree with Lisa's idea that having so many boyfriends would make her seem attractive and wanted?
3. What could be the reason(s) behind Lisa's reported mood swings?
4. What is the connection, if any, between Lisa's behaviors and her mother's illness?

Assessment and Evaluation

Lisa was assessed with an *unstructured diagnostic interview,* the *Beck Depression Inventory-II (BDI-II),* and a psychiatric evaluation. She was also asked some more specific questions relating to alcohol and drug usage. More useful information came out in subsequent sessions.

We also sent Lisa to get a complete physical, just in case her mood swings had a physical cause. "Yeah, I've been thinking about that as well. I'm not on the pill or anything else, but I've often thought that my hormones may be messed up somehow. Maybe that's the cause of all of my problems!" It took 2 weeks to get the results back and everything checked out normally for Lisa. We had suspected as much, but because hormonal and "chemical" imbalances can create psychological symptoms, patients sometimes need to have a complete physical to *rule out* other disorders.

Lisa returned after we received her physical results and we spent more time discussing her situation. "So it's not the hormones. Well, am I nuts? I don't think so. Could the booze and the pot be messing up my mind? I really need to know. The boyfriend I told you about? He's history. We had a bad fight, and I dumped him, and then he dumped me! What a load of crap. So I'm single again, but it won't be for long. I guess I could stop using. At least that would help, and I wouldn't get so many hangovers."

We asked Lisa about her mother and if she could come in and talk to us. "My mom? I don't know what good that will do but go on ahead. She'll be more than happy to speak with you. She's not that sharp, you know, not the sharpest blade in the drawer. But she might be able to help. Sure, bring her in."

Her mother provided some insight into Lisa's mood swings and past. It is not that unusual to ask family members and friends of the patient to come in for a session or two. Some psychologists do not like to do this, but it is one way to gain additional knowledge and see the patient's situation from another perspective. This was also presented at a staff meeting and to the clinic's supervisor. The majority of the staff, as well as the clinic's supervisor, agreed to bring her mother in for some questions. The staff also hoped that if need be her mother would be willing to get involved with family therapy.

Her mother was quite talkative during the one session we saw her. She made good eye contact and displayed an appropriate affect. Her mother was 5'5" tall, had an olive complexion, and was slim. She wore glasses ("for my reading. I wasn't supposed to be using this here magnifying glass, so the doc gave me these. Like them?") and a large diamond ring on her left hand. Her mother was very pleasant and open with us, and we were pleasantly surprised at her candor.

"Lisa has been mixed up lately. I knew about her thing, having so many boyfriends and one-night stands. Did she tell you that she also has a lot of one-night stands, especially during the past year or so? That's what really worries me. A mother knows these things. She doesn't really tell me, but since this is small town you hear them things, and they ain't good things. I did that stuff when I was younger. I liked my fun, and in this s . . . town there isn't much else to do except have sex and booze it up. There are so many kooks out there and her judgment with these guys is not good. I don't know what's going on with her. She's also in trouble at work. They knew about the sex in the stockroom but kept real quiet about it. But she's been warned and an 'incident' was noted in her record. I'm worried about her health and her safety."

We then asked her mother about Lisa's mood swings. "The moods have been going on for at least 9 years, and possibly longer. She can be SO angry and blow up at someone (even me) and then the next day she's as sweet as can be. She doesn't always apologize. She also seems to be tense quite often, which is not surprising since her job situation is somewhat messed up right now. I hope you can find out what's up with her." Before we continue, what is your position on asking a relative to come into a therapy session to gather more information? Will her mother's information prove to be helpful to the psychologist?

We then asked Lisa to come back in and she asked her mother to stay the rest of the session. Lisa's mother told her what they discussed. "Well, she's right. I didn't want to tell you about the one-night stands because you might think that I'm a slut or something. I'm not; I just really like my sex. Do I worry about these strangers? Of course. That's why we usually go to a motel or stay in my car. It's safer that way. I usually go to a motel that I know, or a place that I know well, like by the bridge. My temper is a problem. It never used to be this bad. It's just gotten worse lately, but I'm not sure if my job is the main reason. Certainly these boyfriend problems don't help much. I did have the mood swings for quite awhile, but they've gotten worse lately, during the past 2 years. It always seems that my temper problems involve a man. I rarely have bad mood swings when a woman is involved."

Lisa's BDI-II score was 15, indicating mild to moderate depression. We asked Lisa about this in a subsequent session. "I've been down a lot lately but not so down that I want to kill myself or stuff. The job situation, the guy thing, and Lucy (this is her best friend) telling me that I may need help have brought me down. My mom's cancer really affected me."

We discussed her mother's cancer next. "Well, my mom seems to be in remission, but all doctors lie about stuff like that. What does remission mean anyway? I'm really close to my mom, even though I'm not super-close to either of my parents. Yeah, I love my mom . . . but what does close mean? She knows stuff about me. She's a real gossip. What do you expect? I'm her only daughter and she screwed up bad when she was younger. My dad? Not really. He's been gone so much that he really doesn't matter to me that much. My mom held the family together in spite of my dad. She's been through so much . . . (Lisa begins to cry here). Sorry. She's been through so much, basically raising us kids as a single mom and working so hard, and now the cancer. The chemo did a number on her. She got an infection and had to be hospitalized. They thought she might die. Ever since she got sick, I've really been in bad shape. I thought a lot about who I am and I really don't know anymore. It's like that with the guys. The sex, physically, is nice and all, but the rest leaves me empty. I can't get close to anyone except my best friend Lucy."

Well. Do you have any idea what might be occurring with Lisa? Based on her symptoms, she might be suffering from a *mood disorder,* but this is somewhat unlikely based on her behaviors. Lisa's problems seemed to begin around age 18 or so, have been persistent patterns of behavior, and have specific symptoms. Some of the key symptoms include the problems of controlling her anger, her unstable relationships marked by intense feelings, her uncertainty as to her identity, and her fears of being abandoned. Additionally, many of her behaviors have self-destructive features, either directly or indirectly.

These symptoms, among others, usually lead to the diagnosis of *Borderline Personality Disorder (BPD).* One way to look at this disorder is that those who have it are on the "border" between *psychosis* and what used to be termed *neurosis* (today this is known as having an anxiety disorder). Because of the "in-between" nature of the disorder, treatment is difficult. The psychologist will be handling anxiety and what seems, at times, to be psychotic features.

Lisa was referred to our psychiatrist, since we needed to check on her possible depression and her mood swings. The psychiatrist ruled out depression, stating that it was not significant enough to warrant a diagnosis or medication at the time of the evaluation. He did note that her depressive symptoms needed to be monitored. The psychiatrist was somewhat more concerned about her mood swings. *Lithium (lithium carbonate)* is one medication that is indicated for *Bipolar Disorder.* However, the psychiatrist noted that "her depressive symptoms were not severe enough to warrant extensive concern, and there were no symptoms of manic episodes. The anger and outbursts were a concern, but these alone do not warrant Lithium usage. Conclusion: Borderline Personality Disorder; continue to monitor depressive symptoms. Refer back if needed."

Lisa was presented at a case conference. The clinicians and the psychiatrist reviewed her data and symptoms and came to an agreement on the following preliminary diagnoses. See if you agree with any or all of them:

Borderline Personality Disorder	301.83
Rule Out (R/O) Major Depressive Disorder, Recurrent, Mild, With Melancholic Features	296.31
Cannabis Abuse	305.20

Theoretical Etiologies

Personality disorders are relatively common in the adult population in the United States. A common viewpoint is that they have their onset in childhood and become "hardened" in adulthood, which is why treatment is so difficult. The field lacks information about the courses of certain personality disorders such as *avoidant personality disorder.* Fortunately, more information exists regarding borderline and antisocial personality disorders, but it does not make treatment easier. Research has shown that people with borderline personality disorder will improve (or their symptoms will improve) if they manage to survive into their 30s, which is easier said than done. Many of these individuals attempt suicide, and one study states that about 6% are successful (Perry, 1993). As you have seen, people like Lisa have unstable and emotional relationships, depression, and suicidal gestures. At the very least these individuals want to hurt themselves. This disorder also affects primarily females (75% versus 25% for men).

Evidence supports familial components and early trauma as factors leading to borderline personality disorder (BPD). It is more prevalent when a biological family member has the disorder, and is more prevalent among women who were sexually abused as children. These factors may predispose an individual to develop borderline personality disorder, but we cannot say if these factors cause the disorder. These women also made the most serious attempts to kill themselves and also reported feeling abandoned by their families (Zanarini, Williams, Lewis, Reich, Vera, Marino, Levin, Yong, & Frankenberg, 1997). Some researchers see a link between borderline personality disorder and depression, while others question such a link.

Zanarini, Frankenburg, Dubo, Sickel, Trikha, Levin, & Reynolds (1998) discuss how borderline personality disorder is similar to posttraumatic stress disorder (PTSD). For example, both disorders have problems with moods and impulse control, and both disrupt interpersonal relationships. This follows the concept that borderline personality disorder is partially caused by early exposure to some type of trauma. Regardless, not all borderlines resemble individuals who have PTSD; this discussion is still ongoing and more research is needed.

Cultural issues may play an interesting role. People who have gone through a significant change in culture may end up getting borderline personality disorder. Identity issues and fears of abandonment have been discovered in recent immigrants; these symptoms also occur in BPD. Thus, early trauma, even cultural, may lead to BPD. On the other hand, this of course may not occur at all. The movie *Crocodile Dundee,* while a complete fantasy, demonstrates that people from a less advanced culture do not necessarily collapse when brought into a more technologically advanced situation. It depends on how well they adapt to the situation and more importantly, on their *social support* systems.

Otto Kernberg, a key psychodynamic researcher, sees BPD occurring due to the failure of the child to properly form his/her self-image during the Oedipal stage. The child is unable to resolve and unify the images of what is good and what is bad. Thus the child will view all people, including him/herself, as either all good or all bad. Additionally, parents cannot meet all of their child's needs. During development infants need to unify and consolidate the image of the all-good mother who nurtures with the all-bad mother who withholds and frustrates. If infants cannot do this, they become fixated before they reach the Oedipal complex and thus, due to the fixation, may keep these all-or- none images of their parents.

Finally, we have little data on the biological aspects of BPD. We can hypothesize that since BPD is more common when a biological family member has it, it must have some familial component and therefore genetics must somehow play a role (DiLalla, Carey, Gottesman, & Bouchard, 1996). However, since family members share the same environment, how can we be certain of this? As we have stated, genetics may predispose an individual to develop a disorder, but it seems like stress in the environment, among other factors, must somehow bring this condition out.

Treatment Plan

Treatment for any of the personality disorders is somewhat problematic, since many professionals agree that there is no cure for these disorders. There are other concerns. Personality disorders are notorious for not responding well to most types of therapy. Those suffering from these disorders also tend to be charming (to a degree) and highly manipulative. Because of this, it is easy for the therapist to get "drawn in" and manipulated by the patient. *Countertransference* is also a significant concern. Long-term insight therapies (such as psychoanalysis) also tend to not be very effective, since the patient generally lacks insight into his/her troubles. For example, Lisa sees nothing unusual about her having multiple one-night stands, even at age 27. Many borderline patients also tend to be very dependent and needy, and they demand all of your attention and time. It is difficult for a therapist to meet all of the demands of someone with BPD. At times they will sing your praises to no end, while later in the day they will condemn you to Hades and say you do not care about them at all.

An interesting rule of thumb used to be applied by a former colleague. If you are not sure of a diagnosis but suspect that your patient may have a personality disorder, see how **you** feel at the end of a session. If you feel emotionally drained, exhausted, and as though you have been in a prolonged conflict or battle, most like the patient is suffering from borderline personality disorder. I have mentioned this to many colleagues and many of them agree with this **unscientific** diagnostic criterion.

The key treatment goals for Lisa (and similar patients) are to manage the symptoms and try to change the behaviors, not to try and cure them. Because they tend to be so manipulative, the therapist needs to outline at the onset who is in charge and not move from that position. We decided to use both family and group therapy with Lisa, since some of her issues involved her mother and father. Predictably, her father could (or would) not come in, citing job responsibilities. "What did you expect? He's never been home as long as I can remember. Who cares." Lisa's mother did manage to come in, and some nice progress was made initially. Lisa's brother had no interest, and Lisa's mother did not force him to join, so it remained Lisa and her mother. Issues surrounding Lisa's father, her mother's illness, and Lisa's pot usage were discussed. One of the key concerns was Lisa's sexual behavior. Her mother was not surprised that she was acting this way. "As I told you I suspected and I knew. This is not that big of a town, and people talk a lot. I really thought Lisa would be smarter than this. She's acting like a horse's ass."

The most sensible approach here was using *behavioral modification techniques* and *person-centered therapy*, offering care and support to Lisa. This is easier said than done. Why is that? Offering support to someone who **may** be manipulative is a risk, since they may use that support to manipulate the therapist. One big advantage of behavioral modification techniques is that the therapist can maintain a distance from the patient. This does **not** mean that you do not demonstrate empathy. On the contrary, it means that you make sure not to become overly involved with the patient, do not become their friend, and so on.

Lisa's family therapy went as well as could be expected. We focused on all of Lisa's presenting issues, and her mother finally began to understand Lisa's anger towards her father. Lisa also had some interesting comments for her mother during one of the sessions. "I'm also really angry with you. You are the only one in our family that I really care about, and the only one who really cares about me. And you have the nerve to get sick and potentially leave me alone when I need you the most? I can't believe that. I don't know what I would do without you. You are the one person who keeps me going. Sometimes I think you got sick deliberately to avoid me." These comments were not surprising, since we noted earlier that borderlines tend to feel that all attention must always be focused on them and them alone. This can be seen as a way of seeking approval. What makes these comments quite interesting is that, in effect, Lisa is blaming her mother indirectly for some of her problems.

Lisa was also placed in group therapy; this lasted longer than family therapy. Lisa's mother eventually did not return, saying that she had had enough, and that she was still not fully recovered from her treatments. Lisa was quite angry and upset but generally accepted this. We put Lisa in a *higher functioning group*. These groups contain people that are communicative and sometimes have incentive to gain insight into their problems. They do not necessarily have insight, but the idea is that they have the ability to attain it. Lisa got along well with the group, as many in the group suffered from borderline personality disorder, and many were in her age group. Lisa realized that she was not alone with her concerns, and the group did not hesitate to confront her about her sexual behavior. The group also told Lisa that she needed to grow up, and to stop waiting for her father to demonstrate affection towards her. In other words, Lisa needed to take responsibility for her own actions. If she wanted changes to occur in her family, she needed to be the assertive one.

Lisa also told us "it was time to come clean about the cigarette burns. I hurt myself. There are times when I want to kill myself but I figure it's not worth that much, so I burn myself. It's like a reminder of what I can do if I need to, if things get real bad. See these marks? (She rolls up both sleeves). These represent one year's worth of work. (We saw seven separate burn marks.) I really hate myself at times and how can I help it? Everyone wants to leave me, guys only use me, and you constantly ask me stuff. No, I haven't burned myself since I started here." At this point Lisa looked like she was about to cry but broke into a smile and said "Gotcha!" We then made a behavioral contract with her that she would not hurt or burn herself while she was in treatment with us. She readily signed this document.

We noticed some positive changes in Lisa during the year she was in therapy. She finally settled down with one boyfriend for 6 months, and she stopped her infidelity. She stopped smoking pot "since I want to have kids soon and I heard that can screw up your genes. I also need to save some money. Besides, the group told me how bad it is, and that it's illegal. That stuff can really mess with your head, and my head is already really messed up, scrambled like." She continued to drink sporadically and "I'm not going to stop since that does not cause me many problems." Lisa was referred to and completed an anger management class run by the local hospital, and we noted that her moods were better controlled at termination. "I still get quite angry but I know how to stop it and how to deal with it. If it's necessary I will let it out, but I found out a lot of times the anger is meaningless."

At the last follow-up, Lisa appeared to have relapsed. She had returned to having multiple one-night stands and short-term, intense relationships. She was having some problems controlling her anger, but she told us her mood swings were not as bad as they were in the past. "I realized that I missed the various guys and the sex, and it was too tempting. Temptation got the best of me there. I love the attention. It makes me feel pretty."

"Because of this, I started staying out too late and was late for work too many times. I lost my job at the supermarket, but I found another one at a shopping mall. That seems better for me; less pressure and stuff. I never went back to pot, and I still have little contact with my dad. As for my mom? We still fight . . . a lot. But I'll always love her." Sadly, because personality disorders consist of problems that have been occurring for quite awhile, relapse is quite common. We were dismayed at Lisa's situation, but not terribly surprised.

Certain cognitive-behavioral techniques have been found to be effective in treating BPD. Aaron Beck and his colleagues work on the cognitive distortions where the individual sees everything (including him/herself and other people) as all good or all bad. Linehan and her colleagues (1994) describe a technique which we used, *dialectical behavior therapy (DBT)*. This technique combines behavioral techniques with supportive psychotherapy. Psychotherapy provides support and acceptance, and the behavioral treatment focuses on social and problem-solving skills. Lisa received a lot of support from the group as well as in her family (later individual) therapy. She also learned how to relate better to people and, we had hoped, would use these skills once she was discharged.

No one medication stands out as the ideal treatment option for borderline personality disorder. Antidepressants and antianxiety medications may help calm some of the emotions of an individual with BPD, but they will not alter the long-term maladaptive behavioral patterns. *Prozac (fluoxetine)* seems to be helpful in reducing aggression and impulsivity in individuals with personality disorders, not necessarily BPD (Bezchlibnyk-Butler & Jeffries, 2002). For Lisa, no medications were indicated while she was in treatment with us.

Prognosis

Lisa's prognosis is "guarded". Since the symptoms tend to be long-term, and since these disorders typically do not respond well to treatment, a guarded prognosis is indicated. This prognosis is also based upon the fact that Lisa seems to have relapsed, at least as far as her sexual behaviors are concerned. She does show some degree of progress with her anger management, and she no longer (based on self-report only) smokes pot. She also realizes that she still has issues that need to be addressed, but whether she will address them, and whether she will be successful, is unable to be answered at the present time.

Antisocial Personality Disorder

The Case of Adam: Serial Killers Only?

Presenting Problem

Adam is a 19-year-old white married male; his wife Tisch gave birth to his first child, a son, while he was in treatment. They got married shortly after their son's birth. His wife just turned 17 years old and had to drop out of the tenth grade when she became pregnant. As you are about to see, Adam's history, and subsequent treatment and outcome, is one of the most interesting in this book.

Adam was thin with a very pale complexion. He had a pencil-thin mustache and his face was scarred with acne. He displayed an inappropriate affect, laughing at inappropriate times during the sessions. Adam is 5'6" tall. He wore no jewelry and always wore the same brown leather jacket into the sessions. He smoked at least two packages of cigarettes a day. (Smoking was allowed in the clinic at this time.) Once those rules changed, he would always smoke outside before the sessions began. Adam seemed very angry during all of the sessions; at times it seemed like he was on the verge of an explosive outburst, but we never saw this happen.

Adam explained what brought him in to see us, "One night after work, an old friend from home called up, and we went out and had a few. We hung around for awhile after that, played some cards and sobered up. Then my friend had an idea to make some money. He knew of a house that had a lot of valuable stuff, and the owners were away for the weekend. He told me to come with him; we'd get the stuff, fence it, and have a lot of bucks for a long time. Well, he was right about the house. It was stacked! He thought he had cut the alarms but I guess he missed one. The cops showed up and of course we got caught. This time the judge was not so easy on me. I lost my job, almost lost my girl, and this time went to jail for 11 months, 30 days. (You can only be sent to jail for a sentence of less than 1 year.) They said I was drunk when this happened but I wasn't. I was drinking but I sure wasn't drunk! I knew what I was doing."

Adam was released from jail early (he served 7 months) because of good behavior. Once Adam was released from jail he received 5 years probation and was sent to us for an alcohol evaluation. At this time Tisch was also brought to our attention. As you will see, she provided some very valuable insight and information into Adam's life.

Background Information

We first knew Adam when he was 14 years old. He was a court referral and had been charged with breaking and entering. The court did not wish to incarcerate him, so he was sent to us for an alcohol and drug abuse evaluation. Adam showed up to the first session and came for four subsequent sessions, at which time he disappeared. Shortly thereafter his *probation officer* (P.O.) was contacted; the police located him in a parking lot. He was on the bad end of a vicious fight. He needed to be hospitalized and was then released into the county jail.

When Adam came into the clinic the following summary was presented by the staff social worker, "Adam is a pleasant, bright young man who is very appealing to talk to. He has a significant drinking problem and states that he does not use drugs at all. He is presently involved with a 13-year-old who aborted his child. Adam told her that he was not going to have anything to do with this child, so she either had to abort, or raise it herself and he would leave her."

"Adam had been involved with numerous fights before this one. He also has a rap sheet that involves petit larceny and destruction of property (vandalism). Adam's drinking has progressed to the point where he has alcoholic blackouts, has built up a tolerance and has withdrawal symptoms. He has been drinking heavily since he was 12 and has been unable to give up drinking. Based on this information, Adam has the following diagnoses:

> *Alcohol Dependence*
>
> R/O (Rule Out) Cannabis Dependence
>
> *Conduct Disorder*

Adam spent 30 days in jail for his involvement in the fight. Once he was released he was placed on 3 years probation, with the mandate that he use no alcohol and that he does not break any laws. Adam did his best to follow these orders. He got a job as a locksmith and made good money "even though the hours were not good. You're on call 24 hours at times, but it's a lot of fun. It's like a constant puzzle, to open doors and such." We found it ironic that Adam had a job where he was required to pick locks.

Adam was doing very well in his job and received an early release from probation. He then met Tisch, his problems returned and subsequently increased. Before we continue, do you have any idea as to what might be occurring with Adam? At the very least, he has had legal troubles in the past. It should be noted that with chronic offenders (known as *recidivists*), it is very useful to get an extensive history and background information. This information will help you not only to figure out what is occurring with the patient, but will give you better insight into any possible future occurrences.

Adam was still sober and still working as a locksmith when Tisch came into his life. Tisch worked at a fast food establishment and Adam always used to get dinner there. After a short time Adam asked Tisch out, she accepted, and they began dating. Things progressed quickly, and shortly after this (about 3 months into the relationship), Tisch got pregnant. Adam, as he had done in the past, insisted that Tisch abort the child. She refused, but this time Adam decided to stay "because I really loved this girl. This was very very different." However, Adam's past would cause him and Tisch a lot of problems.

Adam has an 11th grade education. He "dropped out" once he was arrested for breaking and entering (and was subsequently expelled once convicted). Adam's home life and upbringing were not terribly pleasant. "I come from a broken home. My mom is a pass-out drunk, and my dad would beat me a lot. He would also beat my mom, but she would pass out so much that it really didn't matter."

"I have no brothers or sisters, and I've always been pissed about that. The real crap is that, here I was, the only child, and my mom isn't sober enough to show me love or pay attention to me, and my dad only pays attention to me when he beats me up. We had Child Protective Services called in, but they didn't do anything. My dad's a real charmer. They bought his line and left us alone. My dad told me that he was beaten as a child, but that's no excuse to hit a woman. That's b.s., you don't do that stuff. I'm not the best kid, but don't hit me."

"He first hit me when I was about 7 years old. I didn't do well on a school project, and when he got home he got really mad. So he hit me a few times. He never knocked out any teeth or anything, but it really hurt a lot. After that, these beatings really didn't stop. He didn't hit me every day, and there were some times when I had it coming."

Adam reached all of his developmental milestones at the appropriate ages, and initially, aside from the above, he presented no history of mental illness in his family. We asked Adam what happened to him while he was in school. "I had okay grades, low Bs basically. My best subjects were shop and physical education. I wasn't too interested in the other things. Girls became my main interest at about age 11 (laughs). But I was always good at shop. I made a lot of things, got high grades on all of the projects. I am really good with my hands."

We also asked Adam about his social life while in school. "I had a lot of girls interested in me. My first sex was when I was 12 years old; she was 11. It really wasn't a lot of fun. Kids in school used to pick on me a lot, so I'd get into lots of fights. They knew about my mom and her drinking, so they'd tease me about it, and I had to beat them up. I also hung with a kid when we were 14, and we'd do stuff. Stuff like set fires, put our tags (graffiti) on buildings, throw rocks at squirrels and pigeons, stuff like that. Hitting the squirrels was great. They'd move slow, and not move after you really bopped them. We'd do this a lot. We would boost stuff from stores; small stuff like CDs and snacks. Nothing really big."

Let us pause for a moment. Adam certainly seems to have a very colorful history so far. Since you are an astute reader, does any of what Adam has said sound like *Antisocial Personality Disorder (ASPD)*? We need more information, but see if you can discover any warning signs in the above information.

"So, basically what happened is that I was arrested for B and E (breaking and entering) did my stretch, and Nancy (his probation officer) sent me here for an evaluation. She thinks I might have a drinking problem, but I doubt it. She wants to make sure I stay straight, which I will do this time, I promise. Got a child on the way, a wedding to do, and I can't go back inside. Too much to lose this time."

We decided to ask Adam if we could bring in Tisch to assess the possibility of couples' therapy. "Well, I don't know. You can bring her in. I doubt she'd mind it. She might learn a bit more about me in couples' therapy. Understand that she's 8 months pregnant, so I don't know how this will go over. She also has her special classes, so it has to be after that. Tisch takes classes for pregnant school kids. Her school did that because so many kids were dropping out due to getting pregnant. I guess we just added to the numbers (laughs)." Since he agreed, we called Tisch in to the office. She drove Adam everywhere since his license had been revoked due to two *DWIs (Driving While Intoxicated)* he had received within the past three years. His *Blood Alcohol Concentrations (BACs)* were .20 and .24, respectively. This is equivalent to having 10 or 12 drinks in one hour, respectively. Tisch closed the door, Adam chose to leave the office for a while, went outside to smoke, and we then began to question Tisch.

Thought Questions

1. How important is the fact that Adam was hit when he was a child in your evaluation and diagnosis?
2. Discuss the psychologist's decision to bring in Tisch. Give your opinion about doing couple's therapy with such a young couple.

3. What warning signs for Antisocial Personality Disorder, if any, do you detect in the above information?
4. Adam notes that **only** his mother and father suffer from mental illnesses. Is he being accurate? Why or why not?
5. Does the fact that Adam was hit a lot when he was younger lead you to predict how he behaves with Tisch? His past girlfriend?

Assessment and Evaluation

The initial assessment, performed by the staff social worker Adam saw when he was 14, determined that Adam suffered from *alcohol dependence* and *conduct disorder*. This was logical, especially since Adam seemed unable to control his drinking and had two DWIs within a short period of time. We gathered some more information which made us re-examine this diagnosis.

As noted, we questioned Tisch alone initially, and she proceeded to provide us with a lot of valuable information. We asked her for the reasons she decided to stay with Adam while he was in jail, and that opened the proverbial floodgates. "I loved Adam, and I still do. I was pregnant while he was in jail and I decided that my child needed a father. You see, I didn't have a father. He got my mom knocked up and he left before I was born. My momma never saw him again by her choice. He calls sometimes, asking after me, but she doesn't let him see me. That's better I think. My momma says my dad hit her, but I don't know that. I'm an only child also and I want something of my own, and now I'm gonna have this baby. It's a boy; we're so excited. Adam has a lot of love in him and he wants to share that with our child."

We then asked Tisch if Adam was drinking when she got pregnant. "Well, yes, but my doctor said everything's okay with the child from what they can tell. Adam doesn't drink that much. His problem is his temper, not the drinking. He's never hit me, never really hit me I mean. But I usually deserve it. He's the smart one, and he's older, so he knows. I really love him. I'm learning a lot in my classes, and I'll be a great mother. He never says he's sorry when he does hit me, but it doesn't happen so much. I just want us to be a happy family; I never had that."

Tisch was asked what she would expect if she were to participate in couple's therapy. "Well, I don't know. I know we've got troubles like all people, but we can fix them. Adam's been sober ever since he went into jail, and if he breaks it he goes on back. He needs to do something about his temper and his friends. I don't know what would happen. I think it would make us a better family."

Adam was then brought in, and we agreed to have some follow-up appointments. After this initial session we met with Adam alone over the next few sessions, since Tisch was about to give birth and was under doctor's orders to stay in bed. "Well, I have hit her a bit in the past, because she didn't do what I told her to do. Like I said, my dad hit me and it taught me to be a stronger person. Tisch thinks because she's in classes that she's smarter than me. It also shows her what'll happen if she cheats on me. And I suppose the P.O. (probation officer) told you about the fights I had in jail and at school before I dropped out. Those guys had it coming to them. It was their fault. I usually ended up on the good end of those fights. Knocked out a lot of teeth . . . gave some black eyes. Even busted up a guy's ribs once. I'm wiry but tough. And the B and E and other stuff, that was just for fun. No one was hurt by it. I learned a lesson to never break the law again."

We noted that, in fact, he had **not** learned a lesson since he had broken the law repeatedly after that. We confronted him on this. "Well, I make mistakes like everyone else. What the hell do you want from me? I'm only 19! I haven't had a drop since I got out, and I've only hit Tisch once, but that was for sassing me bad. I love Tisch and I love my future family."

Let us pause again. Do you notice any patterns now? Adam's behaviors demonstrate a lack of remorse and/or guilt on his part, aggressiveness, and an inability to plan ahead by not foreseeing the consequences of his actions. He also repeatedly breaks the law. Two key questions: Is he drunk or drinking when all of these things occur, and why does Tisch stay with him?

"Well . . . maybe . . . sometimes I may have had something to drink . . . yeah, I did sometimes. It helped me to get the balls up to do this stuff. I'm not drinking when I give Tisch a crack. I need to be clearheaded so I know what she's doing at all times. She's real pretty, and I don't really trust her. You shouldn't listen to her all the time either. She had a bad life but not as bad as mine. For the B and E, I didn't have anything to drink, since I was driving. I never smoked pot for a long time either. That's illegal you know. I don't wanna mess with the law; they'll bust me right back to stir (jail)."

"Do I feel sorry for the people that got hurt, or the people whose houses I tagged or broke into? Not at all. They've all got so much money; they can get all the stuff back from insurance. It's not like they earned their stuff. One of the houses I tagged, I know the husband. Looked at me in a bad way. I know what he was thinking. The guys I hurt? Too f . . . bad, they deserved it. One looked at me in a funny way, got upside my face. Some other dude was checking out Tisch. They had it coming. Lay off my woman. But I'm not worried. I've talked to psychologists before, and I always get better. I know what I'm about, and you won't tell me any new stuff about me. I'm not dumb. I learn from my past"

We believed that we had enough information to make accurate diagnoses for Adam. Adam supplied us with some key diagnostic criteria. First, he repeatedly broke the law. (Like many in his situation, he broke the law far more times than he was caught.) He had many physical fights and was aggressive toward a lot of people, including Tisch. He showed a tremendous lack of remorse for his victims and for Tisch, *rationalizing* his behaviors. For example, he stated that the houses he robbed or "tagged" deserved it. He is also unable to plan ahead and he lacks insight.

Based on this information, and on what Tisch told us, we arrived at the following initial diagnoses for Adam:

Antisocial Personality Disorder	301.7
Alcohol Dependence	303.90
Partner Relational Problem	V61.10

For Tisch we arrived at the following diagnosis:

Partner Relational Problem	V61.10

Theoretical Etiologies

Men are more likely to receive the diagnosis of Antisocial Personality Disorder (ASPD). ASPD affects about 3% of males and about 1% of females; prevalence ranges anywhere from 3% to 30% in a **clinical setting** (APA, 2000). The diagnosis of ASPD is only given to individuals who are 18 or older. However, the symptoms need to have begun since age 15, which we can see in Adam's situation. Additionally, there needs to be evidence of conduct disorder before age 15 (APA, 2000). Adam satisfies all of these requirements.

In the past individuals with ASPD were called *psychopaths* and *sociopaths*. Some clinicians still use these terms today but they are clinically inaccurate. Like the term *lunatic* they have no diagnostic relevance as far as the DSM-IV-TR is concerned. (We hope no clinicians use the term lunatic.) The term psychopath implies that something is pathological with the individual's mind or with their psychological makeup. The term sociopath implies that the individual is socially deviant. Since some of the etiologies we are about to discuss use the term "psychopath," we will do so to maintain consistency where necessary.

There are two general schools of thought when attempting to diagnose ASPD. Hervey Cleckly (1982) spent a lot of time researching psychopaths, as he called them, and came up with 16 key characteristics for these individuals. They include characteristics that Adam has already demonstrated: lack of remorse, superficial charm, poor judgment, and inability to learn by experience. Hare (1991) created the Revised Psychopathology Checklist. He notes that information should be gathered from the patient as well as from significant others through interviews. Additionally, *permanent products* (i.e., past case notes, prison records, etc.) should also be gathered to help diagnose ASPD. The permanent products can be gathered from the significant others and from various institutions familiar with the patient. Once the information has been collected, the patient is assigned scores on the checklist.

The other school of thought focuses on observable behaviors to diagnose ASPD (APA, 2000). For example, does this individual impulsively and repeatedly change sex partners, jobs, or employment? Clekley and Hare focus on underlying personality traits. Thus, ASPD is not equal in structure to psychopathy as defined by Clekley and Hare. Some psychopaths may never have significant legal issues, and some may never demonstrate overly aggressive behaviors like Adam has done. Finally, there are criminals who do not suffer from ASPD but are defined as those who break the law, including repeat offenders. Which of the two schools of thought do you prefer?

We will first focus on genetic factors that may lead to the development of ASPD. There seems to be a strong genetic link between the development of ASPD and criminality (DiLalla & Gottesman, 1991). What this may indicate is that genes may predispose someone to develop ASPD, but the environment or stressors bring it out. Additionally, unstable family situations may increase the individual's vulnerability to develop ASPD. The most important consideration here, as with all of the disorders we have discussed, is that genetic factors may contribute to ASPD, but certain environmental factors appear to be needed as well.

Biological factors have also been extensively researched. We will briefly consider two theories: The *underarousal hypothesis* (Quay, 1965) and the *fearlessness hypothesis* (Lykken, 1982). The underarousal hypothesis states that psychopaths have low levels of arousal in their brain's cortex. This is the main reason for their antisocial behaviors. They specifically seek out thrill-seeking behaviors and other stimulation in order to boost their arousal levels. These levels are presumed to be constantly low. Adam got involved in petty crimes, but his breaking and entering approached a more daring, thrill-seeking type of felony. There was a risk he would get caught. Based on this theory, this is exactly what Adam sought, a more challenging and **stimulating** situation. Marrying Tisch should also prove to be stimulating, since he will have a child and can also more easily "smack her" when he feels the need.

The fearlessness hypotheses states that psychopaths have a higher fear threshold, i.e., frightening things for most people (a fire, gunshots) have little if any effect on these individuals. Adam figured he would not get caught and so continued to commit his crimes. Jail seems like an inconvenience to him, not a place that should be avoided at all costs. The possibility of getting shot or killed while committing a crime did not seem to deter Adam. We can conclude that because of this fearlessness, punishment will have little or no effect on these individuals. The individual must also be able to learn from his mistakes and learn from being punished. It is also possible that these individuals do not associate certain stimuli or cues with punishment or danger, such as an alarm going off. For Adam this means "S . . ., I just need to move faster, get my stuff and book the house." In other words, move quickly, steal as much as he can, and leave the premises.

Research into psychological factors has discovered an interesting concept. Psychopaths appear to persist in situations where failure is guaranteed. Even when they were informed about this they continued to engage in the situation (Newman, Patterson, & Kosson, 1987)! Newman et al concluded that once a psychopath sets his eyes on a goal, very little if anything will stop him from attaining that goal. Let us use two examples to clarify this interesting hypothesis.

Imagine that you are in Las Vegas and have been told that you may continue to play the slots but there is zero chance that you will win. You tell the manager that your goal is to hit the jackpot. Most people, upon hearing this news, will stop playing. The psychopath, goal-fixated, will continue, not believing this information.

It has been reported that bin Laden and al-Qaeda were involved in the 1993 bombing of the World Trade Center. They were upset and frustrated that more people were not killed. Thus, they targeted it again and succeeded in 2001. In other words, failure seems to motivate and strengthen the psychopath's determination.

Family members, especially parents, may contribute to the development of ASPD (Patterson, 1982). Parents in these situations gave in to their child's problems. Parents, losing their patience with a child who does not listen, may walk away or just give in and say "fine, go ahead and do it, see if we care." The child ends up learning not to give up, but the parent's behavior is also reinforced since the fighting has ceased. If this is combined with other factors involved in a dysfunctional household (parental lack of involvement for example), the antisocial behaviors will continue and thus be strengthened. The Columbine killers' parents were reportedly uninvolved and unaware of what their sons were doing in their basements. Adam's father was involved but in negative ways. Finally, for unknown reasons antisocial behaviors seem to decrease after age 40. This area requires further research.

In sum, as with many of the disorders, an integrative model best explains the etiology of ASPD. Perhaps the individual has no fears and is also chronically underaroused. He comes from a dysfunctional family and environment. Looking for some way to arouse himself, he decides to get involved with crime. Once his family background is examined, it is discovered that his parents gave in to his demands and punishment, when administered, was ineffective. Thus the deviant behaviors continued. Does this sound like anyone you might know?

Treatment Plan

As with borderline personality disorder, treatment of patients with ASPD is very difficult due to their lack of empathy and insight (Andreasen & Black, 1995). Treatment is also problematic because these individuals rarely come into treatment voluntarily. Compounding matters is the fact that these individuals can be extremely manipulative with their therapists. It is not surprising that many clinicians do not predict successful treatment for an individual with ASPD. Additionally, research has demonstrated that a link appears between ASPD and alcohol abuse/dependence (Andreasen & Black, 1995). It is very difficult to treat comorbid disorders when alcohol usage complicates the treatment scenario. Fortunately, we had some help in this matter from two sources.

We decided to perform *couple's therapy* with Adam and Tisch. A female co-therapist was brought in at this time. Adam and Tisch began couples' therapy together, but this soon became individual therapy. The individual therapy with Adam was more successful than the couple's treatment. There are a number of reasons for this. Can you guess what some of them might be?

His probation officer Nancy oversaw the initial problem of Adam's sobriety. She saw Adam twice a week because she was concerned about him and was afraid he might drink again and go back to jail. She saw some hope for Adam and took special interest in him. She also told us how personable and likeable he was. As we noted earlier, those with ASPD are usually very charming individuals.

While Adam was in treatment with us he offered no proof that he had broken his sobriety. We contacted his probation officer weekly, and we also asked Tisch about his sobriety. "Like I told you, I won't drink again. If I have a slip I'll let you know. I can't afford that."

We decided to use *person-centered techniques*, *reality therapy*, and *cognitive-behavior therapy* for Adam and Tisch. Adam worked hard in therapy, but he still did not take responsibility for his legal infractions. He never really gained a lot of insight into his issues, but he told us he did not hit Tisch while he was in treatment. Tisch supported him on these assertions, but this is what we expected.

The couple's sessions were also interesting and successful at first. Tisch told Adam that she never felt appreciated and demanded that he stop hitting her. Adam admitted that he had a hard time controlling his temper, and Tisch told him that if things continued or got worse, she'd take their son and leave Adam. Adam took this threat seriously and promised to work on his temper and on other issues. "I feel like Adam never tries to communicate with me. He comes home, has dinner and passes out from exhaustion. He expects me to do everything with the baby and I won't. I had no father growing up, and this baby will not have the same thing happen to him. This is all new to us, and with all of these appointments for Adam it makes it harder." We referred them to a parenting class at the hospital and they both attended, telling us it really helped a lot.

Tisch also admitted some surprising things while she was in therapy. "I was never sure I loved Adam and I really am not sure I do now. I don't know what love is, since I rarely got it at home. I have to try and love him for our son. I stayed with him because he made me feel wanted and loved. He'd buy me things, say sweet things to me, and suddenly he'd hit me for no reason. I was confused and I still am." Tisch was hoping that the sessions would help her to get to know Adam better, and herself better as well. She told us that Adam is a very sweet person who lacks love and guidance. She was willing to give him a chance.

Tisch was absent for many of the subsequent sessions, so eventually we turned the couple's sessions into individual and saw Adam once a week. Tisch showed up twice after that, both times with her infant son. We tried to be accommodating and attempted therapy with him in the office, but that was not successful. Tisch understood and also "could not see why I need to keep on coming. It's just too hard on me. I could see you individually, but I don't see why."

Adam looked at his temper in our sessions and was eventually referred to a higher functioning group. Adam "never really felt tempted to drink while he was in therapy;" he and Tisch stayed together throughout his time with us. Adam discussed the "hatred I feel for my dad, what he did to me and my mom," and he discussed how his mom's drinking affected him and "ruined my life. Tisch and my son are the best things that happened to me."

After 7 months in treatment, Adam's probation officer decided that he did not have to continue in therapy. We disagreed, but Adam told us "I feel like I'm better, cured. I know what I have to do to get along and the mistakes I made. I paid my price." Adam left against our advice (sometimes called *Against Medical Advice* or *AMA*), and we lost contact with him for a while. Many in the clinic were concerned, since they knew Adam from his past, and remarked how difficult it would be for Adam and Tisch to have a successful marriage. We eventually did discover what happened to Adam and to Tisch, and we will discuss their fate in a moment.

There are some other treatment modalities that could be used for the treatment of ASPD. Some therapists state that individuals with ASPD should be incarcerated in order to protect the public and to discourage future deviant acts. Nancy and the clinic decided against this, since it was our view to give anyone a chance at rehabilitation and treatment. As you will soon see, this perspective may have made more sense.

There are no specific medications, nor any medications indicated, for the treatment of antisocial personality disorder. Sometimes medications such as *Lithium carbonate* and *Tegretol* (*carbamazepine;* an anticonvulsant) have been prescribed for the anger or rage that ASPD patients may have, but the data substantiating their usage are scarce. *Antianxiety medications (Valium)* may be used, but because impulse control for ASPD is poor, using highly addictive medicines is not wise. ASPD remains poorly understood in many ways, so at the present time medication usage is not recommended.

Prognosis

Adam's prognosis is "guarded to poor." We say this for a number of reasons. (We will address Tisch in a moment.) First, even though Adam was sober while in treatment, there is no guarantee that he will remain so. Additionally, we looked at Adam's past and realized that it was quite "eventful" for someone so young. His lawbreaking in the past does not bode well for the future. The lack of remorse and insight that Adam has is also a concern. This is something that cannot be taught and cannot really be remedied in therapy. *Freud* would say that those who lack guilt or remorse have a very weak *superego,* which comes from poor parenting.

Tisch's prognosis is "guarded to fair." She knows that she is in a troublesome relationship, and she knows that her needs and health (and her son's) come before Adam's. She implied that she got trapped and needed a strong man in her life, and Adam came along. "Adam, I guess, manipulated me, got me knocked up, and here we are." Tisch was completing the eleventh grade and was going to take her *GED* and graduate the following year. Due to budget cuts, the county and school cut the teen parent special classes. Tisch took a job at night at a pizza parlor and made decent money.

At last contact Adam had gotten in trouble again. Adam showed up late one day to work and his boss docked him 1 hour's pay, since Adam was the only one on that night. This happened again, Adam was sent home, and he took a swing at his boss. Unfortunately for both of them, Adam connected, the police were called, and eventually his boss decided not to press charges. Adam lost his job, which meant that Tisch was supporting them. Adam moved in with Tisch and her mother, but Tisch, at last contact, had thrown him out. Adam threatened Tisch. She got very scared and did what she had to do. Adam, who was still on probation, was being sought by his probation officer. As for Tisch, "I guess if he comes back I'll take him back. Like I said, our son needs a father. I can't do this alone. Adam needs some help bad." Unfortunately, those of us at the clinic were not surprised at this outcome. Very saddened, but not surprised.

Review and Study Questions

Lisa

1. How accurate is the psychologist's diagnosis of Lisa? Does she have an anxiety disorder?

2. Would you be concerned about Lisa's sexual behavior? Or is she just enjoying her sexuality?

3. Where does Lisa's father figure in all of this?

4. Lisa does not mention her brother much. What might the reasons be for this?

5. Based on your knowledge, how difficult would it be to do therapy with someone who suffers from borderline personality disorder?

6. Does Lisa suffer from Bipolar I or II Disorder? Discuss and support your response.

7. Once again the issue of alcohol and substance abuse arises. How much does Lisa's usage contribute to her difficulties?

Adam and Tisch

1. What is your prognosis for Adam? For Tisch? Justify your responses.

2. Are you surprised that Adam "relapsed" as far as his temper is concerned?

3. Discuss the reasons why Tisch waited for, and stayed with, Adam.

4. How much did Adam's upbringing contribute to his present situation? Tisch's?

5. What type of upbringing do you think their son will experience?

6. Would you prescribe a medication to help Adam control his anger? Why or why not?

7. Do you believe Adam when he says he has no remorse for his victims?

8. "I thought all individuals with ASPD were serial killers!" What is your response to this?

Key Terms to Know

Personality disorders

underarousal hypothesis

fearlessness hypothesis

Borderline Personality Disorder (BPD)

Cluster A

Cluster B

Cluster C

Non-Hodgkin's Lymphoma

mood disorder

cannabis

Rule Out (R/O)

countertransference

higher functioning group

Bipolar Disorder

behavioral modification techniques

person-centered therapy

social support

Lithium (lithium carbonate)

Antisocial Personality Disorder (ASPD)

Conduct Disorder

recidivists

Alcohol Dependence

probation officer (P.O.)

person-centered techniques

reality therapy

cognitive-behavior therapy

Couple's therapy

Against Medical Advice (AMA)

Freud

superego

Tegretol (carbamazepine)

antianxiety medications

Valium

GED

DWI (Driving While Intoxicated)

character disorders

dialectical behavior therapy (DBT)

unstructured diagnostic interview

Beck Depression Inventory–II (BDI–II)

avoidant personality disorder

psychosis

neurosis

Prozac (fluoxetine)

Blood Alcohol Concentrations (BAC)

rationalizing

permanent products

psychopaths

sociopaths

Chapter 11

Applying What You Have Learned: The Cases of Estelle and Diane

As we approach the end of this casebook, we want you to understand how psychologists think, where we get our information, and how we perform our jobs as diagnosticians, treatment planners, therapists, and so on. The purpose of this chapter is **not** to get you to be (or act) like a psychologist and to be "amateur" diagnosticians, but to begin to understand the things psychologists do in their everyday jobs.

Our goal is to make your assessments of Estelle and Diane a classroom exercise. This can be approached on an individual or on a group basis. We suggest that each student work by him/herself on each case, and then compare and contrast results with other students in a small group during class, or with the class as a whole. We want you to think about what might be occurring with these two cases, and we want you to support your hypotheses with data. We believe that these exercises are the next best thing to actual hands-on training.

Introduction

Imagine this: You are a brand new psychologist, and you have just begun your first week at the mental health clinic. You are very excited to have a chance to practice your skills and to begin therapy. Your supervisor believes in "learning on the fly;" i.e., she has decided to give you two new intakes (new cases) with limited background information. You eagerly take these cases and look at the referral notes: A lot of the information is missing!

She tells you that it will be **your** job to figure out what key facts you would focus on in each case, and what additional information you would need before you could attempt to make a diagnosis. That sounds like a fair challenge! Let us then examine the notes you have for the first case:

Case 1
The Case of Estelle

Presenting Problem

Estelle is a 19-year-old Hispanic woman who was raised in Puerto Rico but came to the United States as a 14-year-old. She was raised as a Catholic and remains very devout, attending church on a regular basis and observing all of the holidays. She is 5'5" tall, weighs 148 pounds and is pleased with how she looks. Estelle wore slacks, high-heeled shoes and a long-sleeved shirt to her first visit. This was typical attire for her no matter what the weather. Estelle made fair eye contact and seemed very intense during the sessions. She rarely smiled and seemed on the verge of tears at times but she never really cried during the sessions. She wore a fair amount of eye shadow and lipstick and carried a small purse. She first appeared wearing headphones and carrying a CD player. She spoke with a slight accent and sat with a defensive posture throughout the earlier sessions. Estelle is a freshman at a community college and has no idea what to major in or what to do with her life. She presently works at a hair salon.

Estelle described her reasons for coming to the clinic. "It was a bad day at the salon. My boss yelled at me because a color treatment went bad on a regular. Somehow I used the wrong mix and it came out too reddish. I was yelled at and sent home for the rest of the day. Of course my dad happened to come home early and he found me and yelled at me and asked if I was fired. I mouthed off at him and was sent to my room with no dinner. My mom as usual sided with him and further grounded me for the weekend. Can you believe stuff like this for a 19-year-old?? Anyway, I decided not to go in the next day so I stayed at home and did a lot of thinking. I was tired of the abuse, tired of not finding the right guy, tired of my life. You know how they say I was sick and tired of being sick and tired of all of this crap? I was."

Estelle then decided to do something about these feelings. In the past she cut herself on her arms and legs but had no intention of doing major damage or of taking her life. This time she wanted to do something more dramatic. "I wanted to do something but I was not sure if I wanted to kill myself. I figured if I really really hurt myself the pain would vanish and my family would finally apologize for the way they treat me. So I went to the kitchen and found some Drano. I swallowed it and it hurt like nobody's business. I freaked and called 911 immediately, since I realized something was really wrong here. They arrived quickly with an ambulance and took me to the hospital to pump my stomach." The paramedics told Estelle NOT to make herself vomit. Drano, if vomited back up, could cause as much damage coming up as it did going down.

Her parents arrived at the hospital and were beside themselves with worry and remorse. Estelle told us this was the first time she saw her father crying. "For once they had nothing mean to say to me. My dad wanted to know what went wrong and how, and what they could do to fix it." The hospital kept her for a longer period of time, made a complete evaluation and placed her in group and individual therapy. "I told work I was sick and would be out for awhile and they understood completely. The incident of my messing up a client's color was not mentioned. It was wild. All of a sudden everyone couldn't be nicer to me and they felt sorry for me."

Once Estelle was discharged she went home and returned to work. She was referred to us by the hospital's social worker, who sent us her discharge summary as well as some case notes on Estelle's treatment. Estelle contacted us and we set up a time for an initial intake with her, which led to the initial session.

Background Information

Estelle has two older sisters, 24 and 21, and one older brother, 27. Estelle is the "youngest; I'm often treated like the baby. Everyone always watches out for me." Her mother recently returned to work as a secretary for a large company; her father has worked for the past 5 years as a superintendent in a large apartment building. Estelle still lives at home; her other siblings are all out of the house. "But you need to know that they all live very close to my family and to me, no more than 20 minutes away. We believe in being close, sometimes too close."

Estelle had an unremarkable childhood, reaching all of her developmental milestones at the age-appropriate times. She had her first sexual experience at age 16 with a man who was 10 years older. "I made a mistake and I realize it now. It's okay to have sex when you love someone even if you are not married to him. He never loved me; he lied to me to get me into bed. I felt like a jerk."

In school Estelle's grades ranged from C-plus to B-minus. She graduated with a C-plus average "because I have this tendency to think in Spanish while I'm trying to speak English, and I get confused. My writing is not good. We also do not speak English at home. But that's not really an excuse. I was not the best student. I didn't take school seriously." She could not decide whether to go on to college or not, but her family convinced her to go. Her siblings were all either employed or home taking care of their children, but none of them had a college degree. Estelle "would be the first; I also was not really ready to go out and work full time right now."

Estelle eventually took a job in a hair salon. "I do nails and hair. I went to beauty school and I'm a trained beautician so they let me do the cutting and coloring. It's actually a lot of fun and I made some contacts through the shop. For example, there was Harry. . . ."

Harry was an agent for a local modeling company who told Estelle that she had "the look" to be a professional model. She signed a limited contract and did some work for local newspapers and advertising circulars. Harry promised that she would graduate to bigger and better things. Whether or not this was true, Estelle finally felt good about herself and decided that she was good enough to get a college degree.

"I never really liked myself. My dad would always tell me I was a nothing, that I would not amount to anything, that I would end up pregnant at a young age because I didn't take school seriously. No, he never really beat me. He hit me a few times but he always apologized afterwards for that. He was just mean to me, verbally abusive, and that really hurt. No matter what I did I could never win with him. After hearing this crap for so many months I just snapped."

Thus, at age 14 Estelle cut her wrists and arms repeatedly and waited in the bathroom for her parents to come home that evening. When they arrived "Wooo, were they surprised! I felt like I made my dad pay for all the abuse. Now look at your little girl with her arms all sliced up. What do you think of that?" Her parents immediately called the police, and they took her to the emergency room of the local hospital. Her arms were treated (All of the cuts were superficial. They would leave scars but no permanent damage was done) and she was kept 72 hours for observation. Once it was determined (after this time) that she was not a threat to herself she was discharged.

"It was odd because they really did not do too much to me. They asked me a bunch of questions and told me that I would be staying there for awhile. The only thing they kept asking me was 'Did I really want to off myself? I told them heck no! I just wanted my family to realize how much they would miss me if I DID really do it. But you can guess what happened next." Can you?

When they arrived home from the hospital Estelle expected her family to be upset. Her entire family was there and they all screamed at her, telling her that she was an idiot, especially after everything her family had done for her. "The worst was my dad. He sent me to my room right before a family dinner; that really hurt. He also hit me . . . only once . . . in the face and I got a black eye. He was really mad at me, telling me how scared he was and how my little 'trick' cost him a fortune. Things just seemed to get worse after that for me."

Estelle began withdrawing from everyone and would periodically cut herself, again not with the intent to kill herself. "I wanted to hurt myself. I don't really know why. It was like I couldn't stop." She then showed us her legs. "You see, I needed to stop with the arms because it was too obvious. I switched to my legs because it's easier to wear long pants in the summer. The cuts are not too deep, just enough to burn and hurt." Estelle's grades also began to drop in school. She experimented with alcohol and cocaine and began to have strange mood swings. "I would just have these emotional outbursts for no reason, no matter who was there or what they said." Estelle was about to turn 16 and had been seeing her boyfriend for 8 months. Her parents were furious and forbade him from entering their house. Right after Estelle had intercourse with this man she dropped him and "went crazy with guys. I would have many short relationships but real intense. We'd have sex the first date, see each other as often as we could and then after a month or so I would dump him and move on to the next. The pattern stayed the same, never longer than two months for any guy. And always sex, no matter what I felt. It was like I would have sex, fall in love, and then get sick of them so fast I'd dump them. This was causing me trouble though."

Her parents were called into school because her grades were getting too low. The guidance counselor blamed it on home problems and Estelle being boy crazy. Drug usage was never discussed. Estelle's parent's severely restricted her behavior, forbade her from seeing any more boys, and required her to stay at home on the weekends until her grades came back up. "My grades eventually got better but I really hated my parents now. They were trying to ruin my life."

Estelle graduated high school and went to beauty school as soon as she could, never really having the intention to continue her education. She still lived at home and still suffered from the verbal abuse of her father. She was also seeing guys as often as she could, and the volatility of these relationships did not change. Finally, one day she had enough, which led to her swallowing Drano and eventually to see us.

Assessment and Evaluation

Estelle was assessed with an *unstructured diagnostic interview* and the *Beck Depression Inventory-II (BDI-II)*. Some further information that you might find useful came out in our initial sessions.

Estelle reported no history of mental illness is her family, and also reported no history of drug or alcohol abuse. She emphatically stated that she was clean and that she only "experimented" with cocaine and alcohol and never got in trouble because of her usage. All the drug screens performed at the hospital came up negative, so Estelle was being truthful here. Investigation into the hospital's case notes also confirmed the absence of mental illness in her **immediate** family. What did arise in the ninth session was the fact that her maternal great-grandmother was hospitalized for the treatment of "depression I think, but I'm not so sure. Hispanics tend not to talk about these things. It's kept in the family, but I think something went on there."

Estelle told us that when she was a young child she never seemed to get much attention except when she did something wrong. Her school projects were never displayed at home, and she was sure her family favored her brother. He was the oldest, and her father was especially close to him and was very proud he was male so he could "lead" the family once her father passed on. In many cultures and societies women are seen as not being equals to men. They do not get as much attention and they are not expected to be successful career-wise.

Estelle's BDI-II score was 15, indicating mild to moderate depression. However, she displayed no symptoms of depression and seemed jumpy in the office during the first interview. She was animated and very verbal.

Thought Questions

1. Tell us what key facts you will focus on to help you make a diagnosis of Estelle.
2. Estelle attempted suicide; this appears to be a symptom of depression. Support or refute this statement.
3. How important is Estelle's history of abuse by her father in relation to her difficulties?
4. Discuss what may have led Estelle to get involved in so many self-destructive relationships with men.
5. What additional information would you need in order to make an accurate diagnosis of Estelle?

Case 2
The Case of Diane

Presenting Problem

Diane is a 22-year-old university junior majoring in English. Diane is white, weighs 125 pounds and stands 5'4" tall. She is slim and reports that she has had no weight problems in her life, "I have a fast metabolism so I can eat all the junk I want. In the Midwest this is an asset, since we tend to be "big" out here . . . I guess it's so we can survive the freezing winters!" Diane has taken a bit longer than average to complete her education. Her "problems" have caused her to go part time for a while until she "can get things under control." Diane made good eye contact but often looked at us with suspicion in her eyes. At times she would appear "spooked" when we mentioned certain possible explanations for her behaviors. She displayed a blunted affect and bit her nails. When we asked personal questions the nail biting would increase. She was dressed in a turtleneck sweater and jeans with sneakers. She did not wear any jewelry. It took awhile to get Diane to volunteer certain information.

Diane's problems did not start until she moved away from home to attend university. She was 17 at the time. "I'd never been away from home before. Sure I went to camp for 2 weeks but that was near to where we lived. That was not an issue. I'm not sure what happened but during my freshman year things started to happen to me. I still can't explain them." What were these "things?"

Diane discovered that whenever she would be in a car with other people (She was always a passenger) she would "get sick. That means that I would get all queasy and nauseous and sometimes vomit, but not always. This happened infrequently at first and then happened regularly, which sucks. I watched what I ate and there didn't seem to be any relation between that and getting sick. It would also happen when I ate nothing. So after this went on for awhile, like 4 months, I decided that something is wrong with me and I went to a medical doctor at the clinic on campus."

The doctor performed a thorough examination and found nothing physically wrong with Diane. "Well that blew me away, since I knew for a fact that something was physically wrong with me. Why was I getting sick so often if nothing was physically wrong? I thought they were quacks so I got another opinion. This doctor ran even more tests including hormonal checks and stuff . . . and they still found nothing wrong with me! Well shoot. We then had a nice talk and they suggested that I see a shrink or something. So here I am! Now it's your turn. Am I crazy or what? Get the nets!"

Background Information

Diane has three older brothers and one older sister; her oldest brother is 17 years older than she. "My parents had me later in life; after I was born they said that was it. I'm very close to all my siblings, but I tend to disagree often with my sister Brooke. I'm not sure if it's competition or whatever, but we usually don't see eye to eye. We love each other, but. . . . I'm also seen as the baby in the family. My family is always correcting me to this day. They never trust my judgment on anything, school, guys, anything. I'm always wrong and always making mistakes. Honestly I'm sick of it. It's no wonder I had to get away from them."

"I was really sheltered as a child. We never traveled out of state so this is really my first time away from home. I guess my parents were surprised since they were supposed to be finished with having kids and bam! I show up, even though they told me I was always wanted and loved. My mom had me when she was quite old, but she didn't have any pregnancy complications."

Diane belongs to the Church of Jesus Christ of Latter Day Saints (Mormon), so the fact that she attends a public university is a surprise to many. "My family wanted me to go to BYU but I said forget it. I guess I'm what you might call a religious rebel. I am a 'reform' Mormon, so to speak. I don't drink or smoke but I do use caffeine and I do get involved with men if I choose to." This has caused a significant strain between Diane and her family but she did not wish to dwell on that too much. Diane's father was a policeman (now retired) and her mother is a retired homemaker. "She was a nurse in the Korean War. After the war she got married and decided to stay home and raise the kids. In our town this was considered to be the norm. My mom has been "retired" from homemaking for many years now; she enjoys being a grandparent and great grandparent."

Diane reports having an unremarkable childhood, reaching all of her developmental milestones at the appropriate ages. Her grades in high school were good (Bs mainly), and she presently has a B-plus average at university. "I could do better but again, these . . . problems . . . hold me back." Diane reported no known history of any mental or physical illnesses in her family, and no history of alcohol or drug abuse. "In MY house? I told you we don't even use caffeine! So forget us being alcoholics or junkies . . . no way." It should be noted that groups that believe in extended families such as Mormons make excellent research populations for examining some types of mental and physical illnesses. Why do you think that is?

Assessment and Evaluation

Diane was assessed with an unstructured diagnostic interview, the *Eating Disorder Inventory-II (EDI-II)* and the BDI-II. A lot of interesting information arose as we continued to question Diane.

Diane stated that she went to the campus medical doctor to find out what was physically wrong with her. In fact this was not the first time or the first doctor she had seen. "I actually go to doctors a lot because of these weird problems. Every time they find nothing wrong with me and send me to a psychologist. Well I know something is wrong with them or with their tests or equipment. I guess they think that a 22-year-old woman must be in perfect health. I actually saw a social worker once, last year on campus. She said that I had some type of disorder that caused my getting sick all of the time. That was a lot of bull. How could something in your head cause you to vomit at the weirdest times? That was the last time I saw her or anyone else who shrinks heads for a living. I KNEW that I had a disease of some sort. I'm not crazy."

As we continued our line of questions and discussion, more information arose. "I also seem to be afraid of closed spaces and of bridges. Every time I'm driving and I get to a bridge I freeze up and stop. I just can't cross them. The swaying, the dropping into the water, I can't deal with that. I hate being trapped in a car. I also hate being in tight spots, especially with men. On my last few dates once I got physically close to a guy or went to his place I would puke. Of course that ended things rather quickly. I never saw any of these guys again. No big losses there, as they were jerks for not showing me compassion when I needed it."

We investigated whether Diane had food allergies. "Nah, not that I know of. I was tested and I'm not allergic to anything that would come out in the tests. No specific food will make me sick if that's what you're thinking. I already went there and came up with nothing. Even things like sushi and eggs and raw shellfish don't do it. Of course there have been times when I've gotten food poisoning but that's different." We suggested that Diane get tested again (by a specialist) to confirm the past results. However we suspected that food allergies were NOT the issue here.

Diane seemed to get sick more often when certain things were happening. "I can usually tell when I'm about to get sick. My stomach gets all gassy and I feel knots inside of me. Usually it occurs when I'm with a new guy or with a guy I really like but nothing has yet happened. I also need to have a place that has an easy exit. I HATE getting sick in front of my friends. I still go out all the time but now I'm more aware of how to get to the bathroom quickly or outside when I feel the vomiting coming on. It makes for an eventful evening." Any ideas so far as to what might be happening?

We investigated the possibility of eating disorders. "I've always been very happy with my body and my weight. I didn't get the "freshman 15" and I've never had a weight problem to speak of. I can't see starving myself and I certainly can't see making myself puke after I eat to lose weight. Gee whiz, I get sick when I'm not supposed to and I hate it, so why would I ever do it deliberately? I can't see that at all. That is truly nuts. I eat like a normal 22-year-old woman except when I get sad or have sweet cravings; then I pig out. But nothing more unusual than that." Diane was happy with her body and she showed no scores that caused us to take note on the EDI-II.

Diane's BDI-II score was 11, indicating mild depression. We discussed that. "Well yeah I get depressed. Who the heck wouldn't if you spend all this time trying to find a doctor who knows what they're doing? These vomiting attacks are making me sad. I can't be around hot guys, I can't really be with my friends and I can't even be by myself in my nice car without this fear of getting sick. I tried deep breathing exercises and those really didn't help. Then to top this off my dentist tells me that I'm bulimic and my tooth enamel has begun to erode because of the vomiting. Can you believe this stuff? So yeah I'm depressed and angry. Are those the same thing?"

We finally investigated Diane's past treatment history. "As I said I only saw a social worker once and that was the last time I saw any mental health worker. It was recommended a number of times that I see someone but I saw, and still see, no reason for it. My problems are physical and I expect you'll send me back to the doctor or, even better, find a good one for me to see."

Thought Questions

1. Tell us what key facts you will focus on to help you make a diagnosis of Diane.
2. How important are the facts that Diane is the youngest child and that she was sheltered (and still is to some degree)?
3. What is the connection (if any) between Diane's leaving home for the first time and the onset of her vomiting in certain situations?
4. Diane gets sick when she is in a car as a passenger. This might be a symptom of an anxiety disorder, specifically some type of phobia. Why might this be so?

5. Discuss your views about Diane being convinced that something MUST be physically wrong with her.
6. What additional information would you need in order to make an accurate diagnosis of Diane?

Review and Study Questions

Estelle

1. Why does Estelle cut herself? Is she looking for attention or is it something else?
2. What would you do if you found out that someone with whom you were performing therapy swallowed drain cleaner?
3. You have seen how family background may relate to someone who has a mental illness. What do you believe the relation is between family history of mental illness and a patient's history (if there is any connection at all)?
4. What are your views on Estelle's relationships with significantly older men?
5. How important is Estelle's ethnicity in investigating etiologies and diagnoses?

Diane

1. How likely is it that a psychological problem causes a physiological problem or reaction?
2. What effect did Diane's religious background have on her concerns? Is this something that psychologists should routinely consider? Why or why not?
3. What might be the cause(s) of Diane's fear of crossing bridges?
4. Diane appears to be somewhat sarcastic. What might be the cause of this?

Terms to Know

Eating Disorder Inventory-II (EDI-II)
Beck Depression Inventory-II (BDI-II)

unstructured diagnostic interview

References

Abikoff, H., & Klein, R. G. (1992). Attention-deficit hyperactivity and conduct disorder: Comorbidity and implications for treatment. *Journal of Consulting and Clinical Psychology, 60,* 881–892.

Abraham, S. (1996). Characteristics of eating disorders among young ballet dancers. *Psychopathology, 29,* 223–229.

American Psychiatric Association (2000). *American Psychiatric Association practice guidelines for the treatment of psychiatric disorders.* Washington, DC.

American Psychiatric Association (2000). *Diagnostic and statistical manual of mental disorders (4th ed.-text revision).* Washington, DC.

Andreasen, N. C., & Black, D. W. (1995). *Introductory textbook of psychiatry (2nd ed.)* Washington, DC: American Psychiatric Press.

Angier, N. (1991, August 4). Kids who can't sit still. *The New York Times,* Section 4A, pp. 30–33.

Bach, A. K., Wincze, J. P., & Barlow, D. H. (2001). Sexual dysfunction. In D. H. Barlow (Ed.), *Clinical handbook of psychological disorders: A step-by-step treatment manual* (3rd ed.). New York: Guilford Press.

Barbach, L. G. (2000). *For yourself: The fulfillment of female sexuality.* New York: Penguin Putnam.

Barlow, D. H. (2002). *Anxiety and its disorders: The nature and treatment of anxiety and panic (2nd ed.)* New York: Guilford Press

Barlow, D. H., Gorman, J. M., Shear, K. M., & Woods, S. W. (2000). Cognitive-behavioral therapy, impiramine, or their combination for panic disorder: A randomized controlled trial. *Journal of the American Medical Association, 283,* 2529–2536.

Bassett, A. S., Chow, E. W., Waterworth, D. M., & Brzustowicz, L. (2001). Genetic insights into schizophrenia. *Canadian Journal of Psychiatry, 46,* 131–137.

Bateson, G. (1959). *Cultural problems posed by a study of schizophrenic process.* In A. Auerback (Ed.), *Schizophrenia: An integrated approach.* New York: Ronald Press.

Begley, S. (1998, January 26). Is everyone crazy? *Newsweek,* pp. 48–56.

Bezchlibnyk-Butler, K. Z., & Jeffries, J. J. (2002). *Clinical handbook of psychotropic drugs.* Seattle, WA: Hogrefe & Huber.

Bouton, M. E., Mineka, S., & Barlow, D. H. (2001). A modern learning theory perspective on the etiology of panic disorder. *Psychological Review, 108,* 4–32.

Bruch, H. (2001). *The golden cage: The enigma of anorexia nervosa.* Cambridge, MA: Harvard University Press.

Butler, A. C., & Beck, A. T. (1995). Cognitive therapy for depression. *The Clinical Psychologist, 48,* 3–5.

Castles, A., Datta, H., Gayan, J., & Olson, R. (1999). Varieties of developmental reading disorder: Genetic and environmental influences. *Journal of Experimental Child Psychology, 72,* 73–94.

Centers for Disease Control and Prevention (1995). Sociodemographic and behavioral characteristics associated with alcohol consumption during pregnancy—United States. *Morbidity and Mortality Weekly Report, 44,* 261–264.

Clark, D. M. (1996). Panic disorder: From theory to therapy. In P. Salkovskis (Ed.) *Frontiers of cognitive therapy* (pp. 318–344). New York: Guilford Press.

Clekley, H. M. (1982). *The mask of sanity* (6th ed.). St. Louis: Mosby.

Comings, D. E. (2000). The role of genetics in ADHD and conduct disorder—Relevance to the treatment of recidivist antisocial behavior. In D. H. Fishbein (Ed.), *The science, treatment, and prevention of antisocial behaviors: Application to the criminal justice system* (pp. 16–1—16–25). Kingston, NJ: Civic Research Institute.

Coyne, J. C. (1976). Toward an interactional description of depression. *Psychiatry, 39,* 14–27.

Craddock, N., & Jones, I. (1999). Genetics of bipolar disorder. *Journal of Medical Genetics, 36,* 585–594.

Craighead, W. E., Craighead, L. W., & Ilardi, S. S. (1998). Psychosocial treatments for major depressive disorder. In P. E. Nathan and J. M. Gorman (Eds.), *A guide to treatments that work* (pp. 226–239). New York: Oxford University Press.

Cuadros, P., Land, G., Scully, S., & Song, S. (2003, July 28). The new science of dyslexia. *Time, 162,* 52–59.

Daley, D. C., & Marlatt, G. A. (1992). Relapse prevention: Cognitive and behavioral interventions. In J.H. Lowinson, P. Ruiz, & R.B. Millman (Eds.), *Substance Abuse: A Comprehensive Textbook (2nd ed.) (pp.533–542).* Baltimore, MD: Williams & Wilkins.

DiLalla, D. L., & Gottesman, I. I. (1991). Biological and genetic contributions to violence—Wisdom's untold tale. *Psychological Bulletin, 109,* 125–129.

DiLalla, D. L., Carey, G., Gottesman, I. I., & Bouchard, T. J. (1996). Heritability of MMPI personality indicators of psychopathology in twins reared apart. *Journal of Abnormal Psychology, 105,* 491–499.

Dodge, K. A. (1993). The future of research on the treatment of conduct disorder. *Development and Psychopathology, 5,* 311–319.

Dougherty, D. M., Bjork, J. M., Marsh, D. M., & Moeller, F. G. (2000). A comparison between adults with conduct disorder and normal controls on a continuous Performance Test: Differences in impulsive response characteristics. *Psychological Record, 50,* 203–219.

Dugger, C. W. (1995, January 23). Slipping through the cracks and out the door. *The New York Times,* Section B, pp. 1–2.

Eisler, I., Dare, C., Russell, G. F. M., Szmukler, G., le Grange, D., & Dodge, E. (1997). Family and individual therapy in anorexia nervosa: A five-year follow-up. *Archives of General Psychiatry, 54,* 1025–1030.

Fairburn, C. G. (1985). Cognitive-behavioral treatment for bulimia. In D. M. Garner & P. E. Garfinkel (Eds.), *Handbook of psychotherapy for anorexia nervosa and bulimia* (pp. 160–192). New York: Guilford Press.

Fairburn, C. G., Welch, S. I., Doll, S. A., Davies, B. A., & O'Connor, M. E. (1997). Risk factors for bulimia nervosa: A community-based case-control study. *Archives of General Psychiatry, 54,* 509–517.

Foy, D. W., Resnick, H.S., Sipprelle, R.C., & Carroll, E.M. (1987). Premilitary, military, and postmilitary factors in the development of combat related post-traumatic stress disorder. *The Behavior Therapist, 10,* 3–9.

Fromm-Reichmann, F. (1948). Notes on the development of treatment of schizophrenics by psychoanalytic psychotherapy. *Psychiatry, 11,* 263–273.

Fuller, M. A., & Sajatovic, M. (2000). *Drug information handbook for psychiatry* (2nd ed.). Cleveland, OH: American Pharmaceutical Association.

Garner, D. M., Garfinkel, P. E., Rockert, W., & Olmsted, M. P. (1987). A prospective study of eating disturbances in the ballet. *Psychotherapy and Psychosomatics, 48,* 170–175.

Getzfeld, A. R. (1992). Characteristics of female bulimics and the effectiveness of desipramine treatment. *Dissertation Abstracts International,* (UMI No. 9331697).

Getzfeld, A. R. (1999, April). *Bulimia nervosa, anorexia nervosa, and alcohol abuse: Differential diagnoses using the DSM-IV, a case study, and some potential treatment methods.* Poster session presented at the meeting of the National Association of School Psychologists, Las Vegas, NV.

Goldstein, D. J. (Ed.) (1999). *The management of eating disorders and obesity.* Totowa, NJ: Humana Press.

Gottesman, I. I. (1991). *Schizophrenia genesis: The origins of madness.* New York: W. H. Freeman.

Greist, J. H. (1990). Treatment of obsessive-compulsive disorder: Psychotherapies, drugs, and other somatic treatments. *Journal of Clinical Psychiatry, 51,* 44–50.

Hall, T. E., Hughes, C. A., & Filbert, M. (2000). Computer-assisted instruction in reading for students with learning disabilities: A research synthesis. *Education and Treatment of Children, 23,* 173–193.

Hammen, C. (1997). *Depression.* East Sussex, UK: Psychology Press Ltd.

Hare, R. D. (1991). *Manual for the Revised Psychopathy Checklist.* Toronto: Multi-Health Systems.

Heiman, J. R. (2000). Orgasmic disorders in women. In S. R. Leiblum & R. C. Rosen (Eds.), *Principles and practice of sex therapy* (3rd ed., pp. 118–153). New York: Guilford Press.

Henggeler, S. W., Schoenwald, S. K., Borduin, C. M., Rowland, M. D., & Cunningham, P. B. (1998). *Multisystematic treatment of antisocial behavior in children and adolescents.* New York: Guilford.

Hill, J. C., & Schoener, E. P. (1996). Age-dependent decline of attention deficit hyperactivity disorder. *American Journal of Psychiatry, 153,* 1143–1146.

Hoffman, S. & Barlow, D. H. (2002). Social phobia (social anxiety disorder). In D. H. Barlow (Ed.), *Anxiety and its disorders: The nature and treatment of anxiety and panic (2nd ed.).* New York: Guilford Press.

Hooley, J. M., & Hiller, J. B. (2001). Family relationships and major mental disorder: Risk factors and preventive strategies. In S. Duck (Ed.), *Handbook of personal relationships (2nd ed.),* (pp. 621–648). Chichester, UK: Wiley.

Hsu, L. K. G. (1990). *Eating disorders.* New York: Guilford Press.

Hudson, J., Pope, H., Jonas, J. M., & Yurgelun-Todd, D. (1983). Family history study of anorexia nervosa and bulimia. *British Journal of Psychiatry, 142,* 133–138.

Hunicutt, C. P., & Newman, I. A. (1983). Adolescent dieting practices and nutrition knowledge. *Health Values: The Journal of Health Behavior, Education, and Promotion, 17,* 35–40.

Huttunen, M. O., & Niskanen, P. (1978). Prenatal loss of father and psychiatric disorders. *Archives of General Psychiatry, 35,* 429–431.

Johnson, S. L., Winnet, C. A., Meyer, B., Greenhouse, W. J., & Miller, I. (1999). Social support and the course of bipolar disorder. *Journal of Abnormal Psychology, 108,* 558–566.

Kallman, F. J. (1938). *The genetics of schizophrenia.* New York: Augustin.

Kaplan, H. S. (1974). *The new sex therapy: Active treatment of sexual dysfunction.* New York: Brunner/Mazel.

Karel, M. J. (1997). Aging and depression: Vulnerability and stress across adulthood. *Clinical Psychology Review, 17,* 847–879.

Katz, R., & McGuffin, P. (1993). The genetics of affective disorders. In L. J. Chapman, J. P. Chapman, & D. Fowles (Eds.), *Progress in experimental personality and psychopathology research.* New York: Springer.

Kazdin, A. E. (1996). Problem solving and parent management training in treating aggressive and antisocial behavior. In E. D. Hibbs & P. S. Jensen (Eds.), *Psychosocial treatments for child and adolescent disorders: Empirically based strategies for clinical practice* (pp. 377–408). Washington, DC: American Psychological Association.

Kazdin, A. E., & Wassell, G. (1999). Barriers to treatment participation and therapeutic change among children referred for conduct disorder. *Journal of Clinical Child Psychology, 28,* 160–172.

Kendler, K. S., McGuire, M., Gruenberg, A. M., O'Hare, A., Spellman, M., & Walsh, D. (1993). The Roscommon family study: Methods, diagnosis of probands, and risk of schizophrenia in relatives. *Archives of General Psychiatry, 50,* 527–540.

Kendler, K. S., & Prescott, C. A. (1999). A population-based twin study of lifetime major depression in men and women. *Archives of General Psychiatry, 56,* 39–44.

Key facts about Down syndrome. (n.d.). Retrieved September 10, 2002, from **http://www.down-syndrome.info/topics/keyfacts/key-facts-EN-GB.htm.**

Klein, D. F. (1994). Klein's suffocation theory of panic. Reply, *Archives of General Psychiatry, 51,* 506.

Krehbiel, K. (2000). Diagnosis and treatment of bipolar disorder. *Monitor on Psychology, 31 (9),* 22.

Lambert, N. M., Hartsough, C. S., Sassone, D., & Sandoval, J. (1987). Persistence of hyperactivity symptoms from childhood to adolescence and associated outcomes. *American Journal of Orthopsychiatry, 57,* 22–32.

Lewinsohn, P. M. (1974). A behavioral approach to depression. In R. J. Friedman & M. M. Katz (Eds.), *The psychology of depression: Contemporary theory and research.* Washington, DC: Winston-Wiley.

Lewis, G., Croft-Jeffreys, C., & Anthony, D. (1990). Are British psychiatrists racist? *British Journal of Psychiatry, 157,* 410–415.

Linehan, M. M., Tutek, D. A., Heard, H. L., & Armstrong, H. E. (1994). Interpersonal outcome of cognitive-behavioral treatment for chronically suicidal borderline patients. *American Journal of Psychiatry, 151,* 1771–1776.

LoPiccolo, J., & Stock, W. E. (1987). Sexual function, dysfunction and counseling in gynecological practice. In Z. Rosenwaks, F. Benjamin, & M. L. Stone (Eds.), *Gynecology.* New York: Macmillan.

Lykken, D. T. (1982). Fearfulness: Its carefree charms and deadly risks. *Psychology Today, 16,* 20–28.

McGue, M. (1999). The behavioral genetics of alcoholism. *Current Directions in Psychological Science, 8,* 109–115.

McKim, W. A. (2003). *Drugs and behavior: An introduction to behavioral pharmacology (5th ed.).* Upper Saddle River, NJ: Prentice-Hall.

McLellan, A. T., Arndt, I. O., Metzger, D. S., Woody, G. E., & O'Brien, C.P. (1993). The effects of psychosocial services in substance abuse treatment. *Journal of the American Medical Association, 269,* 1953–1959.

McMahon, R. J., & Estes, A. M. (1997). Conduct problems. In E. J. Mash & L. G. Terdal (Eds.), *Assessment of childhood disorders* (pp. 39–134). New York: Guilford.

McMahon, R. J., & Wells, K. C. (1998). In E. J. Mash & R. A. Barkley (Eds.), *Treatment of childhood disorders.* (2nd ed.). New York: Guilford Press.

Malkoff- Schwartz, S. F., Frank, E., Anderson, B., Sherrill, J. T., Siegel, L., Patterson, D., & Kupfer, D. J. (1998). Stressful life events and social rhythm disruption in the onset of manic and depressive bipolar episodes: A preliminary investigation. *Archives of General Psychiatry, 55,* 702–707.

Marlatt, G. A., Larimer, M. E., Baer, J. S., & Quigley, L. A. (1993). Harm reduction for alcohol problems: Moving beyond the controlled drinking controversy. *Behavior Therapy, 24,* 461–504.

Marshall, W. L. (1997). Pedophilia: Psychopathology and theory. In D. R. Laws & W. O'Donohue (Eds.), *Sexual deviance: Theory, assessment and treatment* (pp. 152–174). New York: Guilford Press.

Masters, W. H., & Johnson, V. E. (1970). *Human sexual inadequacy.* Boston: Little, Brown.

Maxmen, J. S., & Ward, N. G. (1995). *Psychotropic drugs: Fast facts (2nd ed.).* New York: W.W. Norton & Company.

Milich, R., Wolraich, M. C., & Lindgren, S. (1986). Sugar and hyperactivity: A critical review of empirical findings. *Clinical Psychology Review, 6,* 493–513.

Miller, W. R., & McCrady, B. S. (1993). The importance of research on Alcoholics Anonymous. In B. S. McCrady & W. R. Miller (Eds.), *Research on Alcoholics Anonymous: Opportunities and alternatives.* (pp. 3–11). New Brunswick, NJ: Rutgers Center of Alcohol Studies.

Miller, S. L., & Tallal, P. (1995). A behavioral neuroscience approach to developmental language disorders: Evidence for a rapid temporal processing deficit. In D. Cichetti & D. J. Cohen (Eds.), *Developmental psychopathology: Vol. 2: Risk, disorder, and adaptation* (pp. 274–298). New York: Wiley.

Moncher, M. S., Holden, G. W., & Trimble, J. E. (1990). Substance abuse among Native-American youth. *Journal of Consulting and Clinical Psychology, 58,* 408–415.

Morrison, J. (1995). *DSM-IV made easy: The clinician's guide to diagnosis.* New York: Guilford.

National Institute of Mental Health (1999). *Anxiety disorders research at the National Institute of Mental Health* (NIH Publication No. 99–4504). Washington, DC: US Government Printing Office.

Newman, J. P., Patterson, C. M., & Kosson, D. S. (1987). Response perseveration in psychopaths. *Journal of Abnormal Psychology, 96,* 145–148.

Patterson, G. R. (1982). *Coercive family process.* Eugene, OR: Castalia.

Patton. G.C., Selzer, R., Coffey, C., Carlin, J.B., & Wolfe, R. (1999). Onset of adolescent eating disorders: Population based cohort study over 3 years. *British Medical Journal, 318,* 765–768.

Paykel, E. S. (1982). Life events and early environments. In E. S. Paykel (Ed.), *Handbook of Affective Disorders.* New York: Guilford.

Pelham, W. E., Jr. (1993). Pharmacotherapy for children with attention-deficit hyperactivity disorder. *School Psychology Review, 22,* 199–227.

Perry, S. (1993). Psychiatric treatment of adults with human immunodeficiency virus infection. In D. L. Dunner (Ed.), *Current psychiatric therapy* (pp. 475–482). Philadelphia: W. B. Saunders.

Purvis, K. L., & Tannock, R. (2000). Phonological processing, not inhibitory control, differentiates ADHD and reading disability. *Journal of the American Academy of Child and Adolescent Psychiatry, 39,* 485–494.

Quay, H. C. (1965). Psychopathic personality as pathological stimulation seeking. *American Journal of Psychiatry, 122,* 180–183.

Rosenthal, D., Wender, P. H., Kety, S. S., Schulsinger, F., Welner, J., & Reider, R. (1975). Parent-child relationships and psychopathological disorder in the child. *Archives of General Psychiatry, 32,* 466–476.

Seligman, M. E. P. (1975). *Helplessness: On depression, development, and death.* San Francisco: Freeman.

Shaywitz, S. E. (1998). Dyslexia. *New England Journal of Medicine, 338,* 307–312.

Simonoff, E., Bolton, P., & Rutter, M. (1996). Mental retardation: Genetic findings, clinical implications, and research agenda. *Journal of Child Psychology and Psychiatry, 37,* 259–280.

Sobell, M. B., & Sobell, L. C. (1973). Alcoholics treated by individualized behavior therapy: One year treatment outcome. *Behavior Research and Therapy, 11,* 599–618.

Sobell, M. B., & Sobell, L. C. (1993). *Problem drinkers: Guided self-change treatment.* New York: Guilford Press.

State, M., King, B. H., & Dykens, E. (1997). Mental retardation: A review of the past 10 years: II. *Journal of the American Academy of Child and Adolescent Psychiatry, 36,* 1664–1671.

Steiner, H., & Lock, J. (1998). Anorexia nervosa and bulimia nervosa in children and adolescents: A review of the past ten years. *Journal of the American Academy of Child and Adolescent Psychiatry, 37,* 352–359.

Stice, E. (1994). Review of the evidence for a sociocultural model of bulimia nervosa and an exploration of the mechanisms of action. *Clinical Psychology Review, 14,* 633–661.

Strober, M., Freeman, R., Lampert, C., Diamond, J., & Kaye, W. (2000). Controlled family study of anorexia nervosa and bulimia nervosa: Evidence of shared liability and transmission of partial syndromes. *American Journal of Psychiatry, 157,* 393–401.

Tannock, R. (1998). Attention deficit hyperactivity disorder: Advances in cognitive, neurobiological, and genetic research. *Journal of Child Psychology and Psychiatry, 39,* 65–99.

Thase, M. (1998). The relationship between Down syndrome and Alzheimer's disease. In L. Nadel (Ed.), *The psychobiology of Down syndrome.* Cambridge, MA: MIT Press.

Toupin, J., Dery, M., Pauze, R., Mercier, H., & Fortin, L. (2000). Cognitive and familial contributions to conduct disorder in children. *Journal of Child Psychology and Psychiatry, 41,* 333–344.

Vasterling, J. J., Brailey, K., Constans, J.I., & Sotker, P.B. (1998). Attention and memory dysfunction in posttraumatic stress disorder. *Psychiatric Bulletin, 12,* 125–133.

Vincent, J. B., Masellis, M., Lawrence, J., Choi, V., Gurling, H. M. D., Sagar V. P., & Kennedy, J. L. (1999). Genetic association analysis of serotonin system genes in bipolar affective disorder. *American Journal of Psychiatry, 156,* 136–138.

Vogler, G. P., DeFries, J. C., & Decker, S. N. (1985). Family history as an indicator of risk for reading disability. *Journal of Learning Disabilities, 18,* 419–421.

Wechsler, H., Lee, J. E., Kuo, M., & Lee, H. (2000). College binge drinking in the 1990's: A continuing problem. *Journal of the American College Health, 48,* 199–210.

Weissman, M.M., Bruce, M.L., Leaf, P.J., Florio, L.P., & Holzer, C. (1990). Affective disorders. In L. N. Robins & D. A. Regier (Eds.). *Psychiatric Disorders in America: The Epidemiological Catchment Area Study (pp. 53–80).* New York: Free Press.

Wicks-Nelson, R., & Israel, A. C. (2000). *Behavior disorders of children.* Upper Saddle River, NJ: Prentice-Hall.

Wiegel, M., Wincze, J. P., & Barlow, D. H. (2001). Assessment, treatment planning, and outcome evaluation for sexual dysfunction. In M. M. Anthony & D. H. Barlow (Eds.), *Handbook of assessment, treatment planning, and outcome evaluation: Empirically supported strategies for psychological disorders.* New York: Guilford Press.

Zanarini, M. C., Frankenburg, F. R., Dubo, E. E., Sickel, A. E., Trikha, A., Levin, A., & Reynolds, V. (1998). Axis I comorbidity of borderline personality disorder. *American Journal of Psychiatry, 155,* 1733–1739.

Zanarini, M. C., Williams, A. A., Lewis, R. E., Reich, R. B., Vera, S. C., Marino, M. F., Levin, A., Yong, L., & Frankenberg, F. R. (1997). Reported pathological childhood experiences associated with the development of borderline personality disorder. *American Journal of Psychiatry, 154,* 1101–1106.

Zilbergeld, B. (1999). *New male sexuality.* New York: Random House.

Zubin, J., & Spring, B. (1977). Vulnerability—New view of schizophrenia. *Journal of Abnormal Psychology, 86,* 103–126.